David Guterson
Snow Falling on Cedars

David Guterson **Snow Falling on Cedars**

Herausgegeben von:
Birgit Ohmsieder

Verlagsredaktion:
Dr. Marion Kiffe, Michaela Schmidt

Technische Umsetzung:
Ingo Ostermaier

Umschlagillustrationen:
Großes Bild: © Alan Kearney/Getty Images, München
Kleines Bild: © CINETEXT Bildarchiv, Frankfurt am Main

Herausgeber der Cornelsen Senior English Library:
Prof. Dr. Albert-Reiner Glaap

Copyright © 1994 by David Guterson

www.cornelsen.de

1. Auflage, 1. Druck 2006 / 06

Alle Drucke dieser Auflage sind inhaltlich unverändert
und können im Unterricht nebeneinander verwendet werden.

© 2006 Cornelsen Verlag, Berlin

Das Werk und seine Teile sind urheberrechtlich geschützt.
Jede Nutzung in anderen als den gesetzlich zugelassenen Fällen bedarf
der vorherigen schriftlichen Einwilligung des Verlages.
Hinweis zu § 52a UrhG: Weder das Werk noch seine Teile dürfen ohne eine
solche Einwilligung eingescannt und in ein Netzwerk eingestellt werden.
Dies gilt auch für Intranets von Schulen und sonstigen Bildungseinrichtungen.

Druck: CS-Druck CornelsenStürtz, Berlin

ISBN 978-3-06-031133-0

 Inhalt gedruckt auf säurefreiem Papier aus nachhaltiger Forstwirtschaft.

Konstantin Meidel

Contents

Snow Falling on Cedars 5

The Author 396

Abbreviations and Annotations

adj	adjective	**infml**	informal
adv	adverb	**jdm./jdn.**	jemandem/en
AE	American English	**n**	noun
cf.	confer; see	**pl**	plural
e.g.	exempli gratia; for example	**sb.**	somebody
esp.	especially	**sing**	singular
etc.	et cetera; and so on	**sl**	slang
fig	figurative	**sth.**	something
fml	formal	**usu.**	usually
i.e.	id est; in other words	**v**	verb

The annotations are arranged chronologically; the first time a word is used is where you will find it explained. All pronunciations given are American English. For help about reading and presenting literature in the classroom, cf. **www.learnetix.de/bookshelf**.

Chapter 1

The accused man, Kabuo Miyamoto, sat proudly upright with a rigid grace, his palms placed softly on the defendant's table – the posture of a man who has detached himself insofar as this is possible at his own trial. Some in the gallery would later say that his stillness suggested a disdain for the proceedings; others felt certain it veiled a fear of the verdict that was to come. Whichever it was, Kabuo showed nothing – not even a flicker of the eyes. He was dressed in a white shirt worn buttoned to the throat and gray, neatly pressed trousers. His figure, especially the neck and shoulders, communicated the impression of irrefutable physical strength and of precise, even imperial bearing. Kabuo's features were smooth and angular; his hair had been cropped close to his skull in a manner that made its musculature prominent. In the face of the charge that had been leveled against him he sat with his dark eyes trained straight ahead and did not appear moved at all.

In the public gallery every seat had been taken, yet the courtroom suggested nothing of the carnival atmosphere sometimes found at country murder trials. In fact, the eighty-five citizens gathered there seemed strangely subdued and contemplative. Most of them had known Carl Heine, a salmon gill-netter with a wife and three children, who was buried now in the Lutheran cemetery up on Indian Knob Hill. Most had dressed with the same communal propriety they felt on Sundays before attending church services, and since the courtroom, however stark,

---

1 **rigid**: stiff   2 **grace**: attractive quality of elegance and control   **defendant** [-'--]: the person in a trial who is accused of committing a crime   4–5 **disdain for sth.**: the feeling that sth. does not deserve your respect or attention; contempt
5 **verdict**: Urteil   9 **irrefutable**: that cannot be denied   10 **imperial**: herrschaftlich   **bearing** (n): Haltung   11 **crop sth.**: cut sth. (esp. sb.'s hair) very short
18 **subdued**: unusually quiet and possibly unhappy   **contemplative**: thinking quietly and seriously about sth.   19 **salmon**: Lachs   **gill-netter**: fisherman who fishes with large nets (**gill**: Kieme)   21 **propriety** [prə'praɪəti]: Anstand, Schicklichkeit   22 **stark**: (here) without any color or decoration

mirrored in their hearts the dignity of their prayer houses, they conducted themselves with churchgoing solemnity.

This courtroom, Judge Llewellyn Fielding's, down at the end of a damp, drafty hallway on the third floor of the Island County Courthouse, was run-down and small as courtrooms go. It was a place of gray-hued and bleak simplicity – a cramped gallery, a bench for the judge, a witness stand, a plywood platform for the jurors, and scuffed tables for the defendant and his prosecutor. The jurors sat with studiously impassive faces as they strained to make sense of matters. The men – two truck farmers, a retired crabber, a bookkeeper, a carpenter, a boat builder, a grocer, and a halibut schooner deckhand – were all dressed in coats and neckties. The women all wore Sunday dresses – a retired waitress, a sawmill secretary, two nervous fisher wives. A hairdresser accompanied them as alternate.

The bailiff, Ed Soames, at the request of Judge Fielding, had given a good head of steam to the sluggish radiators, which now and again sighed in the four corners of the room. In the heat they produced – a humid, overbearing swelter – the smell of sour mildew seemed to rise from everything.

Snow fell that morning outside the courthouse windows, four tall, narrow arches of leaded glass that yielded a great quantity of weak December light. A wind from the sea lofted snowflakes against the windowpanes, where they melted and ran toward the casements. Beyond the courthouse the town of Amity Harbor spread along the island shoreline. A few wind-whipped and decrepit Victorian mansions, remnants of a lost era of seagoing optimism, loomed out of the snowfall on the town's sporadic hills. Beyond them, cedars wove a steep mat of still green. The snow blurred from vision the clean contours of these cedar hills. The sea wind drove snowflakes steadily inland, hurling them against the fragrant trees, and the snow began to settle on the highest branches with a gentle implacability.

The accused man, with one segment of his consciousness, watched the falling snow outside the windows. He had been exiled in the county jail for seventy-seven days – the last part of September, all of October and all of November, the first week of December in jail. There was no window anywhere in his basement cell, no portal through which the autumn light could come to him. He had missed autumn, he realized now – it had passed already, evaporated. The snowfall, which he witnessed out of the corners of his eyes – furious, wind-whipped flakes against the windows – struck him as infinitely beautiful.

San Piedro was an island of five thousand damp souls, named by lost Spaniards who moored offshore in the year 1603. They'd sailed in search of the Northwest Passage, as many Spaniards did in those days, and their pilot and captain, Martín de Aquilar of the Vizcaíno expedition, sent a work detail ashore to cull a fresh spar pole from among the hemlocks at water's edge. Its members were murdered almost immediately upon setting foot on the beach by a party of Nootka slave raiders.

Settlers arrived – mostly wayward souls and eccentrics who had meandered off the Oregon Trail. A few rooting pigs were slaughtered in 1845 – by Canadian Englishmen up in arms about the border – but San Piedro Island generally lay clear of violence after that. The most distressing news story of the preceding ten years had been the wounding of an island resident by a drunken Seattle yachtsman with a shotgun on the Fourth of July, 1951.

Amity Harbor, the island's only town, provided deep moorage for a fleet of purse seiners and one-man gill-netting boats. It was an eccentric, rainy, wind-beaten sea village, downtrodden and mildewed, the boards of its buildings bleached and weathered, their drainpipes rusted a dull

---

2 **solemnity**: Erhabenheit   5 **hued** [hju:d] (adj): of a particular shade of a color
7 **plywood**: Sperrholz   **juror** (AE): Geschworene(r)   **scuffed**: in bad condition
8 **prosecutor** (AE): public official who officially charges sb. with a crime
studiously: carefully planned, deliberately   10 **crabber**: fisherman who catches mainly crabs   11 **halibut**: Heilbutt   **schooner deckhand**: unskilled worker on a big ship   14 **alternate** (n; AE): Ersatzmitglied   15 **bailiff** (AE): official who keeps order in court, etc.   16 **sluggish**: slow working or not working well   **radiator**: Heizkörper   18 **swelter**: (here) heat that makes you feel uncomfortable   **mildew**: Schimmel   21 **of leaded glass**: bleiverglast   23 **casement**: Fensterrahmen
25 **decrepit**: very old and not in good condition   25–26 **remnant**: Überbleibsel
26 **loom** (v): appear as a large shape that cannot be seen clearly, esp.in a frightening or threatening way   31 **implacability** [ɪmˈplækəbɪlɪti]: Unerbittlichkeit
38 **evaporate**: disappear gradually   42 **moor sth.**: attach sth. (esp. a boat) to a fixed object or to the land with a rope   45 **cull sth.**: (here) find and cut sth. into shape
spar pole: Rundholz, Mast   46 **hemlock**: Hemlocktanne   48 **wayward**: launisch, eigensinnig   56 **purse seiner**: Kutter mit unten schließbarem Schleppnetz

orange. Its long, steep inclines lay broad and desolate; its high-curbed gutters swarmed, most winter nights, with traveling rain. Often the sea wind made its single traffic light flail from side to side or caused the town's electrical power to flicker out and stay out for days. Main Street presented to the populace Petersen's Grocery, a post office, Fisk's Hardware Center, Larsen's Pharmacy, a dime-store-with-fountain owned by a woman in Seattle, a Puget Power office, a chandlery, Lottie Opsvig's apparel shop, Klaus Hartmann's real estate agency, the San Piedro Cafe, the Amity Harbor Restaurant, and a battered, run-down filling station owned and operated by the Torgerson brothers. At the wharf a fish packing plant exuded the odor of salmon bones, and the creosoted pilings of the state ferry terminal lay in among a fleet of mildewed boats. Rain, the spirit of the place, patiently beat down everything man-made. On winter evenings it roared in sheets against the pavements and made Amity Harbor invisible.

San Piedro had too a brand of verdant beauty that inclined its residents toward the poetical. Enormous hills, soft green with cedars, rose and fell in every direction. The island homes were damp and moss covered and lay in solitary fields and vales of alfalfa, feed corn, and strawberries. Haphazard cedar fences lined the careless roads, which slid beneath the shadows of the trees and past the bracken meadows. Cows grazed, stinking of sweet dung and addled by summer blackflies. Here and there an islander tried his hand at milling sawlogs on his own, leaving fragrant heaps of sawdust and mounds of cedar bark at roadside. The beaches glistened with smooth stones and sea foam. Two dozen coves and inlets, each with its pleasant muddle of sailboats and summer homes, ran the circumference of San Piedro, an endless series of pristine anchorages.

Inside Amity Harbor's courthouse, opposite the courtroom's four tall windows, a table had been set up to accommodate the influx of newspapermen to the island. The out-of-town reporters – one each from Bellingham, Anacortes, and Victoria and three from the Seattle papers – exhibited no trace of the solemnity evident among the respectful citizens in the gallery. They slumped in their chairs, rested their chins in their hands, and whispered together conspiratorially. With their backs only a foot from a steam radiator, the out-of-town reporters were sweating.

Ishmael Chambers, the local reporter, found that he was sweating, too. He was a man of thirty-one with a hardened face, a tall man with the eyes of a war veteran. He had only one arm, the left having been amputated ten inches below the shoulder joint, so that he wore the sleeve of his coat pinned up with the cuff fastened to the elbow. Ishmael understood that an air of disdain, of contempt for the island and its inhabitants, blew from the knot of out-of-town reporters toward the citizens in the gallery. Their discourse went forward in a miasma of sweat and heat that suggested a kind of indolence. Three of them had loosened their ties just slightly; two others had removed their jackets. They were reporters, professionally jaded and professionally immune, a little too well traveled in the last analysis to exert themselves toward the formalities San Piedro demanded silently of mainlanders. Ishmael, a native, did not want to be like them. The accused man, Kabuo, was somebody he knew, somebody he'd gone to high school with, and he couldn't bring himself, like the other reporters, to remove his coat at Kabuo's murder trial. At ten minutes before nine that morning, Ishmael had spoken with the accused man's wife on the second floor of the Island County Courthouse. She was seated on a hall bench with her back to an arched window, just outside the assessor's office, which was closed, gathering herself, apparently. 'Are you all right?' he'd said to her, but she'd responded by turning away from him. 'Please,' he'd said. 'Please, Hatsue.'

She'd turned her eyes on his then. Ishmael would find later, long after the trial, that their darkness would beleaguer his memory of these days. He would remember how rigorously her hair had been woven into a black knot against the nape of her neck. She had not been exactly cold to him, not exactly hateful, but he'd felt her distance anyway. 'Go away,' she'd said in a whisper, and then for a moment she'd glared. He remained

---

1 **incline** (n): slope   3 **flail**: move around without control   6 **fountain** (AE): machine that produces soft drinks   7 **chandlery**: shop that sells equipment for ships   8 **apparel**: clothing   11 **plant**: (hier) Fabrik, Werk   **creosote**: thick brown liquid that is used to preserve wood   16 **verdant**: fresh and green   16–17 **incline sb. toward sth.**: jdn. etwas zuneigen   19 **vale**: small valley   20 **haphazard** [hæp'hæzərd]: with no particular order or plan   21 **bracken**: Farnkraut   22 **addled by**: (here) covered with, bothered by   27 **anchorage**: place where ships or boats can anchor   40 **cuff**: Manschette   43 **miasma** [maɪ'æzmə]: air that is dirty and smells unpleasant   44 **indolence**: laziness   46 **jaded**: tired and bored, because you have done too much of sth.   60 **beleaguer**: (here) affect (with sth. unpleasant)

uncertain afterward what her eyes had meant – punishment, sorrow, pain. 'Go away,' repeated Hatsue Miyamoto. Then she'd turned her eyes, once again, from his.

'Don't be like this,' said Ishmael.

'Go away,' she'd answered.

'Hatsue,' said Ishmael. 'Don't be like this.'

'Go away,' she'd said again.

Now, in the courtroom, with sweat on his temples, Ishmael felt embarrassed to be sitting among the reporters and decided that after the morning's recess he would find a more anonymous seat in the gallery. In the meantime he sat facing the wind-driven snowfall, which had already begun to mute the streets outside the courthouse windows. He hoped it would snow recklessly and bring to the island the impossible winter purity, so rare and precious, he remembered fondly from his youth.

---

8 **temple**: Schläfe   10 **recess** (n): (here) short break in a trial at court

Chapter 2

The first witness called by the prosecutor that day was the county sheriff, Art Moran. On the morning Carl Heine died – September 16 – the sheriff was in the midst of an inventory at his office and had engaged the services of the new court stenographer, Mrs. Eleanor Dokes (who now sat primly below the judge's bench recording everything with silent implacability), as an aide in this annual county-mandated endeavor. He and Mrs. Dokes had exchanged surprised glances when Abel Martinson, the sheriff's deputy, reported over the newly purchased radio set that Carl Heine's fishing boat, the *Susan Marie*, had been sighted adrift in White Sand Bay.

'Abel said the net was all run out and drifting along behind,' Art Moran explained. 'I felt, well, concerned immediately.'

'The *Susan Marie* was on the move?' asked Alvin Hooks, the prosecutor, who stood with one foot perched on the witnesses' podium as if he and Art were talking by a park bench.

'That's what Abel said.'

'With its fishing lights on? Is that what Deputy Martinson reported?'

'That's right.'

'In *day*light?'

'Abel called in nine-thirty A.M., I believe.'

'Correct me if I'm wrong,' Alvin Hooks asked. 'Gill nets, by law, must be on board by nine o'clock – is that right, Sheriff Moran?'

'That's correct,' said the sheriff. 'Nine A.M.'

The prosecutor swiveled with a faintly military flourish and executed a tight circle over the courtroom's waxed floor, his hands against the small of his back neatly. 'What did you do then?' he inquired.

---

6 **county-mandated**: von der Bezirksverwaltung erlassen 9 **adrift**: floating without being controlled by anyone 14 **perched on sth.**: sitting or resting on sth., esp. on the edge of sth. 24 **swivel**: turn or move around quickly to face another direction **flourish** (n): (here) an exaggerated movement that you make when you want sb. to notice you 26 **small of sb.'s/the back**: Kreuz

'I told Abel to stay put. To stay where he was. That I would pick him up in the launch.'

'You didn't call the coast guard?'

'Decided I'd hold off just yet. Decided to have a look myself.'

Alvin Hooks nodded. 'Was it your jurisdiction, sheriff?'

'It's a judgment call, Mr. Hooks,' Art Moran said. 'I felt it was the right thing to do.'

The prosecutor nodded one more time and surveyed the members of the jury. He appreciated the sheriff's answer; it cast a favorable moral light on his witness and gave him the authority of the conscientious man, for which there was ultimately no substitute.

'Just tell the court your whole story,' Alvin Hooks said. 'The morning of September 16.'

The sheriff stared at him doubtfully for a moment. By nature Art Moran was an uneasy person, nervous in the face of even trivial encounters. He'd come to his vocation as if driven ineluctably; he had never formed the intention of being sheriff, yet, to his astonishment, here he was. In his liver-colored uniform, black tie, and polished shoes he looked inevitably miscast in life, a man uncomfortable with the accoutrements of his profession, as if he had dressed for a costume party and now wandered about in the disguise. The sheriff was a lean figure, unimposing, who habitually chewed a stick of Juicy Fruit gum (though he wasn't chewing any at the moment, mostly out of deference to the American legal system, which he believed in wholeheartedly despite its flaws). He'd lost much of his hair since turning fifty, and his belly, always undernourished in appearance, now suggested a shriveled emaciation.

Art Moran had lain awake the night before fretting about his role in this trial and remembering the sequence of events with his eyes shut, as if they were occurring in a dream. He and his deputy, Abel Martinson, had taken the county launch into White Sand Bay on the morning of September 16. The tide, steadily on the rise, had turned about three and a half hours before, at six-thirty; by midmorning sunlight lay like a glaze over the water, warming his back pleasantly. The preceding night a fog as palpable as cotton had hung suspended over Island County. Later it gently separated at the seams and became vast billows traveling above the sea instead of a still white miasma. Around the launch as it churned toward the *Susan Marie* the last remnants of this night fog sailed and drifted in shreds of vapor toward the sun's heat.

Abel Martinson, one hand on the launch's throttle, the other on his knee, told Art that a Port Jensen fisherman, Erik Syvertsen – Erik the younger, he pointed out – had come across the *Susan Marie* adrift off the south side of White Sand Point with her net set and, it appeared, no one on board. It was more than an hour and a half past dawn and the running lights had been left on. Abel had driven to White Sand Point and walked out to the end of the community pier with his binoculars dangling from his neck. Sure enough, the *Susan Marie* lay drifting on the tide well into the bay on an angle north by northwest, he'd found, and so he'd radioed the sheriff.

In fifteen minutes they came abreast of the drifting boat and Abel turned back the throttle. In the calm of the bay their approach went smoothly; Art set the fenders out; and the two of them made fast their mooring lines with a few wraps each around the forward deck cleats. 'Lights're *all* on,' observed Art, one foot on the *Susan Marie*'s gunnel. 'Every last one of 'em, looks like.'

'He ain't here,' replied Abel.

'Doesn't look like it,' said Art.

'Went over,' Abel said. 'I got this bad feeling.'

---

1 **stay put** (infml): remain where you are   2 **launch** (n): large boat with a motor
5 **jurisdiction**: area of legal responsibility   9 **jury**: group of members of the public who listen to the facts of a case in a court and decide whether or not sb. is guilty of a crime   10 **conscientious** [ˌkɑːnsiˈenʃəs]: taking care to do things carefully and correctly   16 **vocation**: Berufung   **ineluctable** (fml): that cannot be avoided
19 **miscast**: (of an actor) chosen to play a role for which they are not suitable
20 **accoutrements** (fml): equipment needed for a particular activity   23 **deference** [ˈ- - -]: behavior that shows that you respect sb./sth.   25 **flaw**: mistake; thing that does not work properly   26 **emaciation**: state of being thin and weak, usu. due to illness or lack of food   27 **fret about sth.**: worry about sth.   34 **palpable**: that can be touched   35 **billow**: moving cloud   36 **churn**: move about violently
38 **shred**: (here) very small amount   **vapor**: Nebel   39 **throttle**: Gashebel
41 **off sth.**: away/at a distance from a particular place   44 **running lights**: lights kept on at night   45 **binoculars** (pl) [bɪˈnɑːkjəlɚz]: Fernglas   49 **abreast of sth.**: next to sth. and facing the same way   51 **fender**: soft solid object that is hung over the side of a boat so the boat is not damaged when it touches another boat
52 **cleat**: small bar on a boat to which ropes are fastened   53 **gunnel**: the upper edge of the side of a boat

Art winced at hearing this. 'Let's hope not,' he urged. 'Don't say that.'

He made his way just abaft of the cabin, then stood squinting up at the *Susan Marie*'s guys and stays and at the peaks of her stabilizer bars. The red and white mast lights had been left on all morning; the picking light and the jacklight at the end of the net both shone dully in the early sun. While Art stood there, pondering this, Abel Martinson dragged the hatch cover from the hold and called for him to come over.

'You got something?' Art asked.

'Look here,' answered Abel.

Together they crouched over the square hold opening, out of which the odor of salmon flew up at them. Abel maneuvered his flashlight beam across a heap of inert, silent fish. 'Silvers,' he said. 'Maybe fifty of 'em.'

'So he picked his net least once,' said Art.

'Looks like it,' answered Abel.

Men had been known to fall into empty holds before, crack their heads, and pass out even in calm weather. Art had heard of a few such incidents. He looked in at the fish again.

'What time you figure he put out last night?'

'Hard to say. Four-thirty? Five?'

'Where'd he go, you figure?'

'Probably up North Bank,' said Abel. 'Maybe Ship Channel. Or Elliot Head. That's where the fish been running.'

But Art already knew about these things. San Piedro lived and breathed by the salmon, and the cryptic places where they ran at night were the subject of perpetual conversation. Yet it helped him to hear it aloud just now – it helped him to think more clearly.

The two of them crouched by the hold a moment longer in a shared hiatus from their work. The still heap of salmon troubled Art in a way he could not readily articulate, and so he looked at it wordlessly. Then he rose, his knees creaking, and turned away from the dark hold.

'Let's keep looking,' he suggested.

'Right,' said Abel. 'Could be he's up in his cabin, maybe. Knocked out one way or t'other.'

The *Susan Marie* was a thirty-foot stern-picker – a standard, well-tended San Piedro gill-netter – with her cabin just abaft of midship. Art ducked through its stern-side entry and stood to port for a moment. In the middle of the floor – it was the first thing he noticed – a tin coffee cup lay tipped on its side. A marine battery lay just right of the wheel. There was a short bunk made up with a wool blanket to starboard; Abel ran his flashlight across it. The cabin lamp over the ship's wheel had been left on; a ripple of sunlight, flaring through a window, shimmered on the starboard wall. The scene left Art with the ominous impression of an extreme, too-silent tidiness. A cased sausage hanging from a wire above the binnacle swayed a little as the *Susan Marie* undulated; otherwise, nothing moved. No sound could be heard except now and again a dim, far crackle from the radio set. Art, noting it, began to manipulate the radio dials for no other reason than that he didn't know what else to do. He was at a loss.

'This is bad,' said Abel.

'Take a look,' answered Art. 'I forgot – see if his dinghy's over the reel.'

Abel Martinson stuck his head out the entry. 'It's there, Art,' he said. 'Now what?'

For a moment they stared at one another. Then Art, with a sigh, sat down on the edge of Carl Heine's short bunk.

'Maybe he crawled in under the decking,' suggested Abel. 'Maybe he had some kind of engine trouble, Art.'

'I'm sitting on top of his engine,' Art pointed out. 'There's no room for anyone to crawl around down there.'

'He went over,' said Abel, shaking his head.

'Looks like it,' answered the sheriff.

They glanced at each other, then away again.

'Maybe somebody took him off,' suggested Abel. 'He got hurt, radioed, somebody took him off. That –'

---

1 **wince**: make a sudden expression with your face that shows that you feel pain
2 **abaft**: in a backwards direction   3 **guys and stays**: Teile der Masten
4–5 **picking light**: Fanglicht   5 **jacklight**: Licht am Netz   7 **hatch**: Luke
hold (n): part of a ship where goods are stored   12 **inert**: not moving   **silvers**: Silberlachs   16 **pass out**: become unconscious   18 **put out**: (bei einem Schiff) auslaufen   24 **cryptic**: mysterious   28 **hiatus** [haɪˈeɪtəs]: pause in an activity when nothing happens   34 **stern-picker**: fishing boot with a net at the back (**stern**: Heck)   36 **to port**: nach Backbord   39 **bunk**: narrow bed that is fixed to a wall
42 **starboard**: Steuerbord   44 **binnacle**: Kompasshaus   **undulate** (fml): move gently up and down on the waves   50 **dinghy**: small open often rubber boat

'They wouldn't let the boat drift,' put in Art. 'Besides, we'd a heard about it by now.'

'This is bad,' repeated Abel Martinson.

Art tucked another stick of Juicy Fruit between his teeth and wished this was not his responsibility. He liked Carl Heine, knew Carl's family, went to church with them on Sundays. Carl came from old-time island stock; his grandfather, Bavarian born, had established thirty acres of strawberry fields on prime growing land in Center Valley. His father, too, had been a strawberry farmer before dying of a stroke in '44. Then Carl's mother, Etta Heine, had sold all thirty acres to the Jurgensen clan while her son was away at the war. They were hard-toiling, quiet people, the Heines. Most people on San Piedro liked them. Carl, Art recalled, had served as a gunner on the U.S.S. *Canton*, which went down during the invasion of Okinawa. He'd survived the war – other island boys hadn't – and come home to a gill-netter's life.

On the sea Carl's blond hair had gone russet colored. He weighed two hundred and thirty-five pounds, much of it carried in his chest and shoulders. On winter days, picking fish from his net, he wore a wool cap knitted by his wife and an infantryman's battered field jacket. He spent no time at the San Piedro Tavern or drinking coffee at the San Piedro Cafe. On Sunday mornings he sat with his wife and children in a back pew of the First Hill Lutheran Church, blinking slowly in the pale sanctuary light, a hymnbook open in his large, square hands, a calm expression on his face. Sunday afternoons he squatted on the aft deck of his boat, silently and methodically untangling his gill net or knitting its flaws up patiently. He worked alone. He was courteous but not friendly. He wore rubber boots almost everywhere, like all San Piedro fishermen. His wife, too, came from old island people – the Varigs, Art remembered, hay farmers and shake cutters with a few stump acres on Cattle Point – and her father had passed away not so long ago. Carl had named his boat after his wife, and, in '48, built a big frame house just west of Amity Harbor, including an apartment for his mother, Etta. But – out of pride, word had it – Etta would not move in with him. She lived in town, a stout, grave woman with a slight Teutonic edge to her speech, over Lottie Opsvig's apparel shop on Main. Her son called at her door every Sunday afternoon and escorted her to his house for supper. Art had watched them trudge up Old Hill together, Etta with her umbrella turned against the winter rain, her free hand clutching at the lapels of a coarse winter coat, Carl with his hands curled up in his jacket pockets, his wool cap pulled to his eyebrows. All in all, Art decided, Carl Heine was a good man. He was silent, yes, and grave like his mother, but the war had a part in that, Art realized. Carl rarely laughed, but he did not seem, to Art's way of thinking, unhappy or dissatisfied. Now his death would land hard on San Piedro; no one would want to fathom its message in a place where so many made their living fishing. The fear of the sea that was always there, simmering beneath the surface of their island lives, would boil up in their hearts again.

'Well, look,' said Abel Martinson, leaning in the cabin door while the boat shifted about. 'Let's get his net in, Art.'

'Suppose we better,' sighed Art. 'All right. We'd better do it, then. But we'll do it one step at a time.'

'He's got a power takeoff back there,' Abel Martinson pointed out. 'You figure he hasn't run for maybe six hours. And all these lights been drawing off the battery. Better choke it up good, Art.'

Art nodded and then turned the key beside the ship's wheel. The solenoid kicked in immediately; the engine stuttered once and then began to idle roughly, rattling frantically beneath the floorboards. Art slowly backed the choke off.

'Okay,' he said. 'Like that?'

'Guess I was wrong,' said Abel Martinson. 'She sounds real good and strong.'

They went out again, Art leading. The *Susan Marie* had veered off nearly perpendicular to the chop and angled, briefly, to starboard. With the thrust of the engine she'd begun to bobble a little, and Art, treading across the aft deck, stumbled forward and grabbed at a stanchion, scraping his palm at the heel of the thumb, while Abel Martinson looked

---

7 **acre** ['eɪkər]: ca. 4000m²   16 **russet**: reddish-brown   19 **battered**: old, well-used and not in very good condition   21 **pew**: long wooden seat in a church
22 **sanctuary**: holy place   24 **squat**: hocken, kauern   **aft**: back   26 **courteous** ['kɜːrtiəs]: polite and respectful   29 **shake cutter**: Schindelmacher
30 **pass away**: die   38 **lapel**: Revers, Kragenaufschlag   44 **fathom sth.**: find out the deep meaning of sth.   52 **figure**: think   55 **solenoid**: Magnetspule   61 **veer off**: change direction   62 **perpendicular**: at an angle of 90°   **chop**: (hier) Dünung
63 **bobble**: (hier) hüpfen, holpern   64 **stanchion**: (here) vertical pole used to support the rail (= Reling) of a ship

on. He rose again, steadied himself with a foot on the starboard gunnel, and looked out across the water.

The morning light had broadened, gained greater depth, and lay in a clean sheet across the bay, giving it a silver tincture. Not a boat was in sight except a single canoe traveling parallel to a tree-wreathed shoreline, children in life jackets at the flashing paddles a quarter mile off. *They're innocent*, thought Art.

'It's good she's come about,' he said to his deputy. 'We'll need time to get this net in.'

'Whenever you're ready,' answered Abel.

For a moment it occurred to Art to explain certain matters to his deputy. Abel Martinson was twenty-four, the son of an Anacortes brick mason. He had never seen a man brought up in a net before, as Art had, twice. It happened now and then to fishermen – they caught a hand or a sleeve in their net webbing and went over even in calm weather. It was a part of things, part of the fabric of the place, and as sheriff he knew this well. He knew what bringing up the net really meant, and he knew Abel Martinson didn't.

Now he put his foot on top of the beaver paddle and looked across at Abel. 'Get over there with the lead line,' he said softly. 'I'll bring her up real slow. You may need to pick some, so be ready.'

Abel Martinson nodded.

Art brought the weight of his foot down. The net shuddered for a moment as the slack went out of it, and then the reel wound it in against the weight of the sea. Surging, and then lowering a note, the engine confronted its work. The two men stood at either end of the gunnel roller, Art with one shoe on the beaver paddle and Abel Martinson staring at the net webbing as it traveled slowly toward the drum. Ten yards out, the float line fell away and bobbled in a seam of white water along the surface of the bay. They were still moving up the tide about north by northwest, but the breeze from the south had shifted just enough to bring them gently to port.

They had picked two dozen salmon from the net, three stray sticks, two dogfish, a long convoluted coil of kelp, and a number of ensnarled jellyfish when Carl Heine's face showed. For a brief moment Art understood Carl's face as the sort of illusion men are prone to at sea – or hoped it was this, rather, with a fleeting desperation – but then as the net reeled in Carl's bearded throat appeared too and the face completed itself. There was Carl's face turned up toward the sunlight and the water from Carl's hair dripped in silver strings to the sea; and now clearly it *was* Carl's face, his mouth open – Carl's *face* – and Art pressed harder against the beaver paddle. Up came Carl, hanging by the left buckle of his rubber bib overalls from the gill net he'd made his living picking, his T-shirt, bubbles of seawater coursing under it, pasted to his chest and shoulders. He hung heavily with his legs in the water, a salmon struggling in the net beside him, the skin of his collarbones, just above the highest waves, hued an icy but brilliant pink. He appeared to have been parboiled in the sea.

Abel Martinson vomited. He leaned out over the transom of the boat and retched and cleared his throat and vomited again, this time more violently. 'All right, Abel,' Art said. 'You get ahold of yourself.'

The deputy did not reply. He wiped his mouth with a handkerchief. He breathed heavily and spat into the sea a half-dozen times. Then, after a moment, he dropped his head and pounded his left fist against the transom. 'Jesus Christ,' he said.

'I'll bring him up slow,' answered Art. 'You keep his head back away from the transom, Abel. Get ahold of yourself. Keep his head back and away now.'

But in the end they had to rattle up the lead line and pull Carl fully into the folds of his net. They cupped the net around him like a kind of hammock so that his body was borne by the webbing. In this manner they brought Carl Heine up from the sea – Abel yarding him over the net roller while Art tapped gingerly at the beaver paddle and squinted over the transom, his Juicy Fruit seized between his teeth. They laid him, together, on the afterdeck. In the cold salt water he had stiffened quickly; his right foot had frozen rigidly over his left, and his arms,

---

5 **wreathe sth.**: surround or cover sth.   19 **beaver paddle**: Netzwindenpedal
24 **slack** (n): looseness   **reel**: Winde   28 **drum = net drum**: Netztrommel/~winde
34 **convoluted**: having many twists or curves   **coil**: series of circles formed by winding up sth.   **kelp**: type of brown seaweed   **ensnarl sth.**: entangle sth.
43 **bib overall**: Latzhose   47 **hue** (v): (here) produce a particular shade of a color
48 **parboil sth.**: boil sth. until it is partly cooked   49 **transom**: ledge at the back of a boat   50 **retch**: make the sound of vomiting   62 **yard sb./sth. over sth.**: jdn. über etwas hinweg hineinheben   63 **gingerly**: carefully

locked at the shoulders, were fixed in place with the fingers curled. His mouth was open. His eyes were open too, but the pupils had disappeared – Art saw how they'd revolved backward and now looked inward at his skull. The blood vessels in the whites of his eyes had burst; there were two crimson orbs in his head.

Abel Martinson stared.

Art found that he could not bring forward the least vestige of professionalism. He simply stood by, like his twenty-four-year-old deputy, thinking the thoughts a man thinks at such a time about the ugly inevitability of death. There was a silence to be filled, and Art found himself hard-pressed in the face of it to conduct himself in a manner his deputy could learn from. And so they simply stood looking down at Carl's corpse, a thing that had silenced both of them.

'He banged his head,' whispered Abel Martinson, pointing to a wound Art hadn't noticed in Carl Heine's blond hair. 'Must have banged it against the gunnel going over.'

Sure enough, Carl Heine's skull had been crushed just above his left ear. The bone had fractured and left a dent in his head. Art Moran turned away from it.

---

1 **lock sth.** (v): (here) fix sth. in one position   5 **orb**: Kugel   7 **vestige**: all that remains of sth.   11 **conduct yourself**: behave in a particular way   18 **dent**: hollow place in a hard surface, usu. caused by sth. hitting it

Chapter 3

Nels Gudmundsson, the attorney who had been appointed to defend Kabuo Miyamoto, rose to cross-examine Art Moran with a slow and deliberate geriatric awkwardness, then roughly cleared the phlegm from his throat and hooked his thumbs behind his suspenders where they met their tiny black catch buttons. At seventy-nine, Nels was blind in his left eye and could distinguish only shades of light and darkness through its transient, shadowy pupil. The right, however, as if to make up for this deficiency, seemed preternaturally observant, even prescient, and as he plodded over the courtroom floorboards, advancing with a limp toward Art Moran, motes of light winked through it.

'Sheriff,' he said. 'Good morning.'

'Good morning,' replied Art Moran.

'I just want to make sure I'm hearing you right on a couple of matters,' said Nels. 'You say the lights on this boat, the *Susan Marie*, were all on? Is that right?'

'Yes,' said the sheriff. 'They were.'

'In the cabin, too?'

'That's right.'

'The mast lights?'

'Yes.'

'The picking lights? The net lights. *All* of them?'

'Yes, sir,' said Art Moran.

'Thank you,' Nels said. 'I thought that was what you said, all right. That they were all on. All the lights.'

---

1 **attorney** (AE): lawyer who can act for sb. in court   2 **cross-examine sb.**: question sb. in court about answers that they have already given   3 **geriatric**: related to old age   **phlegm** [flem]: Schleim   4 **suspenders** (AE): Hosenträger
7 **transient**: (here) that cannot remain focussed   8 **preternatural** (fml): that does not seem natural   **prescient** ['presiənt] (fml): appearing to know about things before they happen   10 **mote** (old-fashioned): very small piece of dust, etc.
wink (v): (here) shine with an unsteady light

He paused and for a moment seemed to study his hands, which were riddled with liver spots and trembled at times: Nels suffered from an advancing neurasthenia. Its foremost symptom was a sensation of heat that on occasion flamed in the nerve endings of his forehead until the arteries in his temples pulsed visibly.

'You say it was foggy on the night of September 15?' Nels asked. 'Is that what you said, sheriff?'

'Yes.'

'Thick fog?'

'Absolutely.'

'Do you remember this?'

'I remember, yes. I've thought about it. Because I went out on my porch about ten o'clock, see. Hadn't seen fog for more than a week. And I couldn't see more than twenty yards.'

'At ten o'clock?'

'Yes.'

'And then?'

'I went to bed, I guess.'

'You went to bed. What time did you get up, sheriff? Do you remember? On the sixteenth?'

'I got up at five. At five o'clock.'

'You remember this?'

'I'm always up at five. Every morning. So on the sixteenth, yes, I was up at five.'

'And was the fog still there?'

'Yes, it was.'

'Just as thick? As thick as at ten o'clock the night before?'

'Almost, I'd say. Almost. But not quite.'

'So it was still foggy in the morning, then.'

'Yes. Until nine or so. Then it started burning off – was mostly gone by the time we set out in the launch, if that's what you're driving at, sir.'

'Until nine,' answered Nels Gudmundsson. 'Or thereabouts? Nine?'

'That's right,' replied Art Moran.

Nels Gudmundsson raised his chin, fingered his bow tie, and pinched experimentally the wattles of skin at his neck – a habit of his when he was thinking.

'Out there on the *Susan Marie*,' he said. 'The engine started right up, sheriff? When you went to start it you had no trouble?'

'Right away,' said Art Moran. 'No trouble at all.'

'With all those lights drawing, sheriff? Batteries still strong?'

'Must have been. Because she started with no trouble.'

'Did that strike you as odd, sheriff? Do you remember? That with all those lights drawing, the batteries still had plenty of charge, enough to turn the engine over with no trouble, as you say?'

'Didn't think about it at the time,' said Art Moran. 'So no is the answer – it didn't strike me as odd, at least not then.'

'And does it strike you as odd now?'

'A little,' said the sheriff. 'Yes.'

'Why?' Nels asked.

'Because those lights do a lot of drawing. I'd reckon they can run a battery down quick – just like in your car. So I have to wonder a little, yes.'

'You have to wonder,' said Nels Gudmundsson, and he began to massage his throat again and pull at the dewlaps of skin there.

Nels made his way to the evidence table, selected a folder, and brought it to Art Moran. 'Your investigative report,' he said. 'The one just admitted into evidence during Mr. Hooks's direct examination. Is this it, sheriff?'

'It is.'

'Could you turn to page seven, please?'

The sheriff did so.

'Now,' said Nels, 'is page seven an inventory of items found on board Carl Heine's boat, the *Susan Marie*?'

'Could you read for the court the item listed as number twenty-seven?'

'Of course,' said Art Moran. 'Item twenty-seven. A spare D-8 battery, six celled.'

'A spare D-8 battery, six celled,' said Nels. 'Thank you. A D-8. Six celled. Would you turn now to item forty-two, sheriff? And read one more time for the court?'

---

3 **neurasthenia** (old-fashioned): a condition that makes sb. feel tired all the time   31 **be driving at sth**: try to say sth.   35 **bow tie**: Fliege   36 **wattle**: (here) loose skin   43 **odd** (adj): strange or unusual   54 **dewlap**: (altersbedingte) Halsfalte

'Item forty-two,' replied Art Moran. 'D-8 and D-6 batteries in battery well. Each six celled.'

'A 6 and an 8?' Nels said.

'Yes.'

'I did some measuring down at the chandlery,' said Nels. 'A D-6 is wider than a D-8 by an inch. It wouldn't fit into the *Susan Marie*'s battery well, sheriff. It was an inch too large for that.'

'He'd done some on-the-spot refitting,' Art explained. 'The side flange was banged away to make room for a D-6.'

'He banged out the side flange?'

'Yes.'

'You could see this?'

'Yes.'

'A metal flange that had been banged aside?'

'Yes.'

'Soft metal?'

'Yes. Soft enough. It'd been banged back to make room for a D-6.'

'To make room for a D-6,' Nels repeated. 'But sheriff, didn't you say that the spare was a D-8? Didn't Carl Heine have a D-8 available that would have fit into the existing well with none of this banging and refitting?'

'The spare was dead,' Art Moran said. 'We tested it after we brought the boat in. It didn't have any juice to it, Mr. Gudmundsson. Didn't have any juice at all.'

'The spare was dead,' Nels repeated. 'So, to summarize, you found on the deceased's boat a dead spare D-8 battery, a working D-8 down in the well, and beside it a working D-6 that was in fact too large for the existing space and which forced someone to do some refitting? Some banging at a soft metal flange?'

'All correct,' said the sheriff.

'All right now,' said Nels Gudmundsson. 'Would you please turn to page twenty-seven of your report? Your inventory of items aboard the *defendant's* boat? And read for the court item twenty-four, please?'

Art Moran turned the pages. 'Item twenty-four,' he said after a while. 'Two D-6 batteries in well. Each six celled.'

'Two D-6s on Kabuo Miyamoto's boat,' Nels said. 'And did you find a spare aboard, sheriff?'

'No. We didn't. It isn't in the inventory.'

'The defendant had no spare battery aboard his boat? He'd gone out fishing without one?'

'Apparently, yes, sir, he did.'

'Well, then,' Nels said. 'Two D-6s in the well and no spare to be found. Tell me, sheriff. These D-6s on the defendant's boat. Were they the same sort of D-6 you found in the deceased's battery well? On board the *Susan Marie*? The same size? The same make?'

'Yes,' replied the sheriff. 'All D-6s. The same battery.'

'So the D-6 in use on the deceased's boat could have – hypothetically, since it was identical – made a perfect spare for the defendant's batteries?'

'I suppose so.'

'But, as you say, the defendant *had* no spare on board. Is that right?'

'Yes.'

'All right, sheriff,' Nels said. 'Let me ask you about something else, if you don't mind, for a moment. Tell me – when you brought the deceased in was there some sort of trouble? When you hauled him up from the sea in his fishing net?'

'Yes,' said Art Moran. 'I mean, he was heavy. And, well, his lower half – his legs and feet? – they wanted to slide out of the net. He was hanging by one of his rain gear buckles. And we were afraid if we pulled him out of the water maybe we'd lose him altogether, he'd come out and the buckle would give or the rubber around it would and he'd be gone. His legs were hanging in the water, you understand. His legs weren't quite in the net.'

'And,' said Nels Gudmundsson, 'can you tell us what you and Deputy Martinson did about this?'

'Well, we cupped the webbing. And then we pulled on the lead line. We made a sort of cradle with the net, got his legs inside it. Then we brought him in.'

'So you had some trouble,' Nels said.

'A little, yes.'

1–2 **battery well**: Batterieschacht   8 **on-the-spot**: (here) done by himself
9 **flange**: side of an object that keeps sth. in place   54 **haul sb./sth.**: pull sb./sth. with a lot of effort   58 **gear**: outfit, equipment   **buckle**: Schnalle   60 **give**: break under pressure   65 **cup sth.**: make sth. into the shape of a cup   **webbing**: (Gurt)band

'He didn't come in cleanly?'

'Not at first, no. We had to jerk the net around, work it. But once we had him in and the webbing grabbed it was fairly smooth from there, yes.'

'Sheriff,' said Nels Gudmundsson, 'with all of this jerking of the net and this trouble you're mentioning now – is it possible the deceased hit his head on the transom of the boat as you were bringing him in? Or somewhere else? On the stern gunnel, say, or on the net roller? Is it possible?'

'I don't think so,' said Art Moran. 'I would have seen it if we did.'

'You don't think so,' said Nels Gudmundsson. 'What about when you pulled him out of the net? When you laid him on the deck? He was a big man, as you say, two hundred and thirty-five pounds, and stiff, as you've pointed out. Was he difficult to move around, sheriff?'

'He was heavy, yes, real heavy. But there were two of us and we were careful. We didn't hit him on anything.'

'Are you sure of this?'

'I don't remember hitting him on anything, no, Mr. Gudmundsson. We were careful, as I've said already.'

'But you don't remember,' Nels said. 'Or to put it another way, do you have any uncertainty at all about this? That in moving this awkward and heavy corpse about, in operating this winch equipment you'd rarely operated before, in doing this difficult job of bringing in a drowned man of two hundred and thirty-five pounds – is it possible, Sheriff Moran, that the deceased banged his head sometime *after* his death? Is that possible?'

'Yes,' said Art Moran. '*Possible*. I guess it is – but not likely.'

Nels Gudmundsson turned toward the jury. 'No more questions,' he said. And with a slowness that embarrassed him – because as a young man he had been lithe and an athlete, had always moved fluidly across the floorboards of courtrooms, had always felt admired for his physical appearance – he made his way back to his seat at the defendant's table, where Kabuo Miyamoto sat watching him.

---

28 **lithe**: (of a person or their body) graceful, moving or bending easily

Chapter 4

Judge Lew Fielding called for a recess at ten forty-five that first morning. He turned to observe the silent sweep of the snowfall, rubbed his graying eyebrows and the tip of his nose, then rose in his black robe, slid his hands through his hair, and lumbered into his chambers.

The accused man, Kabuo Miyamoto, leaned to his right and nodded just perceptibly while Nels Gudmundsson spoke into his ear. Across the aisle Alvin Hooks rested his chin in his hands, drumming the floorboards with the heel of his shoe, impatient but not dissatisfied. In the gallery the citizens stood and yawned, then wandered off into the less stultifying atmosphere of the hallway or gazed out the windows with awed expressions, watching the snow lash toward them in parabolas before it struck against the leaded panes. Their faces, bathed in the attenuated December light from the tall windows, appeared quiet and even faintly reverent. Those who had driven into town felt fretful about getting home.

The jurors were led away by Ed Soames to drink cone-shaped cups of lukewarm cooler water and to make use of the lavatory. Then Soames reappeared and plodded about like a parish beadle, backing down the steam radiator valves. Yet it remained too hot in the courtroom despite this; the trapped heat wouldn't dissipate. Steam began to coalesce in a film of vapor on the upper reaches of the windows, closing the courtroom in a little, muffling the pale morning light.

---

4 **lumber** (v): move in a slow, heavy and awkward way   10 **stultifying** (fml): making you feel very bored and depressed   11 **lash** (v): hit sb./sth. with great force   11–12 **parabola**: Parabel   12 **pane**: single sheet of glass in a window   13 **attenuate sth.** (fml): make sth. weaker   14 **reverent** (adj, fml): showing great respect and admiration   **fretful**: restless or worried   18 **plod about**: walk slowly with heavy steps   **beadle**: Kirchendiener   20 **dissipate**: gradually become weaker and then disappear   **coalesce** [ˌkəʊəˈles]: come together to form one substance   22 **muffle sth.**: make sth. less clear or loud, esp. a sound

Ishmael Chambers found a seat in the gallery and sat tapping his pencil's eraser against his bottom lip. Like others on San Piedro Island, he'd first heard about the death of Carl Heine on the afternoon of September 16 – the day the body was discovered. He'd been calling the Reverend Gordon Groves of the Amity Harbor Lutheran Congregation to ask about the sermon topic for Sunday in order that he might paraphrase the reverend's answer in his 'At Our Island Churches' column, a weekly feature in the *San Piedro Review* that ran beside the Anacortes ferry schedule. The Reverend Groves was not in, but his wife, Lillian, informed Ishmael that Carl Heine had drowned and been found tangled in his gill net.

Ishmael Chambers did not believe her: Lillian Groves was a gossip. He was not inclined to believe such a thing and when he hung up sat brooding over it. Then, disbelieving, he dialed the sheriff's office and asked Eleanor Dokes, a person he did not entirely trust either: yes, she replied, Carl Heine had drowned. He'd been fishing, yes. He'd been found in his net. The sheriff? Not in just now. She supposed he was seeing the coroner.

Ishmael immediately called the coroner, Horace Whaley. That's right, said Horace, you'd better believe it. Carl Heine was dead. Terrible thing, wasn't it? The man had survived Okinawa. Carl *Heine*, it was *unbelievable*. He'd hit his head on something.

The sheriff? said Horace. You just barely missed him. He and Abel both; just barely gone. Heading for the docks, they said.

Ishmael Chambers put down the receiver and sat with his forehead held in his palm, remembering Carl Heine from high school. They had both graduated in '42. They had played on the football team together. He remembered riding the team bus with Carl to a game against Bellingham in the fall of '41. They rode wearing their uniforms, their helmets in their laps, each boy carrying his own towel. He remembered how Carl looked sitting beside him with his gym towel draped around his thick German neck, glaring out the window at the fields. It was dusk, a brief November twilight, and Carl was watching snow geese land in low flooded wheat, his square chin set, his head tilted up, a man's blond stubble on his jaw. 'Chambers,' he'd said. 'You see the geese?'

Ishmael slid a notepad into the pocket of his pants and went outside into Hill Street. Behind him he left unlocked the office of the *Review* –

three rooms that had once housed a book and magazine shop and still contained its many wall shelves. The bookshop had ultimately not been profitable because of the steep hill on which it was situated; Hill Street discouraged tourists. Ishmael, though, liked this feature of it. He had nothing in principle against the vacationers from Seattle who frequented San Piedro all summer long – most islanders disliked them because they were city people – but on the other hand he did not especially enjoy seeing them as they wandered up and down Main Street. Tourists reminded him of other places and elicited in him a prodding doubt that living here was what he wanted.

He had not always been so ambivalent about his home. Once he'd known how he felt about it. After the war, a man of twenty-three with an amputated arm, he'd left San Piedro without reluctance to attend school in Seattle. He'd lived in a boardinghouse on Brooklyn Avenue and taken, at first, history classes. He had not been particularly *happy* in this period, but in that regard he was like other veterans. He was keenly aware of his pinned-up sleeve, and troubled because it troubled other people. Since they could not forget about it, neither could he. There were times when he visited taverns near campus and allowed himself to act gregarious and animated in the manner of younger students. Afterward he inevitably felt foolish, however. It was not in him to drink beer and shoot pool. His more natural domain was a high-backed booth near the rear of Day's Restaurant on University Way where he sipped coffee and read his history.

The next fall Ishmael took up American literature. Melville, Hawthorne, Twain. He was prepared, in his cynicism, to find *Moby Dick*

---

9 **schedule** ['skedʒuːl]: timetable   14 **brood over sth.**: think seriously/worry about sth.   19 **coroner** ['kɔːrənər]: official whose job is to investigate the cause of any violent or suspicious death   21 **Okinawa**: battle fought between Japan and the USA in 1945 over the island of Okinawa; after the battle the USA occupied the island   32 **dusk**: time of day when the light is almost gone   34 **set your chin**: fix your face into a firm expression   35 **stubble**: short stiff hairs that grow on a man's face when he has not shaved recently   46 **elicit sth. in sb.** (fml): (here) make sth., esp. a feeling or reaction, grow in sb.   **prodding** (adj): continual   50 **reluctance**: unwillingness   57 **gregarious**: liking to be with other people   59 **shoot pool**: Billard spielen   60 **booth** [buːθ]: place to sit in a restaurant which consists of two long seats with a table between them

unreadable – five hundred pages about chasing a whale? – but, as it turned out, it was entertaining. He read the whole thing in ten sittings in his booth at Day's and began pondering the whale's nature at an early juncture. The narrator, he found upon reading the first sentence, bore his own name – Ishmael. Ishmael was all right, but Ahab he could not respect and this ultimately undermined the book for him.

Huckleberry Finn he had read as a child, but he couldn't remember much of it. He recalled only that it was funnier then – everything was funnier – but the story had fled his mind. Other people spoke fondly and knowingly of books they had read decades before. Ishmael suspected this was pretense. He sometimes wondered what had become of the books he'd read many years earlier – if they were still somewhere inside him. James Fenimore Cooper, Sir Walter Scott, Dickens, William Dean Howells. He didn't think any of them were still there. He couldn't remember them, anyway.

The Scarlet Letter he read in six sittings. He closed down Day's finishing it. The cook came out from behind the swinging doors and told him it was time to leave. Ishmael was on the last page when this occurred and ended up reading 'ON A FIELD, SABLE, THE LETTER A, GULES,' while standing on the sidewalk outside. What did it mean? He could only guess what it might fully mean, even with the explanatory footnote. People hurried past him while he stood there with his book open, an October gust blowing in his face. He felt troubled by this ending to the story of Hester Prynne; the woman, after all, deserved better.

All right, he decided, books were a good thing, but that was all they were and nothing else – they couldn't put food on his table. And so Ishmael turned to journalism.

His father, Arthur, had been a logger at Ishmael's age. Wearing a handlebar mustache and calf-high caulk boots, frayed suspenders and woolen long johns, he'd labored in the service of the Port Jefferson Mill Company for four and a half years. Ishmael's grandfather had been a Highland Presbyterian, his grandmother an Irish zealot from the bogs above Lough Ree; they met in Seattle five years before the Great Fire, wed, and raised six sons. Arthur, the youngest, was the only one to remain on Puget Sound. Two of his brothers became mercenary soldiers, one died of malaria on the Panama Canal, one became a surveyor in

Burma and India, and the last made tracks for the eastern seaboard at seventeen, never to be heard from again.

The *San Piedro Review*, a four-page weekly, was the invention of Arthur's early twenties. With his savings he acquired a printing press, a box camera, and a damp, low-ceilinged office in the rear of a fish-processing warehouse. The inaugural edition of the *Review* displayed a banner headline: JURY ACQUITS SEATTLE'S GILL. Brushing shoulders with reporters from the *Star*, the *Times*, the *Evening Post*, the *Daily Call*, and the *Seattle Union-Record*, Arthur had covered the trial of Mayor Hiram Gill, accused in a liquor scandal. He ran a long feature on George Vandeveer, charlatan attorney for the Wobbly defense in the Everett Massacre deliberations. An editorial pleaded for the exercise of common sense as Wilson moved to declare war; another celebrated the recent extension of ferry service to the leeward side of the island. A meeting of the Rhododendron Society was announced, as was an evening of square dancing at the Grange and the birth of a son, Theodore Ignatius, to the Horatio Marches of Cattle Point. All of this appeared in Centurion bold type – already antiquated in 1917 – with delicate hairlines separating seven columns and subheads in bold serif relief.

Shortly thereafter Arthur was drafted to serve in General Pershing's army. He fought at Saint-Mihiel and Belleau Wood, then came home to

---

4 **juncture** (fml): particular point in an activity   5 **Ahab**: captain in *Moby Dick*, who is obsessed with taking revenge on the whale to whom he lost his leg
6 **undermine sth.**: make sth. less effective   11 **pretense** (AE = BE pretence): act of behaving in a certain way in order to make other people believe sth. that is not true
28 **logger**: lumberjack, person whose job is cutting down trees   29 **handlebar mustache**: Schnauzbart   **caulk boots**: (here) waterproof boots   **frayed**: ausgefranst   30 **long johns**: lange Unterhose   **labor** (v): work, esp. physically
32 **zealot**: fanatic   **bog**: area of wet soft ground, formed of decaying plants
33 **Great Fire**: fire in 1889 that destroyed much of Seattle   35 **mercenary**: soldier who will fight for payment   36 **surveyor**: person whose job is to examine and record the details of a piece of land   42 **inaugural**: first, and marking the beginning of sth. important   **display sth.**: show sth.   43 **acquit sb.**: decide and state officially in court that sb. is not guilty of a crime   43–44 **brush shoulders with sb.**: (here) spend time with sb. of importance   48 **deliberations** (pl): process of carefully considering sth.   **editorial**: article in a newspaper that expresses the editor's opinion   50 **leeward**: on the side of sth. that is sheltered from the wind
56 **draft sb.**: jdn. einziehen (zum Kriegsdienst)

his newspaper. He married a Seattle woman of Illini stock, corn blond, svelte, and somber eyed. Her father, a haberdasher on Seattle's First Avenue and a real estate speculator, frowned on Arthur, who seemed to him a lumberjack posing as a reporter, a man without prospects and unworthy of his daughter; nevertheless the two were married and settled down to the business of rearing children. They had only one, though, after much effort; they lost a second at birth. They built a house at South Beach with a view of the sea and cleared a path to the beach. Arthur became an astute and deliberate vegetable gardener, an inveterate observer of island life, and gradually a small-town newspaperman in the truest sense: he came to recognize the opportunity his words provided for leverage, celebrity, and service. For many years he took no vacations. He put out extra editions on Christmas Eve, during election week, and on the Fourth of July. Ishmael remembered running the press with his father every Tuesday evening. Arthur had bolted it to the floor of a boat-building warehouse on Andreason Street, a dilapidated barn that smelled permanently of lithographic ink and of the ammonia in the typesetting machine. The press was an enormous lime green contraption, rollers and conveyor pulleys in a cast-iron housing; it started with the hesitancy of a nineteenth-century locomotive and shrieked and bleated while it ran. It was Ishmael's job to set the impression meters and water fountains and to act in the role of fly boy; Arthur, who had formed over the years a symbiotic relationship with the machine, ducked in and out inspecting the plates and printing cylinders. He stood mere inches from the clattering rollers, seemingly oblivious to the fact that – as he'd explained to his son – were he caught by a sleeve he'd be instantly popped open like a child's balloon and splattered across the walls. Even his bones would disappear – this was part of Arthur's warning – until somebody found them scattered among the stained newsprint on the floor, looking like strips of white confetti.

A group of businessmen from the chamber of commerce had tried to persuade Arthur to run for the Washington state legislature. They came to the house dressed in overcoats and checkered scarves, reeking of pomade and shaving soap, and sat down to snifters of blackberry cordial, after which Arthur declined to run for office, telling the gentlemen from Amity Harbor that he harbored no illusions, that he preferred to turn sentences and prune his mulberry hedges. The sleeves of his striped oxford shirt lay rolled to his elbows so that the hairs on his forearms showed; his back formed a long hard wedge of muscle against which his suspenders rode tautly. On his nose, a bit low, sat his steel-rimmed full moons, gently prosthetic and handsomely discordant with the sinewy length of his jawline. The cartilage in his nose was twisted – it'd been broken by the lash of a wayward logging cable in the winter of 1915. The men from Amity Harbor couldn't argue with this or with the fixed upward tilt of his chin and jaw. They left unsatisfied.

An unflagging loyalty to his profession and its principles had made Arthur, over the years, increasingly deliberate in his speech and actions, and increasingly exacting regarding the truth in even his most casual reportage. He was, his son remembered, morally meticulous, and though Ishmael might strive to emulate this, there was nevertheless this matter of the war – this matter of the arm he'd lost – that made such scrupulosity difficult. He had a chip on his shoulder: it was a sort of black joke he shared with himself, a double entendre, made silently. He didn't like very many people anymore or very many things, either. He preferred not to be this way, but there it was, he was like that. His cynicism – a veteran's cynicism – was a thing that disturbed him all the time. It seemed to him after the war that the world was thoroughly altered. It was not even a thing you could explain to anybody, why it was that everything was folly. People appeared enormously foolish to him. He understood that they were only animated cavities full of jelly

---

2 **svelte**: (esp. of women) slim and attractive   **haberdasher** (old-fashioned): Kurzwarenhändler   9 **astute**: clever and quick-thinking   **inveterate**: (here) always doing sth. and unlikely to stop   12 **leverage** ['levərɪdʒ] (fml): influence
16 **dilapidated**: old and in a very bad condition   18 **contraption**: merkwürdiger Apparat   20 **bleat**: make the sound that sheep make   22 **fly boy**: boy in a printing office who lifts the printed sheets from the press   25 **oblivious**: not aware of sth.   27 **splatter** (v): cover sth./sb. with large drops of a liquid   29 **stain** sth.: leave a mark on sth., esp. one that is difficult to remove   32 **reek** (v): smell very strongly of sth. unpleasant   33 **snifter**: large glass used for drinking brandy
cordial (n, AE): liqueur   40 **prosthetic**: wie eine Prothese   **discordant** (fml): not in agreement   41 **sinewy** ['sɪnjuːi]: sehnig   **cartilage**: Knorpel   45 **unflagging**: remaining strong   48 **meticulous**: paying careful attention to every detail
49 **emulate sth.** (fml): try to do sth. as well as sb. else because you admire them
51 **have a chip on your shoulder** (infml): be sensitive about sth. that happened in the past and become easily offended if it is mentioned   59 **cavity**: hole or empty space

and strings and liquids. He had seen the insides of jaggedly ripped-open dead people. He knew, for instance, what brains looked like spilling out of somebody's head. In the context of this, much of what went on in normal life seemed wholly and disturbingly ridiculous. He found that he was irritated with complete strangers. If somebody in one of his classes spoke to him he answered stiffly, tersely. He could never tell if they were relaxed enough about his arm to say what they were really thinking. He sensed their need to extend sympathy to him, and this irritated him even more. The arm was a grim enough thing without that, and he felt sure it was entirely disgusting. He could repel people if he chose by wearing to class a short-sleeved shirt that revealed the scar tissue on his stump. He never did this, however. He didn't exactly want to *repel* people. Anyway, he had this view of things – that most human activity was utter folly, his own included, and that his existence in the world made others nervous. He could not help but possess this unhappy perspective, no matter how much he might not want it. It was his and he suffered from it numbly.

Later, when he was no longer so young and back home on San Piedro Island, this view of things began to moderate. He learned to be cordial to everyone – a sophisticated and ultimately false front. Add to the cynicism of a man wounded in war the inevitable cynicism of growing older and the professional cynicism of the journalist. Gradually Ishmael came to view himself as a one-armed man with a pinned-up sleeve, past thirty and unmarried. It was not so bad, and he was not so irritated as he had once been in Seattle. Still, though, there were those tourists, he thought, as he walked down Hill Street toward the docks. All summer they looked at his pinned-up sleeve with the surprised, unaccustomed faces his fellow islanders had stopped making. And with their ice cream and clean faces they elicited in his gut again that bilious, unwanted irritation. The strange thing was, he wanted to like everyone. He just couldn't find a way to do it.

His mother, who was fifty-six and lived alone in the old family house on the south end of the island – the house where Ishmael had lived as a child – had pointed out to him when he'd come home from the city that this cynicism of his, while understandable, was on the other hand entirely unbecoming. His father before him had had it, she said, and it had been unbecoming in him, too.

'He loved humankind dearly and with all his heart, but he disliked most human beings,' she'd told Ishmael. 'You're the same, you know. You're your father's son.'

Art Moran was standing with one foot up on a piling, talking to half a dozen fishermen, when Ishmael Chambers arrived that afternoon on the Amity Harbor docks. They were gathered in front of Carl Heine's gillnetter, which was moored between the *Erik J* and the *Tordenskold* – the former a bow-picker owned by Marty Johansson, the latter an Anacortes purse seiner. As Ishmael came their way a south breeze blew and caused the mooring lines of boats to creak – the *Advancer*, the *Providence*, the *Ocean Mist*, the *Torvanger* – all standard San Piedro gillnetters. The *Mystery Maid*, a halibut and black cod schooner, had fared badly of late and was in the process of being overhauled. Her starboard hull plate had been removed, her engine dismantled, and her crankshaft and rod bearings lay exposed. On the dock at her bow lay a pile of pipe fittings, two rusted diesel barrels, a scattering of broken plate glass, and the hulk of a marine battery on which empty paint cans were stacked. A sheen of oil lay on the water just below where scraps of rug had been nailed down to act as dockside bumpers.

Today there were a lot of seagulls present. Normally they foraged around the salmon cannery, but now they sat on drag floats or buoy bags without stirring a feather, as if made of clay, or rode the tide in Amity Harbor, occasionally flaring overhead, riding the winds with their heads swiveling. Sometimes they alighted on unattended boats and scavenged desperately for deck scraps. Fishermen sometimes shot

---

1 **jagged**: ungleichmäßig   10 **disgusting**: very unpleasant   **repel sb.**: (here) make sb. feel horror or dislike   17 **numb** [nʌm]: unable to feel, think or react in a normal way   19 **cordial** (fml): friendly, polite   29 **bilious**: feeling as if you might vomit soon   36 **unbecoming**: (here) not suiting a particular person
45 **bow-picker**: Seitentrawler   49 **cod**: Dorsch   49–50 **fare badly**: be unsuccessful   50 **of late**: recently   51 **hull plate**: Außenplanke   **dismantle sth.**: take apart a machine or structure   **crankshaft**: Kurbelwelle   52 **rod bearing**: Kolben   **bow** (n): Bug   57 **forage**: (here) search for food   58 **cannery**: factory where food is put into cans in order to preserve it   **buoy** ['buːi]: Boje
59 **clay**: Lehm, Ton   62 **scavenge for sth.**: search through waste for things that can be used or eaten

duck loads at them, but for the most part the gulls were given free rein on the docks; their gray white droppings stained everything.

An oil drum had been turned onto its side before the *Susan Marie*, and on it sat Dale Middleton and Leonard George, dressed in mechanics' grease suits. Jan Sorensen leaned against a plywood garbage Dumpster; Marty Johansson stood with his feet planted wide, his forearms folded across his bare chest, his T-shirt tucked into his pants waist. Directly beside the sheriff stood William Gjovaag with a cigar lodged between his fingers. Abel Martinson had perched himself on the bow gunnel of the *Susan Marie* and listened to the fishermen's conversation with his boots dangling above the waterline.

San Piedro fishermen – in those days, at least – went out at dusk to work the seas. Most of them were gill-netters, men who traveled into solitary waters and dropped their nets into the currents salmon swam. The nets hung down like curtains in the dark water and the salmon, unsuspecting, swam into them.

A gill-netter passed his night hours in silence, rocking on the sea and waiting patiently. It was important that his character be adapted to this, otherwise his chances of success were dubious. At times the salmon ran in such narrow waters that men had to fish for them in sight of one another, in which case arguments brewed. The man who'd been cut off by another man up tide might motor abreast of the interloper in order to shake a gaff at him and curse him up and down as a fish thief. There were, on occasion, shouting matches at sea, but far more often a man was alone all night and had no one, even, to argue with. Some who had tried this lonely sort of life had given up and joined the crews of purse seiners or of long-line halibut schooners. Gradually Anacortes, a town on the mainland, became home to the big boats with crews of four or more, the Amity Harbor fleet home to one-man gill-netters. It was something San Piedro prided itself on, the fact that its men had the courage to fish alone even in inclement weather. An ethic, with time, asserted itself in island souls, that fishing alone was better than fishing other ways, so that the sons of fishermen, when they dreamed at night, dreamed of going forth in their lonely boats and hauling from the sea with their nets large salmon that other men would find impressive.

Thus on San Piedro the silent-toiling, autonomous gill-netter became the collective image of the *good* man. He who was too gregarious, who spoke too much and too ardently desired the company of others, their conversation and their laughter, did not have what life required. Only insofar as he struggled successfully with the sea could a man lay claim to his place in things.

San Piedro men learned to be silent. Occasionally, though, and with enormous relief, they communicated with one another on the docks at dawn. Though tired and still busy, they spoke from deck to deck of what had happened during the night and of things only they could understand. The intimacy of it, the comfort of other voices giving credence to their private myths, prepared them to meet their wives with less distance than they might otherwise bring home after fishing. In short, they were lonely men and products of geography – island men who on occasion recognized that they wished to speak but couldn't.

Ishmael Chambers knew, as he approached the knot of men gathered before the *Susan Marie*, that he was not a part of this fraternity of fishermen, that furthermore he made his living with words and was thus suspect to them. On the other hand he had the advantage of the prominently wounded and of any veteran whose war years are forever a mystery to the uninitiated. These latter were things that solitary gill-netters could appreciate and offset their distrust of a word shaper who sat behind a typewriter all day.

They nodded at him and with slight alterations in posture included him in their circle. 'Figure'd you'd a heard by now,' said the sheriff. 'Probably know more 'n I do.'

'Hard to believe,' answered Ishmael.

William Gjovaag tucked his cigar between his teeth. 'It happens,' he grunted. 'You go fishing, it happens.'

'Well, yeah,' said Marty Johansson. 'But Jesus Christ.' He shook his head and rocked on his heels.

1 **duck loads**: Schrot   **give sb. free rein**: give sb. freedom of action   9 **perch on sth.** (v): sit on sth., esp. on the edge of it   14 **current** (n): Strömung   22 **interloper**: person who is somewhere where they do not belong   23 **gaff**: Fischhaken   31 **inclement**: not pleasant; cold, wet   31–32 **assert itself**: start to have an effect   47 **credence** ['kriːdns]: quality of an idea or a story that makes you believe it is true   56 **uninitiated**: uneingeweiht   **these latter**: diese Letzteren   57 **offset sth.**: balance sth.

The sheriff brought his left leg down from the piling, hitched his trousers at the thigh and brought his right up, then settled his elbow on his knees.

'You see Susan Marie?' asked Ishmael.

'I did,' said Art. 'Boy.'

'Three kids,' said Ishmael. 'What's she going to do?'

'I don't know,' said the sheriff.

'She say anything?'

'Not a word.'

'Well, what's she *going* to say?' put in William Gjovaag. 'What can she say? Jesus Christ.'

Ishmael understood by this that Gjovaag disapproved of journalism. He was a sunburned, big-bellied, tattooed gill-netter with the watery eyes of a gin drinker. His wife had left him five years before; William lived on his boat.

'Excuse me, Gjovaag,' said Ishmael.

'I don't need to excuse nothing,' Gjovaag answered. 'Fuck you anyhow, Chambers.'

Everybody laughed. It was all good-natured, sort of. Ishmael Chambers understood that.

'Do you know what happened?' he asked the sheriff.

'That's just what I'm trying to straighten out,' said Art Moran. 'That's just what we're talking about.'

'Art wants to know where we all was fishing,' Marty Johansson explained. 'He – '

'Don't need to know where *everyone* was at,' Sheriff Moran cut in. 'I'm just trying to figure out where Carl went last night. Where he fished. Who maybe saw him or talked to him last. That kind of thing, Marty.'

'I saw him,' said Dale Middleton. 'We ran out of the bay together.'

'You mean you *followed* him out,' said Marty Johansson. 'I bet you followed him out, didn't you?'

Younger fishermen like Dale Middleton were apt to spend considerable time each day – at the San Piedro Cafe or the Amity Harbor Restaurant – rooting for information. They wanted to know where the fish were running, how other men had done the night before, and where – exactly – they had done it. The seasoned and successful, like Carl Heine, ignored them as a matter of course. As a result he could count on being tailed to the fishing grounds: if a man wouldn't speak he was followed. On a foggy night his pursuers had to run in close and were more apt to lose their quarry altogether, in which case they turned to their radios, checking in with various compatriots whom they invariably found to be checking in with them: hapless voices tuned to one another in the hope of some shred of knowledge. The most respected men, in accordance with the ethos that had evolved on San Piedro, pursued no one and cultivated radio silence. Occasionally others would approach them in their boats, see who it was, and turn immediately away, knowing there would be neither idle conversation nor hard information about the fish they pursued. Some men shared, others didn't. Carl Heine was in the latter category.

'All right, I followed him,' said Dale Middleton. 'The guy'd been bringing in a lot of fish.'

'What time was that?' asked the sheriff.

'Six-thirty, around there.'

'You see him after that?'

'Yeah. Out at Ship Channel Bank. With a lot of other guys. After silvers.'

'It was foggy last night,' said Ishmael Chambers. 'You must have been fishing in close.'

'No,' said Dale. 'I just saw him setting. Before the fog. Maybe seven-thirty? Eight o'clock?'

'I saw him, too,' said Leonard George. 'He was all set. Out on the bank. He was in.'

'What time was that?' said the sheriff.

'Early,' said Leonard. 'Eight o'clock.'

'Nobody saw him later than that? Nobody saw him after eight?'

'I was outa there by ten myself,' Leonard George explained. 'There was nothing doing, no fish. I ran up to Elliot Head real slow like. A fog run. I had my horn going.'

---

26 **cut in**: interrupt   32 **be apt to do sth.**: have the tendency to do sth.   34 **root for sth.**: search for sth.   36 **seasoned**: (here) experienced   37 **as a matter of course**: as usual, out of habit   40 **quarry**: (here) animal that is being hunted or followed   41 **invariably**: always   42 **hapless** (fml): unlucky, unfortunate   61 **be all set**: (here) with the fishing nets cast (= auswerfen) into the sea

'Me, too,' said Dale Middleton. 'Most everybody took off 'fore long. We came over and got into Marty's fish.' He grinned. 'Had a pretty fair night there, too.'

'Did Carl go up to Elliot?' asked the sheriff.

'Didn't see him,' Leonard said. 'But that don't mean nothing. Like I said, fog soup.'

'I doubt he moved,' put in Marty Johansson. 'I'm just guessing on that, but Carl never moved much. He made up his mind 'n' stuck where he was. Probably pulled some fish off Ship Channel, too. Never did see him at the head, no.'

'Me neither,' said Dale Middleton.

'But you saw him at Ship Channel,' said the sheriff. 'Who else was there? You remember?'

'Who else?' said Dale. 'There was two dozen boats, easy. Even more, but Jesus, who knows?'

'Soup,' said Leonard George. 'Real thick fog. You couldn't see nothing out there.'

'Which boats?' asked Art Moran.

'Well, okay,' said Leonard, 'let's see now. I saw the *Kasilof*, the *Islander*, the *Mogul*, the *Eclipse* – this was all out at Ship Channel I'm talking about – '

'The *Antarctic*,' said Dale Middleton. 'She was out there.'

'The *Antarctic*, yeah,' said Leonard.

'What about over the radio?' said Art Moran. 'You hear anybody else? Anybody you didn't see?'

'Vance Cope,' said Leonard. 'You know Vance? The *Providence*? I talked with him a little.'

'You talked with him a lot,' said Marty Johansson. 'I heard you guys all the way over to the head. Jesus Christ, Leonard –'

'Anybody else?' said the sheriff.

'The *Wolf Chief*,' answered Dale. 'I heard Jim Ferry and Hardwell. The *Bergen* was out at Ship Channel.'

'That it?'

'I guess,' said Leonard. 'Yeah.'

'The *Mogul*,' said Art. 'Whose boat is that?'

'Moulton,' replied Marty Johansson. 'He got it from the Laneys last spring.'

'What about the *Islander*? Who's that?'

'The *Islander* is Miyamoto,' said Dale Middleton. 'Ain't that right? The middle one?'

'The oldest,' Ishmael Chambers explained. 'Kabuo – he's the oldest. The middle is Kenji. He's working at the cannery.'

'Suckers all look alike,' said Dale. 'Never could tell them guys apart.'

'Japs,' William Gjovaag threw in. He tossed the stub of his cigar into the water beside the *Susan Marie*.

'All right, look,' said Art Moran. 'You see those guys like Hardwell or Cope or Moulton or anybody, you tell them they ought to come talk to me. I want to know if anybody spoke with Carl last night, from all those guys – you got this? From every last one of them.'

'Sheriff's sounding like a hard-ass,' said Gjovaag. 'Ain't this just a accident?'

'Of course it is,' said Art Moran. 'But still, a man's dead, William. I've got a report to write up.'

'A gud man,' said Jan Sorensen, who spoke with a hint of Danish in his voice. 'A gud fisherman.' He shook his head.

The sheriff brought his leg down from the piling and with care repaired the tuck of his shirt. 'Abel,' he said. 'Why don't you square away the launch and meet me back up at the office? I'm going to walk up with Chambers here. Me and him've got things to discuss.'

But it was not until they'd left the docks altogether and turned onto Harbor Street that Art Moran quit speaking idly and came to the point with Ishmael. 'Look,' he said. 'I know what you're thinking. You're gonna do an article that says Sheriff Moran suspects foul play and is investigating, am I right?'

'I don't know what to say,' said Ishmael Chambers. 'I don't know anything about it yet. I was hoping you'd fill me in.'

'Well, sure, I'll fill you in,' said Art Moran. 'But you got to promise me something first. You won't say anything about an investigation, all right? If you want to quote me on the subject here's my quote: Carl

1 **off'fore** = off before   43 **sucker** (sl): term for sb. who is not liked
45 **Jap** (sl): offensive word for a Japanese person   58 **tuck** (n): (hier) Saum
58–59 **square sth. away**: (here) put sth. in its right place   67 **fill sb. in**: tell sb. what has happened

Heine drowned by accident, or something like that, you make it up, but don't say anything about no investigation. Because there isn't one.'

'You want me to lie?' asked Ishmael Chambers. 'I'm supposed to make up a phony quote?'

'Off the record?' said the sheriff. 'Okay, there's an investigation. Some tricky, funny little facts floating around – could mean anything, where we stand now. Could be murder, could be manslaughter, could be an accident – could be *any*thing. Point is, we just don't know yet. But you go telling everyone that on the front page of the *Review*, we aren't ever going to find out.'

'What about the guys you just talked to, Art? You know what they're going to do? William Gjovaag's going to be telling everyone he can you're snooping around looking for a killer.'

'That's different,' insisted Art Moran. 'That's a rumor, isn't it? And around here there's always going to be rumors like that even if I'm *not* investigating *any*thing. In this case we want to leave it to the killer – if there is a killer, remember – to figure what he hears is just gossip. We'll just let rumor work for us, confuse him. And anyway I've got to be asking questions. I don't have much choice about that, do I? If people want to guess what I'm driving at it's their business, I can't help it. But I'm not going to have any announcement in the newspaper about any sheriff's investigation.'

'Sounds like you think whoever it is, he lives right here on the island. Is that what – '

'Look,' said Art Moran, halting. 'As far as the *San Piedro Review* is concerned there *is* no "whoever", okay? Let's you and I be clear on that.'

'I'm clear on it,' said Ishmael. 'All right, I'll quote you as calling it an accident. You keep me posted on what develops.'

'A deal,' said Art. 'A deal. I find anything, you're the first to know. How's that? You got what you want now?'

'Not yet,' said Ishmael. 'I've still got this story to write. So will you give me a few answers about this *accident*?'

'Now you're talking,' said Art Moran. 'Fire away. Ask.'

---

4 **phony** (AE): fake, false   5 **off the record**: not official   7 **manslaughter**: Totschlag (im Unterschied zu 'murder' = Mord)

Chapter 5

After the morning recess had drawn to a close, Horace Whaley, the Island County coroner, swore softly on the courtroom Bible and edged into the witness box, where he seized the oak armrests between his fingers and blinked behind steel-rimmed spectacles at Alvin Hooks. Horace was by inclination a private man, nearing fifty now, with a sprawling portwine stain on the left side of his forehead that he often fingered unconsciously. In appearance he was tidy and meticulous, storklike and slender – though not so thin as Art Moran – and wore his starched trousers high on his narrow waist and his scant hair slicked from right to left with pomade. Horace Whaley's eyes bulged – his thyroid gland was overactive – and swam, too, behind his spectacles. Something attenuated, a nervous caution, suggested itself in all his movements.

Horace had served as a medical officer for twenty months in the Pacific theater and had suffered in that period from sleep deprivation and from a generalized and perpetual tropical malaise that had rendered him, in his own mind, ineffective. Wounded men in his care had died, they'd died while in his sleepless daze Horace was responsible for them. In his head these men and their bloody wounds mingled into one recurring dream.

Horace had been at his desk doing paperwork on the morning of September 16. The evening before, a woman of ninety-six had died at the San Piedro Rest Home, and another of eighty-one had expired while splitting kindling wood and had been discovered sprawled across her chopping block, a milk goat nuzzling her face, by a child delivering apples in a wheelbarrow. And so Horace was filling in the blanks on two

---

3 **witness box**: Zeugenstand   5 **by inclination**: (here) by nature   8 **storklike**: storchenartig   9 **scant**: spärlich   11 **thyroid gland**: Schilddrüse   15 **Pacific theater**: (here) part of WWII which was fought between the USA and Japan
16 **malaise** (fml): feeling of being ill

certificates of death, and doing so in triplicate, when the phone beside him rang. He brought the receiver to his ear irritably; since the war he could not do too many things at once and at the moment, busier than he liked to be, did not wish to speak to anyone.

It was under these circumstances that he heard about the death of Carl Heine, a man who had endured the sinking of the *Canton* and who, like Horace himself, had survived Okinawa – only to die, it now appeared, in a gill-netting boat accident.

The body, on a canvas stretcher, its booted feet sticking out, had been borne in by Art Moran and Abel Martinson twenty minutes later, the sheriff wheezing under his end of the load, his deputy tight-lipped and grimacing, and laid on its back on Horace Whaley's examination table. It was wrapped by way of a shroud in two white wool blankets of the type issued to navy men and of which there was a great surplus nine years after the war, so that every fishing scow on San Piedro Island seemed to have half a dozen or more. Horace Whaley peeled back one of these blankets and, fingering the birthmark on the left side of his forehead, peered in at Carl Heine. The jaw had set open, he saw, and the vast mouth was a stiffened maw down which the dead man's tongue had disappeared. There were a large number of broken blood vessels in the whites of the deceased's eyes.

Horace pulled the blanket over Carl Heine again and turned his attention to Art Moran, who stood immediately at his side.

'Goddamn,' he said. 'Where'd you find him?'

'White Sand Bay,' Art replied.

Art told the coroner about the drifting boat, the silence and the lights on board the *Susan Marie* and about bringing the dead man up in his net. How Abel went to fetch his pickup truck and the canvas stretcher from the fire station and how together, while a small crowd of fishermen looked on and asked questions, they'd loaded Carl up and brought him in. 'I'm going over to see his wife,' Art added. 'I don't want word to reach her some other way. So I'll be back, Horace. Real soon. But I've got to see Susan Marie first.'

Abel Martinson stood at the end of the examination table exerting himself, Horace observed, to grow accustomed to this idea of conversing in the presence of a dead man. The toe of Carl Heine's right boot poked out of the blankets just in front of him.

'Abel,' said Art Moran. 'Maybe you better stay here with Horace. Give him a hand, if he needs it.'

The deputy nodded. He took the hat he held in his hand and placed it beside an instrument tray. 'Good,' he said. 'Okay.'

'Fine,' said the sheriff. 'I'll be back soon. Half an hour to an hour.'

When he was gone Horace peered in at Carl Heine's face again – letting Art's young deputy wait in silence – then washed his glasses at the sink. 'Tell you what,' he said at last and shut the water off. 'You go on across the hall and sit in my office, all right? There's some magazines in there and a radio and a thermos of coffee if you want it. And if it comes about I've got to shift this body around and I need your help, I'll call for you. Sound fair enough, deputy?'

'Okay,' said Abel Martinson. 'You call me.'

He picked up his hat and carried it out with him. *Damn kid*, Horace said to himself. Then he dried his steel-rimmed glasses on a towel and, because he was fastidious, got his surgical gown on. He pulled on his gloves, removed the shroud of blankets from Carl Heine, and then, methodically, using angled scissors, cut away the rubber bib overalls, dropping pieces of them in a canvas bin. When the overalls were gone he began on the T-shirt and cut away Carl Heine's work pants and underwear and pulled off Carl's boots and socks, out of which seawater ran. He put all the clothes in a sink.

There was a pack of matches, mostly used, in one pocket, and a small shuttle of cotton twine stuffed in another. A knife sheath had been knotted to a belt loop on his work pants, but no knife was in it. The sheath had been unsnapped and left open.

In Carl Heine's left front pocket was a watch that had stopped at one forty-seven. Horace dropped it into a manila envelope.

---

1 **in triplicate**: in dreifacher Ausführung   9 **stretcher**: thing made of strong cloth used for carrying an injured person   11 **wheeze**: breathe noisily and with difficulty   13 **shroud** (n): piece of cloth that a dead person's body is wrapped in before it is buried   15 **scow**: Schute, eine Art Fischerboot   19 **maw**: Schlund   34–35 **exert yourself**: make a big physical or mental effort   53 **fastidious**: being careful that every detail of sth. is correct   61 **shuttle**: (hier) Weberschiffchen **cotton twine**: dicker Baumwollfaden   63 **sheath**: cover for a blade   65 **manila envelope**: envelope made of strong brown paper

The body – despite the two hours it had spent in transport from White Sand Bay to the dock east of the ferry terminal and from there in the back of Abel Martinson's truck up First Hill and into the alley behind the courthouse (where the morgue and the coroner's office could be found beyond a set of double doors that gave onto the courthouse basement) – had not thawed perceptibly, Horace noted. It was pink, the color of salmon flesh, and the eyes had turned back in the head. It was also blatantly and exceedingly powerful, stout and thick muscled, the chest broad, the quadriceps muscles of the thighs pronounced, and Horace Whaley could not help but observe that here was an extraordinary specimen of manhood, six foot three and two hundred thirty-five pounds, bearded, blond, and built in the solid manner of a piece of statuary, as though the parts were made of granite – though, too, there was something apelike, inelegant, and brutish in the alignment of the arms and shoulders. Horace felt a familiar envy stirring and despite himself noted the girth and heft of Carl Heine's sexual organs. The fisherman had not been circumcised and his testicles were taut and hairless. They had pulled up toward his body in the frigid seawater, and his penis, at least twice as large as Horace's own, even frozen, lay fat and pink against his left leg.

The Island County coroner coughed twice, dryly, and circumnavigated his examination table. He began, consciously, for this would be necessary, to think of Carl Heine, a man he knew, as *the deceased* and not as Carl Heine. The deceased's right foot had locked itself behind the left, and Horace now exerted himself to free it. It was necessary to pull hard enough to tear ligaments in the deceased's groin, and this Horace Whaley did.

A coroner's job is to do certain things most people would never dream of doing. Horace Whaley was ordinarily a family physician, one of three on San Piedro. He worked with fishermen, their children, their wives. His peers were unwilling to examine the dead, and so the job had fallen to him, by default as it were. Thus he'd had these *experiences*; he'd seen things most men couldn't look at. The winter before he'd seen a crabber's body recovered out of West Port Jensen Bay after two full months' immersion. The crabber's skin resembled soap more than anything; he seemed encased in it, a kind of ambergris. On Tarawa he had seen the bodies of men who had died facedown in shallow water. The warm tides had washed over them for days, and the skin had loosened from their limbs. He remembered one soldier in particular from whose hands the skin had peeled like fine transparent gloves; even the fingernails had come away. There were no dog tags, but Horace had been able to obtain excellent fingerprints and make an identification anyway.

He knew a little about drowning. He had seen a fisherman in '49 who had been eaten about the face by crabs and crayfish. They'd fed steadily on the softest portions – the eyelids, the lips, to a lesser extent the ears – so that in these areas the face was intensely green. This he had seen in the Pacific war, too, along with other men who had died in tidal pools, astonishingly intact beneath the waterline but entirely eaten – to the bone – by sand flies wherever flesh lay exposed to air. And he had seen a man half-mummy, half-skeleton, floating in the waters of the China Sea, eaten from below while his back side, sun dried, gradually turned brown and leathery. After the sinking of the *Canton* there were parts of men floating around for miles that even the sharks had forsaken. The navy had not taken time to collect these parts; there were living men to attend to.

Carl Heine was the fourth deceased gill-netter Horace had examined in five years. Two others had died in a fall storm and washed up on the mud flats of Lanheedron Island. The third, recalled Horace, was an interesting case – the summer of '50, four years earlier. A fisherman named Vilderling – Alec Vilderling. His wife typed for Klaus Hartmann, who sold real estate in Amity Harbor. Vilderling and his partner had set their net and underneath the summer moon had shared in the lee of their bow-picker's cabin a bottle of Puerto Rican rum. Then Vilderling, it seemed, had decided to empty his bladder into the salt water. With his

4 **morgue**: building in which dead bodies are kept before they are buried or burnt 6 **thaw**: turn back into water after being frozen   8 **blatant**: offenkundig   12 **piece of statuary** (fml): statue   14 **alignment**: arrangement   15 **girth**: measurement around sth. (esp. a person's waist)   16 **heft**: weight   17 **circumcise sb.**: jdn. beschneiden   **testicle**: Hoden   **taut**: firm, not flabby   20 **circumnavigate sth.**: (here) walk around sth.   25 **ligament**: strong band of tissue in the body that connects bones and keeps organs in position   **the deceased** (fml): dead person   **groin**: Lende   30 **default**: sth. that happens if you do not make any other choice   32 **crabber**: person whose job is to fish and sell crabs (= Krabben)   33 **immersion**: state of being completely covered by a liquid   34 **ambergris**: substance won from whales and used for making some perfumes(= Ambra)   39 **dog tag** (AE, sl): metal identification necklace worn by US soldiers   51 **forsake sb.** (fml): auf jdn. verzichten   55 **mud flat**: Watt   58 **real estate**: land or buildings   61 **bladder**: Blase

pants undone he had fallen in and, to his partner's horror, had thrashed once or twice before disappearing altogether beneath the surface of the moon-addled sea. Vilderling, it appeared, could not swim.

His partner, a boy of nineteen named Kenny Lynden, hurled himself in after him. Vilderling, hung up in his net, struggled as the boy tried to free him. Though bleary with rum, Kenny Lynden somehow managed to cut Vilderling loose with a pocketknife and haul him back to the surface. But that was all he could do. Vilderling had ceased to live.

The interesting thing, Horace Whaley recalled, was that in the purely technical sense Alec Vilderling had not drowned. He had inhaled a large volume of seawater, yet his lungs were entirely dry. Horace had at first offered the conjecture in his notes that the deceased's larynx had clamped down – a spastic closure – to prevent liquid from reaching the deeper air passages. But this could not explain the clear distension of the lungs, which had to have been caused by the pressure of the sea, and so he revised his initial hypothesis and entered in his final report that the salt water swallowed by Alec Vilderling had been absorbed into his bloodstream while he yet lived. In this case the official cause of death, he wrote, was anoxia – a deprivation of oxygen to the brain – as well as an acute disturbance to the composition of the blood.

Chief among his current considerations as he stood brooding over Carl Heine's naked form was to determine the precise cause of Carl's demise – or rather to determine how the deceased had become the deceased, for to think of the slab of flesh before him as *Carl*, Horace reminded himself, would make doing what he had to do difficult. Only the week before, the deceased, in rubber boots and a clean T-shirt – perhaps the T-shirt just now cut to pieces with a pair of angled surgical scissors – had carried his eldest, a boy of six, into Horace's office in Amity Harbor and pointed out a cut on the boy's foot, sliced open against the metal strut of an overturned wheelbarrow. Carl had held the boy against the table while Horace put in the sutures. Unlike other fathers to whom this task had fallen, he gave no instructions to his son. He did not allow the boy to move, and the boy cried only when the first stitch went in and thereafter held his breath. When it was over Carl lifted the boy from the table and held him in the cradling manner one holds an infant. Horace had said that the foot must be elevated and went for a set of crutches. Then, as was his habit, Carl Heine paid for the work in cash, taking neat bills from his wallet. He was not profusely thankful and there was that silence about him, that bearded, gruff, and giant silence, that unwillingness to engage the protocols of island life. A man of his size, Horace thought, must take it as a duty to imply no menace or risk that his neighbors will be wary of him. Yet Carl did little to assuage the natural distrust an ordinary man feels for a man of physical stature. He went about his life deliberately instead, taking no time and making no gestures to suggest to others his harmlessness. Horace remembered seeing him one day flicking his lock blade open and then shutting it against the flank of his leg, flicking and shutting it again and again, but as for whether this was a habit or a threat, a nervous tic or an announcement of his prowess, Horace Whaley couldn't tell. The man seemed to have no friends. There was no one who could insult him in jest or speak lightly with him about unimportant matters, though on the other hand he was on courteous terms with almost everyone. And furthermore other men admired him because he was powerful and good at his work, because on the sea he was thoroughly competent and even in his rough way elegantly so; still, their admiration was colored by their distrust of his size and his brooding deliberation.

No, Carl Heine was not amiable, but neither was he a bad sort. He had once, before the war, been a boy on the football team, like other schoolboys in most ways: he'd had a large group of friends, he'd worn a letterman's jacket, he'd spoken when there was no reason to speak, for fun. He had been that way and then the war had come – the war Horace himself had been to. And how to explain? What could he say to others? There was no longer any speaking for the hell of it, no opening one's

---

1 **thrash**: beat   3 **moon-addled**: (here) reflecting the light of the moon irregularly because of the waves moving   8 **cease to do sth.**: stop doing sth.   12 **conjecture** (n): guess   **larynx**: Kehlkopf   12–13 **clamp down**: sich schließen   14 **distension**: swelling   21 **current** (adj): present   23 **demise**: death   24 **slab**: thick, flat piece of sth.   30 **strut** (n): Strebe, Stütze   31 **suture** ['suːtʃər] (n): stitch   37 **crutch**: Krücke   38 **profusely**: overwhelmingly   39 **gruff**: unfriendly   40 **protocol**: system of fixed rules and formal behavior   42 **menace**: threat   **wary**: careful, fearing a danger   43 **assuage sth.** (fml): make sth. (esp. an unpleasant feeling) less severe   49 **prowess** ['praʊəs] (fml): great skill   51 **in jest**: jokingly   57 **amiable**: friendly   60 **letterman**: Mannschaftsjacke

mouth just to have it open, and if others would read darkness into his silence, well then, darkness was there, wasn't it? There'd been the darkness of the war in Carl Heine, as there was in Horace himself.

But – *the deceased*. He must think of Carl as the deceased, a bag of guts, a sack of parts, and not as the man who had so recently brought his son in; otherwise the job could not be done.

Horace Whaley placed the heel of his right hand against the solar plexus of the dead man. He placed his left hand over it and began to pump in the manner of someone attempting to resuscitate a drowning victim. And as he did so a foam, something like shaving cream though flecked with pink-hued blood from the lungs, mushroomed at the deceased's mouth and nose.

Horace stopped and inspected this. He leaned down over the deceased man's face, scrutinizing the foam closely. His gloved hands were still clean, they had touched nothing except the chilled skin of the deceased's chest, and so he took from beside his instrument tray a pad and pencil and noted for himself the color and texture of this extruded foam that was abundant enough to cover the deceased's bearded chin and his mustache almost entirely. It was a result, Horace knew, of air, mucus, and seawater all mingled by respiration, which meant the deceased had been alive at submersion. He had not died first and then been cast beneath the waves. Carl Heine had gone in breathing.

But anoxia, like Alec Vilderling, or a waterlogged, choking asphyxiation? Like most people, Horace felt the need not merely to know but to envision clearly whatever had happened; furthermore it was his obligation to envision it clearly so that in the official register of Island County deaths the truth, however painful, might be permanently inscribed. Carl Heine's dark struggle, his effort to hold his breath, the volume of water that had filled the vacuum of his gut, his profound unconsciousness and final convulsions, his terminal gasps in the grip of death as the last of the air leaked out of him and his heart halted and his brain ceased to consider anything – they were all recorded, or not recorded, in the slab of flesh that lay on Horace Whaley's examination table. It was his duty to find out the truth.

For a moment Horace stood with his hands linked across his belly and debated silently the merits of opening the deceased man's chest so as to get at the evidence in the heart and lungs. It was in this posture that he noted – how had he missed it before? – the wound to the skull over the dead man's left ear. 'I'll be damned,' he said aloud.

⁴⁰ With a pair of barber's shears he cut hair out of the way until the outlines of this wound emerged cleanly. The bone had fractured and caved in considerably over an area of about four inches. The skin had split open, and from the laceration of the scalp a tiny strand of pink brain material protruded. Whatever had caused this wound – a narrow,
⁴⁵ flat object about two inches wide – had left its telltale outline behind in the deceased man's head. It was precisely the sort of lethal impression Horace had seen at least two dozen times in the Pacific war, the result of close-in combat, hand to hand, and made by a powerfully wielded gun butt. The Japanese field soldier, trained in the art of *kendo*, or stick
⁵⁰ fighting, was exceptionally proficient at killing in this manner. And the majority of Japs, Horace recalled, inflicted death over the left ear, swinging in from the right.

Horace inserted a razor into one of his scalpels and poked it into the deceased's head. He pressed the razor to the bone and guided it through
⁵⁵ the hair, describing an arc across the top of the deceased's skull literally from ear to ear. It was a skillful and steady incision, like drawing a curved line with a pencil across the crown of the head, a fluid and graceful curve. In this manner he was able to peel back the dead man's face as though it were the skin of a grapefruit or an orange and turn his
⁶⁰ forehead inside out so that it rested against his nose.

Horace peeled down the back of the head, too, then lay his scalpel in the sink, rinsed his gloves, dried them, and brought out a hacksaw from his instrument cupboard.

5 **guts** (pl): organs around the stomach   9 **resuscitate sb.** [rɪˈsʌsɪteɪt]: revive sb.
14 **scrutinize sb./sth.**: examine sb./sth. carefully   17 **texture**: the way a surface or substance feels when you touch it   **extrude sth.**: push sth. out of sth. else
20 **mucus** [ˈmjuːkəs]: thick liquid that is produced in parts of the body, such as the nose   21 **submersion**: act of going under the surface of water   23 **waterlogged**: completely full of water   23–24 **asphyxiation** [əsˌfɪksiˈeɪʃn]: Erstickung
42 **cave in**: eingedrückt sein   43 **laceration**: wound   **strand**: single thin piece of sth.   44 **protrude**: stick out   45 **telltale**: showing that sth. has happened
49 **butt**: Kolben   **kendo**: martial art of Japanese fencing practised using 'swords' made of wood or split bamboo   51 **inflict sth. (upon sb.)**: make sb. suffer sth.
56 **incision**: sharp cut   62 **hacksaw**: tool with a narrow frame used for cutting metal

He set about the work of sawing through the dead man's skullcap. After twenty minutes it became necessary to turn the body over, and so with reluctance Horace crossed the hall to Abel Martinson, who sat in a chair doing nothing at all, his legs crossed, his hat in his lap.

'Need a hand,' said the coroner.

The deputy rose and put his hat on his head. 'Sure,' he said. 'Glad to help.'

'You won't be glad,' said Horace. 'I've made an incision across the top of his head. His skull is exposed. It isn't pretty.'

'Okay,' said the deputy. 'Thanks for telling me.'

They went in and without speaking turned the body over, Abel Martinson pushing from one side, the coroner reaching across and pulling from the other, and then, with his head hung over the sink, Abel Martinson vomited. He was dabbing his mouth with the corner of his handkerchief when Art Moran came through the door. 'Now what?' asked the sheriff.

Abel, in answer, pointed a finger at Carl Heine's corpse. 'I puked again,' he said.

Art Moran looked at Carl's face turned inside out, the skin of it peeled back like a grape, a bloody foam that looked like shaving cream clinging to his chin. Then he turned away from seeing it.

'Me, too,' said Abel Martinson. 'I got no stomach for this neither.'

'I'm not blaming you,' the sheriff answered. 'Jesus H. Christ. *Jesus Christ*.'

But he stood there watching anyway while Horace, in his surgical gown, worked methodically with his hacksaw. He watched while Horace removed the dead man's skullcap and placed it beside the dead man's shoulder.

'This is called the dura mater.' Horace pointed with his scalpel. 'This membrane here? Right under his skull? This right here is the dura mater.'

He took the dead man's head between his hands and with some effort – the ligaments of the neck were extremely rigid – twisted it to the left.

'Come over here, Art,' he said.

The sheriff seemed aware of the necessity of doing so; nevertheless, he didn't move. Certainly, thought Horace, he had learned in his work that there were distasteful moments about which he had no choice. In the face of these it was best to move quickly and without reservations, as

Horace himself did as a matter of principle. But the sheriff was a man of inherited anxieties. It was not really in him to go over there and see what was under Carl Heine's face.

Horace Whaley knew this: that the sheriff did not want to see what was inside of Carl Heine's head. Horace had seen Art this way before, chewing his Juicy Fruit and grimacing, rubbing his lips with the ball of his thumb and squinting while he thought things over. 'It'll just take a minute,' Horace urged him. 'One quick look, Art. So you can see what we're up against. I wouldn't ask if it wasn't important.'

Horace indicated for Art Moran the blood that had clotted in the dura mater and the tear in it where the piece of brain protruded. 'He got hit pretty hard with something fairly flat, Art. Puts me in mind of a type of gun butt wound I saw a few times in the war. One of those *kendo* strikes the Japs used.'

'*Kendo*?' said Art Moran.

'Stick fighting,' Horace explained. 'Japs are trained in it from when they're kids. How to kill with sticks.'

'Ugly,' said the sheriff. 'Jesus.'

'Look away,' said Horace. 'I'm going to cut through the dura mater now. I want you to see something else.'

The sheriff turned his back deliberately. 'You're pale,' he said to Abel Martinson. 'Why don't you go sit down?'

'I'm okay,' answered Abel. He stood looking into the sink with his handkerchief in his hand and leaned hard against the counter.

Horace showed the sheriff three fragments of the deceased's skull that had lodged in the tissue of his brain. 'That what killed him?' Art asked.

'That's complicated,' answered Horace Whaley. 'Could be he took a hit to the head, then went over the side and drowned. Or maybe he hit his head *after* he drowned. Or *while* he was drowning. I don't know for sure.'

'Can you find out?'

'Maybe.'

'When?'

'I have to look inside his chest, Art. At his heart and lungs. And even that might not tell me much.'

---

39 **inherit sth.**: have qualities that are similar to those of your parents   44 **squint**: partially shut your eyes so as to keep out the sun   48 **tear** (n) [ter]: Riss

'His chest?'

'That's right.'

'What're the possibilities?' said the sheriff.

'Possibilities?' said Horace Whaley. 'All kinds of possibilities, Art. Anything could have happened, and all kinds of things *do* happen. I mean, maybe he had a *heart* attack that pitched him over the side. Maybe a stroke, maybe alcohol. But all I want to know just now is did he get knocked in the head first and *then* go over? Because I know from this foam' – he pointed at it with his scalpel – 'that Carl went in breathing. He was respiratory when he hit the water. So my guess right now is that he drowned, Art. With the head wound an obvious contributing factor. Banged himself on a fairlead, maybe. Setting his net and got a little careless – hung up his buckle and went over. I'm inclined to put all that in my report just now. But I don't know for sure yet. Maybe when I see his heart and lungs everything is going to change.'

Art Moran stood rubbing his lip and blinked hard at Horace Whaley. 'That bang to the head,' he said. 'That bang to the head is sort of … *funny*, you know?'

Horace Whaley nodded. 'Could be,' he said.

'Couldn't it be somebody hit him?' asked the sheriff. 'Isn't that a possibility?'

'You want to play Sherlock Holmes?' asked Horace. 'You going to play detective?'

'Not really. But Sherlock Holmes isn't here, is he? And this wound in Carl's head is.'

'That's true,' said Horace. 'You got that part right.'

Then – and afterward he would remember this, during the trial of Kabuo Miyamoto, Horace Whaley would recall having spoken these words (though he would not repeat them on the witness stand) – he said to Art Moran that if he were inclined to play Sherlock Holmes he ought to start looking for a Jap with a bloody gun butt – a right-handed Jap, to be precise.

---

6 **pitch sb./sth. over the side of sth. else**: make sb./sth. fall over the side of sth. else   7 **stroke**: Schlaganfall   12 **fairlead**: device on a boat or ship like a ring, a hook or a block with holes in it which keeps ropes in their place
13 **buckle** (n): (here) device used to tighten ropes on a boat

Chapter 6

Horace Whaley scratched the birthmark on his forehead and watched the falling snow beyond the courtroom windows. It was coming harder now, much harder, wind whipped and silent, though the wind could be heard pushing against the beams in the courthouse attic. *My pipes*, thought Horace. *They'll freeze.*

Nels Gudmundsson rose a second time, slipped his thumbs behind his suspenders, and noted with his one good eye that Judge Lew Fielding appeared half-asleep and was leaning heavily on the palm of his left hand, as he had throughout Horace's testimony. He was listening, Nels knew; his tired demeanor shielded an active mind from view. The judge liked to mull things soporifically.

Nels, as best he could – he had arthritis in his hips and knees – made his way to the witness stand. 'Horace,' he said. 'Good morning.'

'Morning, Nels,' answered the coroner.

'You've said quite a bit,' Nels Gudmundsson pointed out. 'You've told the court in detail about your autopsy of the deceased, your fine background as a medical examiner, and so forth, as you've been asked to do. And I've been listening to you, Horace, like everybody else here. And – well – I'm troubled by a couple of matters.' He stopped and pinched his chin between his fingers.

'Go ahead,' urged Horace Whaley.

'Well, for example, this *foam*,' said Nels. 'I'm not sure I understand about that, Horace.'

'The foam?'

'You've testified to having applied pressure to the deceased's chest and that shortly thereafter a peculiar foam appeared at his mouth and nostrils.'

---

4 **pipe**: Rohr, Leitung   9 **testimony**: statement in court of the facts you know about a case   10 **demeanor** [dɪ'miːnər] (fml): the way that sb. looks or behaves
11 **mull sth.**: consider sth.   **soporific** (fml): making you want to go to sleep

'That's right,' said Horace. 'I would say this is usually the case with drowning victims. It may not appear when they're first recovered from the water, but almost as soon as someone starts removing their clothing or attempting resuscitation there it is, generally in copious amounts.'

'What would cause that?' Nels asked.

'Pressure brings it up. It results from a chemical reaction in the lungs when water mixes with air and mucus.'

'Water, air, and mucus,' said Nels. 'But what causes them to mix, Horace? This chemical reaction you speak of – what is it?'

'It's caused by breathing. It happens in the presence of respiration. It – '

'Now this is where I got confused,' interrupted Nels. 'Earlier, I mean. When you were testifying. You say this foam is *only* produced when you've got water, mucus, and air all mixed together by a person's breathing?'

'That's right.'

'But a drowned person doesn't breathe,' said Nels. 'So how does this foam … you can see why I'm confused.'

'Oh, sure,' said Horace. 'I think I can make this clear. It's formed – this foam – in the *early* stages. The victim is submerged and begins to struggle. Finally he begins to swallow water, you see, and as he does the air in his lungs is forced out under pressure – and this gives rise to the foam I've testified about. The chemical reaction occurs at the time the drowning victim is *ceasing* to breathe. Or breathing his final breaths.'

'I see,' said Nels. 'So this foam, then, tells you Carl Heine in fact drowned, doesn't it?'

'Well – '

'It tells you, for example, that he wasn't murdered first – say on the deck of his boat – and then thrown overboard? Because if he was, there would be no foam, would there? Am I understanding the chemical reaction correctly? It can't happen unless the victim is breathing at the time of submersion? Is that what you said about it, Horace?'

'Yes,' said Horace. 'It tells you that. But – '

'Excuse me,' said Nels. 'Just wait a moment, now.' He made his way to where Mrs. Eleanor Dokes sat poised over her stenograph. He worked past her and nodded at the bailiff, Ed Soames, then picked out a document from the evidence table and made his way back to the witness stand.

'All right, Horace,' he said now. 'I'm returning to you the exhibit you identified earlier, in direct examination, as your autopsy report, which you've testified accurately reflects your findings and conclusions. If you would kindly take it and read back to yourself paragraph four on page four, please, we'll all wait.'

While Horace did so Nels returned to the defendant's table and sipped from a glass of water. His throat had begun to bother him; his voice had gone hoarse and reedy.

'All right,' said Horace. 'Done.'

'All right,' said Nels. 'Am I correct in saying, Horace, that paragraph four on page four of your autopsy report identifies *drowning* as the cause of Carl Heine's death?'

'Yes, it does.'

'So your conclusion was that he drowned?'

'Yes.'

'Was that unequivocal? Was there any doubt?'

'Yes, of course there's doubt. There's always doubt. You're not – '

'Just a minute, Horace,' said Nels. 'Do you wish to say that your report is inaccurate? Is that what you're trying to tell us?'

'The report is accurate,' said Horace Whaley. 'I – '

'Can you read for the court the last sentence of paragraph four, page four, of the autopsy report you have in front of you?' said Nels Gudmundsson. 'The paragraph you read silently just a moment ago? Please go ahead and read.'

'All right,' answered Horace. 'It says this, and I quote: "The presence of foam in the airway and around the lips and nose indicates beyond doubt that the victim was alive at the time of submersion." Unquote.'

'*Beyond doubt* that he was alive at the time of submersion? Is that what it says, Horace?'

'Yes, it does.'

---

4 **in copious amounts**: in large amounts   34 **poised over sth.**: holding a particular position above sth. but ready to move at any moment   36–37 **witness stand** = witness box   38 **exhibit** [ɪgˈzɪbɪt] (n): object that is used in court as evidence in a case   45 **hoarse**: sounding rough   **reedy**: high-pitched   53 **unequivocal** [ˌʌnɪˈkwɪvəkl] (fml): definite, beyond doubt   63 **airway**: Luftröhre

'Beyond doubt,' said Nels Gudmundsson, and turned toward the jurors. 'Thank you, Horace. That's important. That's good. But there is something else I'd like to ask about now. Something in that autopsy report.'

'Okay,' said Horace, removing his glasses and biting one stem. 'Go ahead and ask.'

'Well, page two, then,' said Nels. 'At the top? The second paragraph, I believe?' He went to the defendant's table and leafed through his own copy. 'Paragraph two,' he said. 'Yes, that's it. If you could read that back for the court, please? Just the first line will do, Horace.'

'Quote,' answered Horace Whaley stiffly. '"A secondary and minor laceration of the right hand is noted, of recent origin, and extends laterally from the fold between the thumb and forefinger to the outside of the wrist."'

'A cut,' said Nels. 'Is that right? Carl Heine cut his hand?'

'Yes.'

'Any idea how?'

'None, really. I could speculate, though.'

'That won't be necessary,' Nels said. 'But this cut, Horace. You say in your report that it's of "recent origin". Any idea how recent?'

'Very. Very recent, I'd say.'

'Very,' said Nels. 'How much is "very"?'

'*Very* recent,' repeated Horace. 'I would say he cut his hand on the night he died, and in the hour or two just preceding his death. *Very* recent, okay?'

'Hour or two?' said Nels. 'Two hours is possible?'

'Yes.'

'What about three? Or four, Horace? What about *twenty-four*?'

'Twenty-four is out of the question. The wound was fresh, Nels. Four hours – maybe, at the outside. No more than four, absolutely.'

'All right,' said Nels. 'He cut his hand, then. No more than four hours before he drowned.'

'That's correct,' said Horace Whaley.

Nels Gudmundsson began to pull, once again, at the wattles of skin at his throat. 'Just one more thing, Horace,' he said. 'I have to ask about something else that confused me during your testimony. This wound to the deceased's head you mentioned.'

'Yes,' said Horace Whaley. 'The wound. All right.'

'Can you tell us again what it looked like?'

'Yes,' repeated Horace. 'It was a laceration about two and a half inches long just slightly above the left ear. The bone under it had fractured over an area of about four inches. There was also a small bit of brain material showing through the laceration. It was evident from the impression left behind in the skull that something narrow, something flat, had caused this injury. That's about everything, Nels.'

'Something narrow and flat had caused it,' Nels repeated. 'Is that what you saw, Horace? Or is that an inference?'

'It's my *job* to infer,' insisted Horace Whaley. 'Look, if a night watchman is struck over the head with a crowbar during the course of a robbery, the wounds you're going to see in his head will look like they were made with a crowbar. If they were made by a ball-peen hammer you can see that, too – a ball-peen leaves behind a crescent-shaped injury, a crowbar leaves, well, linear wounds with V-shaped ends. You get hit with a pistol butt, that's one thing; somebody hits you with a bottle, that's another. You fall off a motorcycle at forty miles an hour and hit your head on gravel, the gravel will leave behind patterned abrasions that don't look like anything else. So yes, I infer from the deceased's wound that something narrow and flat caused his injury. To *infer* – it's what coroners *do*.'

'The motorcyclist is an interesting example,' Nels Gudmundsson pointed out. 'Are you saying it isn't necessary to be struck by anything to produce one of these telltale wounds? That if the victim is *propelled* against an object – let's say it's gravel – his own forward motion might produce the observed injury?'

'It might,' said Horace Whaley. 'We don't know.'

'So in the present case,' said Nels Gudmundsson, 'might the injury in question, the injury to Carl Heine's skull you've spoken of, might it have

---

5 **stem**: (hier) Brillenbügel   13 **lateral**: located on the side of sth.   47 **inference** ['ɪnfərəns]: Schlussfolgerung   49 **crowbar**: Brechstange   51 **ball-peen hammer** (AE): Kugelhammer   52 **crescent** ['kresnt]: curved shape   56 **abrasion**: damaged area of the skin where it has been rubbed against sth. hard and rough
62 **propel sb./sth.**: force sb./sth. to move in a particular direction

been the result of *either* a blow to the head *or* the propulsion of the victim against some object? Are both possible, Horace?'

'There's no way to tell them apart,' argued Horace. 'Only that whatever made contact with his head – whether it was moving toward him or he toward it – was flat, narrow, and hard enough to fracture his skull.'

'Something flat, narrow, and hard enough to fracture his skull. Like the gunnel of a boat, Horace? Is that possible?'

'Possible, yes. If he was moving fast enough toward it. But I don't see how he might have been.'

'What about a net roller? Or one of these fairleads at the stern of a gill-netter? Are they also flat and narrow?'

'Yes. That is, flat *enough*. They – '

'Might he have hit his head on these? Is that at least a possibility?'

'Sure it's a possibility,' agreed Horace. 'Any – '

'Let me ask you something else,' said Nels. 'Is there any way a coroner can determine if a wound like this one occurred before or after death? I mean – to return to your earlier example – couldn't I poison the night watchman, watch him die, then club his lifeless corpse over the head with a crowbar and leave behind precisely the same sort of injury as if I had *killed* him by the latter method?'

'Are you asking about Carl Heine's wound?'

'I am. I want to know if *you* know something. Did he sustain the injury and then die? Or is it possible the wound to the head occurred postmortem? That he sustained it – or should we say his *corpse* sustained it – *after* Carl Heine drowned? Perhaps, say, when he was being brought up in his net by Sheriff Moran and Deputy Martinson?'

Horace Whaley thought about it. He took off his glasses; he massaged his forehead. Then he fixed the stems of his glasses once again behind his earlobes and folded his arms across his chest.

'I don't know,' he said. 'I can't answer that, Nels.'

'You don't know whether the wound to the head preceded death or not? Is that what you're saying, Horace?'

'That's what I'm saying, yes.'

'But the cause of death – unequivocally – was drowning. Is that right? Am I correct?'

'Yes.'

'It was not a wound to the head, then, that killed Carl Heine?'

'No. But – '

'No more questions,' said Nels Gudmundsson. 'Thank you, Horace. That's all.'

Art Moran, from his place in the gallery, felt a peculiar satisfaction watching Horace Whaley suffer. He remembered the insult: *Sherlock Holmes*. He remembered leaving Horace's office, hesitating before going up to Mill Run Road to bring the news to the dead man's wife.

He'd leaned against the fender of Abel Martinson's truck inspecting the hand he'd scraped that morning against a stanchion on Carl Heine's gill-netting boat. Then he'd dug in his pocket for a stick of Juicy Fruit – first his shirt pockets, next, vaguely irritated, his pants. Two remained; he'd gone through eight already. He popped one in his mouth, saved the other, then slid behind the wheel of Abel's pickup. His own car was parked in town near the docks; he'd left it there earlier that same morning when he'd gone to the harbor for the launch. It made him feel like a fool driving Abel's truck because the boy, frankly, had put too much time into it. It was a high-stacked Dodge painted burgundy in Anacortes, elaborately pin-striped and with decorative exhaust extensions pillared just behind the gleaming cab – a schoolboy's play truck, in short. Just the sort of pickup you saw in mainland towns like Everett or Bellingham, the kind kids drove around after football games or on Saturday nights, late. Art had to figure that in his high school days Abel Martinson had been moderately restless, that in the interim between then and now he had changed, and that this truck was the last vestige of his former self: thus he was loath to part with it. But he would, Art predicted, and soon. That was how things went.

---

1 **propulsion**: force that drives sth. forward   6 **fracture sth.**: break sth.   10 **net roller**: Netzwinde   18 **club** (v): hit sb. with a blunt object (blunt = stumpf)   22 **sustain sth.**: (here) suffer sth., receive sth.   24 **postmortem**: after death   29 **earlobe**: Ohr-läppchen   31 **precede sth.**: happen before sth.   45 **fender**: (hier) Kotflügel   55 **elaborate**: worked on in detail, very carefully done   55–56 **exhaust extension**: aufgesetztes Auspuffrohr   56 **pillared**: (here) installed in an upright position like a pillar (= Säule)   **cab**: Fahrerkabine   62 **be loath to do sth.** [loʊθ] (adj, fml): not be willing to do sth

Driving up to see Susan Marie Heine, Art muddled out his words in silence, revising as he went and planning his demeanor, which ought, he decided, to have a vaguely military architecture with certain nautical decorative touches – to report a man's death at sea to his widow was a task done gravely but with tragic stoicism for centuries on end, he figured. *Excuse me, Mrs. Heine. I am sorry to report that your husband, Carl Gunther Heine, was killed last night in an accident at sea. May I express the condolences of the entire community and ...*

But this would not do. She was not unknown to him; he couldn't treat her like a stranger. After all, he saw her at church every Sunday after services pouring tea and coffee in the reception room. She always dressed impeccably for her duties as hostess, in a pillbox hat, tweed suit, and beige gloves: taking coffee from her sure hand he'd found pleasurable. She wore her blond hair pinned up under her hat and a double strand of costume pearls around her neck, a neck that reminded him of alabaster. In short she was, at twenty-eight, attractive in a way that disturbed him. Pouring coffee she called him 'Sheriff Moran' and afterward pointed out the cake and mints down the table with a gloved index finger, as if he had not noted them himself. Then she would smile at him prettily and set the coffee service down on its tray while he helped himself to the sugar.

The prospect of telling her about Carl's death was more than just unsettling to Art, and as he drove he struggled to find the proper words, the formula of phrases that would free him without too much fumbling from the message he carried to this woman. But it seemed to him there were none.

Just before the Heine place on Mill Run Road there was a turnout where in August the sheriff had picked blackberries. Here he pulled in impulsively, because he was not ready to do what was required, and with the engine of Abel's Dodge idling in neutral he popped the last stick of Juicy Fruit between his teeth and looked down the road toward the Heines'.

It was precisely the sort of home Carl *would* build, he thought – blunt, tidy, gruffly respectable, and offering no affront to the world, though at the same time inviting nobody. It sat back fifty yards from the road on three acres of alfalfa, strawberries, raspberries, and orderly vegetable gardens. Carl had cleared the land himself with a characteristic

David Guterson: **Snow Falling on Cedars**   63

rapidity and thoroughness – he'd sold the timber to the Thorsen brothers, burned his slash piles, and poured his footing all in the space of a single winter. By April the berries were in and a post-and-beam shed-barn, and by summer Carl could be seen framing up walls and mortaring clinker brick. He had meant – or so word at church had it – to build an elaborate bungalow of the sort his father had built years before on the family farm at Island Center. He'd wanted inglenooks, somebody had said, and an overscaled fireplace and alcoves, built-in window seats and wainscoting, a battered porch base and low stone walls along his entrance walk. But in time, as he worked, he'd found himself too straightforward for all of that – he was a builder, an exacting one, but not an artist, as his wife had put it – the wainscoting, for example, was left out entirely, and he had not built the sort of river rock chimney that stood up so prominently at his father's old place (now owned by Bjorn Andreason), preferring clinker brick. What he ended up with was a blunt, sturdy house sheathed carefully with cedar shingles, testimony to its builder's exacting nature.

Art Moran, his foot on the brake, chewing his gum and fretting in silence, took in the gardens first, then the front porch with its tapered posts, and finally the overscaled trusses in the gable roof; he took in the pair of shed-roofed dormers that had, despite the original intent of

1 **muddle sth. out**: try to put an order into sth. confused or mixed up   5 **stoicism** (fml): way of life in which you do not complain or show that you are suffering **on end**: without stopping   8 **condolence** [kən'dəʊləns]: sympathy that you feel for sb. who is grieving   12 **impeccable**: perfect   **pillbox hat**: kleiner runder Damenhut   16 **alabaster:** type of white stone that is often used to make statues   23 **unsettling**: making you feel upset, nervous or worried   30 **idle** (v): (of an engine) run slowly while the vehicle is not moving   **in neutral**: im Leerlauf   36 **alfalfa**: plant grown as food for farm animals and as a salad vegetable   38 **timber**: trees that are grown to be used in building or for making furniture   39 **slash pile**: (here) heap of plants that have been pulled out, esp. weeds   **pour a footing**: ein Fundament gießen   40–41 **post-and-beam shed-barn**: barn (= Scheune) built in a very simple way by putting up upright posts crossed by beams (= Balken) which support the roof   42 **mortar sth.**: use mortar (= Mörtel) to hold bricks and stones together   44 **inglenook**: space at either side of a large fireplace where you can sit   46 **wainscoting**: Täfelung   **battered**: (here) made of battered stone (= Bruchstein)   53 **sheathe sth. with sth.**: cover sth. in a material, esp. in order to protect it   56 **taper sth.**: make sth. become gradually narrower   57 **truss**: frame which supports a roof   58 **dormer**: Gaube

asymmetry, been built formally and in tandem. And he shook his head and recollected having been inside this house, with its exposed roof rafters in the upstairs rooms and Susan Marie's oversized furniture downstairs – he'd attended, last October, an autumn church social there – but he knew he would not go inside this time. He knew that suddenly. He'd stand on the porch to deliver his news with his cap resting against one thigh, and then leave without ever entering. He understood that this was not *right*, but on the other hand what else could he do? It was too difficult; it wasn't in him. He would call Eleanor Dokes at his office when he was done, and she would alert Susan Marie's older sister, and the sister would come here before long. But he himself? There wasn't any way he could think of. It wasn't in him to sit with her through this. He would ask this widow to understand that there were matters he must attend to ... urgent matters of a professional nature ... he would deliver his message, offer condolences, and then in the spirit of one who knows his place simply leave Susan Marie Heine alone.

He coasted down and turned into Susan Marie's drive with Abel's truck still in neutral. From here, looking east across the rows of trained raspberry canes, the sea was visible beyond the tops of the cedars falling away along the hill. It was a fine September day of the sort they saw rarely, cloudless and June warm if you stood where there was no shade, the sunlight glinting among the whitecaps in the far distance, so that Art Moran understood what he hadn't before that Carl had built here not just for the sun it afforded but for the long view to the north and west. While Carl had cultivated his raspberries and strawberries he'd kept one eye always on the salt water.

Art pulled in behind the Heines' Bel-Air and shut the ignition down. And as he did so Carl's sons came around the corner of the house running – a boy of three or four, Art guessed, followed by another of about six, who limped. They stood beside a rhododendron bush staring, in shorts, shirtless and barefoot.

Art took a wrapper out of his shirt pocket and spit his Juicy Fruit into it. He did not want to say what he had to say with Juicy Fruit in his mouth.

'Hey there, men,' he called cheerfully through the window frame. 'Your mother home a-tall?'

The two boys didn't answer. They stared at him instead. A German shepherd came stalking around the corner of the house, and the older boy caught him by the collar and held him. 'Stay,' he said, but nothing else.

Art Moran shoved his door partway open, then took his hat from off the seat and put it on the back of his head. 'Policeman,' said the younger boy, and stepped in beside his brother. 'It's not a policeman,' answered the older boy. 'It's the sheriff or somebody like that.'

'That's right,' said Art. 'I'm Sheriff Moran, boys. Is your mother home a-tall?'

The older boy gave his brother a shove. 'Go get Mom,' he said.

They looked like their father. They were going to be big like their father, he could see that. Sun-browned, thick-limbed German children.

'You go ahead and play,' he said to them. 'I'll just go knock. You play.' He smiled down at the younger one.

But they didn't go. They watched from beside the rhododendron bush while he climbed to the porch with his hat in his hand and rapped his knuckles against the front door, which was thrown open to reveal Carl's living room. Art looked in, waiting. The walls had been paneled with varnished pine board in which the knots shone luminously; Susan Marie's curtains were of a clean, smooth yellow, tied off crisply behind careful bows, ruffled, valenced, and undertiered. The concentric circles of a braided wool rug concealed most of the floorboards. In one far corner an upright piano loomed; in another sat a rolltop desk. There were twin oak rockers with embroidered cushions, twin walnut end tables astride a worn bench sofa, and a plush easy chair beside a gilt

---

2–3 **roof rafters**: Dachsparren   4 **social** (n, old-fashioned): party that is organized by a group or club   18 **train sth.**: (here) make a plant grow in a particular direction, e.g. by cutting it back   19 **cane**: thin stick   22 **glint**: reflect litght in a bright flash   **whitecap**: wave capped with white foam   27 **Bel-Air**: type of car first built by Chevrolet in 1953   **ignition**: Zündung   36 **a-tall** (sl): at all   38 **stalk** (v): move in a threatening way   52–53 **rap your knuckles against sth.** (v): anklopfen   54 **panel sth.**: etwas vertäfeln   55 **varnish sth.**: etwas lackieren   **knot**: (hier) Astloch   **luminous**: shining   56 **crisp** (adj): (of textiles) tidy, carefully arranged   57 **ruffle sth.**: put sth. into decorative folds   **valenced** (adj): (hier) mit Volants versehen   **undertier sth.**: arrange sth. (esp. textiles) in several layers at the bottom   59 **rolltop desk**: desk with a top that you roll back to open it   60 **rocker** (AE): Schaukelstuhl   **embroider sth.**: etwas besticken   61 **easy chair**: Sessel

brass floor lamp. The chair had been pulled up to the oversized fireplace Carl had built, inside of which stood tall, fluted andirons. The sheriff was impressed by the order of this room, its bronze, quiet, and syrupy light, and by the photographs on the wall of the various Heines and assorted Varigs who had preceded Carl and Susan Marie in the world: stout, impressive, blunt-faced Germans who never smiled for photographers.

It was a fine living room, clean and quiet. He gave Susan Marie credit for that, just as he had given Carl credit for the chimney and dormers, and while he stood there admiring her hand in everything she appeared at the top of the stairs.

'Sheriff Moran,' she called. 'Hello.'

He knew then that she hadn't heard. He knew it was up to him to say it. But he couldn't just yet – couldn't bring himself – and so he only stood there with his hat in his hand, rubbing his lips with the ball of his thumb and squinting while she came down the stairs. 'Hello,' he said. 'Mrs. Heine.'

'I was just putting the baby down,' she answered.

It was a far different woman from the one at church – the winsome fisher wife serving tea and coffee. Now she wore a dull skirt, no shoes, and no makeup. She had a diaper draped over her left shoulder, spittle stained, and her hair had not recently been washed. In her hand was a baby bottle.

'What can I do for you, sheriff?' she asked. 'Carl hasn't come home yet.'

'That's why I'm here,' Art replied. 'I'm afraid I have some ... bad news to report. The worst sort of news, Mrs. Heine.'

She seemed at first not to understand. She looked at him as if he'd spoken in Chinese. Then she pulled the diaper from her shoulder and smiled at him, and it was his duty to make clear this mystery.

'Carl is dead,' said Art Moran. 'He died last night in a fishing accident. We found him this morning tangled in his net out in White Sand Bay.'

'Carl?' said Susan Marie Heine. 'That can't be.'

'It is, though. I know it can't be. I don't want it to be. Believe me, I wish it wasn't true. But it is true. I've come to tell you.'

It was strange, the way she reacted. There was no way to have predicted it ahead of time. Suddenly she backed away from him, blinking, sat down hard on the bottom stair, and set the baby bottle on the floor beside her toes. She dug her elbows into her lap and began to rock with the diaper between her hands, wringing it between her fingers. 'I knew this would happen one day,' she whispered. Then she stopped rocking and stared into the living room.

'I'm sorry,' Art said. 'I'm … I'm going to call your sister, I think, and ask her to come on over. Is that all right with you, Mrs. Heine?'

But there was no answer, and Art could only repeat that he was sorry and step past her in the direction of the telephone.

---

2 **fluted**: with a pattern of curves   **andiron**: Feuerblock   3 **syrupy:** (here) romantic but overdone   6 **blunt-faced**: without significant features or visible emotions   19 **winsome**: pleasant and attractive   21 **diaper** ['daɪpər]: Windel

Chapter 7

In the back of Judge Lew Fielding's courtroom sat twenty-four islanders of Japanese ancestry, dressed in the clothes they reserved for formal occasions. No law compelled them to take only these rear seats. They had done so instead because San Piedro required it of them without calling it a law.

Their parents and grandparents had come to San Piedro as far back as 1883. In that year two of them – Japan Joe and Charles Jose – lived in a lean-to near Cattle Point. Thirty-nine Japanese worked at the Port Jefferson mill, but the census taker neglected to list them by name, referring instead to Jap Number 1, Jap Number 2, Jap Number 3, Japan Charlie, Old Jap Sam, Laughing Jap, Dwarf Jap, Chippy, Boots, and Stumpy – names of this sort instead of real names.

By century's turn over three hundred Japanese had arrived on San Piedro, most of them schooner hands who jumped ship in Port Jefferson Harbor in order to remain in the United States. Many swam ashore with no American currency and wandered island trails eating salmonberries and matsutake mushrooms until they found their way to 'Jap Town': three bathhouses, two barbershops, two churches (one Buddhist, the other a Baptist mission), a hotel, a grocery store, a baseball diamond, an ice cream parlor, a tofu shop, and fifty unpainted and slatternly dwellings all fronting onto muddy roads. Within a week the ship jumpers possessed mill jobs – stacking lumber, sweeping sawdust, hauling slab wood, oiling machines – worth eleven cents an hour.

Company books preserved in the Island County historical archives record that in 1907 eighteen Japanese were injured or maimed at the Port Jefferson mill. Jap Number 107, the books indicate, lost his hand to a ripping blade on March 12 and received an injury payment of $7.80. Jap Number 57 dislocated his right hip on May 29 when a stack of lumber toppled over.

In 1921 the mill was dismantled: all of the island's trees had been fed to the saws, so that San Piedro resembled a bald stump desert. The mill owners sold their holdings and left the island behind. The Japanese cleared strawberry fields, for strawberries grew well in San Piedro's climate and required little starting capital. All you needed, the saying went, was one horse, one plow, and a lot of children.

Soon some Japanese leased small plots of land and entered into business for themselves. Most, though, were contract farmers or sharecroppers who worked in fields owned by *hakujin*. The law said they could not own land unless they became citizens; it also said they could not become citizens so long as they were Japanese.

They saved their money in canning jars, then wrote home to their parents in Japan requesting wives be sent. Some lied and said they'd gotten rich, or sent pictures of themselves as younger men; at any rate, wives came across the ocean. They lived in cedar slat huts lit by oil lamps and slept on straw-filled ticks. The wind blew in through the cracks in the walls. At five o'clock in the morning bride and groom both could be found in the strawberry fields. In the fall, squatting between the rows, they pulled weeds or poured fertilizer out of buckets. They spread slug and weevil bait in April. They cut back the runners on the yearlings first and then on the two- and three-year-old plants. They weeded and watched for fungus and spit bugs and for the mold that grew when it rained.

---

2 **ancestry**: origin   3 **compel sb. to do sth.**: force sb. to do sth.   8 **lean-to**: small building with its roof leaning against the side of a large building   9 **census taker**: (hier) Volkszähler   14 **hand** = deckhand   19 **baseball diamond**: baseball field (which takes the shape of a diamond)   20 **slatternly** (adj): dirty and untidy   22 **mill**: (here) factory that processes timber   **slab**: (here) thick flat piece of wood   25 **maim sb.**: injure sb. seriously, causing permanent damage to their body   28 **dislocate sth.**: (here) put a bone out of its normal position by accident   30 **dismantle sth.**: (here) systematically take sth. to pieces   36 **lease sth.**: etwas pachten   37 **contract farmer**: sb. who is paid to cultivate a piece of land that is owned by sb. else   37–38 **sharecropper**: farmer who gives part of his or her crop as rent to the owner of the land   38 ***hakujin***: Japanese for 'white person'   41 **canning jar**: Einmachglas   44 **slat**: Holzlatte   45 **tick**: (here) kind of mattress   49 **slug**: snail without a shell   **weevil**: kind of bug that eats grain and nuts and destroys crops (= Feldfrüchte)   **bait**: Köder   **runner**: (here) plant stem that grows along the ground and puts down roots   51 **fungus**: Pilz   **spit bug**: insect which feeds on strawberry leaves and covers its eggs with a substance that looks like spit (= Spucke)   **mold** (AE = BE mould): Schimmel

In June, when the berries ripened, they took their caddies into the fields and began the task of picking. Canadian Indians came down each year to join them at working for the *hakujin*. The Indians slept at the verges of fields or in old chicken houses or barns. Some worked in the strawberry cannery. They stayed for two months, through raspberry season, then they were gone again.

But for at least a solid month each summer there were endless strawberries to pick. By an hour after dawn the first flats were mounded over, and the foreman, a white man, stood writing Roman numerals in a black book beside the name of each picker. He sorted the berries in cedar bins while men from the packing company loaded them onto flatbed trucks. The pickers went on filling flats, squatting in the numbered rows.

When the harvest was over in early July they were given a day off for the Strawberry Festival. A young girl was crowned Strawberry Princess; the *hakujin* put on a salmon bake; the Volunteer Fire Department played a softball game against the Japanese Community Center team. The Garden Club displayed strawberries and fuchsia baskets, and the chamber of commerce awarded trophies for a float competition. In the dance pavilion at West Port Jensen the night lanterns were kindled; tourists from Seattle poured forth from the excursion steamers to perform the Svenska polka, the Rhinelander, the schottische, and the hambone. Everybody came out – hay farmers, clerks, merchants, fishermen, crabbers, carpenters, loggers, net weavers, truck farmers, junk dealers, real estate brigands, hack poets, ministers, lawyers, sailors, squatters, millwrights, cedar rats, teamsters, plumbers, mushroom foragers, and holly pruners. They picnicked at Burchillville and Sylvan Grove, listened while the high school band played sluggish Sousa marches, and sprawled under trees drinking port wine.

One part bacchanal, one part tribal potlatch, one part vestigial New England supper, the entire affair hinged on the coronation of the Strawberry Princess – always a virginal Japanese maiden dressed in satin and dusted carefully across the face with rice powder – in an oddly solemn ceremony before the Island County Courthouse at sundown of the inaugural evening. Surrounded by a crescent of basketed strawberries, she received her crown with a bowed head from Amity Harbor's mayor, who wore a red sash from shoulder to waist and carried a decorated scepter. In the hush that ensued he would announce gravely that the Department of

David Guterson: **Snow Falling on Cedars** 71

Agriculture – he had a letter – credited their fair island with producing America's Finest Strawberry, or that King George and Queen Elizabeth, on a recent visit to the city of Vancouver, had been served San Piedro's Best for breakfast. A cheer would fly up as he stood with scepter high, his free hand about the young maiden's shapely shoulder. The girl, it turned out, was an unwitting intermediary between two communities, a human sacrifice who allowed the festivities to go forward with no uttered ill will.

The next day, at noon traditionally, the Japanese began picking raspberries.

Thus life went forward on San Piedro. By Pearl Harbor Day there were eight hundred and forty-three people of Japanese descent living there, including twelve seniors at Amity Harbor High School who did not graduate that spring. Early on the morning of March 29, 1942, fifteen transports of the U.S. War Relocation Authority took all of San Piedro's Japanese-Americans to the ferry terminal in Amity Harbor.

They were loaded onto a ship while their white neighbors looked on, people who had risen early to stand in the cold and watch this exorcising of the Japanese from their midst – friends, some of them, but the merely curious, mainly, and fishermen who stood on the decks of their boats out in Amity Harbor. The fishermen felt, like most islanders, that this exiling of the Japanese was the right thing to do, and leaned against the cabins of their stern-pickers and bow-pickers with the conviction that the Japanese must go for reasons that made sense: there was a war on and that changed everything.

1 **caddy:** (here) type of basket   8 **flat** (n): (hier) flacher Korb   19 **kindle sth.**: set sth. alight   20 **steamer**: ship that is driven by steam   24 **real estate brigand**: Immobilienhai   **hack poet**: poet with little skill or fame   25 **millwright**: Sägemaschinenbauer   **cedar rats**: Schindelmacher   **teamster**: truck driver   26 **forage** (n): search for food, esp. in the wood   **holly**: Stechpalme   **pruner**: (here) person who cuts off some of the branches from a tree so that it will grow better   28 **sprawl** (v): sit or lie with your arms and legs spread out   29 **bacchanal**: Gelage   **potlatch** ['pɒtlætʃ]: wild party   **vestigial**: (here) being a poor copy of a formerly great tradition   30 **hinge on sth.**: depend on sth. completely   36 **sash**: Schärpe   37 **hush**: period of silence, following a lot of noise, esp. when people are expecting sth. to happen   **ensue**: follow   42 **shapely**: having an attractive shape   43 **unwitting**: not aware of sth.   **intermediary**: Vermittler   51 **relocation**: act of moving sb./sth. to a new place   54 **exorcise sb. from sth.**: (here) remove sb. who is thought to be bad for a community from sth.

CHAPTER 7

During the morning recess the accused man's wife had come alone to the row of seats behind the defendant's table and asked permission to speak with her husband.

'You'll have to do it from back there,' said Abel Martinson. 'Mr. Miyamoto can turn and face you all right, but that's about it, you see. I'm not supposed to let him move around much.'

Once each afternoon, for seventy-seven days, Hatsue Miyamoto had appeared at the Island County Jail for a three o'clock visit with her husband. At first she came alone and spoke with him through a pane of glass, but then he asked her to bring the children. Thereafter she did so – two girls, eight and four, who walked behind her, and a boy of eleven months whom she carried in her arms. Kabuo was in jail on the morning their son began to walk, but in the afternoon she brought the boy and he took four steps while his father watched from behind the visiting room windowpane. Afterward she'd held him up to the glass and Kabuo spoke to him through the microphone. 'You can go further than me!' he'd said. 'You take some steps for me, okay?'

Now, in the courtroom, he turned toward Hatsue. 'How are the kids?' he said.

'They need their father,' she answered.

'Nels is working on that,' said Kabuo.

'Nels is going to move away,' said Nels. 'Deputy Martinson ought to do the same. Why don't you stand where you can watch, Abel? But give these people some privacy.'

'I can't,' replied Abel. 'Art'd kill me.'

'Art won't kill you,' Nels said. 'You know darn well Mrs. Miyamoto isn't going to slip Mr. Miyamoto any kind of weapon. Back off a little. Let them talk.'

'I can't,' said Abel. 'Sorry.'

But he sidled back about three feet anyway and pretended not to be listening. Nels excused himself.

'Where are they staying?' asked Kabuo.

'They're at your mother's. Mrs. Nakao is there. Everybody is helping out.'

'You look good. I miss you.'

'I look terrible,' answered Hatsue. 'And you look like one of Tojo's soldiers. You'd better quit sitting up so straight and tall. These jury people will be afraid of you.'

He fixed his gaze directly on hers, and she could see he was thinking about it. 'It's good to be out of that cell,' he said. 'It feels great to be out of there.'

Hatsue wanted to touch him then. She wanted to reach out and put her hand on his neck or place her fingertips against his face. This was the first time in seventy-seven days that they had not been separated by a pane of glass. For seventy-seven days she'd heard his voice only through the filter of a microphone. During this time she had never once felt composed, and she had stopped imagining their future. At night she'd brought the children into her bed, then exerted herself fruitlessly toward sleep. She had sisters, cousins, and aunts who called mornings and asked her to come for lunch. She went because she was lonely and needed to hear the sound of voices. The women made sandwiches, cakes, and tea and chattered in the kitchen while the children played, and this is how the autumn passed, with her life arrested, on hold.

Sometimes in the afternoons, Hatsue fell asleep on a sofa. While she slept these other women cared for her children, and she didn't neglect to thank them for it; but in the past she would never have done such a thing, fall asleep, drop away in the middle of a visit while her children ran about recklessly.

She was a woman of thirty-one and still graceful. She had the flat-footed gait of a barefoot peasant, a narrow waist, small breasts. She very often wore men's khaki pants, a gray cotton sweatshirt, and sandals. It was her habit in the summer to work at picking strawberries in order to bring home extra money. Her hands were stained in the picking season with berry juice. In the fields she wore a straw hat low on her head, a thing she had not done consistently in her youth, so that now around her eyes there were squint lines. Hatsue was a tall woman – five foot eight – but nevertheless able to squat low between the berry rows for quite some time without pain.

26 **darn** (infml): mild swear word (= Schimpfword) used instead of 'damn'
30 **sidle**: walk somewhere in a shy or uncertain way as if you do not want to be noticed   35 **Tojo** = Tojo Hideki (1884–1948): president of Japan from 1941 to 1944, executed for war crimes in 1948   46 **composed**: (here) calm and in control of your feelings   47 **exert yourself**: make a big physical or mental effort
52 **on hold**: delayed until a later time   57 **reckless**: wild, showing a lack of care about oneself and others   59 **gait**: way of walking

Recently she had begun to wear mascara and lipstick. She was not vain, but she understood that she was fading. It was all right with her, at thirty-one, if she faded, for it had come to her slowly over the years, an ever-deepening realization, that there was more to life than the extraordinary beauty she had always been celebrated for. In youth she had been so thoroughly beautiful that her beauty had been public property. She had been crowned princess of the Strawberry Festival in 1941. When she was thirteen her mother had dressed her in a silk kimono and sent her off to Mrs. Shigemura, who taught young girls to dance *odori* and to serve tea impeccably. Seated before a mirror with Mrs. Shigemura behind her, she had learned that her hair was *utsukushii* and that to cut it would be a form of heresy. It was a river of iridescent onyx – Mrs. Shigemura described it in Japanese – the salient feature of her physical being, as prominent and extraordinary as baldness might have been in another girl of the same age. She had to learn that there were many ways to wear it – that she might tame it with pins or weave it in a thick plait hanging over one breast or knot it intricately at the nape of her neck or sweep it back in such a manner that the broad, smooth planes of her cheeks declared themselves. Mrs. Shigemura lifted Hatsue's hair in her palms and said its consistency reminded her of mercury and that Hatsue should learn to play her hair lovingly, like a stringed musical instrument or a flute. Then she combed it down Hatsue's back until it lay opened like a fan and shimmered in unearthly black waves.

Mrs. Shigemura, on Wednesday afternoons, taught Hatsue the intricacies of the tea ceremony as well as calligraphy and scene painting. She showed her how to arrange flowers in a vase and how, for special occasions, to dust her face with rice powder. She insisted that Hatsue must never giggle and must never look at a man directly. In order to keep her complexion immaculate – Hatsue, said Mrs. Shigemura, had skin as smooth as vanilla ice cream – she must take care to stay out of the sun. Mrs. Shigemura taught Hatsue how to sing with composure and how to sit, walk, and stand gracefully. It was this latter that remained of Mrs. Shigemura: Hatsue still moved with a wholeness of being that began in the balls of her feet and reached right through to the top of her head. She was unified and graceful.

Her life had always been strenuous – field work, internment, more field work on top of housework – but during this period under Mrs.

Shigemura's tutelage she had learned to compose herself in the face of it. It was a matter in part of posture and breathing, but even more so of soul. Mrs. Shigemura taught her to seek union with the Greater Life and to imagine herself as a leaf on a great tree: The prospect of death in autumn, she said, was irrelevant next to its happy recognition of its participation in the life of the tree itself. In America, she said, there was fear of death; here life was separate from Being. A Japanese, on the other hand, must see that life embraces death, and when she feels the truth of this she will gain tranquillity.

Mrs. Shigemura taught Hatsue to sit without moving and claimed that she would not mature properly unless she learned to do so for extended periods. Living in America, she said, would make this difficult, because here there was tension and unhappiness. At first Hatsue, who was only thirteen, could not sit still for even thirty seconds. Then later, when she had stilled her body, she found it was her mind that would not be quiet. But gradually her rebellion against tranquillity subsided. Mrs. Shigemura was pleased and claimed that the turbulence of her ego was in the process of being overcome. She told Hatsue that her stillness would serve her well. She would experience harmony of being in the midst of the changes and unrest that life inevitably brings.

But Hatsue feared, walking home over forest trails from Mrs. Shigemura's, that despite her training she was not becalmed. She dallied and sometimes sat under trees, searched for lady's slippers or white

---

2 **vain**: too proud of your own appearance, abilities or achievements   6 **public property**: sth. belonging to everybody in a community   9 *odori*: traditional Japanese dance   11 *utsukushii*: Japanese for 'beautiful'   12 **heresy**: Ketzerei   **iridescent** (fml): showing many bright colors that seem to change in different lights   13 **salient**: most important or noticeable   16 **tame sth.**: etwas zähmen/bändigen   **plait**: geflochtener Zopf   17 **intricate**: having a lot of different parts and small details that fit together   18 **plane**: Fläche, Ebene   20 **mercury**: silver liquid metal with an iridescent surface (used in thermometers)   25 **calligraphy** [-'---]: art of beautiful handwriting   29 **immaculate**: pure, without flaws   31 **composure**: state of being calm and in control of your feelings or behavior   35 **unified**: (hier) in sich ruhend   36 **internment** [-'--]: act of putting sb. in prison during a war or for political reasons, although they have not been charged with a crime   38 **tutelage** ['tu:təlɪdʒ] (fml): teaching and instruction   46 **tranquillity** [træŋ'kwɪləti]: state of inner calmness   53 **subside**: become calmer or quieter   59 **dally** (old-fashioned): do sth. too slowly

trilliums to pick, and contemplated her attraction to the world of illusions – her craving for existence and entertainment, for clothes, makeup, dances, movies. It seemed to her that in her external bearing she had succeeded only in deceiving Mrs. Shigemura; inwardly she knew her aspiration for worldly happiness was frighteningly irresistible. Yet the demand that she conceal this inner life was great, and by the time she entered high school she was expert at implying bodily a tranquillity that did not in fact inhabit her. In this way she developed a secret life that disturbed her and that she sought to cast off.

Mrs. Shigemura was open and forthright with Hatsue about matters of a sexual nature. With all the seriousness of a fortune-teller she predicted that white men would desire Hatsue and seek to destroy her virginity. She claimed that white men carried in their hearts a secret lust for pure young Japanese girls. Look at their magazines and moving pictures, Mrs. Shigemura said. Kimonos, sake, rice paper walls, coquettish and demure geishas. White men had their fantasies of a passionate Japan – girls of burnished skin and willowy long legs going barefoot in the wet heat of rice paddies – and this distorted their sex drives. They were dangerous egomaniacs and utterly convinced that Japanese women worshiped them for their pale skin and for their ambitious courage. Stay away from white men, said Mrs. Shigemura, and marry a boy of your own kind whose heart is strong and good.

Her parents had sent Hatsue to Mrs. Shigemura with the intent that the girl would not forget that she was first and foremost Japanese. Her father, a strawberry farmer, had come from Japan, from people who had been pottery makers for as long as anyone in his prefecture could remember. Hatsue's mother, Fujiko – the daughter of a modest family near Kure, hardworking shopkeepers and rice wholesalers – had come to America as Hisao's picture bride on board the *Korea Maru*. The marriage was arranged by a *baishakunin* who told the Shibayamas that the potential groom had made a fortune in the new country. But the Shibayamas were owners of a respectable house, and it seemed to them that Fujiko, the daughter in question, could do better than to marry a hired hand in America. Then the *baishakunin*, whose work was to procure brides, showed them twelve acres of prime mountain land, which, he said, the potential bridegroom intended to purchase upon his return from America. There were peach and persimmon trees there, and slender, tall cedars, and a beautiful new home with three rock gardens. And finally, he pointed out, Fujiko *wanted* to go: she was young, nineteen, and wished to see something of the world beyond the sea before settling into her married life.

But she had been sick all the way across the ocean, prostrate, clench bellied, and vomiting. And once in the new country, arriving in Seattle, she found she had married a pauper. Hisao's fingers were callused and sun blistered, and his clothing smelled powerfully of field sweat. He had nothing, it turned out, but a few dollars and coins, for which he begged Fujiko's forgiveness. At first they lived in a Beacon Hill boardinghouse where the walls were plastered with pictures from magazines and where the white people on the streets outside treated them with humiliating disdain. Fujiko went to work in a waterfront cookhouse. She, too, sweated beneath her clothes and cut her palms and knuckles working for the *hakujin*.

Hatsue was born, the first of five daughters, and the family moved to a Jackson Street boardinghouse. It was owned by people from Tochigiken prefecture who had done astoundingly well for themselves: the women among them wore silk crepe kimonos and scarlet, cork-soled slippers. Jackson Street, though, smelled of rotting fish, cabbages and radishes fermenting in sea brine, sluggish sewers and diesel streetcar fumes. Fujiko cleaned rooms there for three years, until one day Hisao came home with the news that he had procured jobs for them with the National Cannery Company. In May the Imadas boarded a boat for San Piedro, where there was work to be had in the many strawberry fields.

---

1 **trillium**: plant with a central flower with three petals (= Blütenblätter)
5 **aspiration**: strong desire to have or to do sth.   9 **cast sth. off** (fml): (here) get rid of sth. because you no longer want or need it   16 **demure**: modest   17 **burnished**: (here) shiny   **willowy**: (of a woman) tall, thin and attractive   18 **rice paddy**: rice field   26 **prefecture**: an area of local government   29 **Korea Maru**: ocean liner sold by an American to a Japanese company in 1916 which transported many immigrants to the USA until 1930   34 ***baishakunin***: Japanese for 'matchmaker', sb. who is paid to arrange a marriage   35 **procure sth.** (fml): obtain sth., esp. with difficulty   37 **persimmon**: kind of plum tree   42 **prostrate** ['--] (adj): lying face down   44 **pauper**: very poor person   **callused**: (of the skin) made rough and hard, usually by hard work   49 **humiliate sb.**: make sb. feel ashamed or stupid
58 **brine**: salt water   **sewer**: Abwasserkanal

It was hard work, though – Hatsue and her sisters would do a lot of it in their lives – stoop labor performed in the direct sun. But despite that it was infinitely better than Seattle: the neat rows of strawberries flowed up and down the valleys, the wind brought the smell of the sea to their nostrils, and in the morning the gray light evoked something of the Japan Hisao and Fujiko had left behind.

At first they lived in the corner of a barn they shared with an Indian family. Hatsue, at seven, cut ferns in the forest and pruned holly trees beside her mother. Hisao sold perch and made Christmas wreaths. They filled a grain sack with coins and bills, leased seven acres of stumps and vine maple, purchased a plow horse, and started clearing. Autumn came, the maple leaves curled into fists and dropped away, and the rain ground them into an auburn paste. Hisao burned piles and pried stumps from the earth in the winter of 1931. A house of cedar slats went up slowly. The land was tilled and the first crop planted in time for the pale light of spring.

Hatsue grew up digging clams at South Beach, picking blackberries, collecting mushrooms, and weeding strawberry plants. She was mother, too, to four sisters. When she was ten a neighborhood boy taught her how to swim and offered her the use of his glass-bottomed box so that she could look beneath the surface of the waves. The two of them clung to it, their backs warmed by the Pacific sun, and together watched starfish and rock crabs. The water evaporated against Hatsue's skin, leaving a residue of salt behind. Finally, one day, the boy kissed her. He asked if he might, and she said nothing either way, and then he leaned across the box and put his lips on hers for no more than a second. She smelled the warm, salty interior of his mouth before this boy pulled away and blinked at her. Then they went on looking through the glass at anemones, sea cucumbers, and tube worms. Hatsue would remember on the day of her wedding that her first kiss had been from this boy, Ishmael Chambers, while they clung to a glass box and floated in the ocean. But when her husband asked if she had kissed anyone before, Hatsue had answered *never*.

'It's coming down hard,' she said to him now, lifting her eyes to the courtroom windows. 'A big snow. Your son's first.'

Kabuo turned to take in the snowfall, and she noticed the thick sinews in the left side of his neck above where his shirt was buttoned. He had not lost any of his strength in jail; his strength, as she understood it, was an inward matter, something he tuned silently to the conditions of life: in his cell he had composed himself to preserve it.

'Check the root cellar, Hatsue,' he said. 'You don't want anything to freeze.'

'I've been checking,' she answered. 'Everything's fine.'

'Good,' said Kabuo. 'I knew you would.'

He watched the snow for a silent moment, the needles of it blurring past the leaded panes, then turned again to look at her. 'Do you remember that snow at Manzanar?' he said. 'Whenever it snows I think of that. The drifts and the big wind and the potbellied stove. And the starlight coming through the window.'

It was not the sort of thing he would normally have said to her, these romantic words. But perhaps jail had taught him to release what otherwise he might conceal. 'That was jail, too,' said Hatsue. 'There were good things, but that was jail.'

'It wasn't jail,' Kabuo told her. 'We thought it was back then because we didn't know any better. But it wasn't jail.'

She knew, as he spoke, that this was true. They'd been married at the Manzanar internment camp in a tar paper Buddhist chapel. Her mother had hung woolen army blankets to divide the Imadas' cramped room in half and had given them, on their wedding night, two cots adjacent to the stove. She had even pushed the cots together to form one bed and smoothed their sheets with her palms. Hatsue's sisters – all four of them – had stood beside the curtain watching while their mother went about her silent business. Fujiko loaded coal into the potbellied stove and wiped her hands on her apron. She nodded and said they should close the damper when forty-five minutes had gone by. Then she took her daughters out with her and left Hatsue and Kabuo behind.

---

2 **stoop** (v): bend your body forwards and downwards   8 **fern**: Farn   9 **perch** (n): Barsch   **wreaths** [riːðz]: round decorative arrangements of flowers and leaves   11 **vine maple**: kleine Ahornart   13 **auburn**: reddish-brown   13–14 **pry sth. from sth. else** (AE): use force to separate sth. from sth. else   15 **till sth.**: prepare and use land for growing crops   17 **clam** (n): Venusmuschel   22 **starfish**: Seestern   23 **residue** [rezɪduː]: small amount of sth. that remains at the end of a process   47 **potbellied stove = potbelly stove** (AE): small round stove with a large and bulging middle part for burning coal or wood   58 **cot** (AE): Feldbett   **adjacent**: located next to sth.   63 **apron**: Schürze   64 **damper**: Ofenklappe

They stood beside the window in their wedding clothes and kissed, and she smelled his warm neck and throat. Outside snow had drifted against the barracks wall. 'They'll hear everything,' Hatsue whispered.

Kabuo, his hands at her waist, turned and spoke to the curtain. 'There must be something good on the radio,' he called. 'Wouldn't some music be nice?'

They waited. Kabuo hung his coat on a peg. In a little while a station from Las Vegas came on – country-and-western music. Kabuo sat down and removed his shoes and socks. He put them under the bed neatly. He unknotted his bow tie.

Hatsue sat down beside him. She looked at the side of his face for a moment, at the scar on his jaw, and then they kissed. 'I need help with my dress,' she whispered. 'It unhooks in the back, Kabuo.'

Kabuo unclasped it for her. He ran his fingers along her spine. She stood and pulled the dress from her shoulders. It dropped to the floor, and she picked it up and hung it on the peg beside his coat.

Hatsue came back to the bed in her bra and slip and sat down beside Kabuo.

'I don't want to make a lot of noise,' she said. 'Even with the radio. My sisters are listening.'

'Okay,' said Kabuo. 'Quietly.'

He unbuttoned his shirt, stripped it off, and set it on the end of the cot. He pulled his undershirt off. He was very strong. She could see the muscles flowing in his abdomen. She was glad to have married him. He, too, came from strawberry farmers. He was good with the plants and knew which runners to cut. His hands, like hers, were berry stained in the summer months. The red fruit mingled with his skin and scented it. She knew that in part because of this smell she wanted to tie her life to his; it was something she understood in her nose, finally, as odd as that might seem to others. And she knew that Kabuo wanted what she wanted, a San Piedro strawberry farm. That was all, there was nothing more than that, they wanted their farm and the closeness at hand of the people they loved and the scent of strawberries outside their window. There were girls Hatsue's age she knew very well who felt certain their happiness was something other, who wanted to go to Seattle or Los Angeles. They could not say in any precise way exactly what it was they sought in the city, only that they wanted to go there. It was something Hatsue herself had once felt but had since emerged from as if from a dream, discovering the truth of her private nature: it was in her to have the composure and tranquillity of an island strawberry farmer. She knew in her bones what she wanted, and she knew why she wanted it, too. She understood the happiness of a place where the work was clear and there were fields she could enter into with a man she loved purposefully. And this was what Kabuo felt, too, and what he wanted from life. And so they made plans together. When the war was over they would return to San Piedro. Kabuo was rooted there just as she was, a boy who understood the earth and the working of it and how it was a good thing to live among people one loved. He was precisely the boy Mrs. Shigemura had described for her so many years ago when she'd spoken of love and marriage, and now she kissed him, hard, because of that. She kissed his jaw and forehead more softly, and then she put her chin against the top of his head and held his ears between her fingers. His hair smelled like wet earth. Kabuo put his hands against her back and pulled her deeply to him. He kissed the skin just over her breasts and put his nose against her bra.

'You smell so good,' he said.

He drew away and stripped his pants off and laid them next to his shirt. They sat there beside each other in their underwear. His legs shone in the light from the window. She could see beneath the fabric of his underpants how his penis stood erect. The end of it pushed his shorts into the air.

Hatsue brought her feet up onto the bed and propped her chin on her knees. 'They're listening,' she said. 'I know they are.'

'Could you turn the radio up?' Kabuo called. 'We can't hear it so well in here.'

The country-and-western music grew louder. And they were very quiet at first. They lay on their sides and faced one another, and she felt his hardness against her belly. She reached down and touched it beneath the fabric of his shorts, the tip of it and the ridge just below. She could hear the coal burning in the potbellied stove.

She remembered how she had kissed Ishmael Chambers, clinging to that wooden box. He was a brown-skinned boy who lived down the

7 **peg**: (hier) (Kleider)haken   24 **abdomen**: part of the body below the chest that contains the stomach

road – they'd picked blackberries, climbed trees, fished for perch. She thought of him while Kabuo kissed the undersides of her breasts, and then her nipples through the fabric of her bra, and she recognized Ishmael as the beginning of a chain, that she had kissed a boy when she was ten years old, had even then felt something strange, and that tonight, soon, she would feel another boy's hardness deep inside of her. But it was not difficult for her, on her wedding night, to then cast Ishmael out of her mind completely; he had only crept in by accident, as it were, because all romantic moments are associated willy-nilly – even when some are long dead.

In a little while her husband took off her slip and underpants and unhooked her bra, and she pulled down his shorts. They were naked, and she could see his face in the starlight from the window. It was a good face, strong and smooth. The wind was blowing hard outside now, and the sound of it whistled between the boards. She put her hand around Kabuo's hardness and squeezed it, and it pulsed once in her hand. Then, because she wanted it this way, she fell onto her back without letting go, and he was on top of her with his hands on her buttocks.

'Have you ever done this before?' he whispered.

'Never,' answered Hatsue. 'You're my only.'

The head of his penis found the place it wanted. For a moment he waited there, poised, and kissed her – he took her lower lip between his lips and gently held it there. Then with his hands he pulled her to him and at the same time entered her so that she felt his scrotum slap against her skin. Her entire body felt the rightness of it, her entire body was seized to it. Hatsue arched her shoulder blades – her breasts pressed themselves against his chest – and a slow shudder ran through her.

'It's right,' she remembered whispering. 'It feels so right, Kabuo.'

'*Tadaima aware ga wakatta*,' he had answered. '*I understand just now the deepest beauty.*'

Eight days later he left for Camp Shelby, Mississippi, where he joined the 442nd Regimental Combat Team. He *had* to go to the war, he told her. It was necessary in order to demonstrate his bravery. It was necessary to demonstrate his loyalty to the United States: his country.

'You can die demonstrating all of that,' she told him. '*I* know you are brave and loyal.'

He went despite these words of hers. She had spoken them many times before their wedding, often she'd urged him not to go, but he had not been able to bring himself to stay away from the fighting. It was not only a point of honor, he'd said, it was also a matter of having to go because his face was Japanese. There was something extra that had to be proved, a burden this particular war placed on him, and if he would not carry it, who would? She saw that in this he would not be swayed and recognized the hardness buried in him, the part of her husband that was attracted to the fighting and wanted to enter it desperately. There was a place in him she could not reach where he made his choices in solitude, and this made her not only uneasy about him but afraid for their future, too. Her life was joined to his now, and it seemed to her that every corner of his soul should be opened to hers because of this. It was the war, she persistently told herself, it was the prison of camp life, the pressures of the times, their exile from home, that explained his distance. Many men were going off to the war against the wishes of women, a lot of them leaving the camp each day, droves of young men going. She told herself she must endure it in the way her mother and Kabuo's mother counseled her and not struggle against those larger forces that could not be struggled against. She was in the stream of history now, as her mother before her had been. She must travel in it easily or her own heart would devour her and she would not endure the war unwounded, as she still hoped to do.

Hatsue settled into missing her husband and learned the art of waiting over an extended period of time – a deliberately controlled hysteria that was something like what Ishmael Chambers felt watching her in the courtroom.

9 **willy-nilly:** (here) whether you want to or not   24 **scrotum**: Hodensack
33 **bravery**: courage   43 **sway (sb.)**: (here) persuade sb. to change their mind
50 **persistent**: beharrlich   53 **droves**: large group of people or animals
58 **devour sth.**: etwas verschlingen   60 **settle into sth.**: (here) become used to sth.

Chapter 8

Ishmael Chambers, watching Hatsue, remembered digging geoduck clams with her below the bluff at South Beach. Hatsue, carrying a garden shovel and a metal pail rusted through in its bottom, dripped water behind her as she walked the tide flats; she was fourteen and wore a black bathing suit. She went barefoot, avoiding barnacles, picking her way along the flats with the tide drawn out and the salt chuck grass sleek against the mud in sun-dried fans. Ishmael wore rubber boots and clutched a gardener's hand spade; the sun struck his shoulders and back as he walked and dried the mud on his knees and hands.

They wandered for nearly a mile. They stopped to swim. At the turning of the tide the geoducks emerged, shooting jets of water like miniature geysers hidden among the eelgrass. Down the mud flats small fountains erupted, dozens of them, spurting two feet or more, then again, then lower, then dwindling and stopping. The geoducks raised their necks from the mud and aimed their lips at the sun. The siphons at the ends of their necks glistened. They blossomed delicately white and iridescent out of the tidal morass.

The two of them knelt beside a clam siphon to discuss the particulars of its appearance. They were quiet and made no sudden movements – movement inspired shyness among clams and encouraged them to withdraw. Hatsue, her bucket beside her, her shovel in one hand, pointed out the darkness of the exposed clam's lip, its size, its hue and tone, the circumference of its watery dimple. She decided they'd stopped beside a horse clam.

They were fourteen years old; geoducks were important. It was summer and little else really mattered.

They came to a second siphon and knelt again. Hatsue, sitting on her ankles, twisted the salt water out of her hair so that it dripped along her arm. She lofted her hair out neatly behind her and let it spread against her back to catch the sun.

'Geoduck,' she said quietly.

'A good one,' Ishmael agreed.

Hatsue bent forward and slipped a forefinger inside the siphon. They watched while the clam seized up around it and drew its neck into the mud. She followed its retreating path with the point of an alder stick; its two feet of length disappeared. 'He's way down there,' she said, 'and he's big.'

'My turn to dig,' answered Ishmael.

Hatsue handed him her shovel. 'The handle's coming loose,' she warned. 'Be careful it doesn't break.'

The shovel brought butter clams, sticks, and sea worms up with it. Ishmael built a dike against the turning of the tide; Hatsue bailed with the leaking pail, stretched out flat against the warm mud, the backs of her legs smooth and brown.

When the alder stick fell over, Ishmael dropped down beside her and watched while she scraped with the hand spade. The clam's siphon came into view; they saw the aperture through which its neck had retreated. They lay at the edge of the hole together, each with a muddy arm hung in, and excavated around it until a third of the shell showed. 'Let's pull it now,' suggested Ishmael.

'We'd better get under it,' answered Hatsue.

He had taught her to dig geoducks, and they had dug them for four summers, but in the end she'd surpassed him in it. There was this way she had of speaking with certainty that he found entirely convincing. 'He's still got a good grip,' she pointed out. 'He'll break if we start pulling. Let's be patient and dig some more. It's better if we keep digging.'

1–2 **geoduck clam**: Pacific sea shell that digs deep into the mud (= Schlamm) for safety   2 **bluff**: steep cliff or slope, esp. by the sea or a river   3 **pail**: bucket   5 **barnacle**: (here) small shellfish   6 **salt chuck grass**: type of grass growing at the seafront   7 **sleek** (adj): glatt, flach   **fan**: Fächer   11 **jet**: (here) strong, narrow stream of gas or liquid that is ejected under pressure   13 **spurt**: (of a liquid) burst out suddenly   14 **dwindle**: become gradually less or smaller   23 **circumference** [sər'kʌmfərəns]: (Kreis)umfang   **dimple**: (here) any small hollow place in a surface   29 **loft sth. out**: (hier) etwas auswerfen   35 **alder**: Erle   39 **handle** (n): part of an object that you use to hold it   42 **bail** (v): (hier) schöpfen   47 **aperture** ['æpətʃʊr]: small opening   49 **excavate**: dig   53 **surpass sb. in sth.** [sər'pæs]: do or be better in sth. than sb.

When the time came to pull he slid his hand down as far as he could so that the side of his face lay against the mud, turned toward Hatsue's knee. He was close enough so that her knee was his whole view of things, and he smelled the salt on her skin.

'Gentle,' she urged. 'Slow. Easy is the way. Don't hurry it. Slow is best.'

'He's coming,' Ishmael grunted. 'I can feel him.'

Afterward she took the clam from between his fingers and rinsed it off in the shallows. She rubbed the shell with the heel of her palm and cleaned the long neck and foot. Ishmael took the clam back and put it in the bucket. Clean and delicate, as large as any he had seen, it was approximately the size and shape of a turkey breast carved away from the bone. He admired it, turned it in his hand. He was always surprised at the thickness and heft of a geoduck. 'We found a good one,' he said.

'He's huge,' answered Hatsue. 'Enormous.'

She stood in the shallows rinsing mud from her legs while Ishmael filled in the hole. The tide skated in over sun-heated flats, and the water was as warm as a lagoon. The two of them sat side by side in the shallows, facing out toward the expanse of the ocean, kelp draped across their legs. 'It goes forever,' said Ishmael. 'There's more water than anything in the world.'

'It ends somewhere,' answered Hatsue. 'Or it just goes around and around.'

'That's the same thing. It's forever.'

'There's a shore somewhere right now where the tide is up,' explained Hatsue. 'And that's the end of the ocean.'

'It doesn't end. It meets another one and pretty soon the water is back and it all mixes together.'

'Oceans don't mix,' said Hatsue. 'They're different temperatures. They have different amounts of salt.'

'They mix underneath,' said Ishmael. 'It's all really just one ocean.' He lay back on his elbows, draped a strand of seaweed across his thighs, and settled in again.

'It's not one ocean,' said Hatsue. 'It's four oceans – Atlantic, Pacific, Indian, Arctic. They're different from each other.'

'Well, how are they different?'

'They just are.' Hatsue lay back on her elbows beside him and let her hair fall behind. 'Just because,' she added.

'That's not a good reason,' Ishmael said. 'The main thing is, water is water. Names on a map don't mean anything. Do you think if you were out there in a boat and you came to another ocean you'd see a sign or something? It – '

'The color would change, I've heard that,' said Hatsue. 'The Atlantic Ocean is brown, sort of, and the Indian Ocean is blue.'

'Where'd you hear that?'

'I don't remember.'

'It isn't true.'

'Yes, it is.'

They were silent. There was the lapping of the water and no other sound. Ishmael was aware of her legs and arms. The salt had dried at the corners of her lips and left a residue behind. He noticed her fingernails, the shape of her toes, the hollow place at her throat. He had known her for six years and he had not known her. The detached part of her, the part she kept to herself, had begun to interest him deeply.

It made him unhappy when he thought about her lately, and he had passed a lot of time, all spring long, mulling how to tell her about his unhappiness. He'd sat on top of the bluff at South Beach thinking about it in the afternoons. He'd thought about it during school. His thoughts, however, yielded no clue as to how to talk to Hatsue. Words evaded him completely. He felt in her presence that to reveal himself would be a mistake he might never correct. She was closed up and offered him no opening for talk, though for years now they had walked from the school bus together, met on the beach and in the woods to play, picked berries on the same nearby farms. They had played together as children in a group that included her sisters and other kids – Sheridan Knowles, Arnold and Bill Kruger, Lars Hansen, Tina and Jean Syvertsen. They had passed autumn afternoons when they were nine years old in the hollowed-out base of a cedar tree, where they sprawled on the ground looking out at the rain as it pummeled the sword ferns and ivy. At school they were strangers for reasons unclear to him, though at the same time

---

7 **rinse sth.**: remove dirt from sth. by washing it with clean water   8 **shallows** (pl): seichte Stelle   **heel of the palm**: Handballen   13 **heft**: weight   18 **expanse** [-'-]: wide and open area or surface   58 **yield sth.**: offer or provide sth.   **evade sb.** (fml): (here) not come to sb.   68 **pummel sth.** (v): beat/hit sth. hard

he understood it had to be that way because she was Japanese and he wasn't. It was the way things were and there was nothing to be done about such a basic thing.

She was fourteen and her breasts were beginning to show beneath her bathing suit. They were small and hard, like apples. He could not put his finger on how else she had changed, but even her face was different. The texture of its skin had changed. He had watched her change, and when he sat close to her, as he did now in the water, he felt driven and nervous.

Ishmael's heart began the fretful pounding he'd experienced of late in her presence. There were no words for what he had to say and his tongue felt paralyzed. He couldn't stand another moment without explaining his heart to her. A knot of pressure was building inside him to declare the love he felt. It was not only that her beauty moved him but that they already had a history together that included this beach, these waters, the very stones, and the forest at their backs, too. It was all theirs and always would be, and Hatsue was the spirit of the place. She knew where to find matsutake mushrooms, elderberries, and fern tendrils, and she had found them now for years at his side, and they had taken each other for granted, they had been as easy as friends about it all – until these last few months. Now he was in pain about her, and he understood that he would continue in his pain unless he did something about it. It was up to him. It took courage and it made him feel ill, this unasked-for thing. It was too hard. He shut his eyes.

'I like you,' he confessed with his eyes still shut. 'Do you know what I mean? I've always liked you, Hatsue.'

She didn't answer. She didn't even look at him; she looked down. But having started it he moved into the warmth of her face anyway and put his lips against hers. They were warm, too. There was the taste of salt and the heat of her breathing. He pushed too hard, and she planted one hand beneath the water behind her to keep from falling over. She pushed back against him, and he felt the pressure of her teeth and smelled the inside of her mouth. Their teeth clashed a little. He shut his eyes and then opened them again. Hatsue's eyes were tightly shut, she wouldn't look at him.

Just as soon as they were no longer touching she leapt up and went for her geoduck pail and ran away down the beach. She was very fast, he knew that. He stood up only to watch her go. Then, after she had disappeared into the woods, he lay in the water for another ten minutes feeling the kiss many times. He decided then that he would love her forever no matter what came to pass. It was not so much a matter of deciding as accepting the inevitability of it. It made him feel better, though he felt perturbed, too, worried that this kiss was *wrong*. But from his point of view, at fourteen years old, their love was entirely unavoidable. It had started on the day they'd clung to his glass box and kissed in the sea, and now it must go on forever. He felt certain of this. He felt certain Hatsue felt the same way.

For ten days after that Ishmael worked – odd jobs and stray chores, weeding and window washing – and worried about Hatsue Imada. She stayed away from the beach intentionally, it seemed to him in his fretfulness, and gradually he became dark and morose. He battened down the guy wires over which Mrs. Verda Carmichael's raspberries were trellised, straightened out the contents of her shadowy toolshed, and bundled up her cedar kindling – all of it permeated by thoughts about Hatsue. He helped Bob Timmons scrape paint from his shed and weeded flower beds with Mrs. Herbert Crow, a woman who concerned herself with flower arrangements and treated Ishmael's mother formally. Now, seated on a knee pad, Mrs. Crow worked beside Ishmael with a maple-handled claw, stopping every now and then to wipe sweat from her brow with the back of her forearm and to exclaim that he seemed blue. Later she decided they would sit on the back porch and sip tall glasses of iced tea and lemon wedges. She pointed to a fig tree and told Ishmael she'd planted it more years ago than she could remember; against all

---

12 **paralyze sb./sth.**: make sb./sth. unable to move their body   18 **tendril**: thin curling stem that grows from a climbing plant   43 **perturbed**: alarmed, worried   48 **odd:** (here) various   **stray chores**: verschiedene Aufgaben im Haushalt   49 **weed** (v): Unkraut jäten   51 **morose**: unhappy and bad-tempered   **batten sth. down**: fix sth. firmly in position   52 **guy wire**: Spanndraht   53 **trellise sth.** ['trelɪs]: (hier) etwas an ein Spalier anbinden   **straighten sth. out:** (here) make sth. neat and tidy   54 **kindling**: small dry pieces of wood that are used to start a fire   **permeate sth.**: affect every part of sth.   58 **maple:** (hier) Ahornholz   59 **claw:** (here) tool used for holding, pulling or lifting things   60 **brow** (fml): (hier) Stirn   **blue:** (here) depressed   62 **wedge** (n): piece or slice   **fig**: Feige

odds it had taken hold and produced enormous quantities of sweet figs. Mr. Crow greatly approved of figs, she added. She sipped her tea, then changed the subject: the families up and down South Beach, she said, were thought of by folks in Amity Harbor as self-styled aristocrats and malcontents, seclusion seekers and eccentrics – Ishmael's family included. Did he know that his grandfather had helped to drive the pilings for the wharf at South Beach Bay landing? The Papineaus, she said, were dirt poor for a reason: none of them did any work. The Imadas, on the other hand, were consistently hard workers, including the five little girls. The Eberts hired professional gardeners and various domestic troubleshooters – plumbers, electricians, and handymen arrived in step vans to do *their* dirty work – but the Crows always hired neighborhood people. For forty years, she reminded Ishmael, she and Mr. Crow had lived right there at South Beach. Mr. Crow had been in coal mining and the manufacturing of pallet boards but had recently gone into the shipbuilding business and was right now in Seattle financing the construction of frigates and minesweepers for Roosevelt's navy (though he didn't care a lick for Roosevelt, she said) – but why was Ishmael so blue? Cheer up, urged Mrs. Crow, and sipped her tea. Life was wonderful.

Fishing with Sheridan Knowles that Saturday – rowing the shoreline and worrying about Hatsue – Ishmael saw Mr. Crow, with his hands on his knees, peering into a telescope mounted on a tripod in the center of his terraced lawn. From this vantage point he jealously inspected the yachts of the Seattlites who cruised past South Beach on their way to anchorages in Amity Harbor. Mr. Crow was a man of uncertain temper with a high, severe forehead like Shakespeare's. His vista of the sea was a wide and windy one; his gardens were planted with low azalea hedges, camellias, starina roses, and espaliered boxwoods, all framed by the white-caps on the shuffling waters and the annealed gray of the beach stones. His house turned a great, immaculate wall of shuttered windows to the sun, cedars surrounding it on three sides imperiously. Mr. Crow had entered into a sort of border war with Bob Timmons, his neighbor to the north, claiming that Bob's grove of western hemlocks actually grew on his property. One morning when Ishmael was eight years old a pair of surveyors had showed up with their transits and alidades and knotted red flagging everywhere. This ceremony was repeated at odd

intervals over the years, and while the faces of the surveyors changed nothing else did except that the hemlocks grew taller, their limber tips
40 bent like green whips against the sky. Bob Timmons – a transplanted son of the New Hampshire uplands and a pale, wordless, determined man of puritanical sensibilities – looked on without expression, hands braced against his hips, while Mr. Crow grumbled and paced with his high forehead glistening.

45 Ishmael worked, too, for the Etheringtons, who were vigorous summer people from Seattle. In June each year the summer people arrived *en force* to take up balmy residence along South Beach. Here they meandered in their tiny sailboats, tacking and coming about; they painted, hoed, swept, and planted when the mood for therapeutic work
50 struck them, and lolled on the beach when they felt like it. In the evenings there were bonfires and steamer clams, mussels, oysters, and perch, the boats dragged up beyond the tide line, the shovels and rakes hosed off and put away. The Etheringtons drank gin-and-tonics.

At the head of Miller Bay, beyond the mud flats, lived Captain
55 Jonathan Soderland, who'd plied his decrepit windjammer, the *C. S. Murphy*, to the Arctic each year on trading expeditions. He had finally gotten too old for it and spent his time telling lies to the summer people

---

5 **malcontent**: dissatisfied or troublemaking person who is not satisfied with a situation   **seclusion**: state of being private or of having little contact with other people   7 **piling**: Pfahl   8 **dirt poor** (infml): extremely poor   11 **troubleshooter**: person who helps to solve problems or to repair sth.   **handyman**: (hier) Handwerker   15 **pallet**: heavy wooden base   17 **minesweeper**: ship used for finding and clearing away mines   18 **not care a lick** (infml): not care at all   23 **tripod**: support with three legs   24 **vantage point**: position from which you watch sth.   27 **vista** (fml): panoramic view   29 **espaliered**: als Spalierholz gezo-gen   **boxwood**: Buchsbaum   30 **annealed gray**: stahlgrau   32 **imperious**: with an air of great importance, inspiring respect   34 **grove**: small group of trees   36 **transit**: (here) optical instrument used to measure positions and distances in order to draw maps   **alidade**: optical instrument used to measure directions   39 **limber**: flexible   40 **whip** (n): Peitsche   43 **brace sth. against sth. else**: etwas gegen etwas anderes stemmen   **pace** (v): walk up and down in a small area esp. because you are feeling nervous or angry   47 **balmy**: pleasant   48 **meander**: change direction often, esp. without a particular aim   **tack**: (hier) durch den Wind wenden   49 **hoe** (v): break up soil, remove plants   50 **loll**: lie, sit or stand in a lazy, relaxed way   51 **bonfire**: large outdoor fire, esp. as part of a celebration   53 **hose sth. off**: etwas abspritzen   55 **ply sth.** (fml): travel regularly with a ship/boat along a particular route

– stroking his snowy beard, dressed in woolen long johns and ragtag suspenders – and posing for photographs at the wheel of the *Murphy*, which was permanently lodged in the mud flats. Ishmael helped him split firewood.

The only viable profit-seeking concern on South Beach – other than the Imadas' strawberry enterprise – was Tom Peck's Great American Blue Fox Farm. On the far side of Miller Bay, in the shadows of madrona trees, Tom Peck tugged at his burnt-red goatee, sucked on his pipe stem, and raised American blue foxes for their varnished pelts in sixty-eight overcrowded breeding pens. The world left him thoroughly alone in this, although Ishmael and two other boys were hired that June to clean the cages with wire brushes. Peck had accumulated a personal mythology that included Indian wars, gold mining, and mercenary executions, and was known to carry a derringer pistol in a hidden shoulder holster. Farther up the bay, on the dead-water east arm known as Little House Cove, the Westinghouse family had built a Newport-style mansion on thirty acres of Douglas fir trees. Troubled by the general moral demise of the East – manifest, particularly, in the Lindbergh kidnapping – the well-known home appliance magnate and his high-born Bostonian wife had brought their three sons, a maid, a cook, a butler, and a pair of private tutors to San Piedro's secluded shores. Ishmael, one long afternoon, helped Dale Papineau – self-appointed caretaker for half a dozen summer families – prune back the alder branches overarching their long drive.

Ishmael worked with Dale, too, to clean the Etheringtons' gutters. The Etheringtons mostly humored him, it seemed to Ishmael – for them he was a colorful island character, part of the charm of the place. After a freeze or two days of hard rain, Dale would plod from house to house with a flashlight in hand – limping because the hip he'd dislocated at the creosote plant ached when it was damp or cold or both together, and squinting because he was too vain to wear glasses – and poke around garages and basements, clearing mud from the drains. In the fall he burned brush piles and raked leaves for Virginia Gatewood, a stick figure at twilight in cloth gloves and a threadbare mackinaw coat ragged at the elbows. The veins in his cheeks were broken and smashed flat and appeared as a sort of blue paste beneath his skin; his Adam's apple bulged like a toad's. He looked, to Ishmael, vaguely like an alcoholic scarecrow.

David Guterson: **Snow Falling on Cedars** 93

Four days after the kiss on the beach, just after dusk – it was dark in the woods, but the strawberry fields lay in twilight – Ishmael crouched at the edge of the Imadas' farm and watched for half an hour. To his surprise no boredom overtook him and so he stayed for an hour more. It was a kind of relief to rest his cheek against the earth underneath the stars and to have some hope of seeing Hatsue. The fear of being discovered and labeled a Peeping Tom urged him to move on finally, and he had almost convinced himself to leave, was getting up in fact, when the screen door creaked open, light slipped across the porch, and Hatsue crossed to one of the corner posts. She lifted a wicker basket to the cedar railing and began drawing in her family's laundry.

Ishmael watched Hatsue pull sheets from the line, standing in a pool of muted porch light with her arms illuminated and elegant. Clenching clothespins between her teeth, she folded towels, pants, and work shirts before dropping them into the wicker basket. When she finished she leaned against the corner post for a moment, scratching her neck and looking at the stars, then smelling the dampness in the fresh laundry. Then she took her basket of sheets and clothes and melted back into the house.

Ishmael returned the following evening; five nights in a row he spied religiously. Each night he told himself not to return, but on the next he would take a walk at dusk, his walk would become a pilgrimage, he

---

1 **ragtag**: worn and old   5 **viable**: rentabel   7 **madrona**: strawberry tree
8 **goatee** [goʊˈtiː]: Spitzbart   9 **varnished**: (here) shiny   **pelt**: skin of an animal
10 **pen**: small area surrounded by a fence in which farm animals are kept
14 **derringer**: small handgun   17 **demise** [dɪˈmaɪz]: end or failure of an institution or idea   18 **manifest** ['---] (adj): easy to see and understand   **Lindbergh** = Charles Lindbergh (1902–1974): US pilot who became the first person to fly across the Atlantic Ocean alone, going from New York to Paris on 20 May 1927; in 1932, his baby son was kidnapped and killed in a case that shocked America
19 **appliance**: Haushaltsgerät   **magnate**: person who is rich, powerful and successful, esp. in business   24 **gutter:** (hier) Dachrinne   32 **brush**: Unterholz
33 **threadbare**: old and thin because it has been used a lot   **ragged**: shabby
36 **bulge**: stick out from sth. in a round shape   **toad**: Kröte   37 **scarecrow**: Vogelscheuche   44 **Peeping Tom**: person who likes to watch other people when they are doing sth. private   47 **wicker basket**: Weidenkorb   50 **muted**: (here) dimmed, not bright   59 **pilgrimage**: journey to a holy place for religious reasons

would feel guilt and shame, he would top the groundswell that buttressed her strawberries and pause before the sweep of her fields. He wondered if other boys did this sort of thing, if his voyeurism constituted a disease. He was sustained, though, by seeing her once more reel in laundry – elegant hand over elegant hand – drop the clothespins in a bucket on the railing, then fold shirts, sheets, and towels. Once she stood on the porch for a moment brushing the dust from her summer dress. She corralled the long sweep of her hair in deftly and knotted it before going inside.

On the last night of his spying he saw her empty a bucket of kitchen scraps not fifty yards from where he crouched. She appeared in the porch light, as always, without warning and shut the door behind her gently. As she moved in his direction his heart lurched before freezing altogether in his chest. He could see her face now and hear the *thock* of her sandals. Hatsue turned down between strawberry rows and upended her bucket on the compost heap, glanced at the moon so that its blue light caught her face, then returned to the house by a different route. He caught a glimpse of her through the interstices of raspberry canes before she emerged in front of her porch with one hand knotting her hair at her neck and the bucket dangling from the other. He waited, and in a moment she was at the kitchen window with a nimbus of light around her head. Moving closer, keeping low, Ishmael saw her smoothing hair from her eyes while soapsuds ran from her fingers. There were young strawberries growing on the plants around him and their fragrance filled up the night. He moved closer until the Imadas' dog came loping around the corner of the house and then he froze, prepared to bolt. The dog sniffed for a moment, whined, sidled toward him and allowed him to stroke her head and ears and licked his palm and lay down. She was a jaundiced, stain-toothed, and lopsided old hound, leathery looking and swaybacked, and her sad eyes wept miserably. Ishmael rubbed her belly. The dog's gray tongue lolled in the dust and her rib cage pumped up and down.

A moment later Hatsue's father came onto the porch and called to the dog in Japanese. He called again, a low guttural command, and the dog raised her head, barked twice, sprang to her feet, and limped away.

That was the last time Ishmael spied at the Imada place.

At the start of the strawberry season, at five-thirty in the morning, Ishmael saw Hatsue on the South Beach wood path underneath silent cedars. They were both of them going to work for Mr. Nitta – he paid better than any berry farmer on the island – for thirty-five cents a flat.

He walked behind her, his lunch in hand. He caught up and said hello. Neither said anything about their kiss on the beach two weeks before. They walked the path quietly, and Hatsue suggested there was a chance they'd see a black-tailed deer out feeding on fern tendrils – she'd seen a doe the previous morning.

Where the path met the beach the madrona trees leaned out over the tidal water. Slender and sinuous, olive green, mahogany red, scarlet, and ash, they were weighted with broad, gleaming leaves and velvet berries and shaded the beach stones and mud flats. Hatsue and Ishmael flushed a roosting blue heron with feathers the hue of beach mud; it squawked once and, elongated wing tips wide, graceful even in sudden flight, crossed Miller Bay at a soaring angle to perch in the dead top of a far tree.

The path looped around the head of the bay, then down into a swale known as Devil's Dip – ground fog shrouded its thimbleberry and devil's club, such was the clammy, low wetness of the place – then climbed among cedars and the shadows of spruces before descending into Center Valley. The homesteads here were old and productive ones – the Andreasons, the Olsens, the McCullys, the Coxes; oxen had been used to cultivate their fields, descendants of the oxen brought to San

---

1 **top sth.**: (here) climb or jump on top of sth.   **groundswell**: (hier) Wall
buttress sth.: (here) protect sth.   3 **constitute sth.**: be considered to be sth.
4 **sustained**: (here) satisfied, contented   **reel sth. in**: etwas einholen   7 **corral sth.**: (hier) etwas zusammenfassen   8 **deft**: skilful and quick   12 **lurch**: (hier) sich zusammenziehen   13 **thock**: sound of sb.'s steps   14 **upend sth.**: turn sth. upside down   17 **interstices** (pl, fml): small crack or space in sth.   20 **nimbus**: Aura
22 **soapsuds** (pl): Seifenschaum   24 **lope**: run taking long relaxed steps   25 **bolt** (v): run away in order to escape   26 **whine** (v): make a long high unpleasant sound
28 **jaundiced** ['dʒɔːndɪst]: (here) having yellowish eyes   **stain-toothed**: mit fleckigen Zähnen   **lopsided**: schief, krumm   29 **swaybacked**: mit krummem Rücken
33 **guttural**: made at the back of the throat   44 **doe**: female deer, rabbit or hare
46 **sinuous**: twisting in an elegant way   48 **flush sb./sth.**: (here) force sb./sth., esp. an animal to leave the place where it was hiding   49 **roost**: (of birds) rest or go to sleep somewhere   **heron**: Reiher   50 **elongate sth.**: make sth. longer   51 **soar**: fly very high in the air   52 **swale**: sumpfige Senke   53 **shroud sth.**: cover or hide sth.
53–54 **thimbleberry**, **devil's club**: shrubs native to the Pacific coast of North America   55 **spruce**: Fichte   56 **homestead**: Gehöft

Piedro in the old, log-skidding days. They were enormous, pungent, and hoary beasts, and Ishmael and Hatsue stopped to stare at one rubbing his hindquarters against a fence post.

At Nitta's farm the Canadian Indians were already busy when they arrived. Mrs. Nitta, a small woman with a waist no larger than a soup tin, darted up and down the rows like a hummingbird beneath her straw picking hat. Her mouth – like her husband's – was full of gold fillings and when she smiled the sun glinted in among them. In the afternoons she sat beneath a canvas umbrella with a pencil between her fingers, her accounts laid out on a cedar crate before her, one palm laid against her forehead. Her handwriting was impeccable – small, soft, and elegant numbers filled the pages of her account book. She wrote with the quiet deliberation of a court scribe, sharpening her pencil often.

Ishmael and Hatsue went their separate ways to pick among their friends. The farm was so large that a leased, battered school bus carried workers to its dusty gate at the height of picking season. An aura of manic purpose hung over the fields, for in them went forward a gleeful harvest performed by children only just freed from school. San Piedro children delighted in their field toil in part because of the social life it provided, in part because it furnished the illusion that a job had been included in the summer's proceedings. The rich heat, the taste of berries on the tongue, the easy talk, and the prospect of spending money on soda pop, firecrackers, fishing lures, and makeup all seduced them toward Mr. Nitta's. All day the children knelt beside one another in the fields, hunkered down close against the earth beneath the heat of the sun. Romances began and ended there; children kissed at the verges of fields or walking home through the woods.

Ishmael, from three rows off, watched Hatsue at her work. Her hair soon came loose from its arrangement, and a sheen of sweat appeared against her collarbones. She picked deftly and had a reputation for speed and efficiency; she filled two flats in the time it took other pickers to fill one and a half. She was among friends – a half-dozen Japanese girls squatting in the rows together, their faces shrouded by straw hats – and would not acknowledge that she knew him when he passed her with his own flat mounded high. He passed her again with his emptied flat and saw how intent she was on her picking, never hurrying but never stopping. He squatted again in his spot three rows distant and tried to

concentrate on his own work. When he looked up she was sliding a berry into her mouth, and he stopped to watch her eat it. Hatsue turned
40 and met his eyes, but he could not discern in this her feelings and it seemed to him wholly an accident; she meant nothing by it. Looking away, she ate another berry with no embarrassment, slowly. Then, adjusting herself on her haunches for a moment, she went back to her methodical work.
45 Late in the afternoon, at about four-thirty, heavy clouds shadowed the strawberry fields. The clean June light went softly gray and a breeze came up in the southwest. It was possible, then, to smell the rain coming and to feel the cool pause before the first drops fell. The air turned thick; sudden gusts caught the cedars at the edge of the fields and flailed their
50 tops and branches. The pickers hurried their last flats in and waited in line while Mrs. Nitta put marks beside their names and paid them from underneath her umbrella. The pickers craned their necks to watch the clouds and held their palms out to check for rain. At first just a few drops raised tiny wisps of dust around them and then, as if a hole had
55 been punched in the sky, an island summer rain poured hard against their faces, and the pickers began moving toward shelter of any kind – the doorway of a barn, the inside of a car, the berry storage sheds, the cedar woods. Some stood with flats held over their heads and let their picked strawberries catch the water.
60 Ishmael saw Hatsue cross the Nittas' upper fields and slip into the cedar woods, going south. He found himself following, slowly at first, letting the rain pound him as he moved through the strawberries – he was already soaked so what difference could it make?; the rain was warm and felt good on his face – and then he was trotting through the forest.
65 The South Beach trail, with its canopy of cedars, was as good a place as

1 **log-skidding days**: Holzfällerzeiten   **pungent**: having a strong taste or smell
2 **hoary:** (here) grey and old   6 **hummingbird**: Kolibri   10 **crate**: wooden container for transporting goods   13 **court scribe**: Gerichtsschreiber   17 **gleeful**: happy   23 **lure** (n): Köder   25 **hunker**: sit on your heels with your knees bent up in front of you   29 **sheen**: Schimmer   40 **discern sth.**: know, recognize or understand sth.   43 **haunches** (pl): Gesäß   49 **flail sth.**: make sth. move around without control   52 **crane your neck**: stretch your neck in order to see sth. better   54 **wisp**: long thin line of smoke or cloud   63 **soak sth./sb.**: make sb./sth. completely wet   65 **canopy**: Baldachin

any in a rainstorm, and he wanted to walk it home with her, saying nothing if that was what she desired. But when he caught sight of her below the McCullys' farm it occurred to him to slow to a walking pace and follow along at fifty yards. The rain would cover any noise he made and besides, he didn't know what to say. It would be enough merely to see her, as it had been in the fields or when he'd hid behind the cedar log and watched her fold her family's laundry. He would follow along behind, listening to the rain pelt the trees, and watch her wind her way home.

Where the trail hit the beach on Miller Bay – there was a wall of honeysuckle just past blossom, salmonberries hanging in among it and a few last wild roses blooming – Hatsue cut into the cedar woods. Ishmael followed her through a dell of ferns where white morning glory blossoms dotted the forest floor. A fallen cedar log hung with ivy bridged the dell; she slipped under it and turned up a side path that followed a shallow creek where three years before they'd sailed driftwood boats together. The path made three bends, and then Hatsue crossed the water on a log, hiked halfway up the cedar hillside, and ducked into the hollow tree they'd played in together when they were only nine years old.

Ishmael squatted beneath branches in the rain and watched the tree's entry for half a minute. His hair hung wet in his eyes. He tried to understand what had brought her here; he himself had forgotten about the place, which was a good half mile from his home. He remembered, now, how they'd packed moss underneath their legs and lolled in the tree looking up. It was possible to kneel but not to stand, though on the other hand the room inside the tree was wide enough to lie down in. They'd gone there with other kids and imagined they were hiding out, sharpening alder sticks with pocketknives to be used in their defense. The inside of the tree had been filled with a stock of arrows to be used in a fantasy battle at first, then in a battle fought amongst themselves. From twine and yew wood they'd made miniature bows; they'd used the hollow cedar as a kind of fort and run up and down the hillside shooting at each other. Ishmael squatted there remembering playing war on this hillside and how that had ultimately driven the Syvertsen girls away, and then the Imada sisters, and then he saw that Hatsue was looking at him from the entry of the hollow cedar tree.

He looked back; there was no point in hiding. 'You'd better come in,' she said. 'It's wet.'

'All right,' he answered.

Inside the tree he knelt on the moss with water dripping beneath his
shirt. Hatsue sat on the moss in her damp summer dress, her broad-
rimmed picking hat beside her. 'You followed me,' she said. 'Didn't you.'

'I didn't mean to,' Ishmael apologized. 'It just happened, sort of. I
was going home. You know what I mean? I saw you turn off and … it
just happened, sort of. Sorry,' he added. 'I followed you.'

She smoothed her hair back behind her ears. 'I'm all wet,' she said.
'I'm soaked.'

'So am I. It feels good, sort of. Anyway it's dry in here. Remember
this place? It seems smaller.'

'I've been coming here all along,' said Hatsue. 'I come here to think.
Nobody else comes around. I haven't seen anybody here in years.'

'What do you think about?' Ishmael asked. 'When you're here, I
mean. What do you think about?'

'I don't know. All sorts of things. You know, a place to think.'

Ishmael lay down with his hands propping up his chin and looked
out at the rain. The inside of the tree felt private. He felt they would
never be discovered here. The walls surrounding them were glossy and
golden. It was surprising how much green-tinted light entered from the
cedar forest. The rain echoed in the canopy of leaves above and beat
against the sword ferns, which twitched under each drop. The rain
afforded an even greater privacy; no one in the world would come this
way to find them inside this tree.

'I'm sorry I kissed you on the beach,' said Ishmael. 'Let's just forget
about it. Forget it happened.'

There was no answer at first. It was like Hatsue not to answer. He
himself was always in need of words, even when he couldn't quite
muster them, but she seemed capable of a brand of silence he couldn't
feel inside.

---

8 **pelt sth.**: throw sth. at sth. else   10 **honeysuckle**: Geißblatt   11 **cut** (v): (here) change direction or take a different route, usu. in order to make your way shorter   12 **dell**: small valley with trees growing in or around it   **morning glory**: Trichterwinde   15 **creek**: narrow area of water where the sea flows into the land   30 **yew**: Eibe   54 **prop sth. up**: support sth. by putting sth. under it   57 **tint sth.**: give sth. a certain shade of color   59 **twitch** (v): be forced to make a sudden quick movement   66 **muster sth.**: (here) be able to express sth.   **brand**: kind of sth.

She picked up her straw hat and looked at it instead of him. 'Don't be sorry,' she said with her eyes down. 'I'm not sorry about it.'

'Me, neither,' said Ishmael.

She lay down on her back beside him. The green-tinted light caught her face. He wanted to put his mouth against hers and leave it there forever. He knew now that he might do so without regretting it. 'Do you think this is wrong?' she asked.

'Other people do,' said Ishmael. 'Your friends would,' he added. 'And your parents.'

'So would yours,' said Hatsue. 'So would your mother and father.'

'Yours more than mine,' said Ishmael. 'If they knew we were out here in this tree together …' He shook his head and laughed softly. 'Your father'd probably kill me with a machete. He'd slice me into little pieces.'

'Probably not,' said Hatsue. 'But you're right – he would be angry. With both of us, for doing this.'

'But what are we doing? We're talking.'

'Still,' said Hatsue, 'you're not Japanese. And I'm alone with you.'

'It doesn't matter,' answered Ishmael.

They lay beside each other in the cedar tree talking until half an hour had gone by. Then, once again, they kissed. They felt comfortable kissing inside the tree, and they kissed for another half hour. With the rain falling outside and the moss softly under him Ishmael shut his eyes and breathed the smell of her fully in through his nostrils. He told himself he had never felt so happy, and he felt a sort of ache that this was happening and would never again happen in just this way no matter how long he lived.

Chapter 9

Ishmael found himself sitting in the courtroom where Hatsue's husband was on trial for murder. He found he was watching her as she spoke to Kabuo, and he exerted himself to look away.

The jurors returned, and then Judge Fielding, and Carl Heine's mother took the stand. Despite living in town a full ten years she retained the look of a farmer's wife: stout, faded, and wind worn. Etta adjusted her girth in the witness chair so that the hitching and sliding of her undergarments was heard – heavy nylons, a girdle purchased in Lottie Opsvig's shop, a back brace prescribed by a doctor in Bellingham for the sciatica she attributed to her farm days. For twenty-five years she had worked in all weather beside her husband, Carl senior. Winters, with steam puffing from her mouth, she'd worn mud boots, a greatcoat, and a scarf over her head firmly knotted below her heavy chin. In fingerless wool gloves knitted late at night – sitting up in bed while Carl snored – she'd perched on a stool, milking cows. In summer she'd sorted berries, cut runners, pulled weeds, and kept one eye on the Indians and Japanese who yearly picked on the Heine farm.

She'd been born in Bavaria – still carried its accent – on a dairy farm near Ingolstadt. She'd met her husband when he came to her father's wheat farm near Hettinger, North Dakota. They'd eloped on the Northern Pacific to Seattle – she remembered eating breakfast in the dining car – where he worked for two years in a Harbor Island foundry and for one loading lumber on the waterfront. Etta, a farmer's daughter,

---

6 **stout**: rather fat   7 **girth**: (here) her stout figure   **hitch** (v): (of clothes) move or be pulled up   **slide**: move easily over a surface   8 **girdle**: (hier) Hüfthalter
9 **brace**: device that supports sth. firmly in order to keep it in position   10 **sciatica** [saɪˈætɪkə]: pain caused by pres-sure on the sciatic nerve (= Ischias)   12 **greatcoat**: long heavy coat   15 **stool**: Schemel   20 **elope**: run away with sb. in order to marry them secretly   21 **Northern Pacific** = Northern Pacific Railway   22 **foundry**: factory where metal or glass is melted and made into different shapes or objects

found Seattle to her liking. She was a seamstress on Second Avenue and made Klondike coats at piece rate. The strawberry farm on San Piedro, where they visited at Christmas, belonged to Carl's father, a portly man; Carl'd left it at seventeen, seeking adventure in the world. When his father died he migrated back, bringing Etta with him.

She tried to like San Piedro. It was damp, though, and she developed a cough, and her lower back began to bother her. She had four children and raised them to work hard, but the oldest went off to Darrington to set choker cables, and the second and third went off to war. Only the second – Carl junior – returned. The fourth was a girl who, like Etta herself, eloped and went off to Seattle.

Etta grew tired, gut weary, of strawberries: she didn't even like to eat them. Her husband was a true lover of the fruit, but Etta couldn't feel anything for it. To him strawberries were a holy mystery, jewels of sugar, deep red gems, sweet orbs, succulent rubies. He knew their secrets, the path they took, the daily responses they made to sunlight. The rocks between the rows collected heat, he said, and kept his plants warmer at night than they would otherwise have been – but to this sort of thing she made no answer. She brought him his eggs and went to the barn for milk. Threw feed from her apron pockets to the turkeys and chickens. Scrubbed the field muck from the mudroom floor. Filled the hog trough and walked through the pickers' cabins to see that they hadn't relieved themselves in pilfered canning jars.

Carl's heart failed him one clear October night in 1944. She'd found him on the toilet with his head against the wall, his pants clumped around his ankles. Carl junior was away at the war, and Etta took advantage of this circumstance to sell the farm to Ole Jurgensen. That gave Ole sixty-five acres in the middle of Center Valley. It also provided Etta with enough money to get by on, if she was mindful of her pennies. Fortunately this mindfulness accorded with her nature: it brought her the same depth of pleasure Carl had derived from nurturing his strawberries.

Alvin Hooks, the prosecutor – he appeared more nimble than ever in her presence – was keenly interested in Etta's finances. He paced in front of her with his left elbow cradled in his right palm neatly and his chin resting on his thumb. Yes, she said, she'd kept the books for the farm. No, it had never been very profitable, but the thirty acres had gotten them by for twenty-five years – better some years than others, she added: depended what the cannery was paying out. They'd cleared their debts by '29, that helped, but then the Depression came along. The price of berries dropped, the Farmall needed a rod bearing from Anacortes, the sun didn't shine every year. One spring a touch of night cold ruined the fruit, another you couldn't get the fields to dry out and the low-hanging berries rotted. One year the fungus got you, another you couldn't keep the spit bugs down. On top of all that Carl broke his leg in '36 and spent his time hobbling up and down the rows, chasing after posts or buckets he couldn't carry on account of his homemade crutches. Then he went and put five acres into raspberries and dumped money into *that* experiment – wire and cedar posts, labor to build trellises – it set them back until he figured how to cull the canes and train them to produce. Another time he tried a new variety – Rainiers – that wouldn't take because he used too much nitrogen: lots of green, plants high and fluffy, but small hard fruit, a piddling harvest.

Yes, she'd known the defendant, Kabuo Miyamoto, for a good long time, she figured. It was more than twenty years since his family came to pick – the defendant, his two brothers, his two sisters, his mother and father – she remembered them well enough. They were hard workers, kept to themselves mostly. They brought their caddies in mounded up, she marked them off and paid out. They lived in one of the pickers' cabins at first: she could smell the perch they cooked there. She saw them some evenings sitting under a maple tree eating rice and fish off of tin plates. They would have their laundry strung between two saplings in a field of fireweed and dandelions. They had no automobile for getting about, she didn't know how they did it. In the mornings, early, two or

---

1 **seamstress** ['siːmstrəs]: woman who makes clothes   2 **at piece rate**: paid per piece not per hour   3 **portly**: (esp. of an older man) stout, rather fat   9 **choker cable**: Starterkabel   12 **grow gut weary (of sth.)** ['wɪri]: eine Sache leid sein   15 **succulent**: (here) juicy   **ruby**: dark red jewel   21 **hog**: pig   22 **cabin**: small house, usually made of wood   23 **pilfer sth.**: steal sth. of little value or in small quantities   33 **nimble**: (here) able to think and understand quickly   40 **Depression**: Weltwirtschaftskrise   41 **Farmall**: Traktor (Markenname)   49 **trellis**: Spalier   50 **cull sth.**: (hier) etwas zurückschneiden   51 **Rainiers**: Himbeersorte   53 **piddling**: small and unimportant   62 **sapling**: young tree   63 **fireweed**: Weidenröschen   **dandelion** ['dændɪlaɪən]: Löwenzahn

three of their children went down to Center Bay with hand lines and fished from the pier or swam out to the rocks and tried for cod. She'd seen them on the road at seven in the morning coming home with their strings of fish or with mushrooms, with fern tendrils, butter clams, searun trout if they got lucky. They walked barefoot; they kept their faces down. All of them wore woven straw pickers' hats.

Oh, yes, she remembered them well. How was it she was supposed to forget such people? She sat in the witness stand staring at Kabuo, and tears pooled in her eyes.

Judge Fielding called for a recess then, seeing that her emotions had overwhelmed her, and Etta followed Ed Soames into the anteroom, where she sat in silence, remembering.

Zenhichi Miyamoto had appeared at her door at the end of his family's third picking season. Etta had been at the kitchen sink, and from there, looking through the parlor, she saw him watching her. He nodded at her, and she stared at him and then went back to her dishes. Then Carl – her husband – came to the door and spoke to Zenhichi with his pipe between his thumb and forefinger. It was difficult to hear exactly what they were saying so she turned the water off. Etta stood quietly and listened.

In a little while the two men left the doorway and went out into the fields together. From the window over the sink she could see them: they would stop, one of them would point, they would move on. They stopped again, pointed, swept their arms this way and that. Carl lit his pipe and scratched behind his ear, and Zenhichi pointed with his hat to the west, made a sweep, put his hat on his head. The two men walked between the rows some more, made the crest of the rise, and turned west behind some raspberry canes.

When Carl returned she'd put coffee on the table. 'What did *he* want?' she said.

'Land,' said Carl. 'Seven acres of it.'

'Which seven?'

Carl had set his pipe on the table. 'Due west seven, middle west seven. Leaves plots north and south. I told him better the northwest seven. If I was going to sell. It's hilly anyway.'

Etta poured coffee for both of them. 'We ain't going to sell,' she said firmly. 'Not in such times as these, when land is cheap. Not until better times come.'

'It's hilly,' repeated Carl. 'Hard to work. Good sun, bad drainage. Least productive acres on the property. He knows that. That's why he asked for it. Knows it's the only piece I'd think of letting go.'

'He wanted the *middle* seven,' Etta pointed out. 'Figured he might get a good two acres 'thout your noticing it.'

'Maybe,' said Carl. 'Anyway, I noticed.'

They drank their coffee. Carl ate a slice of bread spread with butter and sugar. He ate another. He was always hungry. Feeding him was a challenge. 'So what did you tell him?' she asked.

'Told him I'd think on it,' answered Carl. 'I was getting ready to let five of them west acres go to weeds, you know, they're so choresome to keep the thistle out of.'

'Don't sell,' said Etta. 'You do, you'll regret it, Carl.'

'They're decent folks,' answered Carl. 'You can bet it'd be quiet over there. Nobody carousing or carrying on. Somebody you can work with when you have to. Better than a lot of other people that way.' He picked up his pipe and fiddled with it; he liked the feel of it in his hand. 'Anyway, I told him I'd think on it,' said Carl. 'Doesn't mean I have to sell to him, does it? Just means I'm going to think.'

'Think hard,' warned Etta. She got up and started in clearing the coffee things. She felt willing to push and pull about this; seven acres was near one-quarter of the property, one-quarter of their holdings. 'That seven will be worth plenty more later,' she advised. 'You're better off keeping a good hold to it.'

'Maybe,' said Carl. 'I'll have to think about that, too.'

Etta stood at the sink with her back to him. She did her dishes hard.

'Sure be nice to have the money, though, wouldn't it?' Carl said after a while. 'There's things we've been needing and – '

1 **hand line**: fishing line   5 **searun trout**: Forellenart   11 **anteroom**: waiting room
27 **crest**: top part of a hill   39 **drainage**: system of ditches (= Gräben) or drains by which water is carried from an area   49 **choresome** ['tʃɔːrsəm]: mühselig
53 **carouse** [kə'raʊz]: spend time drinking alcohol, laughing and enjoying yourself in a noisy way   59 **push and pull**: (here) fight constantly until you get what you want

'If you're going to get on to *that*,' Etta told him, 'it won't do any good by *me*. Don't try waving new church clothes at me, Carl. I can get myself clothes when I need them. We're not such paupers as to sell to Japs, are we? For new clothes? For a pouch of fancy pipe tobacco? I say you'd better keep hold of your land, keep a tight hold, Carl, and a new frilly hat from Lottie's won't change that. Besides,' she added, turning toward him now and wiping her hands on her apron, 'you think that man's got a treasure chest or something buried in the fields somewhere? That what you think? You think he's going to slap it down all at once in front of you or some such like? Do you? He doesn't have a thing but what we give him for picking and what he gets cutting firewood for Thorsens and those Catholic people – who are they? – on South Beach, by the pier. He doesn't *have* it, Carl. He's going to pay up two bits at a time, and you're going to carry it for pocket change to town. Pipe tobacco aplenty. Magazines to read. Your seven acres is going to be swallowed up by the dime store in Amity Harbor.'

'Them Catholic people is the Hepplers,' returned Carl. 'Miyamoto don't do any work for them anymore, I don't think. Last winter he cut cedar bolts for Torgerson, made good money would be my guess. He works hard, Etta. You know that. You've seen him in the fields. Don't have to tell you that. He don't spend none of it either. Eating sea perch all the time, big sack wholesale rice from Anacortes.' Carl scratched beneath his arm, massaged his chest with his thick, heavy fingers, picked up his pipe again and fiddled with it. 'Miyamotos live clean,' he pressed on. 'You never been in their cabin? Person could eat off the floor in there, kids sleep on mats, somebody even been scrubbing mildew off the walls. Kids don't run around their faces all stained. Laundry all strung out neat with clothespins somebody *carved*. Don't wake up late, don't holler, don't complain, don't ask for nothing – '

'Like the Indjuns do,' put in Etta.

'Don't treat the Indians like dirt, neither,' Carl said. 'Kind to 'em. Showed 'em to the latrine, showed them new ones the trail to the salt chuck, showed 'em the best place for butter clams. Now,' said Carl, 'to me it don't make one bit of difference which way it is their eyes slant. I don't give a damn 'bout that, Etta. People is people, comes down to it. And these are clean-living people. Nothing wrong with them. So the question is, do we want to sell? Because Miyamoto, what he said, he's got five hundred to put down *now*. Five *hundred*. And the rest we can spread over ten years.'

Etta turned to her sink again. If this wasn't Carl all over! She thought. Liked to wander in his fields, chat with his pickers, taste his berries, smack his lips, smoke his pipe, go to town for a sack of nails. Put himself on the board for the Strawberry Festival Association, judged the floats, helped barbecue the salmon. Got himself all involved buying up the new fairgrounds, getting folks in Amity Harbor to donate lumber and whatnot for the dance pavilion at West Port Jensen. Joined the Masons and the Odd Fellows both, helped out with the record keeping at the Grange. Stood around evenings up at the pickers' cabins jawing with the Japs and taking pains with the Indians, watching the women weave sweaters and such, drawing the men out on the subject of the old days before the strawberry farms went in. Carl! Come end of picking season, he'd wander out to some old lonely place they'd told him about and look for arrowheads and bits of old bones, clamshell, and whatnot. Once some old chief went with him; they came back with arrowheads and sat on the porch smoking pipes until two o'clock in the morning. Carl gave the man rum to drink – she could hear them going at it from the bedroom, the both of them getting tipsy. She lay there with her eyes open and her ears tuned to the night and listened to Carl and his chief do their rum, some horse laughs, all the while the chief telling stories about totem poles and canoes and an old potlatch he'd been to where some other chief's daughter had gotten married and the old chief himself had won a spear-throwing contest and the next day the other chief died suddenly in his sleep, just like that he was dead and his daughter married, and the others went and punched a hole in his canoe and stuck him in it and put it up in a tree for some god-awful reason.

---

4 **pouch**: Beutel   5 **frilly**: gekräuselt   32–33 **salt chuck** (Chinook, the language of a native tribe on the northwest coast of the US): salt water, the sea or the ocean
43 **board** (n): group of people (esp. volunteers) responsible for organizing an event
45 **fairgrounds** (pl, AE): outdoor area where a fair is held for farmers to offer their products and/or for public entertainment   **donate sth.**: give sth. as a gift, esp. for charity (= Wohltätigkeit)   48 **Grange**: Genossenschaft der Landwirte/Farmer
jaw (v, infml): talk   59 **horse laugh**: loud uncontrolled laughter

Etta had come to the door at two A.M. in her robe and told the chief to get on home, it was late, there were stars to walk by, she didn't like the smell of rum in her house.

'Well,' she said to Carl now, folding her arms in the kitchen doorway, where she knew she would have the last word. 'You're the man of the house, you wear the pants, go ahead and sell our property to a Jap and see what comes of it.'

The arrangement, she explained at the behest of Alvin Hooks when the court had been called into session again, included a five-hundred-dollar down payment and an eight-year 'lease-to-own' contract. Carl to collect two hundred and fifty dollars every six months, June 30 and December 31, with six and a half percent interest figured annually. Papers to be held by Carl, another set by Zenhichi, a third set for any inspector wanted to see them. The Miyamotos – this was back in '34, said Etta – couldn't really own land anyway. They were from Japan, both of them *born* there, and there was this law on the books prevented them. Carl'd kept the title in his own name, held it for them, called it a lease in case they got checked. *She* hadn't figured it, Carl had – she just kept track, was all. Watched the money come and go, made sure the interest was right. *She* didn't ever arrange no such thing.

'One moment,' Judge Fielding interrupted. He smoothed his robe and blinked at her. 'Excuse me for interrupting, Mrs. Heine. The court has a few things to say about these matters. Pardon me for interrupting.'

'All right,' said Etta.

Judge Fielding nodded at her, then turned his attention toward the jury. 'We'll skip all the whispering at the bench,' he began. 'Mr. Hooks and I might discuss matters for a bit, but if we did, no doubt it would come down to this – I'm going to have to interrupt the witness in order to explain a point of law.'

He rubbed his eyebrows, then drank some water. He put down his glass and began again. 'The witness makes reference to a currently defunct statute of the State of Washington which made it illegal at the time of which she speaks for an alien, a noncitizen, to hold title to real estate.

This same statute furthermore stipulated that no person shall hold title *for* an alien – a noncitizen – in any way, shape, or form. Furthermore, in 1906, I believe it was, the U.S. attorney general ordered all federal courts to deny naturalized citizenship to Japanese aliens. Thus it was impossible, in the strict legal sense, for Japanese immigrants to own land in Washington state. Mrs. Heine has told us that her deceased husband, in joint *conspiracy* with the defendant's deceased father, entered into an agreement which, shall we say, was predicated on a rather liberal, albeit mutually satisfying, interpretation of these laws. They quite simply made their way *around* them. At any rate, the witness's husband and the defendant's father entered into a so-called "lease" agreement that concealed an actual purchase. A substantial down payment changed hands, false papers were drawn up for state inspection. These papers, in fact – along with the others Mrs. Heine has described, the ones her husband and his "buyer" held – were entered, as you may recall, as state's evidence in this trial. The *perpetuators* of all this, as Mrs. Heine has taken pains to point out, are no longer among us, so their culpability is not at issue. If counsel or witness feel any further explanation is required they may inquire further,' the judge added. 'However,' he said, 'let it be known that this court is not concerned with any perpetuators of violations against our state's now – blessedly so – defunct Alien Land Law. Mr. Hooks, you may proceed.'

'One thing,' said Etta.

'Yes, of course,' the judge answered.

'Them Japanese couldn't own land,' said Etta. 'So I don't see how them Miyamotos could think they owned ours. They – '

'Mrs. Heine,' said the judge. 'Excuse me one more time. I apologize for interrupting. But I must remind you that Mr. Miyamoto here is on trial for murder in the first degree, that such is the focus of this court's concern, and that any contentiousness about legal ownership of land will have to be addressed in a civil court, madam. You will confine yourself, please, to answering the questions put to you. Mr. Hooks,' said the judge. 'Proceed.'

'Thank you,' Alvin Hooks replied. 'For the record let me point out that the witness has attempted only to reconstruct the facts about ownership of her land in direct response to a question put to her in the course of examination. That furthermore such information is vital to the state's case and that a clear portrait of the agreement between the defendant and the witness will illuminate the defendant's motive for committing murder. That – '

'That's enough,' said Judge Fielding. 'You've made your opening statement, Alvin. Let's get on with it.'

Alvin Hooks nodded and paced again. 'Mrs. Heine,' he said. 'Let's back up just a moment. If the law, as you say, prevented the Miyamotos from owning land, what was the point of this sale agreement?'

'So they could make payments,' said Etta. 'The law let 'em own land if they were citizens. Them Miyamoto kids were born here so they're citizens, I guess. When they turned twenty the land'd go over into their name – law said they could do that, put it in their kids' name at twenty.'

'I see,' Alvin Hooks replied. 'And they – the defendant's family, the Miyamotos, that is – had no children in 1934 who were twenty years of age, Mrs. Heine? As far as you know, ma'am?'

'Oldest one's sitting right there,' said Etta, pointing a finger at Kabuo. 'He was twelve, I believe, back then.'

Alvin Hooks turned to look at the defendant as though he was uncertain who she meant. 'The defendant?' he asked. 'In '34?'

'Yes,' said Etta. 'The defendant. That's what the eight-year lease was all about. When eight years was up, he'd be twenty.'

'In '42,' said Alvin Hooks.

'Forty-two, that's right,' said Etta. 'November of '42 he'd be twenty, they'd make the last payment December 31, the land'd go over into his name, that was going to be that.'

'*Going* to be?' said Alvin Hooks.

'Missed the last payment,' said Etta. 'Missed the last *two* payments, in fact. Never made 'em. The last two. Out of sixteen total.'

She folded her arms across her chest. She set her mouth and waited.

Nels Gudmundsson coughed.

'Now Mrs. Heine,' said Hooks. 'When they missed two successive payments in 1942, what did you do about that?'

It took her awhile to answer. She rubbed her nose. She adjusted her arms. She remembered how Carl'd come home one afternoon with a posting he'd picked up in Amity Harbor. He'd sat at the table, smoothed it down in front of him, and read every word slowly. Etta had stood over him reading, too.

'INSTRUCTIONS TO ALL PERSONS OF JAPANESE ANCESTRY LIVING IN THE FOLLOWING AREAS,' it said, and then it listed Anacortes and Bellingham, San Juan and San Piedro, a lot of other places in the Skagit Valley; she forgot the others. At any rate, it told the Japs they had to leave by noon on March 29. They were to be evacuated by the Fourth Army.

Etta had counted on her fingers. The Japs had eight days exactly. They could bring bedding, linen, toilet articles, extra clothing, knives, spoons, forks, plates, bowls, cups. They had to tie it in neat bundles and put their names on everything. The government would give them a number. The Japs could bring what they could carry, but no pets. The government said it would store their furniture. The furniture would stay, the Japs had to report to an assembly center at the Amity Harbor dock on March 29, eight A.M. The government would provide transportation.

'By God,' said Carl. He smoothed the bill with his thumb, shook his head.

'Won't be pickers this year,' replied Etta. 'Maybe get some Chinamen from Anacortes, the Japs aren't going to be around.'

'Plenty of time for that,' said Carl. 'By God, Etta.' He shook his head.

Carl took his fingers from the bill on the table. It rolled up of its own accord. 'By God,' he repeated. 'Eight days.'

'They'll be selling everything off,' said Etta. 'Just you wait and see. All their knickknacks, pots and pans. A lot of yard sales – you watch. That's what those people'll do with their things – sell them off as fast as they can to whoever'll take them off their hands.'

---

1 **contentiousness**: Streitsucht   60 **bill**: (here) notice in a public place announcing sth.   68 **knickknack**: small decorative object in a house

'People are going to take advantage, too,' said Carl, still wagging his big head. He sat with his forearms on the table. Soon, she knew, he was going to eat something, spread crumbs across her kitchen. He looked as though he was ready to eat, as if he was contemplating food. 'It's too bad,' he said. 'It ain't *right*.'

'They're Japs,' answered Etta. 'We're in a war with them. We can't have spies around.'

Carl shook his head and, heavy as he was, swiveled in his chair to face her.

'We ain't right together,' he told Etta flatly. 'You and me, we just ain't right.'

She knew, indeed, what he meant by that. But just the same she didn't answer. Anyway, he had said this sort of thing before. It didn't hurt very much.

For a moment Etta stood with her wrists against her hips, letting him know how she felt about matters, but Carl didn't look away. 'Have some Christian compassion,' he said. 'My grace, Etta. Don't you feel nothing?'

She went out. There was weeding to be done, and she had to fill the hog trough. She stopped in the mudroom, hung her apron on a hook, sat down to pull her boots on. She was sitting there like that, struggling with a boot, worrying over what Carl had said – the two of them not being right for each other, that old thing – when Zenhichi Miyamoto came to the door, took his hat off, and nodded.

'We heard,' she said, 'about you people.'

'Is Mr. Heine home, Mrs. Heine?' Miyamoto propped his hat against his leg, but then he shifted it behind his back.

'He's here,' said Etta. 'Yes.'

She stuck her head around the mudroom door and called loudly for Carl. 'Someone's here!' she added.

When Carl showed she said to him, 'You may as well talk about it right here in front of me, I'm a part of this.'

'Hello, Zenhichi,' said Carl. 'Why don't you come on in?'

Etta pried her boots off. She followed the Jap into the kitchen.

'Sit down, Zenhichi,' Carl said. 'Etta will get you some coffee.'

He stared at her and she nodded. She took a fresh apron from its hook and put it on. She filled the coffeepot.

'We saw the posting,' said Carl. 'Eight days just isn't near enough time. How can a body be ready in eight days? It ain't right,' he added. 'It just ain't right.'

'What can we do?' Zenhichi said. 'We will put boards with nails on our windows. Leave everything. If you will like, Mr. Heine, you can work our fields. We are grateful that you have sold them to us. Good two-year plants now, most. We will have plenty berries. You pick them, please. Sell them to the cannery, keep what money. Otherwise they rot, Mr. Heine. And nobody gets nothing.'

Carl began to scratch his face. He sat across from Zenhichi scratching. He looked large and coarse, the Japanese man smaller and clear-eyed. They were about the same age, but the Jap looked younger, fifteen years younger at least. Etta put cups and saucers on the table, opened the sugar bowl. *Pretty shrewd, for openers*, she thought. Offer the berries, they're worth nothing to him now. Real clever. Then talk about payments.

'I'm obliged,' said CARL. 'We'll pick them, then. I'm much obliged, Zenhichi.'

The Japanese man nodded. He was always nodding, thought Etta. It was how they got the better of you – they *acted* small, thought big. Nod, say nothing, keep their faces turned down; it was how they got things like her seven acres. 'How are you going to make your payments if me and Carl's picking your berries?' she asked from her place by the stove.

'It's not – '

'Just hold on now, Etta,' Carl broke in. 'We don't need to talk about that just yet.' He turned his attention back to the Jap. 'How is everyone to home?' he said. 'How is everyone taking it?'

'Very busy at home,' said Miyamoto. 'Packing everything, making ready.' He smiled; she saw his big teeth.

'Can we help somehow?' said Carl.

'You pick our berries. That is big help.'

'But can we help? Can we do something else?'

1–2 **wag your head**: shake your head from side to side, often as a sign of disapproval   17 **compassion**: strong feeling of sympathy for people who are suffering and a desire to help them   33 **pry sth. off** (AE): (here) take sth. off quickly   38 **a body** (infml): any-body   47 **coarse**: (hier) ungeschlacht   50 **shrewd**: clever   **for openers** (infml): as a beginning   63 **to home** (infml): at home

Etta brought the coffeepot to the table. She saw that Miyamoto had his hat in his lap. Well, Carl was being a real gracious host, but he'd forgotten about that, hadn't he? The Jap had to sit there with his hat under the table like a man who'd wet his pants.

'Carl will pour,' she announced. She sat down, smoothed her apron. She folded her hands on the tabletop.

'Let it sit a minute,' answered Carl. 'Then we'll have our coffee.'

They were sitting there like that when Carl junior barged through the kitchen door. Home from school already. Three thirty-five and home already. Must've *run* or something. Had one book with him – mathematics. His jacket was grass stained, his face ruddy with the wind, a little sweaty, too. She could see he was hungry, like his father that way, ate everything in sight. 'There's some apples in the pantry,' she pointed out.

'You may get one, Carl. Get a glass of milk and go outside. Somebody's here, we're talking.'

'I heard about it,' said Carl junior. 'I – '

'Go on and get your apple,' said Etta. 'Somebody's here, Carl.'

He went. He came back with two apples. Went to the refrigerator, took out the milk pitcher, poured himself a glass of milk. His father reached for the coffeepot and filled Miyamoto's cup, then Etta's, then his own. Carl junior looked at them, the apples in one hand, the glass of milk in the other. He went on into the living room.

'You go outside,' called Etta. 'Don't you eat in there.'

The boy came back and stood in the doorway. There was a bite taken out of one of the apples. The milk was gone from his glass. He was already near as big as his father. He was eighteen. It was hard to believe how big he was. He took another bite from the apple. 'Is Kabuo home?' he asked.

'Kabuo just home,' replied Miyamoto. 'Yes, he is there.' He smiled.

'I'm going over,' said Carl junior. He walked across the kitchen and put his glass in the sink. He banged out through the kitchen door.

'Come back for your schoolbook!' Etta called.

The boy came back and took his book up the stairs. He went into the pantry, got another apple, waved as he went by them. 'I'll be back,' he announced.

Carl pushed the sugar bowl toward the Japanese man. 'Take some,' he said. 'Cream, too, if you like.'

Miyamoto nodded. 'Thank you,' he said. 'Very good. Sugar only, please.'

He stirred in half a spoon of sugar. He used his spoon carefully, set it in his saucer. He waited until Carl picked up his cup, then picked up his own and sipped. 'Very good,' he said. He looked over at Etta and smiled her way – a little smile, that was all he ever gave.

'Your boy is very big now,' he said. He was still smiling. And then he lowered his head. 'I want to make payment. Two more payment, everything done. Today I have one hundred twenty dollar. I – '

Carl senior was shaking his head. He put his coffee down, shook his head some more. 'Absolutely not,' he said. 'Absolutely not, Zenhichi. We'll get your harvest in, see what comes of that July. Maybe then we can work out something. Maybe, where you're going, they'll have work for you to do. Who knows? It'll turn out. Point is, though, no way am I going to take your savings off your hands at a time like this, Zenhichi. Don't even *talk* about that now.'

The Jap put his one hundred and twenty dollars on the table – a lot of tens, some fives, ten ones; he spread them out in a fan. 'You take this, please,' he said. 'I send more from where I am going. Make payment. Maybe payment is not enough, you still have seven acres strawberries this year. Then, December, there is one more payment. You see? One more.'

Etta folded her arms across her chest; she knew he wasn't giving his strawberries for nothing! 'Your berries,' she said. 'What can we figure? After all, nobody sets the price 'til June. All right, say you've got good plants, two-year plants, like you say you do. Everything goes right. We get people in there weeding. No spit bugs, good sun, everything comes out right, berries come in, good crop. All right, after labor and what we put into fertilizer maybe you've got two hundred worth of berries? In a good year? If the price is good? If everything goes right? But let's just say it's a bad year. An average year. Fungus gets 'em, too much rain, any one of a dozen things – now we're talking about a hundred, maybe a hundred

---

8 **barge** (v): move in an awkward way 11 **ruddy** (here): looking red and healthy
13 **pantry**: cupboard or small room in a house that is used for storing food
66 **fertilizer**: substance added to soil to make plants grow more successfully

twenty worth of berries. Okay? What then? I'll tell you what. It won't be enough to cover your payment, two hundred and fifty dollars.'

'You take this,' said Zenhichi. He made a stack of the bills, moved them toward her. 'This one hundred and twenty dollar. Strawberries bring one hundred and thirty, next payment is made.'

'Thought you was *giving* the berries,' said Etta. 'Didn't you come in here giving them away? Didn't you tell us to sell them to the cannery and keep whatever comes from that? Now what you want is one hundred thirty.' She reached out and took his neat stack of bills, counted the money while she spoke. 'One hundred and thirty on the risk they bring it, plus this here as an early payment, the risk in exchange for getting this March instead of us waiting on all of it 'til June? Is that what you came here hoping on?'

The Japanese man blinked at her steadily. He said nothing, didn't touch his coffee either. He'd gone rigid, gone cold. She could see that he was angry, that he was holding it in, not exposing his rage. *He's proud*, she thought. *I just spit on him, he's pretending it didn't happen that way. Blink away*, she thought.

Etta finished counting his money, set the stack of bills back on the table, and folded her arms across her chest again. 'More coffee?' she asked.

'No, thank you,' the Jap replied. 'You take money, please.'

Carl's big hand slid across the table. His fingers covered the stack of bills and pushed it in front of the Jap's coffee. 'Zenhichi,' he said. 'We won't take this. Don't matter what Etta says, we won't. She's been rude to you and I apologize for that.' He looked at her then and she looked right back. She knew how he felt, but it didn't matter very much – she wanted Carl to know what was up, how he was being duped. She wasn't going to hang her head. She stared back at him.

'I am sorry,' the Jap said. 'Very sorry.'

'We'll worry about this come picking season,' said Carl. 'You get where you're going, you write to us. We'll get your berries in, write back, we'll go from there. We'll just play this by ear a little bit, far as I'm concerned. One way or another you get your payments finished, maybe down the road somewhere, everything comes out like it should in the long run. Everything comes out satisfactory. But right now you got deeper things to think about. You don't need us bending your ear about payments. You got plenty to do 'thout that. And anything I can do, help you get your things all ready, you let me know, Zenhichi.'

40 'I make payments,' Zenhichi answered. 'I find a way, I send you.'

'That's fine,' said Carl and put his hand out. The Japanese man took it. 'Thank you, Carl,' he said. 'I make payments. No worry.'

Etta watched Zenhichi. It occurred to her that he had not grown old – she noticed this more clearly than ever. For ten years he'd been
45 working these very same fields, his eyes were still clear, his back was straight, his skin was taut, his belly remained lean and hard. Ten years he had worked in the same fields she had, and yet he hadn't aged a day. His clothes were clean, his head erect, his complexion brown and healthy. And all of this was part of his mystery, his distance from what
50 *she* was. Something he knew about kept him from aging while she, Etta, grew worn and weary – something he knew about yet kept to himself, bottled up behind his face. Maybe it was Jap religion, she thought, or maybe it was in his blood. There didn't seem any way to know.

She remembered, on the witness stand, that Carl junior had returned
55 that evening with a bamboo fishing rod. How he had looked to her coming through the door with his hair rumpled by the wind. How big and young, like a Great Dane puppy, bounding into her kitchen. Her son, a big young man.

'Look at this,' he'd said to her. 'Kabuo loaned it to me.'

60 He began to explain it to her. She'd been at the sink peeling supper potatoes. He said it was a good rod for sea-run cutthroat. Split bamboo, made by a Mr. Nishi, the ferrules smooth, silk wrapped. Figured he'd go trolling with it, get Erik Everts or somebody, one of his friends, to take

---

8 **want sth.** (fml): (here) be short of sth.   10 **on the risk**: assuming but not being sure that sth. will happen the right way   18 **blink (sth.) away**: try to control sth., esp. an emotion although it is hard to do   28 **dupe sb.**: trick or cheat sb.
31 **come sth.** (old-fashioned): when the time for sth. comes   33 **play sth. by ear** (infml): improvise   37 **bend sb.'s ear about sth.**: talk to sb. a lot about sth., esp. about a problem that you have   38 **'thout** = without   46 **taut**: (here) with firm muscles, not fat   **lean** (adj): thin and fit   48 **complexion**: natural color and condition of the skin on a person's face   52 **bottle sth. up**: hide sth., esp. negative feelings   56 **rumple sth.**: make sth. untidy or messy   59 **loan sth. to sb.**: lend sth. to sb.   61 **sea-run cutthroat**: kind of trout (= Forelle)   62 **ferrule** ['ferəl]: ring made of metal or rubber that covers part of a stick in order to protect it
63 **troll** (v): mit der Schleppangel fischen

him out in a canoe. Rig it up with light tackle, see how it played. Where was Dad? He'd go show it to him.

Etta didn't stop peeling her potatoes while she said to her son what she had to say: take the fishing rod back to the Japs, they owed them money, the rod confused that.

She remembered how the boy had looked at her. Hurt and trying to hide it. Wanted to argue, didn't want to argue – wouldn't win and already knew it. The look of the defeated – his father's look – big, plodding strawberry farmer. Subdued, pinned to the earth. The boy spoke like his father and moved like his father, but he had a broad brow, small ears, there was a set to his eyes, some of her in him. The boy was not all Carl's. Her son, too, she felt that.

'You turn around and take it right on back,' she'd said again, and pointed with the peeler. And in this, she saw now, on the witness stand, her feelings had not been wrong. He'd taken the rod back, some months had passed, he'd gone to the war, he'd come on home, that Japanese boy had *killed* him. She'd been right about them all along; Carl, her husband, had been wrong.

They didn't meet their payments, she told Alvin Hooks. Simple as that. Didn't meet them. She sold the place off to Ole Jurgensen, sent their equity on down to them in California, didn't try to hold back their money. Gave every penny back. She moved into Amity Harbor Christmastime '44. That was that, she'd figured. Looked, now, like she was wrong about one thing: you were never shut of people where money was concerned. One way or another, they *wanted*. And on account of that, she told the court, her son had been murdered by Kabuo Miyamoto. Her son was dead and gone.

1 **rig sth. up**: (here) fit sth. with equipment   **tackle**: (here) equipment used for catching fish   11 **set** (n): (of the face) particular expression, esp. showing determination   21 **equity**: (here) the value of the share you had in a property or the money you already paid for buying it   24 **be shut of sb.** (infml): be safe of sb., not be bothered by sb.

Chapter 10

Alvin Hooks skirted the edge of his table and resumed the slow, fluid pacing of the floorboards that had been part of his strategy all morning. 'Mrs. Heine,' he said. 'In December of '44 you moved to Amity Harbor?'
'That's right.'
'Your husband had recently passed away?'
'That's right, too.'
'You felt that without him you could not work your land?'
'Yes.'
'So you moved to Amity Harbor,' said Alvin Hooks. 'Where exactly, Mrs. Heine?'
'On Main Street,' said Etta. 'Up above Lottie Opsvig's shop.'
'Lottie Opsvig's? An apparel shop?'
'That's right.'
'In an apartment?'
'Yes.'
'A big apartment?'
'No,' said Etta. 'Just one bedroom.'
'One bedroom above an apparel shop,' said Alvin Hooks. 'So you took a one-bedroom apartment then. And may I ask about your monthly rent?'
'Twenty-five dollars,' said Etta.
'A twenty-five-dollar-a-month apartment,' Alvin Hooks said. 'You're still living there? You currently reside there?'
'Yes.'
'Still paying twenty-five dollars?'
'No,' said Etta. '*Thirty*-five. Price has gone up since '44.'
'Forty-four,' Alvin Hooks repeated. 'The year you moved in? The year you sent the Miyamotos their equity and came to live in Amity Harbor?'
'Yes,' said Etta.

1 **skirt sth.**: go around the edge of sth.   23 **reside** (fml): live in a house or apartment

'Mrs. Heine,' said Alvin Hooks, and stopped pacing. 'Did you hear again from the Miyamotos after that? After you sent them their money?'

'I heard from them,' said Etta.

'When was that?' Alvin Hooks asked.

Etta bit her lip and thought it over; she squeezed her cheeks between her fingers. 'It was July of '45,' she answered finally. 'That one there showed up at my door.' And she pointed at Kabuo Miyamoto.

'The defendant?'

'Yes.'

'He came to your door in 1945? To your apartment door in Amity Harbor?'

'That's right.'

'Did he call ahead? Were you expecting him?'

'No. Just showed up. Just like that.'

'Just showed up unannounced? Out of nowhere, as it were?'

'That's right,' replied Etta. 'Out of nowhere.'

'Mrs. Heine,' said the prosecutor. 'What did the defendant indicate was the nature of his business with you?'

'He wanted to talk about land, he said. Had a few things to say about my land I sold to Ole.'

'Exactly what did he say, Mrs. Heine? Can you remember? For the benefit of the court?'

Etta folded her hands in her lap and glanced at Kabuo Miyamoto. She could see in his eyes – they didn't fool *her* – that he remembered everything. He'd stood in her doorway, neatly dressed, his hands clasped, unblinking. It was July and the heat in her apartment was unbearable; the doorway felt much cooler. They'd stared at each other, and then Etta had folded her arms across her chest and asked him what he wanted.

'Mrs. Heine,' he'd said. 'Do you remember me?'

''Course I do,' Etta had answered.

She hadn't seen him since the day the Japs left – more than three years before, in '42 – but she recollected him clearly enough. He was the boy who'd tried to give Carl a fishing rod, the boy she used to see from her kitchen window practicing in the fields with his wooden sword. He was the oldest of the Miyamoto children – she knew his face but didn't remember his name – the one her son used to hang around with.

'I've been back home three days,' he'd said. 'I guess Carl isn't home yet.'

'Carl's passed on,' replied Etta. 'Carl junior's fighting the Japs.' She stared at the man in the doorway. 'They're just about licked,' she added.

'Just about,' Kabuo had replied. He unclasped his hands and put them at his back. 'I was sorry to hear about Mr. Heine,' he said. 'I heard about it in Italy. My mother sent me a letter.'

'Well, I told you people about it when I sent on down the equity,' returned Etta. 'Said in my letter Carl'd passed on and that I'd had to go and sell the place.'

'Yes,' said Kabuo. 'But Mrs. Heine, my father had an agreement with Mr. Heine, didn't he? Didn't – '

'Mr. Heine was passed away,' Etta interrupted. 'I had to make a decision. Couldn't farm the place myself, could I? I sold to Ole and that's that,' she said. 'You want to talk about that piece of land, you're going to have to talk to *Ole*. I don't have nothing to do with it.'

'Please,' replied Kabuo. 'I talked to Mr. Jurgensen already. I got back to the island just last Wednesday and went out to see what had become of the place. You know, have a look around. Mr. Jurgensen was out there, up on his tractor. We talked for a while about things.'

'Well, good,' said Etta. 'So you talked to him.'

'I talked to him,' said Kabuo. 'He said I'd better talk to you.'

Etta folded her arms more tightly. '*Humpf*,' she said. 'It's his land, isn't it? Go on back and tell him that. Tell him I said so. You tell him.'

'He didn't *know*,' said Kabuo. 'You didn't tell him we were one payment away, Mrs. Heine. You didn't tell him Mr. Heine had – '

'He didn't know,' sneered Etta. 'Is that what Ole told you? He didn't know – is that it? Was I supposed to say, "Ole, there's these folks made an illegal agreement with my husband hands over seven acres to them"? Is that what I was supposed to say? He didn't *know*,' repeated Etta. 'Most ridiculous thing I ever heard. I'm supposed to tell someone's buying up my land there's an illegal contract muddling matters up? And what if I did? Huh? Fact is you people didn't meet your payments. That's a fact. And just suppose you done that to a bank 'round here. Just suppose. You don't make your payments, what do you think happens? Somebody waits real polite on you? No. Bank repossesses your land, that's what

38 **pass on**: die   39 **lick sb.** (infml): (here) easily defeat sb.   67 **muddle sth. up**: etwas durcheinander bringen   71 **repossess sth.**: etwas wieder in Besitz nehmen

happens. I haven't done anything a bank wouldn't do. I haven't done anything wrong.'

'You haven't done anything *illegal*,' the Jap replied. 'Wrong is a different matter.'

Etta blinked. She stepped back and put her hand on the doorknob. 'Get out of here,' she said.

'You sold our land,' the Jap continued. 'You sold our land out from under us, Mrs. Heine. You took advantage of the fact that we were gone. You – '

But she'd shut the door so as not to listen. *Carl made such a mess*, she'd thought. *Now I have to clean it all up.*

'Mrs. Heine,' said the prosecutor, Alvin Hooks, when she'd finished telling of these things. 'Did you see the defendant thereafter? Did he approach you again about these land matters?'

'Did I see him?' asked Etta. 'Sure I saw him. Saw him in town, saw him at Petersen's, here and there … I saw him now and again, yes.'

'Did he speak to you?'

'No.'

'Ever?'

'No.'

'There was no further communication between you?'

'None I can think of. 'Less you want to call dirty looks a way of speaking.' And she glanced at Kabuo again.

'Dirty looks, Mrs. Heine? What exactly do you mean?'

Etta smoothed the front of her dress and sat more erectly in the witness stand. 'Ever time I saw him,' she insisted, 'there he'd be with his eyes narrowed at me. You know, watchin', *glarin'*.'

'I see,' said the prosecutor. 'And how long did this continue?'

'Been going on ever since,' said Etta. 'Never stopped. I never saw a sociable look from him, not once in all the times I saw him. Always narrowin' his eyes at me, giving me his *mean* face.'

'Mrs. Heine,' said Alvin Hooks. 'Did you ever have a conversation with your son about the defendant in this regard? Did you tell Carl junior that Kabuo Miyamoto had come to your door and argued with you about the sale of your family's land?'

'My son knew all about it. When he got back, I told him.'

'Got back?'

'From the war,' said Etta. 'Couple months later, 'bout October, I think it was.'

'And you told him then the defendant had come to your door?'

'Yes.'

'Do you recall his response?'

'Yes,' said Etta. 'He said he'd keep an eye on it. Said that if Kabuo Miyamoto was giving me dirty looks he'd keep an eye on him.'

'I see,' said Alvin Hooks. 'And did he?'

'Yes. Far as I know, yes.'

'He kept an eye out for Kabuo Miyamoto?'

'Yes, he did. He watched for him.'

'To your knowledge, Mrs. Heine, were the two of them on unfriendly terms? They were both fishermen, they shared that in common. They were, as you have said, neighbors in adolescence. And yet there was this ... dispute. This family dispute over land. So were they, the defendant and your son, on friendly or unfriendly terms from 1945 on?'

'No,' said Etta. 'The defendant wasn't no friend of my son's. Isn't that obvious? They were enemies.'

'Enemies?' said Alvin Hooks.

'Carl told me more 'n once he wished Kabuo would forget about his seven acres and stop lookin' at me cross-eyed.'

'When you told him the defendant had given you dirty looks your son reacted exactly how, Mrs. Heine?'

'Said he wished Kabuo'd stop doing that. Said he'd have to keep an eye out for Kabuo.'

'*Keep an eye out*,' Alvin Hooks repeated. 'He saw some danger from Mr. Miyamoto?'

'Objection,' cut in Nels Gudmundsson. 'The witness is being asked to speculate as to her son's state of mind and his emotional status. He's – '

'All right, all right,' said Alvin Hooks. 'Tell us what you *observed*, Mrs. Heine. Tell us what your son said or did – was there anything to suggest he saw some kind of danger from Kabuo Miyamoto?'

7–8 **out from under sb.** (infml): without sb.'s knowledge, esp. against their will
30 **sociable**: (here) friendly, interested in people   65 **objection**: (bei Gericht) Einspruch

'Said he'd keep an eye out for him,' repeated Etta. 'You know, he'd watch out.'

'Did your son say he felt he had to watch for Mr. Miyamoto? That there was danger from him of some kind?'

'Yes,' said Etta. 'He kept an eye on him. Every time I told him that man was glarin' at me, that's what he said – he'd watch out.'

'Mrs. Heine,' said Alvin Hooks. 'Do you think that the term "family feud" could be accurately applied to the relationship between your family and that of the defendant? Were you enemies? Was there a feud?'

Etta looked directly at Kabuo. 'Yes,' she said. 'We're enemies all right. They've been botherin' us over those seven acres for near ten years now. My son was killed over it.'

'Objection,' said Nels Gudmundsson. 'The witness is speculating as to – '

'Sustained,' agreed Judge Fielding. 'Witness will confine herself to answering questions put to her without further speculation. I hereby instruct you jury members to disregard her last words. Witness's comment will furthermore be struck from the record. Let's move on, Mr. Hooks.'

'Thank you,' Alvin Hooks said. 'But I can't think of anything else I want to ask, Your Honor. Mrs. Heine, I want you to know that I appreciate your coming down, though, what with this weather we've been having. Thank you for testifying in a snowstorm.' He swiveled, now, on the toe of one shoe; he pointed a forefinger at Nels Gudmundsson. 'Your witness,' he said.

Nels Gudmundsson shook his head and frowned. 'Just three questions,' he grumbled, without getting up. 'I've done some calculating, Mrs. Heine. If I've multiplied correctly, the Miyamoto family purchased seven acres from you for forty-five hundred dollars – is that right? Forty-five hundred dollars?'

'Tried to buy it for that much,' said Etta. 'Never finished their payments.'

'Second question,' Nels said. 'When you went to Ole Jurgensen in 1944 and told him you wanted to sell him your land, what was the price per acre?'

'A thousand,' said Etta. 'Thousand per acre.'

'I guess that makes what would have been forty-five hundred dollars into seven thousand dollars instead, doesn't it. A twenty-five-hundred-dollar increase in the land's value if you sent the Miyamotos their equity and sold the land to Ole Jurgensen?'

'Is that your third question?' said Etta.

'It is,' said Nels. 'Yes.'

'You done your math right. Twenty-five hundred.'

'That's all then, thank you,' Nels replied. 'You may step down, Mrs. Heine.'

Ole Jurgensen came out of the gallery leaning hard on his cane. Alvin Hooks held the swinging door for him, and Ole shuffled past with his cane in his right hand and his left at the small of his back. He shuffled half sidewise, an injured crab, making his way toward where Ed Soames stood proffering the Holy Bible. When Ole arrived he bobbled his cane from hand to hand before settling on the expediency of hanging it from his wrist. The stroke he'd suffered in June caused his hands to tremble. He'd been out among his pickers, sorting berries in a bin, when the sensation that the earth was tilting under his feet grew on him out of a more general dizziness and nausea that had inhabited him all morning. Ole reared up and made a last desperate effort to shrug off what was happening, but the sky seemed to crowd around his head, the earth buckled, and he keeled over into a strawberry bin. There he lay blinking up at the clouds until two Canadian Indian pickers pulled him out by the armpits. They took him up to his house in the tractor bucket and laid him on his porch like a corpse. Liesel shook him until he grunted at her and drooled, and in the face of this she began a hysterical interrogation into the nature of his symptoms. When it became apparent he didn't intend to answer she stopped talking and kissed his forehead. Then she hurried in and called Dr. Whaley.

---

8 **feud**: conflict between two people or groups of people, esp. families, that continues over a long period of time   14 **sustained** = objection sustained: (bei Gericht) stattgegeben   **confine yourself to sth.**: restrict yourself to sth.
16 **disregard sth.**: ignore sth.   21 **what with**: (here) considering   46 **shuffle**: walk slowly without lifting your feet completetly off the ground   49 **proffer sth.**: (here) offer sth. to sb. by holding it out to them   50 **expediency**: Zweckdienlichkeit
53 **tilt**: sich neigen, kippen   54 **nausea** ['nɔːzɪə]: feeling of sickness   **rear up**: (here) stand up suddenly   56 **buckle** (v): (hier) sich neigen   56–57 **keel over**: (here) fall over unexpectedly, esp. because you feel ill or sick   60 **grunt**: make a short low sound in your throat, esp. to show that you are in pain   **drool**: sabbern

Since then he had withered rapidly. His legs were stilts, his eyes leaked water, his beard ended in wisps at the third button of his vest, his skin appeared pink and chafed. He perched in the stand, both hands wrapped around the head of his cane now, a tremulous and gangling old man.

'Mr. Jurgensen,' Alvin Hooks began. 'You were for many years a neighbor of the Heine family in Center Valley? Is that correct, sir?'

'Yes,' said Ole Jurgensen.

'How many years?'

'Yust always,' said Ole. 'Why, I can remember back fo-forty years to when Carl – old Carl – cleared his land next to mine.'

'Forty years,' said Alvin Hooks. 'For forty years you were a berry farmer?'

'Yes, sir. More than forty.'

'How many acres did you own, Mr. Jurgensen?'

Ole seemed to think about it. He licked his lips and squinted at the courthouse ceiling; his hands roamed up and down the length of his cane. 'Thirty-five, start out,' he said. 'Then I ac-acquired thirty more from Etta, you see, like Etta tell before when she was up here. So that brought me up-up to sixty-five acre; big farm, it was.'

'Yes,' said Alvin Hooks. 'So you purchased thirty acres from Etta Heine, then?'

'Yes, sir. I did so.'

'And when was that, Mr. Jurgensen?'

'Yust like she tell. Nineteen hundred and forty-four.'

'She handed over to you the property deed at that time?'

'Yes, sir.'

'In your mind, Mr. Jurgensen, did the deed read free and clear? That is, were there any encumbrances or conditions? Easements? Liens? That sort of thing?'

'No,' said Ole Jurgensen. 'No ting like that. The contract was good. Every ting look right with it.'

'I see,' said Alvin Hooks. 'So you were not aware of any claim, then, that the Miyamotos might have had to any seven of your newly purchased thirty acres?'

'Not aware, no,' said Ole. 'I bring it up with Etta, you see, because the Miyamoto family, they have-have a house on the property, I know

David Guterson: **Snow Falling on Cedars** 127

seven acres has been sold to them. But Etta says to me they don' make no payment so she is ... to repossess. She don' have any choice after
40 Carl passed away, says she. Every ting looks good with the contract, says she. The Miyamoto family away in the camp, says she, maybe they won' come b-back. She is going to give them their money, says she. They don' have any claim, no, sir.'

'So you heard nothing about any claim the Miyamotos might have
45 had to seven acres of your newly purchased land?'

'No. I hear no ting about it until that man' – he aimed his nose at the defendant – 'come round about and tell me.'

'Do you mean the defendant there – Kabuo Miyamoto?'

'Him,' said Ole. 'Yes, that's right.'

50 'He came around when, Mr. Jurgensen?'

'Let's see,' said Ole. 'He come summer of '45, he does. He sh-shows up at my place and say Mrs. Heine robbed him, Mr. Heine never would have let no such ting like that happen, he says.'

'I'm not following,' said Alvin Hooks. 'The defendant showed up at
55 your farm in the summer of 1945 and accused Etta Heine of *robbing him*?'

'Yes, sir. That's what I remember.'

'And what did you say?'

'I say no to him, she sell the land to me, and I don't see *his* name any place on the contract.'

60 'Yes?'

'He wants to know will I sell it back to him.'

'Sell it back?' said Alvin Hooks. 'The thirty acres?'

'He don't want all thirty,' answered Ole. 'He just want the seven in the northwest, where his family was one time living. Before the war.'

65 'And did you talk about that? Did you consider selling?'

---

1 **wither**: (here) become weaker   **stilt**: Stelze   2 **wisp**: (hier) Strähne   3 **chafed**: wund   4 **tremulous** (fml): trembling or shaking slightly, esp. because you are nervous   **gangling**: (of a person) tall, thin and awkward (= ungelenk)
10 **yust** = just   26 **property deed**: legal document that you sign that proves that you own a house or a building   29 **encumbrance**: Belastung (von Eigentum)
easement: right to use the property of another person for a specific purpose like cultivating plants, etc.   **lien** ['liːən]: right to keep sb.'s property until a debt is paid

'He didn't have no money,' said Ole. 'Anyway, I'm not thinking of s-selling then. It was before ... my stroke. I had a good farm, sixty-five acres. I don't want to sell one piece to anybody.'

'Mr. Jurgensen,' said Alvin Hooks. 'When you purchased Etta Heine's thirty acres did you acquire her home as well?'

'No. She sold it separate. Just the house, to Bjorn Andreason. And he is still living there now.'

'And the house the *defendant's* family had lived in, Mr. Jurgensen?'

'This one,' said Ole, 'I bought.'

'I see,' said Alvin Hooks. 'And what did you do with it?'

'I use it for my pickers, you see,' said Ole. 'My f-farm was so big now, I need to have a manager with me year around. So he is living there, plus room for pickers come picking time.'

'Mr. Jurgensen,' Alvin Hooks said. 'Did the defendant say anything else to you during his visit in the summer of 1945? Anything you can remember?'

Ole Jurgensen's right hand left the head of his cane. It clawed its way into the side pocket of his coat and fumbled about for something. 'Yes, one ting,' said Ole. 'He said some day he would get his land back.'

'That he would get it back?'

'Yes, sir. And he is angry.'

'And what did you say?'

'I said to him why is he angry to *me*? I don't know any ting about this land, except that I don't want to sell it to nobody.' Ole lifted a handkerchief to his mouth and dried his lips with it. 'I say to him go talk with Etta Heine, she is moved into Amity Harbor. I tell him where he can look for her, she is the person to talk to.'

'And did he leave then?'

'Yes.'

'And did you see him again?'

'I see him, yes. This island is small. You live hereabouts you see everybody.'

'All right,' Alvin Hooks said. 'You've had a stroke, Mr. Jurgensen, as you say. And that was in June of this year?'

'Yes, sir. June 28.'

'I see,' said Alvin Hooks. 'And it incapacitated you? So that you felt you could no longer run your farm?'

Ole Jurgensen didn't answer at first. His right hand, with the handkerchief in it, returned to the head of his cane. He chewed on the inside of his cheek; his head shook. Ole struggled to speak.

'I – I ... yes,' he said. 'I yust couldn't do it, you see.'

'You couldn't run your farm?'

'N-no.'

'So what did you do?'

'I – I put it on the market. For sale,' said Ole Jurgensen. 'September 7. Yust after Labor Day.'

'Of this year?'

'Did you list your property with a real estate agent, Mr. Jurgensen?'

'Yes, sir.'

'With Klaus Hartmann?'

'Yes, sir.'

'Did you advertise in any other way?'

'We had a sign on the barn,' said Ole. 'That was everyting.'

'And what happened then?' asked Alvin Hooks. 'Did anybody come to look?'

'Carl Heine came,' said Ole. 'C-Carl Heine, Etta's son.'

'When was that?' Alvin Hooks asked.

'That was September 7,' said Ole. 'Round about comes Carl Heine, wantin' to buy my farm.'

'Tell us about that,' Alvin Hooks asked gently. 'Carl Heine was a ... successful fisherman. He owned a fine place on Mill Run Road. What did he want with your farm?'

Ole Jurgensen blinked half a dozen times. He dabbed at his eyes with his handkerchief. The young man, he remembered, Carl junior, had driven into his yard that morning in a sky blue Bel-Air, scattering chickens before him. Ole, from his place on the porch, knew who it was immediately; he guessed what it was he wanted. The young man had come by each picking season; he'd brought along his wife and children. They'd taken their caddies into the fields and picked berries together.

---

31 **hereabouts**: near this place   36 **incapacitate sb.**: make sb. unable to live or work normally   46 **Labor Day**: public holiday in honor of working people held in the US and Canada on the first Monday of September   48 **real estate agent**: Immobilienmakler   63 **dab at sth.**: touch sth. lightly, usually several times

Ole had always refused Carl's money, but Carl'd pressed it on him. When Ole shook his head Carl put the bills on the weighing table next to the scales, beneath a stone. 'Don't care if it was my father's land once,' he'd say. 'It's yours now. We'll pay.'

Now here he was, big, like his father, with his father's stature and his mother's face, dressed like a fisherman in rubber boots – he *was* a fisherman, Ole recalled, had named his boat after his wife: the *Susan Marie*.

Liesel had given the young man a glass of iced tea. He'd sat down so that from where they looked the strawberry fields spread out before them. Way in the distance they could just make out the broad side of Bjorn Andreason's house – where Carl junior had once lived.

Small talk, Ole explained now to the court. Carl had asked about the strawberries this year, Ole had asked about the salmon runs. Liesel had inquired as to Etta's health, and then she had asked Carl how the fishing life suited him. 'It doesn't,' Carl had answered.

It'd been, thought Ole, an odd thing for the young man to say aloud. It must have hurt his pride to say it. He'd been admitting something, Ole understood, and admitting it for a reason. He'd wanted to make a point.

The young man had put his glass down, just in front of his rubber boots, and leaned toward them, his elbows on his knees, as if he was about to confess something. He'd looked at the floorboards of the porch for a moment. 'I want to buy your farm,' he'd said.

Liesel had explained to him how Bjorn Andreason had the old Heine house – there was nothing to be done about it. Liesel had explained that she and Ole didn't want to leave the farm at all – but there was nothing to be done about that either. And the young man had nodded and scratched the bristles along his jaw. 'I'm sorry for that,' he'd said quietly. 'I feel bad to take advantage of your health, Mr. Jurgensen. But if you have to sell, I guess ... well, I'm interested.'

Ole had said, 'I am happy. You have lived here, you know this place. We do what is fair. I am happy.' And he'd reached his hand toward the young man.

The young man took it solemnly. 'It's the way I feel, too,' he'd said.

They'd spoken in the kitchen of the arrangements they would make together. Carl's money was tied up in the *Susan Marie* and in his house on Mill Run Road. In the meantime there was a thousand dollars in earnest money – Carl put it on the table. Ten one-hundred-dollar bills. Come November the boat would sell, then the house, said Carl. 'Your wife will be happy,' said Liesel with a smile. 'Fishermen are always gone at night.'

Ole Jurgensen leaned on his cane and remembered another visitor later that same day. Kabuo Miyamoto had come to see him.

'The defendant?' asked Alvin Hooks. 'On September 7 of this year?'

'Yes, sir,' said Ole.

'The same day Carl Heine came to see you to inquire about the sale of your land?'

'Yes, sir.'

'In the afternoon of that same day?'

'Round abouts lunch,' said Ole. 'We were yust about sitting down to lunch, it was. Miyamoto knocked on our door.'

'And did he say, Mr. Jurgensen, what he wanted?'

'Same as Etta's son,' said Ole. 'He wanted to buy my land.'

'Tell us about that,' said Alvin Hooks. 'What exactly did he say to you?'

They'd sat down on the porch together, explained Ole. The defendant had seen the sign on the barn and wanted to buy Ole's farm. Ole had remembered the Japanese man's promise: how he'd stood in the fields and vowed that one day he would get his family's land back. The Japanese man had slipped his mind altogether. Nine years had passed.

He'd remembered, too, that the Japanese man had worked for him years before, part of a crew that put in his raspberries in 1939. Ole remembered him pounding home cedar posts for raspberry canes, standing in the bed of a pickup truck, shirtless, swinging a maul. He must have been sixteen or seventeen.

---

3 **scales** (pl): instrument for weighing people or things 14 **salmon runs** (usu. pl): courses salmon take at sea to get back to the rivers in which they were born in order to spawn (= laichen) and die 29 **bristle**: (Bart)stoppel 37 **tie sth. up in sth.**: invest money in an object or enterprise so that it is not or not easily availabe to spend 39 **earnest money**: Anzahlung 61 **slip sb.'s mind**: be forgotten by sb. 64 **pound sth.**: (hier) etwas einrammen **home** (adv): (here) into the correct position 65 **maul**: schwerer Holzhammer

He remembered seeing him early in the morning, too, swinging a wooden sword in the fields. The boy's father, he remembered, was Zeneechee, something like that. He never could pronounce it.

On the porch he'd asked Kabuo about his father, but the man had long passed away.

The Japanese man had asked about the land then, and asserted his wish to buy the seven acres his family had once held.

'I'm afraid it isn't for sale,' Liesel had said. 'It's already been sold, you see. Somebody else came by this morning. I'm sorry to tell you, Kabuo.'

'Yes,' said Ole. 'We're sorry.'

The Japanese man had stiffened. In a moment the politeness went from his face so that Ole could no longer read him. 'It's sold?' he said. 'Already?'

'Yes,' said Liesel. 'Just like that. We're sorry to disappoint you.'

'All of it?' asked the Japanese man.

'Yes,' said Liesel. 'We're very sorry. We didn't even have time to take our sign down.'

The stiff expression of Kabuo Miyamoto's face didn't change even for a second. 'Who bought it?' he said. 'I want to talk to them.'

'Etta Heine's son Carl,' said Liesel. 'He came by around ten o'clock.'

'Carl Heine,' the Japanese man answered, with a hint of anger in his voice.

Ole had suggested that Kabuo Miyamoto go to see Carl Heine about the matter. Perhaps something could be worked out.

Liesel shook her head and wrung her hands in her apron. 'We've sold it,' she'd repeated apologetically. 'Ole and Carl shook hands, you see. We accepted earnest money. We're bound to our agreement. It's sold, you see. We're sorry.'

The Japanese man had stood then. 'I should have come earlier,' he said.

The next day Carl had come by again – Liesel phoned him about Kabuo Miyamoto – to take the sign down from the barn. Ole, leaning on his cane, stood below and told him about the Japanese man's visit. Carl, he remembered, had been interested in the details of it. He nodded his head and listened closely. Ole Jurgensen told everything – the way the politeness had gone out of the Japanese man, the unreadable Japanese expression on his face when he heard that the land he coveted had been sold. Carl Heine nodded again and again and then came down from the ladder with the sign. 'Thanks for telling me,' he'd said.

---

6 **assert sth.**: state clearly and firmly that sth. is true   26 **wring your hands**: Hände (verzweifelt) ringen   27 **apologetic**: feeling or showing that you are sorry for doing sth.   38 **covet sth.**: want sth. very much, esp. sth. that belongs to sb. else

Chapter 11

After the noon recess was called that day Kabuo Miyamoto ate lunch in his cell, as he had seventy-seven times. The cell was one of two in the courthouse basement and had neither bars nor windows. It was big enough for a low military surplus bunk, a toilet, a sink, and a nightstand. There was a drain in the corner of its concrete floor and a foot-square grate in its door. Other than this there were no openings or apertures through which light could seep. A naked bulb hung overhead, and Kabuo could turn it on and off by screwing and unscrewing it in its socket. Yet before the first week was over he'd discovered in himself a preference for darkness. His eyes adjusted to it. He was less troubled by the closeness of his cell walls with the naked light put out, less conscious that he was jailed.

Kabuo sat on the edge of his bunk with his lunch perched in front of him on the nightstand. A peanut-butter-and-jelly sandwich, two carrot sticks, a mound of lime gelatin, a tin cup of milk, served on a cafeteria tray. At this particular moment his light was on. He'd turned it on in order to see what he was eating but also in order to look at his face in a hand-held shaving mirror. His wife had said he looked like one of Tojo's soldiers. He wanted to see if this was so.

He sat with his tray just in front of his knees, confronting his reflection in the hand mirror. He could see how his face had once been a boy's face and how on top of this was laid the face of his war years – a face he was no longer surprised to see, though it had astonished him greatly in the beginning. He had come home from the war and seen in his own eyes the disturbed empty reaches he'd seen in the eyes of other soldiers he'd known. They did not so much seem to stare right through things as to stare past the present state of the world into a world that was permanently in the distance for them and at the same time more immediate than the present. Kabuo remembered much in this manner. Under the surface of his daily life was a life he lived as if underwater. Kabuo remembered how under the helmet of the soldier on the wooded hillside, underneath the steady droning of the bees, it had turned out to be a very young boy he had shot directly through the groin. When Kabuo approached from one side the boy had stared up at him and spoke through clenched teeth in tremulous German. Then the boy panicked and moved his hand toward his gun, and Kabuo shot him one more time in the heart at point-blank range. Yet still the boy refused to die and lay on his back between two trees while Kabuo stood five feet away, frozen, his rifle shouldered still. The boy held his chest in both of his hands and exerted himself to raise his head from the ground, at the same time gathering himself to take a breath, and sucked in the hot afternoon air. Then he spoke again, between his teeth, and it was clear to Kabuo that he was begging, pleading, that he wanted the American who had killed him to save him – he had no choice but to ask him for this, nobody else was present. All of it was too much, and when the boy stopped talking his chest twitched a half-dozen times and blood ran from his mouth and down his cheeks. Then Kabuo went forward with his rifle and squatted beside the German boy, on his right, and the boy put his hand on Kabuo's boot and shut his eyes and gave out. The tension stayed in his mouth for a while, and Kabuo watched until it faded. The smell of breakfast soon rose from the German boy's bowels.

Kabuo sat in his prison cell now and examined his reflection carefully. It was not a thing he had control over. His face had been molded by his experiences as a soldier, and he appeared to the world seized up inside precisely because this was how he felt. It was possible for him all these years later to think of the German boy dying on the hillside and to feel his own heart pound as it had as he squatted against the tree, drinking from his canteen, his ears ringing, his legs trembling. What could he say to people on San Piedro to explain the coldness he projected? The world was unreal, a nuisance that prevented him from focusing on his memory

---

4 **nightstand**: Nachttisch   6 **grate**: (hier) Gitter   9 **socket**: Steckdose   25 **reaches** (n, pl): (hier) Tiefen   32 **drone** (v): make a continuous low noise   35 **clench your teeth**: press your teeth together tightly, showing anger   37 **point-blank** (adj): shot fired very close to the target (= Ziel)   48 **rifle**: Gewehr   49 **give out**: (here) die   51 **bowels**: Gedärme   53 **mold sth.** (AE = BE mould): shape sth., influence sth.   58 **canteen**: Feldflasche   **ring** (v): (hier) dröhnen   59 **project sth.**: (hier) etwas vermitteln/ausstrahlen   60 **nuisance** ['nu:sns] (usu. sing): sth. that causes trouble or problems

of that boy, on the flies in a cloud over his astonished face, the pool of blood filtering out of his shirt and into the forest floor, smelling rank, the sound of gunfire from the hillside to the east – he'd left there, and then he hadn't left. And still there had been more murders after this, three more, less difficult than the first had been but murders nonetheless. So how to explain his face to people? After a while, motionless in his cell, he began to feel objective about his face, and then he saw what Hatsue did. He had meant to project to the jurors his innocence, he'd wanted them to see that his spirit was haunted, he sat upright in the hope that his desperate composure might reflect the shape of his soul. This was what his father had taught him: the greater the composure, the more revealed one was, the truth of one's inner life was manifest – a pleasing paradox. It had seemed to Kabuo that his detachment from this world was somehow self-explanatory, that the judge, the jurors, and the people in the gallery would recognize the face of a war veteran who had forever sacrificed his tranquillity in order that they might have theirs. Now, looking at himself, scrutinizing his face, he saw that he appeared defiant instead. He had refused to respond to anything that happened, had not allowed the jurors to read in his face the palpitations of his heart.

Yet listening to Etta Heine on the witness stand had moved Kabuo to bitter anger. He had felt his carefully constructed exterior crumbling when she spoke to the court so insultingly about his father. The desire had come over him to deny what she said, to interrupt her testimony with the truth about his father, a strong and tireless man, honest to a fault, kind and humble as well. But all of this he suppressed.

Now, in his jail cell, he stared into the mirror at the mask he wore, which had been arranged by its wearer to suggest his war and the strength he'd mustered to face its consequences but which instead communicated haughtiness, a cryptic superiority not only to the court but to the prospect of death the court confronted him with. The face in the hand mirror was none other than the face he had worn since the war had caused him to look inward, and though he exerted himself to rearrange it – because this face was a burden to wear – it remained his, unalterable finally. He knew himself privately to be guilty of murder, to have murdered men in the course of war, and it was this guilt – he knew no other word – that lived in him perpetually and that he exerted himself not to communicate. Yet the exertion itself communicated guilt, and he

could see no way to stop it. He could not change how his face arranged itself while he sat with his hands on the defendant's table with his back
40 to his fellow islanders. In his face, he knew, was his fate, as Nels Gudmundsson had asserted at the start of things: 'There are facts,' he said, 'and the jurors listen to them, but even more, they watch you. They watch to see what happens to your face, how it changes when witnesses speak. For them, at bottom, the answer is in how you appear
45 in the courtroom, what you look like, how you act.'

He liked this man, Nels Gudmundsson. He had begun to like him on the September afternoon when he first appeared at his cell door carrying a folded chessboard beneath his arm and a Havana cigar box full of chess pieces. He'd offered Kabuo a cigar from his shirt pocket, lit his
50 own, then brought two candy bars out of the box and dropped them on the bunk beside Kabuo without acknowledging that he had done so. It was his way of being charitable.

'I'm Nels Gudmundsson, your attorney,' he said. 'I've been appointed by the court to represent you. I – '
55 'I didn't do it,' Kabuo had said. 'I'm not guilty of anything.'

'Look,' said Nels. 'I'll tell you what. We can worry about that later, all right? I've been trying to find someone with the free time to play chess for fifty years now, even more. Seems to me you just might be the fellow.'

'I am,' said Kabuo. 'But – '
60 'You were in the service,' said Nels. 'My guess is you play a mean game of chess. Chess, checkers, rummy, bridge, hearts, dominoes, cribbage. And what about solitaire?' added Nels. 'Solitaire might be the thing for you in here.'

---

2 **rank** (adj): (of smell) strong and unpleasant   9 **haunted**: believed to be visited by ghosts   13 **detachment**: state of not being involved in sth. in an emotional or personal way   15 **sacrifice sth.**: etwas opfern   17 **defiant**: openly refusing to obey sb./sth.   19 **palpitations** (pl): condition in which your heart beats very quickly
21 **crumble**: begin to fail or get weaker or to come to an end   22 **insulting**: make sb. feel offended   24–25 **to a fault**: to such a degree that it is too much
25 **humble**: showing you do not think that you are as important as other people
29 **haughtiness** ['hɔːtiˌnəs]: Hochmut   34 **unalterable**: impossible to change
36 **perpetual**: continuous   37 **exertion**: (hier) Anstrengung   44 **at bottom**: im Grunde   49 **chess piece**: Schachfigur   52 **charitable**: wohltätig   60 **mean** (adj, infml, esp. AE): skilful (at sports or games)

'Never liked solitaire,' Kabuo answered. 'Besides, a guy who starts playing solitaire in jail is just asking to get depressed.'

'Never thought of that,' said Nels. 'We'll have to get you out of here, that's all there is to it.' He smiled.

Kabuo nodded. 'Can you?'

'They're not budging just now on anything, Kabuo. You're here until your trial, I think.'

'There shouldn't even *be* a trial,' said Kabuo.

'Alvin Hooks would disagree,' said Nels. 'He's putting his case together. He's serious about murder in the first degree, and he's serious about asking for the death penalty. We should be, too – we should get serious. We have a lot of work to do, you and I. But first, what about chess?'

The death penalty, Kabuo said to himself. He was a Buddhist and believed in the laws of karma, so it made sense to him that he might pay for his war murders: everything comes back to you, nothing is accidental. The fear of death grew in him. He thought of Hatsue and of his children and it seemed to him he must be exiled from them – because he felt for them so much love – in order to pay his debts to the dead he had left on the ground in Italy.

'You sit on the bunk,' he said to Nels, trying to calm himself. 'We'll draw up the nightstand for the board.'

'Fine,' Nels said. 'Just fine.'

The old man's hands fumbled setting up the chess pieces. They were darkly spotted, and the skin, translucent in appearance, was prominently veined.

'White or black?' Nels asked.

'Advantages to both,' replied Kabuo. 'You choose, Mr. Gudmundsson.'

'Most players prefer to open,' Nels said. 'Why is that, anyway?'

'Must see some advantage in going first,' said Kabuo. 'Must believe in taking the offensive.'

'And you don't?' inquired Nels.

Kabuo took up a pawn in each hand and put them behind his back. 'Best way to settle the problem,' he said. 'This way, all you have to do is guess.' He held his closed fists in front of Nels.

'Left,' the old man said. 'If we're going to leave it to chance, left is as good as right. They're both the same, this way.'

'You don't prefer it?' asked Kabuo. 'You prefer white? Or black?'

'Open your hands,' Nels answered, and tucked his cigar in between his teeth high up on the right side – dentures, it occurred to Kabuo.

As it turned out, the first move was Nels's. As it turned out, the old man never castled. He had no interest in an endgame. His strategy was to give up points for position, to give up men in the early going in return for an undefeatable board posture. He'd won, even though Kabuo could see what he was doing. There was no fiddling around. The game, quite suddenly, was over.

Kabuo set the hand mirror on his tray of food now and ate half of the lime gelatin. He chewed down his carrot sticks and what remained of his sandwich, then poured out the tin cup of milk and filled it twice with water. He washed his hands, removed his shoes, and lay down on the jail bed. After a while he stood up again and turned the lightbulb in its socket. Then in the darkness the accused man lay down again, shut his eyes, and dreamed.

He dreamed without sleeping – daydreams, waking dreams, as had come to him often in his jail cell. In this manner he escaped from its walls and roamed in freedom along San Piedro's wood paths, along the verges of its autumn pastures crusted over with skins of hoarfrost; he followed in his mind certain remnants of trail that gave out suddenly in blackberry riots or in fields of unexpected Scotch broom. In his thoughts were vestiges of old skid roads and forgotten farm paths that bled into vales of ghost fern and hollows filled with skunk cabbage. Sometimes these trails faded at mud bluffs overlooking the sea; other times they wandered down onto beaches where thick cedars, sapling alders, and

---

6 **budge**: move slightly   14 **karma**: (in Buddhism and Hinduism) the sum of sb.'s good and bad actions in one of their lives, believed to decide what will happen to them in the next life   24 **translucent**: allowing light to pass through, but not transparent   32 **pawn**: chess piece of the smallest size and least value   39 **dentures**: artificial teeth   41 **castle** (v): (at chess) move the castle or rook (= Turm) close to the king in order to cover it (= decken)   **endgame**: final stage of a game of chess   44 **fiddle around**: (here) spend much time on playing the game instead of on winning it   55 **roam**: (here) walk or travel around an area without any definite aim or direction   56 **pasture**: Weide(land)   **hoarfrost**: Raureif   58 **riot**: a mass of individual plants of the same kind spreading on the forest floor   **Scotch broom** Ginster   59 **skid road**: road made of logs (= Pfahl) on which freshly cut wood can be transported   **bleed into sth.**: (hier) in etwas hineinfließen   60 **skunk cabbage**: ill-smelling swamp plant of western North America

vine maples, toppled by winter tides, lay with the tips of their desiccated branches buried in sand and gravel. The waves brought seaweed in and draped it across the downed trees in thick oozing skeins. Then his mind moved outward, and Kabuo was at sea again, his net set, the salmon running, and he was standing on the foredeck of the *Islander* with the breeze in his face, the phosphorus in the water brilliant before him, the whitecaps silver in the moonlight. From his bunk in the Island County Jail he felt the sea again and the swells under his boat as it rode over the foam; with his eyes shut he smelled cold salt and the odor of salmon in the hold, heard the net winch working and the deep note of the engine. Rafts of seabirds rose off the water, making way in the first misty light with the *Islander* bound for home on a cool morning, half a thousand kings in her hold, the whine of wind in her rigging. At the cannery he held each fish in his hands before tossing it up and over the side – lambent chinooks, lithe and sleek, as long as his arm and weighing a fourth what he did, slick, glassy eyes held open. He could feel them in his hands again while overhead the gulls flew tangents. When he put off and motored for the docks the gulls followed on high with their breasts opened to the wind. Then he was amid a flock of gulls while he swabbed the deck of the *Islander*. He heard their squawking and watched them circle low, angling for scraps, while Marlin Teneskold or William Gjovaag shot at them with a side-by-side so that the gulls settled out on the water. The gun's report echoed from the hills of Amity Harbor, and then Kabuo remembered what he had missed this year: the birch and alder going golden, the red autumn hue of the vine maples, the rust and russet colors of October, the cider press, pumpkins, and baskets of young zucchini squash. The smell of dying leaves in the motionless gray morning as he shambled up onto the porch after a night's fishing, and the full, fine growth in the cedar trees. The *scritching* sound of leaves underfoot; leaves mashed into paste after rains. He'd *missed* fall rains, the water dripping along the knobs of his spine and mixing with the sea spray in his hair – things he hadn't known he'd miss.

In August he'd taken his family to Lanheedron Island. They'd tied off to a float, and he'd rowed them up onto Sugar Sand Beach in the skiff. His daughters stood in the surf and poked at jellyfish with sticks and collected sand dollars; then they followed the beach creek up through a dell, Kabuo carrying the baby on his right arm, until they came to a waterfall, a cascade tumbling from a wall of moss. They ate their lunch there in the shadows of the hemlocks and gathered salmonberries. Hatsue found under birch trees a half-dozen destroying angels and pointed them out to her daughters. They were pure white and lovely, she explained, but fatal to eat. She pointed out, too, the maidenhair fern nearby; the black stems, she said, retained their shine in a pine needle basket's weave.

He'd admired her fully on that day. She collected the stems of wild ginger for seasoning rice and yarrow leaves for tea. On the beach she dug butter clams with a pointed stick, raking an arc in front of her. She found sea glass and a fossilized crab leg embedded in a concretion. She doused the baby with seawater. The girls helped Kabuo gather beach wood for a fire when evening came up. At the last of dusk they launched their skiff again. His oldest daughter hooked a true cod in the kelp beds off Lanheedron. He filleted it on the deck while Hatsue caught another on a hand line. They ate at sea – the cod, the clams, ginger rice, yarrow tea. His middle daughter and the baby slept on his bunk, his oldest daughter manned the wheel. Kabuo and Hatsue went forward. He stood with his chest against her back and his hands in the rigging until the lights of Amity Harbor came up to the south, and then he went in and repositioned the *Islander* in order to take the channel head on. His daughter leaned

1 **desiccated**: completely dry 3 **ooze** (v): produce liquid from inside **skein**: Strang, Geflecht 8 **swell**: movement of the sea when it rises and falls without the waves breaking 10 **winch**: Winde 11 **raft**: large number or amount 13 **king**: kind of salmon **rigging**: ropes that support the masts and sails of a boat or ship 15 **lambent**: (hier) glitzernd **chinook**: kind of salmon **sleek**: smooth and shiny 16 **slick**: glatt, schlüpfrig 17 **fly tangents**: (hier) kreisen, umherschweifen **put off**: (hier) ablegen 19 **swab sth.**: etwas schrubben 23 **report** (n): sound of an explosion or of a gun being fired 24 **birch**: Birke 28 **shamble**: walk in an awkward or lazy way 33 **tie (sth.) off**: (here) attach sth., esp. a boat, to a fixed object with a rope 34 **float** (n): Floß **skiff**: kleines Ruderboot 35 **surf**: Brandung **jellyfish**: Qualle 36 **sand dollar**: kind of flattened disklike sea urchin (= Seeigel) 40 **destroying angel**: Knollenblätterpilz 42 **maidenhair fern**: Frauenhaarfarn 46 **ginger**: Ingwer **season** (v): add salt, pepper, etc. to food in order to give it more flavour **yarrow**: Scharfgarbe 48 **sea glass**: pieces of broken glass that have been shaped by water and sand so that they have a very smooth surface **concretion**: (here) stone 48–49 **douse sb. with sth.**: pour a lot of liquid over sb. 50 **launch sth.**: (here) put a ship or boat into the water 55 **man sth.**: be in charge of sth.

against him after he took the wheel from her, and he came into the harbor that way at midnight, the girl's head against his arm.

Then he remembered strawberry fields from before Manzanar and he was in them as he'd always been, a sea of strawberries, rows and rows, a labyrinth of runners as intricate as a network of arteries feeding on the surface of a dozen farms he knew from childhood. He was in these mounded rows, stooped and picking with the sun on his neck, low against the land in a sea of green and red with the smell of the earth and its berries rising like a mist, filling by the labor of his hands the twelve woven pine baskets in his caddy. He saw his wife before she'd married him, he saw her picking at Ichikawas' farm, how he'd come toward her carrying his caddy and as if by accident, by happenstance, how she hadn't seen him coming, intent on her work, bent to it, but at the last minute lifted her black eyes, lissome as ever, continuously picking – berries lay gently like red gems between her fingers – and while she met his eyes fed one of her woven pine baskets, three of which already lay full on the caddy, mounded over with ripened fruit. He'd squatted down across from her and, picking, took her in – how she squatted with her chin near her kneecaps, her hair woven tautly into a long, thick rope, the sweat against her forehead and the tendrils of hair that had escaped from their arrangement – loose strands fell across her cheeks and nose. She was sixteen. Low to the ground, folded together with her breasts against her thighs, she wore woven sandals and a red muslin summer dress, its narrow straps running over her shoulders. He saw again the strength of her legs, the brown of her ankles and calves, the suppleness of her spine, the film of sweat at her throat. Then it was evening, and he'd left the South Beach wood path to look at her home of worn cedar slats and across the fields to where she lived: fields circumscribed by tall cedar trees and lit by spindly moonlight. A kerosene lantern flickered orange in the window of Hatsue's home, her door stood open, ajar ten inches, and an angle of lantern light spilled across her porch. Crickets and night toads, the brattle of a dog, laundry billowing on a line against the night breeze. And again he breathed in the green in the strawberry runners, the rain in the cedar duff, and the salt water. She padded toward him with a bucket full of kitchen scraps, her sandals squeaking, moving toward the compost heap, and on her return trip she'd passed between the rows of raspberries. He watched while she held her hair

back with one hand, the other moving in search of the sweetest fruit, grazing among the canes. Her heels lifted from the sandals now and
40 then. She slid the berries in between her lips, still holding her hair, the canes rebounding in quiet arcs when she freed the berry caps from their cores. He stood watching and imagined that if he kissed her that night the taste of the raspberries would be cool in his mouth.

He saw her just as he had seen her in history class, a pencil between
45 her teeth, one hand laid against the nape of her neck, lost behind her effusive hair. She walked through the halls with her books pressed against her breasts, in pleated skirt, argyle sweater, white bobby socks folded down crisply above the polished onyx buckles of her shoes. She looked at him and then away again quickly, saying nothing when he
50 passed by.

He remembered Manzanar, the dust in the barracks, in the tarpapered shacks and cafeteria; even the bread tasted gritty. They'd worked tending eggplants and lettuces in the camp garden. They'd been paid little, the hours were long, they'd been told it was their duty to work hard. He and
55 Hatsue spoke of little things at first, then of the San Piedro fields they'd left behind and the smell of ripening strawberries. He had begun to love her, to love more than just her beauty and grace, and when he saw that in their hearts they shared the same dream he felt a great certainty about her. They kissed in the back of a crew truck coming into camp one
60 night, and the warm wet taste of her, however brief, brought her down for him from the world of angels and into the world of human beings. In this way his love deepened. Working in the gardens he would pass her

5 **intricate**: having a lot of different parts and small details   12 **happenstance** (fml): chance   14 **lissome**: thin and attractive   15 **gem**: precious stone   18 **take sb. in**: look closely at sb.   20 **tendril** (fml): (hier) Locke   25 **calf**: (hier) Wade   **suppleness**: Geschmeidigkeit   29 **spindly**: (here) weak   30 **ajar**: slightly open   31 **cricket**: Grille   32 **brattle**: rattling noise   **billow** (v): fill with air   34 **duff**: decaying leaves and branches covering a forest floor   **pad** (v): walk with quiet steps   39 **graze**: touch sth. lightly while passing it   41 **rebound** (v) [rɪˈbaʊnd]: bounce back   42 **core**: hard central part of a fruit   46 **effusive**: (hier) üppig   47 **pleated skirt**: Faltenrock   **argyle**: knitted pattern of diamond shapes on a plain background   **bobby socks**: short white socks worn by girls or young women with a dress or skirt   48 **crisp**: (here) fresh and clean   51 **tarpapered**: mit Teerpappe beschlagen   52 **gritty**: sandig   53 **eggplant** (AE): Aubergine   **lettuce**: Blattsalat   59 **crew truck**: Mannschaftswagen

by and, for a moment, slide one hand around her waist. She would squeeze his hand between her fingers, which had grown more callused and hard at Manzanar, and he would squeeze back, and they would return to their weeding. The wind blew desert dust in their faces and dried their skin and turned their hair to wire.

He remembered the expression on Hatsue's face when he told her he had enlisted. It was not the being gone, she said – though the being gone was a horrible thing – it was more that he might not ever return, or that he might return not himself. Kabuo had not made promises to her – he could not say if he was coming back, or if he would come back the same man. There was this matter of honor, he'd explained to her, and he had no choice but to accept the duty the war required of him. At first she had refused to understand this and had insisted that duty was less important than love and she hoped Kabuo felt the same way. But he could not bring himself to agree with this; love went deep and meant life itself, but honor could not be turned from. He was not who he was if he didn't go to war, and would not be worthy of her.

She turned from him and tried to stay away, and for three days they didn't speak. At last he'd come to her, at dusk, in the gardens, and said that he loved her more than anything in the world and that he hoped only that she would understand why it was he had to leave. He asked for nothing else from her, only this acknowledgment of who he was, how his soul was shaped. Hatsue stood with her long-handled hoe and said that she had learned from Mrs. Shigemura that character was always destiny. He would have to do what he must do, and she would have to do the same.

He'd nodded and exerted himself to show nothing. Then he turned and walked between the rows of eggplants. He was twenty yards off when she called his name and asked if he would marry her before leaving. 'Why do you want to marry me?' he asked, and her answer came back, 'To hold a part of you.' She dropped the hoe and walked the twenty yards to hold him in her arms. 'It's my character, too,' she whispered. 'It's my destiny now to love you.'

It had been, he saw now, a war marriage, hurried into because there was no choice and because both of them felt the rightness of it. They had not known each other more than a few months, though he had always admired her from a distance, and it seemed to him, when he

thought about it, that their marriage had been meant to happen. His
parents approved, and hers approved, and he was happy to leave for the
war in the knowledge that she was waiting for him and would be there
when he returned. And then he had returned, a murderer, and her fear
that he would no longer be himself was realized.

He remembered, too, his father's face, and the sword his father kept
inside a wooden chest in the days before Pearl Harbor. A *katana* made by
the swordsmith Masamune, it had been in the Miyamoto family, it was
said, for six centuries. His father kept it sheathed and rolled in cloth, an
undecorated and highly useful weapon. Its beauty lay in its simplicity, the
plainness of its curve; even its wooden scabbard was spare and plain. His
father had taken it, along with other things – his wooden *kendo* practice
swords, his *sageo*, his *obi*, his *naginata*, his *hakama* pants, his *bokken* – and
buried them one night in a strawberry field, laid them carefully wrapped
in a hole along with the dynamite he'd used to clear stumps, a case full of
books and scrolls written in Japanese, and a photograph taken of Kabuo
at the San Piedro Japanese Community Center dressed in the feudal costume of a *bugeisha* and wielding a *kendo* stick.

Kabuo's training at *kendo* had begun when he was seven. His father
had taken him one Saturday to the community center hall, where a *dojo*
had been established in a corner of the gym. They knelt before an alcove
at the back of the room and contemplated a shelf on which small bowls
of uncooked rice had been neatly arranged. Kabuo learned to bow from
a seated position. While he sat on his heels his father explained softly

---

23 **hoe**: Hacke   44 *katana*: traditional Japanese sword   46 **sheathe sth.**: put a
knife or sword into its cover   48 **scabbard**: cover or sheath for a sword that is made
of leather or metal   50 *sageo*: cord made of silk or cotton that is used to tie a
sword's sheath to the traditional costume of a samurai   *obi*: sash worn by practitioners of Japanese martial arts   *naginata*: pole weapon of the samurai with a
wooden shaft and a curved blade   *hakama*: type of Japanese clothing traditionally
worn by men that resembles a wide, pleated skirt which is tied at the waist and falls
to the ankles   *bokken*: wooden sword used for training Japanese martial arts
53 **scroll** (n): long roll of paper for writing on   54 **feudal**: (here) traditionally worn
by Japanese noblemen, i.e. the samurai   55 *bugeisha*: Japanese word for 'martial
artist', i.e. sb. who practises martial arts   **wield sth.**: hold sth., ready to use it as a
weapon   57 *dojo*: training hall for martial arts   58 **alcove**: area in a room that is
formed by part of a wall being built farther back than the rest of the wall

the meaning of *zenshin*, which the boy understood to mean a constant awareness of potential danger. His father finished by repeating the word twice – '*zenshin! zenshin!*' – then took down a wooden pole from the wall and, before Kabuo knew what had happened, slammed him with it in the solar plexus.

'*Zenshin!*' said Zenhichi, while the boy caught his breath. 'Didn't you say you understood?'

His father said that if he was to learn *kendo* more would be expected of him than of the average person. Did he wish to learn anyway? The choice was his. He should take some time to consider it.

When Kabuo was eight his father put a weapon in his hands for the first time – a *bokken*. They stood in the strawberry fields early one July morning just after picking season was finished. The *bokken*, a curved piece of cherry wood three feet long, had been Kabuo's great-grandfather's, a man who had been a samurai before the Meiji Restoration and later – after the wearing of swords was outlawed – a farmer of government rice lands on Kyushu for ten days before he joined two hundred other rebellious samurai in Kumamoto. They formed themselves into the League of the Divine Tempest and attacked an imperial garrison with swords aloft, having fasted for three days. Its defenders, wielding rifles, killed all but twenty-nine with their opening volley; the survivors committed suicide on the battlefield, including Kabuo's great-grandfather.

'You come from a family of samurai,' Kabuo's father said to him in Japanese. 'Your great-grandfather died because he could not stop being one. It was his bad fortune to live at a time when the samurai were no longer necessary. He could not adapt to this, and his anger at the world overwhelmed him. I remember what an angry man he was, Kabuo. He lived for revenge against the Meiji. When they told him he could no longer wear his sword in public he conspired to kill men he hardly knew – government officials, men with families who lived near us, who were kind to us, whose children we played with. He became irrational in his behavior and spoke of purifying himself in such a manner that he would afterward be invulnerable to the Meiji rifles. He was always gone at night. We didn't know where he went. My grandmother bit her nails. She argued with him when he came home in the mornings, but he wouldn't change his ways or explain. His eyes were red, his face rigid.

He sat eating from his bowl in silence, wearing his sword in the house. It was said that he had joined other samurai who had been displaced by the Meiji. They roamed the roads disguised, swords in hand, killing government officials. They were bandits, thieves, and renegades. My grandfather – I remember this – was happy to hear of Okubo Toshimichi's assassination, the man who had been responsible for the confiscation of his master's castle and the destruction of his master's army. He smiled, showed his teeth, and drank.

'My grandfather was an expert swordsman,' Zenhichi had explained, 'but his anger overwhelmed him in the end. It is ironic, because how often did he tell me, when I was your age and he was a contented and peaceful man, of the kind of sword a man should wield? *"The sword that gives life, not the sword that takes life, is the goal of the samurai,"* my grandfather said then. The goal of the sword is to give life, not to take it.

'You can be very good with the *bokken* if you concentrate,' said Kabuo's father. 'You have it in you. You have only to decide to learn – now, when you are eight.'

'I want to,' replied Kabuo.

'I know you do,' his father said. 'But look, your hands.'

Kabuo adjusted them.

'Your feet,' said his father. 'The front turned in more. Too much weight on the back.'

They began to work on the vertical stroke, moving along between the strawberries, the boy advancing, the man retreating, the two of them together in it. 'The *bokken* strikes,' Kabuo's father said. 'The hips and stomach cut. You must tighten the stomach muscles as the stroke

1 **zenshin**: state of continuous alertness in which the martial artist is always ready for an attack   15 **samurai**: (in the past) member of a powerful military class in Japan   **Meiji Restoration** (1866–1869): chain of events that led to a change in Japan's political and social structure (e.g. land of Japanese noblemen was repossessed and their military privileges were abolished) and marked the beginning of the rule of emperor Meiji (1867–1912)   16 **outlaw sth.** ['--]: make sth. illegal   19 **imperial**: kaiserlich   **garrison**: Garnison   20 **aloft** (fml): high in the air   **fast** (v): fasten   21 **volley**: Salve   29 **Meiji**: (here) soldiers of the emperor Meiji   41 **renegade**: Abtrünniger   42 **Okubo Toshimichi** (1830–1878): Japanese nobleman and supporter of the Meiji restoration, later Minister of the Interior under emperor Meiji   43 **assassination**: murder of an important or famous person, esp. for political reasons

advances. No, you're locking your knees – they must give when you strike. Elbow soft, too, or there is no follow-through, the *bokken* is cut off from the power of the body. Hips sink, knees and elbows go soft, stomach is hard, cut, turn, again, strike …'

Kabuo's father showed him how to hold the wooden sword so that the wrists were flexible and liberated. An hour went by, and then it was time for field work and they put the *bokken* away. Thereafter, each morning, Kabuo practiced his *kendo* strokes – the vertical slash that would split a man's head down the bridge of the nose, leaving one eye on each side, the skull cleaved into two parts; the four diagonal strokes – from left and right, upward and downward – that would cleave a man beneath a rib or disjoin an arm deftly; the horizontal stroke swinging in from the left that could sever a man just above the hips; and, finally, the most common of *kendo* strokes, a horizontal thrust a right-handed man could propel with great force against the left side of his enemy's head.

He practiced these until they were natural to him, part of who he was, the *bokken* an extension of his hands. By the time he was sixteen there was no one any longer at the community center who could defeat him, not even the half-dozen grown men on the island for whom *kendo* was a serious hobby, not even his father, who acknowledged his son's triumph without shame. It was said by many in the Kendo Club that Zenhichi, despite his years, remained the superior practitioner, the more pure between father and son, but that the boy, Kabuo, had the stronger fighting spirit and a greater willingness to draw on his dark side in order to achieve a final victory.

It was only after he'd killed four Germans that Kabuo saw how right they were, how they had seen deeply into his heart with the clarity of older people. He was a warrior, and this dark ferocity had been passed down in the blood of the Miyamoto family and he himself was fated to carry it into the next generation. The story of his great-grandfather, the samurai madman, was his own story, too, he saw now. Sometimes, when he felt his anger rising because he had lost his family's strawberry land, he gathered it up into the pit of his gut and stood in the yard with his *kendo* stick rehearsing the black choreography of his art. He saw only darkness after the war, in the world and in his own soul, everywhere but in the smell of strawberries, in the good scent of his wife and of his three children, a boy and two girls, three gifts. He felt he did not deserve for a moment the happiness his family brought to him, so that late at night, when he couldn't sleep, he imagined that he would write them a note explicating his sin completely. He would leave them and go to suffer alone, and his unhappiness would overwhelm his anger. The violence might at last die out of him and set him free to contemplate his destiny and his next life on the Great Wheel.

Sitting where he sat now, accused of the murder of Carl Heine, it seemed to him he'd found the suffering place he'd fantasized and desired. For Kabuo Miyamoto was suffering in his cell from the fear of his imminent judgment. Perhaps it was now his fate to pay for the lives he had taken in anger. Such was the nature of cause and effect, such was the impermanence of all things. What a mystery life was! Everything was conjoined by mystery and fate, and in his darkened cell he meditated on this and it became increasingly clear to him. Impermanence, cause and effect, suffering, desire, the precious nature of life. Every sentient being straining and pushing at the shell of identity and distinctness. He had the time and the clarity about suffering to embark on the upward path of liberation, which would take him many lives to follow. He would have to gain as much ground as possible and accept that the mountain of his violent sins was too large to climb in this lifetime. He would still be climbing it in the next and the next, and his suffering inevitably would multiply.

---

1 **give**: (here) bend   8 **slash** (n): sharp movement made with a knife or weapon   10 **cleave sth./sb.**: split or cut sth./sb. into two parts   13 **sever sb./sth.** (fml) ['sevər]: cut sb./sth. into two pieces   28 **ferocity**: violence   34 **rehearse sth.**: practice sth., esp. a play, piece of music, etc., in preparation for a public performance   40 **explicate sth.** (fml): explain sth.in a lot of detail   43 **Great Wheel**: (concept in Buddhism) continuous cycle of birth, decay and death in which all beings in the universe take part   47 **imminent**: likely to happen very soon   49 **impermanence**: Unbeständigkeit   50 **conjoin sth.**: join sth.together   52 **sentient**: able to see or feel sth. through the senses   53 **strain** (v): make an effort to do sth., using all your mental or physical strength   **distinctness**: individuality, qualities that make sb. different from other people

Chapter 12

Outside the wind blew steadily from the north, driving snow against the courthouse. By noon three inches had settled on the town, a snow so ethereal it could hardly be said to have settled at all; instead it swirled like some icy fog, like the breath of ghosts, up and down Amity Harbor's streets – powdery dust devils, frosted puffs of ivory cloud, spiraling tendrils of white smoke. By noon the smell of the sea was eviscerated, the sight of it mistily depleted, too; one's field of vision narrowed in close, went blurry and snowbound, fuzzy and opaque, the sharp scent of frost burned in the nostrils of those who ventured out of doors. The snow flew up from their rubber boots as they struggled, heads down, toward Petersen's Grocery. When they looked out into the whiteness of the world the wind flung it sharply at their narrowed eyes and foreshortened their view of everything.

Ishmael Chambers was out walking aimlessly in the snow, admiring it and remembering. The trial of Kabuo Miyamoto had brought that world back for him.

Inside their cedar tree, for nearly four years, he and Hatsue had held one another with the dreamy contentedness of young lovers. With their coats spread against a cushion of moss they'd stayed as long as they could after dusk and on Saturday and Sunday afternoons. The tree produced a cedar perfume that permeated their skin and clothes. They would enter, breathe deeply, then lie down and touch each other – the heat of it and the cedar smell, the privacy and the rain outside, the slippery softness of their lips and tongues inspired in them the temporary illusion that the rest of the world had disappeared; there was nobody and nothing but the two of them. Ishmael pressed himself against Hatsue while they held each other, and Hatsue pressed back, her hips leaving the moss, her legs open beneath her skirt. He felt her breasts and grazed the waistband of her underwear, and she stroked his belly and chest and back. Sometimes when he was walking home through the forest Ishmael would stop in some lonely place and, because he had no choice in the matter, take himself in his hand. He would think about Hatsue while he touched himself. He would shut his eyes and lean his head against a tree; afterward he felt better and worse.

Sometimes at night he would squeeze his eyes shut and imagine how it might be to marry her. It did not seem so farfetched to him that they might move to some other place in the world where this would be possible. He liked to think about being with Hatsue in some place like Switzerland or Italy or France. He gave his whole soul to love; he allowed himself to believe that his feelings for Hatsue had been somehow preordained. He had been meant to meet her on the beach as a child and then to pass his life with her. There was no other way it could be.

Inside their cedar tree they spoke of everything in the intense and overwrought manner of teenagers and he found that she had many moods. There were times when she went cold and silent and he felt her distance from him so completely that it seemed impossible to reach her. Even when he held her it seemed to him there was a place in her heart he couldn't get to. At times he worked himself up to discussing this, gradually revealing to her how it hurt him to feel there was a part of her love she withheld. Hatsue denied that this was so and explained to him that her emotional reserve was something she couldn't help. She had been carefully trained by her upbringing, she said, to avoid effusive displays of feeling, but this did not mean her heart was shallow. Her silence, she said, would express something if he would learn to listen to it. Yet his suspicion that he loved more deeply than she did nevertheless remained with him, and he worried about it perpetually.

Hatsue, he found, had a religious side he had only sensed when they'd been younger. He drew her out in conversation on this matter,

---

3 **ethereal** [ɪˈθɪriəl] (fml): extremely light   5 **ivory** (adj): elfenbeinfarben
6 **eviscerate sth.** [ɪˈvɪsəreɪt]: (here) make sth. vanish   7 **deplete sth.**: reduce sth.
8 **blurry**: not clear   **snowbound**: (here) restricted because a lot of snow has fallen
fuzzy: not clear in shape   **opaque**: not clear enough to see through or allow light
through   9 **venture** [ˈventʃər]: go somewhere although you know that it might be
dangerous or unpleasant   21 **permeate**: spread to every part of an object or a place
35 **farfetched**: very difficult to believe   40 **preordained**: already decided or
planned by God or by fate   43 **overwrought**: very worried and upset; excited in a
nervous way   47 **work yourself up**: make yourself reach a state of great excitement, anger, etc.   51 **effusive**: showing much or too much emotion   52 **shallow**:
(of a person) not showing serious thought or feelings about sth.

and she told him how she tried to keep in mind certain basic articles of her faith. All of life was impermanent, for example – a thing she thought about every day. It was important for a person to act carefully, for every action, Hatsue explained, had consequences for the soul's future. She confessed to experiencing a moral anguish over meeting him so secretly and deceiving her mother and father. It seemed to her certain that she would suffer from the consequences of it, that no one could maintain such deceit for so long without paying for it somehow. Ishmael argued at length about this, asserting that God could not possibly view their love as something wrong or evil. God, replied Hatsue, was personal; only she could know what God wanted from her. Motive, she added, was very important: what was her motive in concealing from her parents the time she spent with Ishmael? This was the question that worried her most: determining for herself her motive.

Ishmael, at school, feigned detachment in her presence and ignored her in the casual way she gradually taught him to use. Hatsue was a master of the art of false preoccupation; she would pass him in the hallway, in her plaid blouse with its neat tucks, puffed sleeves, and ruffled collar, with a bow in her hair, pleats in her skirt, and books hiked up against her breast, and move on with an apparently artless indifference that in the beginning painfully astonished him. How was it possible for her to feign such coldness without feeling it at the same time? By degrees he learned to enjoy these encounters, though his indifference always appeared more studied than hers and he was always anxious, in a barely concealed way, to meet her gaze. He even said hello to her now and again as one element in his pretense. 'Hard test,' he'd say at the end of a class. 'How'd you do, anyway?'

'I don't know. I didn't study enough.'

'Did you do the essay for Sparling?'

'I tried. It's about a page long.'

'Mine, too. A little longer.'

He would move on, collect his books, and leave the room with Sheridan Knowles or Don Hoyt or Denny Horbach.

At the Strawberry Festival in 1941 he'd watched while the mayor of Amity Harbor had crowned Hatsue Strawberry Princess. The mayor had placed a tiara on her head and hung a sash over her left shoulder. Hatsue and four other girls made a promenade through the crowd and tossed strawberry-flavored candy to the children. Ishmael's father – owner, publisher, editor, chief reporter, photographer, and printer of the *San Piedro Review* – had a special interest in these proceedings. Year after year they provided a lead story, complete with a portrait of the crowned and comely maiden, candids of picnicking families ('The Maltons of Protection Point enjoy Saturday's strawberry festival'), and a beneficent editorial or boilerplate column approving the efforts of local organizers ('... Ed Bailey, Lois Dunkirk, and Carl Heine, Sr., without whom none of this would have been possible ...'). Arthur wandered the picnic grounds in bow tie and suspenders, a porkpie hat pulled low over his forehead and the enormous weight of his camera slung from a thick leather thong around his neck. Ishmael stood beside him while he photographed Hatsue – he winked at her when his father put one eye to the camera, and she gave back the faint trace of a smile.

'Neighbor girl,' his father said. 'South Beach ought to be proud.'

He followed his father that afternoon, and they joined in the tug-of-war and the three-legged race. The strawberry floats, festooned with staghorn ferns, zinnias, and forget-me-nots – and with the royal court of the Strawberry Festival draped theatrically under cherry sprays and spruce boughs trained to wire guy lines – passed like ships before the somber eyes of the Strawberry Festival Association, which included the mayor, the chairman of the chamber of commerce, the fire chief, and

---

5 **anguish** (fml): extreme pain, mental suffering or unhappiness   8 **deceit**: dishonest behavior that is intended to make sb. believe sth. that is not true   15 **feign sth.**: etwas vortäuschen   17 **preoccupation**: state of thinking about sth. or being busy doing sth., esp. while ignoring everything else   18 **plaid**: kariert   **tuck** (n): (here) decorative fold in textiles   **puffed sleeves**: Puffärmel   19 **bow** (n): (hier) Schleife   20 **artless**: simple, natural and honest   24 **studied**: deliberate and carefully planned   36 **tiara**: piece of jewellery like a small crown   42 **comely**: attractive   **candid** (n): photograph taken without the persons in it knowing that they are being photographed   43 **beneficent** (fml): generous; showing kindness   44 **boilerplate** (AE): text using standard expressions that can be reused and adpated to new contexts again and again   **column**: Kolumne   48 **thong**: narrow strip of leather   53–54 **tug-of-war**: Tauziehen   54 **float** (n): (here) large vehicle on which people dressed in special costumes are carried in a festival   **festoon sth. with sth. else**: decorate sth. with flowers, colored paper, etc.   55 **staghorn fern**: kind of fern   **zinnia**: brightly colored garden flower   56 **spray** (n): small branch of a tree or plant   57 **bough**: branch of a tree   **guy lines** = guy wire   58 **somber** (AE): (here) serious

Arthur Chambers. Again Ishmael stood beside his father while Hatsue, on board her float, passed by waving to everybody majestically with her crepe paper scepter in hand. Ishmael waved back and laughed.

September came; they were high school seniors. A gray green stillness settled into things, and the summer people left for their city homes again: soft overcast, night fog, low mists in the dips between hills, road mud, vacant beaches, empty clamshells scattered among rocks, silent shops folded in on themselves. By October San Piedro had slipped off its summer reveler's mask to reveal a torpid, soporific dreamer whose winter bed was made of wet green moss. Cars slumped along the mud and gravel roads at twenty or thirty miles an hour like sluggish beetles beneath the overhanging trees. The Seattle people passed into memory and winter savings accounts; stoves were stoked, fires banked, books taken down, quilts mended. The gutters filled with rust-colored pine needles and the pungent effluvium of alder leaves, and the drainpipes splashed with winter rain.

Hatsue told him, one fall afternoon, about her tutelage under Mrs. Shigemura and the directive she'd been given as a girl of thirteen to marry a boy of her own kind, a Japanese boy from a good family. She repeated that it made her unhappy to deceive the world. Her secret life, which she carried with her in the presence of her parents and sisters at every moment, made her feel she had betrayed them in a way that was nothing less than *evil* – there was no other word for it, she told Ishmael. Outside, the rain dripped from the canopy of cedar boughs down into the under-growth of ivy. Hatsue sat with her cheek against her knees, looking out through the opening in the cedar tree, her hair a single braid down her spine. 'It isn't evil,' Ishmael insisted. 'How can this be evil? It wouldn't make any sense for this to be evil. It's the world that's evil, Hatsue,' he added. 'Don't pay it any mind.'

'That isn't so easy,' said Hatsue. 'I lie every day to my family, Ishmael. Sometimes I think I'll go crazy with it. Sometimes I think this can't go on.'

Later they lay side by side against the moss, looking up into the darkened cedar wood with their hands folded behind their heads. 'This can't go on,' whispered Hatsue. 'Don't you worry about that?'

'I know,' answered Ishmael. 'You're right.'

'What will we do? What's the answer?'

'I don't know,' said Ishmael. 'There isn't one, it looks like.'

'I heard a rumor,' Hatsue replied. 'There's a fisherman who claims to have seen a German submarine just off Amity Harbor. A periscope – he followed it for half a mile. Do you think that can be true?'

'No,' said Ishmael. 'It isn't true. People will believe anything – they're scared, I guess. It's just fear, is all. They're afraid.'

'I'm afraid, too,' said Hatsue. 'Everybody's afraid right now.'

'I'm going to be drafted,' answered Ishmael. 'It's something I just have to face.'

They sat in their cedar tree thinking about this, but the war still seemed far away. The war did not disturb them there, and they continued to view themselves as exceedingly fortunate in the particulars of their secret existence. Their absorption in one another, the heat of their bodies, their mingling smells and the movements of their limbs – these things shielded them from certain truths. Yet sometimes at night Ishmael Chambers would lie awake because there was a war on in the world. He would turn his thoughts toward Hatsue then and keep them there until at the verge of sleep the war swam back to spill forth horribly anyway in his dreams.

---

6 **dip** (n): Senke   9 **reveler**: person who is having fun in a noisy way   **torpid**: lethargic   11 **sluggish**: (here) moving more slowly than normal   13 **stoke a stove**: fill a stove with wood or coal   **bank a fire**: (here) pile coal, etc. on a fire so that it burns slowly for a long time   14 **mend sth.**: repair sth.   15 **effluvium**: Ausdünstung   22 **betray sb.**: jdn. verraten/betrügen   29 **pay sth. a mind**: take notice of sth., worry about sth.   39 **periscope**: Sehrohr   48 **particulars** (pl): Umstände   49 **absorption**: state of sb. being very interested in sb./sth. so that they do not pay attention to anything else   54 **spill forth**: (here) come up in a very forceful way

Chapter 13

Hatsue Imada was standing in the foyer of the Amity Harbor Buddhist Chapel, buttoning her coat after services, when Georgia Katanaka's mother told the people gathered there the news about Pearl Harbor. 'It's very bad,' she said. 'A bombing raid. The Japanese air force has bombed everything. It is bad for us, terribly bad. There is nothing else on the radio. Everything is Pearl Harbor.'

Hatsue pulled her lapels more closely around her throat and turned her eyes toward her parents. Her father – he'd been busy helping her mother into her coat – only stood there blinking at Mrs. Katanaka. 'It can't be true,' he said.

'It's true,' she said. 'Find a radio. Just this morning. They bombed Hawaii.'

They stood in the reception room kitchen with the Katanakas, Ichiharas, Sasakis, and Hayashidas and listened to the Bendix sitting on the counter. Nobody spoke – they merely stood there. They listened for ten minutes without moving, their heads down, their ears turned toward the radio. Finally Hatsue's father began to pace and scratch his head and then to rub his chin, long strokes. 'We'd better get home,' he said.

They drove home and listened to the radio again, the five Imada girls and their parents. They kept the radio on all afternoon and late into the evening, too. Now and then the telephone would ring, and Hatsue's father, in Japanese, would discuss matters with Mr. Oshiro or Mr. Nishi. More than a half-dozen times he made calls himself to discuss matters with other people. He would hang up, scratch his head, then return to his seat by the radio.

Mr. Oshiro called again and told Hatsue's father that in Amity Harbor a fisherman named Otto Willets had put up a ladder in front of Shigeru Ichiyama's movie theater and unscrewed the lightbulbs in the marquee. While he was busy at it two other men had steadied the ladder for him and yelled curses at the Ichiyamas, who were not present. Otto Willets and his friends, on discovering this, had driven out to Lundgren Road and sat in front of the Ichiyamas' in a pickup truck, where they pounded on the horn until Shig came out and stood on his porch to see what they wanted. Willets had called Shig a dirty Jap and told him he ought to have smashed every light in the marquee – didn't he know there was a blackout? Shig said no, he hadn't known, he was glad to have been told, he was thankful to the men for unscrewing the marquee bulbs for him. He ignored Otto Willets's insults.

At ten o'clock Mr. Oshiro called again; armed men had posted themselves around Amity Harbor out of fear of a Japanese attack. There were men with shotguns behind logs along the beach just north and south of town. The defense of San Piedro was being organized; there were men meeting right now at the Masons' lodge. The Otsubos had driven by at eight o'clock and seen at least forty cars and pickup trucks parked along the road near the Masons'. Furthermore three or four gill-netters, it was said, had left the harbor to patrol San Piedro's waters. Mr. Oshiro had seen one drifting on the tide, its engine cut, its running lights out, below the bluff near his home on Crescent Bay, a mere silhouette in the night. Hatsue's father – he spoke in Japanese – asked Mr. Oshiro if in fact there were submarines and if the rumors of an invasion of Oregon and California were factual. 'Anything is possible,' answered Mr. Oshiro. 'You should be prepared for anything, Hisao.'

Hatsue's father took his shotgun from the closet and set it in the corner of the living room, unloaded. He got out a box of squirrel loads, too, and slipped three shells into his shirt pocket. Then he turned off every light but one and hung sheets across all the windows. Every few minutes he would leave his place by the radio to pull back a corner of one of these sheets and peer out into the strawberry fields. Then he would go out onto the porch to listen and to search the sky for airplanes. There were none, but on the other hand the sky was mostly overcast and a plane would not easily be seen.

They went to bed; nobody slept. In the morning, on the school bus, Hatsue looked directly at Ishmael Chambers as she passed him on the way to her seat. Ishmael looked back and nodded at her, once. The bus

4 **raid** (n): Angriff   14 **Bendix**: brandname of a radio   28 **marquee**: covered entrance to a theater, movie theater, hotel, etc.   47 **cut an engine**: einen Motor ausschalten   54 **squirrel load**: leichte Schrotmunition   55 **shell**: (hier) Patrone

driver, Ron Lamberson, had an Anacortes newspaper tucked underneath his chair; at each stop he flung the door open with a flourish, then sat reading a section of the paper while the children boarded in silence. 'Here's the deal,' he called over his shoulder as the school bus wound down Mill Run Road. 'The Japanese are attacking all over the place, not just Pearl Harbor. They're making raids all over the Pacific Ocean. Roosevelt is going to declare war today, but what are we gonna do about these attacks? The whole fleet's been destroyed out there, is the deal. And they're arresting Jap traitors in Hawaii and other places – the FBI's in on it. They're getting them down in Seattle right now, in fact. Arresting the spies and everything. The government's frozen Jap bank accounts, too. Main thing, there's a blackout ordered for tonight all up and down the coast. The navy figures there's gonna be an air raid. Don't want to scare you kids, but could be right here – the transmitter station at Agate Point? The navy transmitter station? Your radio is gonna be off the air from seven tonight until tomorrow morning so the Japs don't pick up any signals. Everyone's supposed to put black cloth on their windows and stay inside, stay calm.'

At school, all day, there was nothing but the radio. Two thousand men had been killed. The voices that spoke were cheerless and sober and suggested a barely suppressed urgency. The young people sat with their books unopened and listened to a navy man describe in detail how to extinguish incendiary bombs, and then to reports of further Japanese attacks, Roosevelt's speech before the Congress, an announcement by Attorney General Biddle that Japanese fifth columnists were being arrested in Washington, Oregon, and California. Mr. Sparling became restive and bitter and began to talk in a desolate monotone about his eleven months in France during the Great War. He said that he hoped the boys in his class would take their duty to fight seriously and that furthermore they should consider it an honor to meet the Japs head-on and do the job of paying them back. 'War stinks,' he added. 'But they started it. They bombed Hawaii on a Sunday morning. On a Sunday morning, of all things.' He shook his head, turned up the radio, and leaned morosely against the blackboard with his arms seized against his narrow chest.

By three o'clock that afternoon Ishmael's father had printed and distributed the first war extra in the history of his island newspaper, a one-page edition with a banner headline – ISLAND DEFENSE SET!

Only a few hours after the outbreak of hostilities between Japan and the United States, San Piedro Island late last night was prepared – temporarily at least – for an air raid bombing or other serious emergency.

A meeting of the local defense commission was called promptly by Richard A. Blackington, local defense commissioner, at the Masons' lodge yesterday afternoon and attended by all defense commission lieutenants. An air raid blackout signal system, details of which can be found elsewhere in this edition, was established. It will rely on church bells, industrial plant whistles, and automobile horns.

Defense leaders, taking the attitude that 'anything can happen,' warned islanders to be on the alert to black out electric lights on extremely short notice.

Island watchers for the Interceptor Command will be on duty on a twenty-four-hour basis. Meanwhile members of the island's Japanese community pledged their loyalty to the United States.

Guards were trebled at the U.S. Navy's Agate Point radio transmitter station and at the Crow Marine Railway and Shipbuilding Company. The Pacific Telephone and Telegraph Company and the Puget Sound Power and Light Company indicated steps would be taken to guard their facilities here.

---

1 **tuck sth. underneath sth. else**: put sth. into a small space   2 **flourish** (n): Schwung   4 **deal** (n, infml): facts about sth. that is happening in the present situation   9 **traitor**: Verräter   **the FBI** = the Federal Bureau of Investigation: a US government police organization that investigates national crimes and is responsible for the safety of the country from international enemies   9–10 **be in on sth.** (infml): (hier) an etwas beteiligt sein   15 **off the air**: (of radio or TV) not broadcasting any programs   20 **sober**: (here) serious and sensible   23 **incendiary bomb**: bomb designed to cause fires   25 **fifth columnist**: member of a group of people working secretly to help the enemy of the country or organization they are in   26 **restive**: unruhig, nervös   28 **the Great War**: World War I   30 **head-on**: in a direct way   33 **morose**: unhappy, bad-tempered and not talking very much   38 **hostility**: aggressive behavior   50 **on the alert**: in Alarmbereitschaft   51 **on short notice** (AE): kurzfristig   52 **interceptor**: (Flug)abwehr   54 **pledge sth.**: formally promise to give sth.   56 **treble sth.**: make sth. three times as big

> Arrangements were being made to bring summer firefighting equipment, stored for the winter in Anacortes, back to the island today.
>
> Ensign R. B. Clawson, representing Comdr. L. N. Channing of the Agate Point radio transmitter station, addressed the defense commission meeting. Military and naval intelligence units, he said, have the situation well in hand and are taking proper local steps to guard against saboteurs and spies. 'The transmitter station went on prearranged war alert status immediately upon news of the Pearl Harbor attack,' added Ensign Clawson. 'Nevertheless, island civilians must do whatever they can independent of naval and military aid to safeguard their homes and businesses against sabotage or bombing.'
>
> The following lieutenants of the defense commission were present at yesterday's meeting:
>
> Bill Ingraham, communications; Ernest Tingstaad, transportation; Mrs. Thomas McKibben, medical supplies; Mrs. Clarence Wukstich, supplies and food; Jim Milleren, auxiliary police; Einar Petersen, roads and engineering; Larry Phillips, auxiliary fire force; Arthur Chambers, publicity.
>
> Also present were Major O. W. Hotchkins, chairman of the separate local defense council; Bart Johannson, an assistant to Major Hotchkins; and S. Austin Coney, organizer of the island's Interceptor Command force.

At the bottom of the page, in bold sixteen-point type, was a message from the island defense commission:

> AT THE SOUND OF PROLONGED RINGING OF CHURCH BELLS, THE PROLONGED SOUNDING OF AUTOMOBILE HORNS, AND THE PROLONGED BLOWING OF WHISTLES AT THE CROW MARINE RAILWAY AND SHIPBUILDING COMPANY, IMMEDIATELY TURN OFF ALL ELECTRIC LIGHTS. THIS INCLUDES THE TURNING OFF OF ALL PERMANENT NIGHT LIGHTS, SUCH AS STORE DISPLAY LIGHTS, WHICH ARE UNDER YOUR CONTROL. KEEP LIGHTS OFF UNTIL THE ALL-CLEAR SIGNAL, WHICH WILL BE A DUPLICATION OF THE AIR RAID WARNING SIGNAL.

There was also a statement issued by Richard Blackington that church bells and automobile horns should be used only in a manner consistent with the air raid warning system. Mrs. Thomas McKibben, in charge of medical supplies, requested that any islander with a station wagon available for use as an emergency ambulance should contact her at Amity Harbor 172-R; she was also registering emergency nurses and those with emergency first-aid training. Finally, the island sheriff, Gerald Lundquist, asked islanders to report suspicious activities or signs of sabotage to his office with all due speed.

Arthur's war extra included an article entitled 'Japanese Leaders Here Pledge Loyalty to America,' in which Masato Nagaishi, Masao Uyeda, and Zenhichi Miyamoto, all strawberry men, made statements to the effect that they and all other island Japanese stood ready to protect the American flag. They spoke on behalf of the Japanese Chamber of Commerce, the Japanese-American Citizens' League, and the Japanese Community Center, and their pledges, said the *Review*, were 'prompt and unequivocal,' including Mr. Uyeda's promise that 'if there is any sign of sabotage or spies, we will be the first ones to report it to the authorities.' Arthur also ran his editor's column under the usual heading of 'Plain Talk,' which he'd composed wearily at two A.M. with a candle propped beside his typewriter:

If ever there was a community which faced a local emergency growing out of something over which it had no control, it is San Piedro Island this Monday morning, December 8, 1941.

This is, indeed, a time for plain talk about things that matter to all of us.

---

4 **ensign** (AE): Fähnrich zur See   12–13 **safeguard sth./sb. against sth.**: protect sth./sb. from loss, harm or damage; to keep sth./sb. safe   20 **auxiliary**: (here) helping or supporting the professional police or fire force on a voluntary basis   27 **prolonged**: continuing for a long time   36 **issue sth.** ['ɪʃuː]: (of news, information, etc.) make sth. known formally   37–38 **consistent with sth.**: in agreement with / not differing from sth.   39 **station wagon**: Kombi(wagen)   44 **with all due speed**: unverzüglich   47–48 **to the effect that**: saying that   52 **unequivocal**: (of opinion or intention) clear, firm   54 **plain** (adj): (here) honest and direct

> There are on this island some 800 members of 150 families whose blood ties lie with a nation which yesterday committed an atrocity against all that is decent. That nation has committed itself to a war against us and has earned our swift and sure action. America will unite to respond courageously to the threat now facing us in the Pacific. And when the dust settles, America will have won.
>
> In the meantime the task before us is grave and invites our strongest emotions. Yet these emotions, the *Review* must stress, should not include a blind, hysterical hatred of all persons who trace their ancestry to Japan. That some of these persons happen to be American citizens, happen to be loyal to this country, or happen to have no longer a binding tie with the land of their birth could all easily be swept aside by mob hysteria.
>
> In light of this, the *Review* points out that those of Japanese descent on this island are not responsible for the tragedy at Pearl Harbor. Make no mistake about it. They have pledged their loyalty to the United States and have been fine citizens of San Piedro for decades now. These people are our neighbors. They have sent six of their sons into the United States Army. They, in short, are not the enemy, any more than our fellow islanders of German or Italian descent. We should not allow ourselves to forget these things, and they should guide us in our behavior toward all our neighbors.
>
> So of all islanders – of all ancestries – the *Review* would seek as calm an approach as possible in this emergency. Let us so live in this trying time that when it is all over we islanders can look one another in the eye with the knowledge that we have behaved honorably and fairly. Let us remember what is so easy to forget in the mad intensity of wartime: that prejudice and hatred are never right and never to be accepted by a just society.

Ishmael sat reading his father's words in the cedar tree; he was rereading them when Hatsue, in her coat and scarf, ducked in and sat down on the moss beside him. 'My father was up all night,' said Ishmael. 'He put this paper out.'

'My father can't get our money from the bank,' Hatsue replied to this. 'We have a few dollars, and the rest we can't get. My parents aren't citizens.'

'What will you do?'

'We don't know.'

'I have twenty dollars from picking season,' said Ishmael. 'You can have all of it – you can just have it. I'll bring it to school in the morning.'

'No,' said Hatsue. 'Don't bring it. My father will figure out something pretty soon. I could never accept your money.'

Ishmael turned onto his side, toward her, and propped himself on his elbow. 'It's hard to believe,' he said.

'It's so unreal,' answered Hatsue. 'It just isn't *fair* – it's not fair. How could they do this, just like that? How did we get ourselves into this?'

'*We* didn't get ourselves in it,' said Ishmael. 'The Japanese *forced* us into it. And on a Sunday morning, when no one was ready. It's cheap, if you ask me. They – '

'Look at my face,' interrupted Hatsue. 'Look at my eyes, Ishmael. My face is the face of the people who did it – don't you see what I mean? My face – it's how the Japanese look. My parents came to San Piedro from Japan. My mother and father, they hardly speak English. My family is in bad trouble now. Do you see what I mean? We're going to have trouble.'

'Wait a minute,' said Ishmael. 'You're not Japanese. You're – '

'You heard the news. They're arresting people. They're calling a lot of people spies. Last night some men stopped at the Ichiyamas' and called them names, Ishmael. They sat out front and honked their horn. How can this be happening?' she added. 'How did things get like this?'

'Who did that?' said Ishmael. 'Who are you talking about?'

'It was Mr. Willets – Otto Willets. Gina Willets's uncle and some other men. They were mad about the lights at the theater. The Ichiyamas left them on.'

'This is crazy,' said Ishmael. 'This whole thing is crazy.'

'They unscrewed his lightbulbs and then drove out to his house. They called him a dirty Jap.'

---

3 **atrocity**: horrific act of violence, esp. in a war   14 **mob**: large crowd of people, esp. one that may become violent or cause trouble   27 **trying**: challenging, difficult to deal with   60 **honk your horn**: hupen

Ishmael had no answer for this. He shook his head instead.

'I went home after school,' said Hatsue. 'My father was talking on the telephone. Everyone is worried about the navy transmitter, the one on Agate Point. They think it's going to be bombed tonight. There are men going out there with shotguns to defend it. They're going to sit in the woods along the beaches. The Shirasakis have a farm on Agate Point, and some soldiers from the transmitter station came there. They took their radio and their camera and their telephone, and they arrested Mr. Shirasaki. And the rest of the Shirasakis can't leave their house.'

'Mr. Timmons was going down there,' Ishmael answered. 'I saw him, he was getting into his car. He said he was going to the Masons' first, where everything is being organized. They're telling people which beaches to watch. And my mother is painting these blackout screens. She's had the radio on all day.'

'Everyone's had their radios on. My mother can't move away from ours. She sits there and listens to everything and talks on the phone to people.'

Ishmael sighed. 'A war,' he said. 'I can't believe this is happening.'

'We'd better go,' replied Hatsue. 'It's getting dark already.'

They crossed the small torrent of the creek below their tree and followed the path down the hillside. It was dusk and the sea wind blew in their faces. Standing in the path with their arms around each other they kissed once and then again, the second time with greater force. 'Don't let this hurt us,' Ishmael said. 'I don't care about what's happening in the world. We're not going to let this hurt us.'

'It won't,' said Hatsue. 'You'll see.'

Ishmael, on Tuesday, went to work for his father. He answered the telephone in the office on Andreason Street and took notes on a yellow legal pad. His father told him to call certain people and made lists of questions to ask. 'Give me a hand?' his father had asked. 'I can't keep up with it all.'

Ishmael made a call to the naval station. The pilot of a daily reconnaissance plane, said an Ensign Clawson, had noticed something he'd never noticed before: the Japanese strawberry farms on San Piedro Island were planted in rows pointing straight toward the radio transmitter at the end of Agate Point. The rows of berry plants could guide Jap Zeroes straight to their target easily. 'But those fields have been there for thirty years,' said Ishmael. 'Not all of them,' replied Ensign Clawson.

The county sheriff called in. Dozens of Japanese farmers, he speculated, had stores of dynamite in their sheds and barns which could be used for sabotage. Others, he'd heard, had shortwave radios. The sheriff asked that as an act of goodwill these farmers turn in such dangerous items to his office in Amity Harbor. He wanted, he said, a message in the *Review*. He was thankful for Ishmael's help.

Arthur printed the sheriff's message. He printed a notice from the defense authority telling Japanese nationals on San Piedro that as of December 14 they could no longer ride the ferries. Twenty-four men, he wrote in a news article, had been named by Larry Phillips to the civilian defense auxiliary fire force, including George Tachibana, Fred Yasui, and Edward Wakayama. 'Yes, I did, I singled those three out,' he explained when Ishmael asked about it. 'Not every fact is just a fact,' he added. 'It's all a kind of ... balancing act. A juggling of pins, all kinds of pins, that's what journalism is about.'

'That isn't journalism,' Ishmael answered. 'Journalism is just the facts.'

He had been learning about journalism at school, from a textbook, and it seemed to him that his father had abridged some basic journalistic principle.

'But which facts?' Arthur asked him. 'Which facts do we print, Ishmael?'

In the next issue Arthur reminded island businesses to extinguish display lights promptly at dusk; it was Christmas and the temptation was to leave them on. He announced that on New Year's Eve a public dance would be held under the slogan 'Remember Pearl Harbor – It Could Happen Here!'; men in uniform would be admitted at no charge; all islanders were encouraged to attend. Arthur informed his readers that a quota of $500 had been set by Mrs. Lars Heineman of the San Piedro Red Cross Relief Fund and that the Japanese-American Citizens'

League had immediately donated $55 – the largest contribution to date. Another article reported that at the Japanese Community Center hall in Amity Harbor a reception had been held for Robert Sakamura, who'd been inducted into the army. Speeches were made and food was served; a salute to the American flag and the loud singing of 'The Star-Spangled Banner' rounded out the evening.

The *San Piedro Review* printed a reminder to its readers that it was pledged to remain silent on military news that might comfort or aid the enemy. It furthermore counseled islanders 'not to talk carelessly of army or navy maneuvers which may be observed.' The construction of the island's first fishing resort, at Protection Point, was delayed, Arthur wrote, because of the war. Nick Olafsen died while stacking wood; the George Bodines escaped death when their kitchen stove exploded, but Mrs. Bodine broke a leg and an arm. The PTA began a paper drive and took a special interest in Christmas wrappings. The island Grange committed itself to the defense of San Piedro and promised in a letter to the secretary of agriculture to 'see to the production of such fruits and vegetables as can be grown on our island and as our fighting forces might need.' The army asked owners of mules and horses on San Piedro to register their animals with the county agent, describing the request in the pages of the *Review* as 'a patriotic obligation'; islanders were also asked to check their automobile tires and to drive in a manner consistent with preserving them: rubber was in short supply.

The navy warned islanders, in a message printed in the *Review*, 'to kill a rumor by refusing to carry it further.' Another benefit dance was held, and the enlisted men at the Agate Point station were invited as guests of honor. The defense fund committee came to the school board with a request that the high school auditorium be made available for two future dances; the board in return asked for written assurance that there would be no smoking or drinking. A draft registration desk was set up at Fisk's Hardware Center; meanwhile a sudden warm spell turned San Piedro's roads to mud and sank automobiles up to their running boards. Eve Thurmann, who was eighty-six, stalled out on Piersall Road in her '36 Buick, then showed up at Petersen's with mud caked on her knees; she'd walked two miles into town. Air raid rules, the Review reminded readers, were now posted on many electrical poles: keep calm and cool; stay home; put out lights; lie down; stay away from windows; don't telephone. Ray Ichikawa scored fifteen points for the Amity Harbor High School basketball team in its victory over Anacortes. A half-dozen residents of West Port Jensen claimed to have seen a mysterious creature sunning itself in the shallows; it appeared to have a swanlike neck, the head of a polar bear, and a cavernous mouth from which emerged puffs of steam. When islanders rowed out to get a closer look the creature disappeared beneath the waves.

'This doesn't go in the paper, does it?' Ishmael asked his father. 'A sea creature at West Port Jensen?'

'Maybe you're right,' answered Arthur. 'But do you remember the bear stories I ran last year? The bear who was responsible for everything, suddenly? Dead dogs, broken windows, missing chickens, scratched cars? A mysterious creature – that's news, Ishmael. The fact that people see it – that's news.'

In the following issue Arthur printed a public service advertisement urging islanders to buy war bonds. He explained that the civilian defense commission was registering boats that might be available in the event of an evacuation. William Blair, he told his readers – son of Zachary and Edith Blair of Amity Harbor – graduated in the U.S. Naval Academy's first emergency class and shipped out for the European theater. The island lost power for four hours one morning when a half-dozen of the army's captive balloons broke away and dragged down power lines. The defense commissioner, Richard Blackington, appointed nine district air raid wardens to be responsible for the effectiveness of an island blackout; he also attended, in Anacortes, a chemical warfare training class and

---

4 **induct sb.** (fml): jdn. einberufen   5–6 **Star-Spangled Banner**: the national anthem of the US   6 **round sth. out**: finish an activity or complete sth. in a good or suitable way   14 **PTA** = 'parent-teacher association': group run by parents and teachers in a school that organizes social events and helps the school in different ways   **drive** (n): organized effort by a group of people to achieve or collect sth.   27 **school board**: (hier) Schulrat   30 **draft** (sing, esp. AE): Einberufung   31 **spell** (n): (here) a short period of time during which sth. lasts, esp. a particular kind of weather   32 **sink sth.**: (hier) etwas versenken   33 **running board**: Trittbrett   **stall out**: (mit dem Auto) liegen bleiben   34–35 **mud caked**: schmutzverkrustet   42 **cavernous**: very large and often empty and/or dark   52 **public service**: (here) issued by government or government departments   53 **war bonds**: Kriegsanleihen   57 **European theater**: the part of World War II which was fought in Europe   59 **captive balloon**: Fesselballon

afterward busied himself disseminating flyers about it. Meanwhile the children of San Piedro Island had been numbered and registered in their school classrooms against the possibility of separation from their families. Arthur published a War Department chart showing wing and tail markings of airplanes. He also printed a photograph of Japanese-Americans in Fresno, California, standing in line to get citizen registration cards.

Four more islanders of Japanese descent – this was a front-page article – enlisted in the United States Army. Richard Enslow, who taught wood shop at the high school, resigned his position and joined the navy. Mrs. Ida Cross of South Beach knitted socks for sailors, sent them off, and received a thank-you note from an antiaircraft gunner stationed near Baltimore. The coast guard banned fishing on the west side of the island and bore down on gill-netters in the middle of the night who had set nets near restricted areas. In late January islanders experienced a temporary fuel shortage and were made to turn their oil heaters down by order of the civilian defense commission. The commission asked farmers for ten thousand sandbag sacks – gunny, feed, or flour. One hundred and fifty islanders attended first-aid courses offered by the Red Cross auxiliary. Petersen's store cut back on deliveries, citing fuel and labor shortages.

'Seems like you're favoring the Japs, Art,' an anonymous *Review* reader wrote one day. 'You're putting them on the front page every week and writing all about their patriotism and loyalty while saying nothing about their treachery. Well, maybe it's time you pulled your head from the sand and realized – there's a war on! And who are you siding with, anyway?'

In January fifteen islanders canceled their subscriptions, including the Walker Colemans of Skiff Point and the Herbert Langlies of Amity Harbor. 'The Japs are the enemy,' wrote Herbert Langlie. 'Your newspaper is an insult to all white Americans who have pledged themselves to purge this menace from our midst. Please cancel my subscription as of this date and send refund immediately.'

Arthur did so; he sent a full refund to each customer who canceled, and a personal note written in a cordial style. 'One day they'll be back,' he predicted. But then the Price-Rite store in Anacortes canceled its weekly quarter-page advertisement; then Lottie's Opsvig's apparel shop on Main Street, then Larsen's Lumberyard and the Anacortes Cafe. 'We won't worry about this,' Arthur told his son. 'We can always put out four pages instead of eight if that's what we have to do.' He printed the letter from Walker Coleman and another one like it from Ingmar Sigurdson. Lillian Taylor, who taught English at the high school, wrote back in angry condemnation of the 'spirit of small-mindedness evident in the letters of Mr. Walker Coleman and Mr. Ingmar Sigurdson, two well-known islanders who quite obviously have lost their grip on their senses while in the grip of war hysteria.' Arthur printed that, too.

---

1 **disseminate sth.**: spread sth., esp. information, knowledge, etc. so that it reaches many people   4 **chart**: Schaubild   10 **wood shop**: Werken   14 **bear down on sb./sth.**: move quickly towards sb./sth. in a determined or threatening way
18 **gunny**: Jute   20 **cite sth.**: mention sth. as a reason for doing sth. else
21 **labor** (AE): (here) people who are available for work in a country or an area
25 **treachery** ['tretʃəri]: Verrat   31 **purge sth.**: (hier) etwas beseitigen   **subscription**: Abonnement   32 **refund** (n) ['--]: sum of money that is paid back to you
44–45 **lose your grip on sb./sth.**: lose your control or power over sb./sth.

Chapter 14

Two weeks later, on February 4, a black Ford threaded through the Imadas' fields, making for the house of cedar slats. Hatsue was standing at the verge of the woodshed, filling her apron with cedar kindling from a pile underneath a sheet of waxed canvas, when she noticed – this was odd – that the Ford's headlights had been blackened; she heard the car before she saw it. It came to a halt just in front of her house; two men emerged in suits and ties. They shut their doors gently and looked at each other; one of them straightened his coat a little – he was bigger than the other, and his sleeves were not long enough to cover even half of his shirt cuffs. Hatsue stood silently with her apron full of kindling while the men mounted the porch and knocked on the door, holding their hats in their hands. Her father answered in his sweater and sandals, his newspaper dangling from his left hand neatly and his reading glasses perched on the bridge of his nose; her mother stood just behind him.

'Allow me to introduce myself,' said the smaller of the men, producing a badge from his coat pocket. 'Federal Bureau of Investigation,' he announced. 'Are you He-say-o Imada?'

'Yes,' said Hatsue's father. 'Is something wrong?'

'Not wrong exactly,' said the FBI man. 'It's just that we've been asked to search this place. You understand, we're going to search. Now if you'll just step inside, please, we'll all sit down.'

'Yes, come in,' said Hatsue's father.

Hatsue dropped her apron full of kindling back onto the pile of cedar sticks. The two men turned to look at her; the larger one came halfway down the porch steps. Hatsue walked out of the shadow of the woodshed and into the glow of the porch light. 'You come in, too,' said the smaller man.

They crowded into the living room. While Hatsue and her sisters sat on the couch, Hisao brought chairs from the kitchen for the FBI men – the larger one followed him everywhere. 'Please, sit down,' offered Hisao.

'You're real polite,' replied the smaller man. Then he took an envelope from his coat pocket; he handed it over to Hisao. 'It's a warrant from the

U.S. district attorney. We're going to search the premises – it's an order, see, an order.'

Hisao held the envelope between his fingers but made no move to open it. 'We are loyal,' he said. That was all.

'I know, I know,' said the FBI man. 'Still, we've got to look around.'

While he spoke the larger man stood and shot his cuffs, then calmly opened Fujiko's glass case and picked up the stack of *shakuhachi* sheet music she kept on the bottom shelf. He picked up Fujiko's bamboo flute, turned it over twice in his hands – small hands for such a thick, cloddish man – then set it on the dining room table. There was a magazine stand beside the wood stove, and he pawed through the magazines there. He picked up Hisao's newspaper.

'We've had some complaints from local citizens that certain enemy aliens on San Piedro Island have in their possession items declared illegal contraband,' said the smaller man. 'It's our job to search the premises for these. We ask for your cooperation.'

'Yes, of course,' said Hisao.

The larger man went into the kitchen. They could see him through the doorway peering beneath the sink and opening the oven door. 'We're going to have to search through your private effects,' the small FBI man explained. He stood and took the envelope from Hisao; he put it back in his coat pocket. 'I hope you won't mind,' he added.

He opened the *tansu* – a chest of drawers in one corner of the living room. He took out Fujiko's silk kimono with its gold brocaded sash. 'That's very nice,' he said, holding it to the light. 'From the old country, it appears. High class.'

The larger man came through the living room from the pantry with Hisao's shotgun seized in one hand and four boxes of shells against his

---

16 **badge**: Dienstmarke   31 **warrant** (n): legal document that is signed by a judge and gives the police authority to do sth.   32 **premises** (pl): Gelände   37 **shoot your cuffs**: stretch out your arms with a quick movement so that the sleeves of your jacket move up, your shirt cuffs become visible and your arms can move more freely   38 ***shakuhachi***: traditional Japanese bamboo flute   38–39 **sheet music**: Notenblätter   41 **cloddish**: tölpelhaft   42 **paw through sth.**: touch sth. in a rough way   46 **contraband**: goods that are sold and owned illegally in a country and/or taken there illegally   51 **effects** (pl): (here) belongings

chest. 'The guy's all armed,' he said to his partner. 'There's a big old sword back there, too.'

'Put it all on the table,' said the small man. 'And tag everything, Wilson – did you bring the tags in?'

'They're in my pocket,' Wilson answered.

The youngest of the Imada girls began to whimper, covering her face with her hands. 'Hey, little girl,' said the FBI man. 'I know this is kind of scary – but guess what? There's nothing to cry about, you hear me? We'll be done and out of your way soon.'

The large man, Wilson, went back for Hisao's sword. Then he turned his attention to the bedrooms.

'Tell you what,' said the first man to Hisao. 'Let's just sit tight until Wilson is finished. Then you and me, we'll take a walk outside. We'll tag these things up and load them in the car. Then you can show me around your outbuildings. We have to check everything – that's the way it is.'

'I understand,' said Hisao. He and Fujiko were holding hands now.

'Don't be nervous,' said the FBI man. 'We'll be out of your hair in a few minutes.'

He stood at the table putting tags on things. For a while he waited in silence. He tapped his foot and put his mouth to the flute. 'Wilson!' he said finally. 'Get your paws off the underwear!' Then he chuckled and picked up Hisao's shotgun.

'We gotta take this,' he said apologetically. 'All this stuff, you understand. They'll hold it for a while – who knows why? – then they'll ship it all back to you. They'll ship it back when they're done with it. It's complicated, but that's the way it is. There's a war on and that's the way it is.'

'The flute is precious,' said Hisao. 'The kimono, the sheet music – you must take those things?'

'Anything like that, yeah,' said the FBI man. 'Any old-country stuff we have to take.'

Hisao was silent, his brow furrowed. Wilson came back from the bedrooms looking solemn; he carried Hatsue's scrapbook. 'Pervert,' said his partner. 'Come on.'

'Crap,' said Wilson. 'I was going through the drawers. You do it next time if you don't like it.'

'He-say-o and I are going out,' the small man said firmly. 'You can sit here with the ladies and finish up with these tags. And be polite,' he added.

'I'm always polite,' said Wilson.

Hisao and the small man went outside; Wilson worked on the tags. When he was done he browsed through Hatsue's scrapbook, chewing on his bottom lip. 'Strawberry Princess,' he said, looking up. 'You must a been flattered by that.'

Hatsue didn't answer. 'It's a good picture,' added Wilson. 'It looks like you. Looks just like you, in fact.'

Hatsue said nothing. She wished Wilson would get his hands off her scrapbook. She was thinking of asking him, politely, to put it down, when Hisao and the other man came through the door, the FBI man carrying a crate. 'Dynamite,' he said. 'Look at this, Wilson.' He set the crate lightly on the table. The two men stood pawing through the dynamite – twenty-four sticks of it. Wilson chewed on his cheek and stared.

'You must believe me,' insisted Hisao. 'This is for tree stumps, for clearing land.'

The smaller FBI man shook his head gravely. 'Maybe,' he said. 'But this is still bad. This stuff' – he pointed a finger at the crate – 'this is illegal contraband. You were supposed to have turned this stuff in.'

They took the gun, the shells, the sword, and the dynamite and put it all in the car trunk. Wilson came back with a duffel bag and stuffed in the scrapbook, the kimono, the sheet music, and finally the bamboo flute.

When everything was loaded in the trunk of their car the FBI men sat down again. 'Well,' said the smaller one. 'This is it. Guess what?' he said to Hisao.

Hisao didn't answer. He sat in his sandals and sweater, blinking, holding his glasses in his hand. He waited for the FBI man to speak.

'We gotta arrest you,' said Wilson. 'You're going on a trip to Seattle.' He unhooked a pair of handcuffs from his belt; they were clipped on next to his gun.

'You don't need those,' urged the smaller man. 'This guy here is a class act, a gentleman. There's no need for any handcuffs.' He turned his

---

3 **tag sth.**: etwas mit einem Etikett versehen   6 **whimper** (v): make low, weak crying noises   17 **be out of sb.'s hair**: stop annoying sb. by always being near them, by asking them many questions, etc.   21 **chuckle** (v): laugh quietly
31 **his brows furrowed**: mit gerunzelter Stirn   57 **duffel bag** (AE): Reisetasche
68 **class act** (AE, infml): sb./sth. of distinctive and superior quality

attention to Hisao. 'They're just going to ask you some questions, okay? We go down to Seattle, a few questions, a few answers, the whole thing is over.'

The two younger girls were both crying. The youngest buried her face in her hands, and Hatsue put an arm around her. She pulled her sister's head in close and stroked her hair gently. Hisao rose from his chair.

'Please not take him,' said Fujiko. 'He has done no bad things. He –'

'Nobody knows about that,' said Wilson. 'There's nobody who can say.'

'Probably in just a few days,' said the other man. 'These things take a little time, you see. We have to take him on down to Seattle. He's gotta be scheduled in and all. Maybe a few days, maybe a week.'

'A week?' said Fujiko. 'But what we do? What do you – '

'Think of it as a war sacrifice,' the FBI man interrupted. 'Figure to yourself there's a war on, you see, and everybody's making some sacrifices. Maybe you could look at it that way.'

Hisao asked if he could change out of his sandals and get his coat from the pantry. He wanted to pack a small bag, he added, if that would be acceptable. 'Both,' said Wilson. 'Go ahead. We're perfectly willing to accommodate.'

They allowed him to kiss his wife and daughters and to say good-bye to each. 'Call Robert Nishi,' Hisao told them. 'Tell him I am arrested.' But when Fujiko called it turned out that Robert Nishi had been arrested as well. Ronald Kobayashi, Richard Sumida, Saburo Oda, Taro Kato, Junkoh Kitano, Kenzi Yamamoto, John Masui, Robert Nishi – they were all in a Seattle jail now. They had all been arrested on the same night.

The arrested men rode on a train with boarded windows – prisoners had been shot at from railroad sidings – from Seattle to a work camp in Montana. Hisao wrote a letter to his family each day; the food, he said, was not very good, but they were not really being mistreated. They were digging trenches for a water system that would double the size of the camp. Hisao had gotten a job in the laundry ironing and folding clothes. Robert Nishi worked in the camp kitchen.

Hatsue's mother gathered her five daughters together, Hisao's letter in her hand. She told her daughters, once again, the story of her odyssey from Japan on board the *Korea Maru*. She told them about the Seattle rooms she had cleaned, the sheets on which white men had vomited

blood, the toilets full of their excrement, the stench of their alcohol and sweat. She told them about the waterfront cookhouse where she'd
40 worked chopping onions and frying potatoes for *hakujin* stevedores who looked right through her as if she weren't even there. She knew, already, about hardship, she said – her life had long been difficult. She knew what it was to be alive without being alive; she knew what it was to be invisible. She wanted her daughters to know how to face this in a
45 manner that would allow them their dignity. Hatsue sat motionless while her mother spoke, trying to guess at her meaning. She was eighteen now, and her mother's story held more weight than it had when she'd heard it earlier. She leaned forward and listened carefully. Her mother predicted that the war with Japan would force all her daughters to
50 decide who they were and then to become more Japanese. Wasn't it true that the *hakujin* didn't really want them in their country? There were rumors that all the Japanese on the coast were going to be forced to leave. There was no point in trying to conceal anything or in trying to pretend they were not Japanese – the *hakujin* could see it in their faces;
55 they were going to have to accept this. They were Japanese girls in America during a time when America was fighting a war with Japan – did any of them want to deny it? The trick was to live here without hating yourself because all around you was hatred. The trick was to refuse to allow your pain to prevent you from living honorably. In Japan,
60 she said, a person learned not to complain or be distracted by suffering. To persevere was always a reflection of the state of one's inner life, one's philosophy, and one's perspective. It was best to accept old age, death, injustice, hardship – all of these were part of living. Only a foolish girl would deny this was so, thus revealing to the world her immaturity and
65 the degree to which she lived in the world of the *hakujin* instead of in the world of her own people. And her people, insisted Fujiko, were Japanese – the events of the past months had proved it so; why else had

12 **schedule sb. in**: (here) fit sb.'s case into a busy time schedule   20 **accommodate (sb.)**: (hier) jdm. entgegenkommen / einen Gefallen tun   27 **board sth. (up)**: cover sth. with wooden boards (esp. a door, a window, etc.)   31 **trench** (n): long deep hole dug in the ground, for example for carrying away water   38 **stench**: strong, very unpleasant smell   40 **stevedore**: person whose job is moving goods on and off ships   61 **persevere** [ˌpɜːrsəˈvɪr]: continue trying to do or achieve sth. despite difficulties   64 **immaturity**: Unreife

their father been arrested? The events of the last two months should teach them something about the darkness in the hearts of the *hakujin* and the more general darkness that was part of living. To deny that there was this dark side to life would be like pretending that the cold of winter was somehow only a temporary illusion, a way station on the way to the higher 'reality' of long, warm, pleasant summers. But summer, it turned out, was no more real than the snow that melted in wintertime. Well, said Fujiko, now your father is gone, folding laundry in a camp in Montana, and we all must get by, endure. 'Do you understand?' she said in Japanese. 'There is no choice in the matter. We will all have to endure.'

'They don't all hate us,' Hatsue replied. 'You're exaggerating, mother – you know you are. They're not so different from us, you know. Some hate, others don't. It isn't all of them.'

'I know what you're saying,' said Fujiko. 'Not all of them hate – you're correct. But on this other matter' – she still spoke in Japanese – 'you don't think they are very much different? In some big way, Hatsue? Different from us?'

'No,' said Hatsue. 'I don't.'

'They are,' said Fujiko, 'and I can tell you how. The whites, you see, are tempted by their egos and have no means to resist. We Japanese, on the other hand, *know* our egos are nothing. We bend our egos, all of the time, and that is where we differ. That is the fundamental difference, Hatsue. We bend our heads, we bow and are silent, because we understand that by ourselves, alone, we are nothing at all, dust in a strong wind, while the *hakujin* believes his aloneness is everything, his separateness is the foundation of his existence. He seeks and grasps, seeks and grasps for his separateness, while we seek union with the Greater Life – you must see that these are distinct paths we are traveling, Hatsue, the *hakujin* and we Japanese.'

'These people seeking union with the Greater Life,' argued Hatsue, 'are the ones who bombed Pearl Harbor. If they're so ready to bend and bow, then what are they doing attacking all over the world and taking over other countries? I don't feel I'm a part of them,' said Hatsue. 'I'm a part of *here*,' she added. 'I'm from this place.'

'Yes, you were born here, that's so,' said Fujiko. 'But your blood – you are still Japanese.'

'I don't want to be!' said Hatsue. 'I don't want anything to do with them! Do you hear me? I don't want to be Japanese!'

Fujiko nodded at her eldest daughter. 'These are difficult times,' she replied. 'Nobody knows who they are now. Everything is cloudy and unclear. Still, you should learn to say nothing that will cause you regret. You should not say what is not in your heart – or what is only in your heart for a moment. But you know this – silence is better.'

Hatsue knew immediately that her mother was right. Her mother, clearly, was serene and unruffled, and her voice carried the strength of truth. Hatsue fell silent, ashamed of herself. Who was she to say how she felt? What she felt remained a mystery, she felt a thousand things at once, she could not unravel the thread of her feelings with enough certainty to speak with any accuracy. Her mother was right, silence was better. It was something – one thing – she knew with clarity.

'I could say,' her mother went on, 'that living among the *hakujin* has tainted you, made your soul impure, Hatsue. This lack of purity envelops you – I see it every day. You carry it with you always. It is like a mist around your soul, and it haunts your face like a shadow at moments when you do not protect it well. I see it in your eagerness to leave here and walk in the woods in the afternoon. I cannot translate all of this easily, except as the impurity that comes with living each day among the white people. I am not asking you to shun them entirely – this you should not do. You must live in this world, of course you must, and this world is the world of the *hakujin* – you must learn to live in it, you must go to school. But don't allow living *among* the *hakujin* to become living *intertwined* with them. Your soul will decay. Something fundamental will rot and go sour. You are eighteen, you are grown now – I can't walk with you where you are going anymore. You walk alone soon, Hatsue. I hope you will carry your purity with you always and remember the truth of who you are.'

Hatsue knew then that her pretense had failed her. For four years now she had taken her 'walks' and come home offering fuki tendrils, water-

---

9 **get by**: manage to live   46 **serene** [sə'riːn]: calm and peaceful   **unruffled**: calm
49 **unravel sth.**: etwas entwirren   53 **taint sb./sth.**: damage or spoil the quality of sb./sth   57 **translate sth.**: (here) understand sth., interpret sth.   59 **shun sb.**: avoid sb.   62–63 **become intertwined with sb./sth.**: become very closely connected with sth./sb. else   69 **fuki**: kind of fern

cress, crawfish, mushrooms, huckleberries, salmonberries, blackberries – even clusters of blue elderberries for making jam – anything to conceal her purpose. She had gone to dances with other girls and stood in a corner refusing requests, while Ishmael stood among his friends. Her girlfriends had sought to concoct dates for her; she was widely encouraged to make use of her beauty and to emerge from the shell of her apparent shyness. It had even been rumored for a while last spring that she had a secret boyfriend who was extraordinarily handsome, somebody she visited in Anacortes, but that rumor gradually evaporated. Through all of it Hatsue had struggled with the temptation to reveal the truth to her sisters and school friends, because the truth was a burden to carry in silence and she felt the need, like most young girls, to speak about love with other girls. But she never did. She persisted in the pretense that her shy demeanor in the presence of boys prevented her from dating them.

Now her mother seemed to know the truth, or to have some inkling of it. Her mother's black hair was bound severely into a gleaming knot pinned to the back of her head. Her hands were folded majestically in her lap – she'd set her husband's letter on the coffee table – and she was perched with great dignity on the edge of her chair, blinking calmly at her daughter. 'I know who I am,' said Hatsue. 'I know exactly who I am,' she asserted again, but they were just more words to feel uncertain about; they were just more words to regret. Silence would have been better.

'You're fortunate,' said Fujiko evenly, in Japanese. 'You speak with great assurance, oldest daughter. The words fly from your mouth.'

Hatsue found herself walking in the woods later that afternoon. It was getting on toward the end of February, a time of only bleak light. In spring great shafts of sun would split the canopy of trees and the litter fall of the forest would come floating down – twigs, seeds, needles, dust bark, all suspended in the hazy air – but now, in February, the woods felt black and the trees looked sodden and smelled pungently of rot. Hatsue went inland to where the cedars gave way to firs hung with lichen and moss. Everything was familiar and known to her here – the dead and dying cedars full of punky heartwood, the fallen, defeated trees as high as a house, the upturned root wads hung with vine maple, the toadstools, the ivy, the salal, the vanilla leaf, the low wet places full of devil's club. These were the woods through which she had wandered on her way home from Mrs. Shigemura's lessons, the woods where she had cultivated the kind of tranquillity Mrs. Shigemura had demanded. She'd sat among sword ferns six feet tall or on a shelf above a vale of trilliums and opened her eyes to the place. As far back as she could recall the content of her days there had always been this silent forest which retained for her its mystery.

There were straight rows of trees – colonnades – growing out of the seedbed of trees that had fallen two hundred years before and sunk and become the earth itself. The forest floor was a map of fallen trees that had lived half a thousand years before collapsing – a rise here, a dip there, a mound or moldering hillock somewhere – the woods held the bones of trees so old no one living had ever seen them. Hatsue had counted the rings of fallen trees more than six hundred years old. She had seen the deer mouse, the creeping vole, the green-hued antlers of the white-tailed deer decaying underneath a cedar. She knew where lady fern grew and phantom orchids and warted giant puffballs.

Deep among the trees she lay on a fallen log and gazed far up branchless trunks. A late winter wind blew the tops around, inducing in her a momentary vertigo. She admired a Douglas fir's complicated bark, followed its grooves to the canopy of branches two hundred feet above. The world was incomprehensibly intricate, and yet this forest made a simple sense in her heart that she felt nowhere else.

She drew up for herself, in the silence of her mind, a list of the things now cluttering her heart – her father was gone, arrested by the FBI for keeping dynamite in his shed; there was talk going around that before too long everyone with a Japanese face on San Piedro would be sent away

1 **crawfish** (AE): Flusskrebs **huckleberry**: amerikanische Heidelbeere 5 **concoct sth.**: (here) arrange sth. that takes a lot of planning or persuasion 15 **inkling**: slight knowledge of sth. 23 **even** (adj): calm 26 **bleak**: trüb 27 **shaft**: narrow strip of light 28 **twig**: small branch of a tree 29 **suspend sth.**: hang sth. **hazy**: dunstig 30 **sodden**: extremely wet 32 **lichen**: Flechte 33 **punky**: morsch **heartwood**: inner layers of wood in a tree 34 **root wad**: Wurzelballen 35 **toadstool**: Pilz **salal**: small evergreen bush with white or pink flowers and edible berries 47 **hillock**: small hill 50 **creeping vole**: Wühlmaus **antlers** (pl): horns that grow on the head of male deer 52 **phantom orchids**: Scheinorchideen **warted**: warzig **puffball**: Pilzart 55 **vertigo**: fear of losing your balance that causes dizziness, esp. caused by looking up or down great heights 56 **groove**: long narrow cut in the surface of sth. hard 60 **clutter sth.**: fill sth. with too many things

until the war was done; she had a *hakujin* boyfriend she could see only in secret, who in a few short months was sure to be drafted and sent to kill the people of her blood. And now, on top of these insoluble things, her mother had only hours before probed into the pit of her soul and discovered her deep uncertainty. Her mother seemed to know about the gulf that separated how she lived from what she was. And what was she anyway? She was of this place and she was not of this place, and though she might desire to be an American it was clear, as her mother said, that she had the face of America's enemy and would always have such a face. She would never feel at home here among the *hakujin*, and at the same time she loved the woods and fields of home as dearly as anyone could. She had one foot in her parents' home, and from there it was not far at all to the Japan they had left behind years before. She could feel how this country far across the ocean pulled on her and lived inside her despite her wishes to the contrary; it was something she could not deny. And at the same time her feet were planted on San Piedro Island, and she wanted only her own strawberry farm, the fragrance of the fields and the cedar trees, and to live simply in this place forever. And then there was Ishmael. He was as much a part of her life as the trees, and he smelled of them and of the clam beaches. And yet he left this hole inside of her. He was not Japanese, and they had met at such a young age, their love had come out of thoughtlessness and impulse, she had fallen into loving him long before she knew herself, though it occurred to her now that she might never know herself, that perhaps no one ever does, that such a thing might not be possible. And she thought she understood what she had long sought to understand, that she concealed her love for Ishmael Chambers not because she was Japanese in her heart but because she could not in truth profess to the world that what she felt for him was love at all.

She felt a sickness overtake her. Her late-afternoon walks had not concealed her meetings with a boy her mother had long had intuition of. Hatsue knew she had not fooled anybody, she had not fooled herself, as it turned out, either, she had never felt completely right. How could they say, she and Ishmael, that they truly loved each other? They had simply grown up together, been children together, and the proximity of it, the closeness of it, had produced in them love's illusion. And yet – on the other hand – what was love if it wasn't the instinct she felt to be on the moss inside the cedar tree with this boy she had always known? He was the boy of this place, of these woods, these beaches, the boy who smelled like this forest. If identity was geography instead of blood – if living in a place was what really mattered – then Ishmael was part of her, inside of her, as much as anything Japanese. It was, she knew, the simplest kind of love, the purest form, untainted by Mind, which twisted everything, as Mrs. Shigemura, ironically, had preached. No, she told herself, she'd merely followed her instincts, and her instincts did not make the kinds of distinctions having Japanese blood demanded. She didn't know what else love could be.

One hour later, inside the cedar tree, she brought this matter up with Ishmael. 'We've known each other forever,' she said. 'I can hardly remember not knowing you. It's hard to remember the days before you. I don't even know if there were any.'

'My memory is like that, too,' said Ishmael. 'Do you remember that glass box I had? The one we took into the water?'

'Of course,' she said. 'I remember it.'

'That must have been ten years ago,' said Ishmael. 'Hanging onto that box. Being out there in the ocean – that's what I remember.'

'That's what I want to talk about,' said Hatsue. 'A box in the ocean – what kind of a start is that? What, really, did we have in common? We didn't even know each other.'

'We knew each other. We've always known each other. We've never been strangers the way most people are when they meet and start going out.'

'That's another thing,' said Hatsue. 'We don't go out – that isn't the right word – we *can't* go out, Ishmael. We're trapped inside this tree.'

'We're going to graduate in three months,' answered Ishmael. 'I think we should move to Seattle after that. It'll be different in Seattle – you'll see.'

'They're arresting people like me there, too, just like here, Ishmael. A white and a Japanese – I don't care if it's Seattle – we couldn't just go walking down the street together. Not after Pearl Harbor. You know that. Besides, you're going to be drafted in June. That's the way it's going to be. You won't be moving to Seattle, either. Let's be honest with ourselves.'

3 **insoluble**: unlösbar   4 **probe into sth.**: examine/investigate sth., esp. to find out secret or hidden information   27 **profess sth.**: state openly that you have a particular belief, feeling etc.   34 **proximity**: state of being near sb./sth.

'Then what will we do? You tell me. What's the answer, Hatsue?'

'There isn't one,' she said. 'I don't know, Ishmael. There isn't anything we can do.'

'We just have to be patient,' Ishmael replied. 'This war won't go on forever.'

They sat in silence inside their tree, Ishmael propped up against one elbow, Hatsue with her head perched against his ribs and her legs up against the glossy wood. 'It's nice in here,' said Hatsue. 'It's always nice in this place.'

'I love you,' answered Ishmael. 'I'll always love you. I don't care what else happens. I'm always going to love you.'

'I know you do,' said Hatsue. 'But I'm trying to be realistic about this. It isn't that simple, is what I'm saying. There are all these other things.'

'They don't really matter,' said Ishmael. 'None of those other things make a difference. Love is the strongest thing in the world, you know. Nothing can touch it. Nothing comes close. If we love each other we're safe from it all. Love is the biggest thing there is.'

He spoke with such confidence and drama about it that Hatsue allowed herself to be convinced by him that nothing was greater than love. She wanted to believe this, and so she indulged herself and tried to be swept up in it. They began to kiss against the moss inside the tree, but the touch of it felt to her false somehow, an attempt to obliterate the truth of the world and to deceive themselves with their lips. 'I'm sorry,' she said, drawing away. 'Everything is complicated. I can't forget about things.'

He held her in his arms and stroked her hair. They didn't speak anymore. She felt safe there, as though she were hibernating at the heart of the forest with time suspended and the world frozen – the temporary safety of a quiet way station one must leave in the morning. They fell asleep with their heads against the moss until the light in the tree went from green to gray, and then it was time to go home.

'Everything is going to work out,' said Ishmael. 'You'll see – it'll work out.'

'I don't see how,' answered Hatsue.

The problem was resolved for them on March 21 when the U.S. War Relocation Authority announced that islanders of Japanese descent had eight days to prepare to leave.

The Kobayashis – they'd planted a thousand dollars' worth of rhubarb on five acres in Center Valley – negotiated an agreement with Torval Rasmussen to tend and harvest their crop. The Masuis weeded their strawberry fields and worked at staking peas in the moonlight; they wanted to leave things in good condition for Michael Burns and his ne'er-do-well brother Patrick, who'd agreed to take care of their farm. The Sumidas decided to sell at cut-rate and close their nursery down; on Thursday and Friday they held all-day sales and watched pruning tools, fertilizer, cedar chairs, birdbaths, garden benches, paper lanterns, fountain cats, tree wrap, caddies, and bonsai trees go out the door with whoever was willing to take them. On Sunday they put padlocks on the greenhouse doors and asked Piers Petersen to keep an eye on things. They gave Piers their flock of laying chickens as well as a pair of mallard ducks.

Len Kato and Johnny Kobashigawa traveled island roads in a three-ton haying truck hauling loads of furniture, packing crates, and appliances to the Japanese Community Center hall. Filled to the rafters with beds, sofas, stoves, refrigerators, chests of drawers, desks, tables, and chairs, the hall was locked and boarded up at six P.M. on Sunday evening. Three retired gill-netters – Gillon Crichton, Sam Goodall, and Eric Hoffman, Sr. – were sworn in as deputies by San Piedro's sheriff for the purpose of guarding its contents.

The War Relocation Authority moved into musty offices at the old W. W. Beason Cannery dock, just outside Amity Harbor. The dock housed not only the Army Transport Command but representatives of the Farm Security Administration and the Federal Employment Service. Kaspars Hinkle, who coached the high school baseball team, stormed into the war relocation office on a late Thursday afternoon – everyone was just then preparing to leave – and slammed his roster on the secretary's desk:

---

20 **indulge yourself**: allow yourself to have or do sth. that you like, esp. sth. that is considered bad for you   22 **obliterate sth.**: remove all signs of sth.   26 **hibernate**: spend the winter in a state like deep sleep   27 **suspend sth.**: stop sth. for a while   37 **rhubarb**: Rhabarber   40 **stake sth.**: (here) support sth., esp. a plant, with a stick   43 **at cut-rate**: at a reduced price   **nursery** = tree nursery: place where young plants and trees are grown for sale   47 **padlock**: Vorhängeschloss   **greenhouse**: Gewächshaus   48 **flock**: group of birds   52 **fill sth. to the rafters** (infml): put many things into sth., esp. a bulding, so that it is extremely full   58 **musty**: smelling damp and unpleasant   64 **roster**: list of people's names

his starting catcher, second baseman, and two outfielders, he said – not to mention his two best pitchers – were going to miss the whole season. Couldn't this matter be thought through again? None of these kids were spies!

On Saturday evening, March 28, the Amity Harbor High School senior ball – its theme this year was 'Daffodil Daze' – went forward in the high school auditorium. An Anacortes swing band, Men About Town, played upbeat dance tunes exclusively; during an interlude the captain of the baseball team stood in front of the microphone on the bandstand and cheerfully handed out honorary letters to the seven team members departing Monday morning. 'We don't have much chance without you,' he said. 'Right now we don't even have enough guys to field a team. But any wins we do get, they're for you guys who are leaving.'

Evelyn Nearing, the animal lover – she was a widow who lived without a flush toilet or electricity in a cedar cabin on Yearsley Point – took goats, pigs, dogs, and cats from a half-dozen Japanese families. The Odas leased their grocery to the Charles MacPhersons and sold Charles their car and two pickup trucks. Arthur Chambers made arrangements with Nelson Obada to act as a special correspondent for his newspaper and to send reports to San Piedro. Arthur ran four articles on the imminent evacuation in his March 26 edition: 'Island Japanese Accept Army Mandate to Move,' 'Japanese Ladies Praised for Last-Minute PTA Work,' 'Evacuation Order Hits Prep Baseball Nine,' and a 'Plain Talk' column called 'Not Enough Time,' which roundly condemned the relocation authority for its 'pointless and merciless speed in exiling our island's Japanese-Americans.' The next morning, at seven-thirty, Arthur fielded an anonymous phone call – 'Jap lovers get their balls cut off,' a shrill tenor voice had explained. 'They get their balls stuffed down – ' Arthur had hung up and gone on typing a story for the next edition of his newspaper: 'Faithful to Praise Christ Easter Morn.'

On Sunday afternoon, at four o'clock, Hatsue told her mother she was going for a walk; her last walk before leaving, she pointed out. She wanted to sit in the forest, she said, and think about matters for a while. She left as if headed toward Protection Point, then circled through the woods to the South Beach trail and followed the path to the cedar tree. Ishmael, she found, was waiting for her there with his head propped up on his jacket. 'This is it,' she said to him, kneeling for a moment in the entry. 'Tomorrow morning we leave.'

'I've got something figured out,' answered Ishmael. 'When you get where you're going you write to me. Then when the school newspaper comes out I'll send you a copy with a letter from me inside it and put Journalism Class for a return address. What do you think of that plan? You think that will be safe?'

'I wish we didn't even need a plan,' said Hatsue. 'Why do we have to do this?'

'Write me at my house,' said Ishmael, 'but put Kenny Yamashita's name for the return address – my parents know I'm friendly with Kenny, you can write me at home with no problems.'

'But what if they want to see Kenny's letter? What if they ask how he's doing?'

Ishmael thought about this for a moment. 'What if they want to see Kenny's letter? What if you collect maybe half a dozen letters and stick them all in one envelope? One from Kenny, one from you, one from Helen, one from Tom Obata – tell them it's a request from the school newspaper. I'll call Kenny tonight and tell him about it so it doesn't sound suspicious when you bring it up. Collect them all, stick yours in last, send them all to me, I'll pull yours out and take the rest to school. That should work out perfectly.'

'You're like me,' said Hatsue. 'We've both gotten good at being devious.'

'I don't think it's devious,' said Ishmael. 'It's just what we have to do.'

Hatsue undid the belt on her coat, a herringbone wraparound from the Penney's in Anacortes. Underneath she wore an austelle dress with a broad embroidered collar. On this day she'd brushed her hair out long and tossed it to flow down the length of her back, unfettered by plaits,

---

1–2 **starting catcher, second baseman, outfielder, pitcher**: positions in baseball 6 **daffodil**: Narzisse **go forward**: take place as planned 8 **upbeat**: happy, cheerful **interlude**: short period of time between the parts of a concert or show that is filled with a different performance (= Auftritt) 10 **honorary letter**: (Ehren)urkunde 12 **field a team**: (hier) ein Team aufstellen 22 **mandate** ['mændeɪt] (n): official order given to sb. to perform a particular task 26 **field sth.**: receive sth. and deal with it 59 **devious**: behaving in a dishonest or indirect way 61 **herringbone**: Fischgrätmuster **wraparound**: Wickel(mantel) 62 **austelle**: brand of clothing that is cut in a particular way 64 **unfettered**: not controlled

braids, or ribbons. Ishmael pressed his nose against it. 'It smells like cedar,' he said.

'So do you,' said Hatsue. 'It's your smell I'll miss as much as anything.'

They lay on the moss, not touching, in silence, Hatsue with her hair coiled over one shoulder now, Ishmael with his hands in his lap. The March wind came up outside the tree and they heard it tossing the ferns together and the suspiration of the wind joined with the sliding of the water in the little creek just below. The tree muted and softened these sounds, and Hatsue felt herself at the heart of things. This place, this tree, was safe.

They began to kiss and touch each other, but the emptiness she felt pervaded it and she found she couldn't put her thoughts away. She placed an index finger against Ishmael's lips and shut her eyes and let her hair fall back against the moss. The smell of the tree was his smell, too, and the smell of the place she was leaving the next day, and she began to understand how she would miss it. The ache of it filled her; she felt sorry for him and sorry for herself and began to cry so quietly that it was only behind her eyes, a tautness in her throat, a tightening of her rib cage. Hatsue pressed against him, crying in this silent way, and breathed in the smell of Ishmael's throat. She buried her nose beneath his Adam's apple.

Ishmael moved his hands beneath the hem of her dress, then slowly up her thighs and over her underpants to the curves of her waist, where they stayed. He held her lightly in the curves of her waist and after a while lower, at her hips, and pulled her hard against him. She felt herself lifted, and she felt how hard he was and she pressed back into his hardness. The length of it pushed against his trousers, and his trousers pressed against her underpants and their smooth, wet silk pushed pleasantly. They kissed harder now, and she began to move as if to gather him in. She could feel the hard length of him and the silk of her underpants and his cotton trousers between. Then his hands left her hips and traced the line of her waist and traveled along up under her dress to the clasp on her bra. She arched off the moss to make room for his hands, and he undid the clasp without struggling and pulled the shoulder straps down onto her arms and softly kissed her earlobes. His hands traveled down her body again, coming out from the dress to hold her neck under her hair, then her shoulder blades. She let her weight rest against his

hands and arched her breasts to meet him. Ishmael kissed the front of
her austelle dress and then began, from just below the embroidered
40 collar, to undo its eleven buttons. It took time. They breathed into one
another, and she took his upper lip between her lips while he worked on
the buttons carefully. After a while the front of her dress came open, and
he pulled her bra up onto her chest and moved his tongue against her
nipples. 'Let's get married,' he whispered. 'I want to marry you, Hatsue.'
45 She was far too empty to answer this; there was no way she could
speak. Her voice felt buried underneath her crying, and there was no way
to bring it to the surface. So instead she ran her fingertips along his spine
and against his hips, and then with both hands she felt his hardness
through the fabric of his pants and felt how, for a moment, he seemed to
50 stop breathing altogether. She squeezed with both hands and kissed him.
'Let's get married,' he said again, and she understood what he meant.
'I just ... I want to marry you.'
She made no move to stop him when he slid his hand inside her
panties. Then he was peeling them down her legs, and she was still
55 crying silently. He was kissing her and pulling his own pants to his
knees, the tip of his hardness was against her skin now and his hands
were cupped around her face. 'Just say yes,' he whispered. 'Just tell me
yes, tell me yes. Say yes to me. Say yes, oh God say yes.'
'Ishmael,' she whispered, and in that moment he pushed himself inside
60 of her, all the way in, his hardness filling her entirely, and Hatsue knew
with clarity that nothing about it was right. It came as an enormous shock
to her, this knowledge, and at the same time it was something she had
always known, something until now hidden. She pulled away from
him – she pushed him. 'No,' she said. 'No, Ishmael. No, Ishmael. Never.'
65 He pulled himself out, away. He was a decent boy, a kind boy, she
knew that. He pulled his trousers up, buttoned them, and helped her
back into her panties. Hatsue straightened her bra and clasped it again
and buttoned up her dress. She put her coat on and then, sitting up,

8 **suspiration**: Seufzen   9 **mute sth.**: make the sound of sth. quieter or softer
13 **pervade sth.**: fill every part of sth.   14 **index finger**: Zeigefinger   19 **tautness**:
Anspannung, Enge   22 **hem**: Saum   33 **bra**: BH   **arch off sth.**: sich von einem
Untergrund aufwölben   49 **fabric**: Stoff

began meticulously to brush the moss from her hair. 'I'm sorry,' she said. 'It wasn't right.'

'It seemed right to me,' answered Ishmael. 'It seemed like getting married, like being married, like you and me were married. Like the only kind of wedding we could ever have.'

'I'm sorry,' said Hatsue, picking moss from her hair. 'I don't want you to be unhappy.'

'I am unhappy. I'm miserable. You're leaving tomorrow morning.'

'I'm unhappy, too,' said Hatsue. 'I'm sick with it, I feel worse than I've ever felt. I don't know anything anymore.'

He walked her home, to the edge of her fields, where they stood for a moment behind a cedar tree. It was nearly dusk and a March stillness had seized everything – the trees, the rotting deadwood, the leafless vine maple, the stones littering the ground. 'Good-bye,' said Hatsue. 'I'll write.'

'Don't go,' said Ishmael. 'Stay here.'

When she finally did leave it was well past dusk, and she walked out of the woods and into the open with the intention of not looking back again. But after ten steps she did so despite herself – it was too hard not to turn around. It was in her to say good-bye forever and tell him she would never see him again, to explain to him that she'd chosen to part because in his arms she felt unwhole. But she didn't say it, that they had been too young, that they had not seen clearly, that they had allowed the forest and the beach to sweep them up, that all of it had been delusion all along, that she had not been who she was. Instead, unblinking, she looked at him, unable to hurt him in the way that was demanded and in some undefined way still loving what he was, his kindness, his seriousness, the goodness in his heart. He stood there, Ishmael, looking at her desperately, and that was the way she would remember him. Twelve years later she would still see him this way, standing at the edge of the strawberry fields beneath the cover of the silent cedars, a handsome boy with one arm outstretched, beckoning her to come back.

---

23 **sweep sb. up**: (here) absorb sb., keep sb. from seeing the facts clearly
delusion: false belief or opinion about yourself or your situation   31 **beckon sb.**: give sb. a signal using your finger or hand to tell them to move nearer

Chapter 15

An army truck took Fujiko and her five daughters to the Amity Harbor ferry dock at seven o'clock on Monday morning, where a soldier gave them tags for their suitcases and coats. They waited among their bags in the cold while their *hakujin* neighbors stood staring at them where they were gathered on the dock between the soldiers. Fujiko saw Ilse Severensen there, leaning against the railing with her hands clasped in front of her; she waved at the Imadas as they passed by. Ilse, a Seattle transplant, had for ten years purchased strawberries from Fujiko and spoke to her as if she were a peasant whose role in life was to make island life pleasantly exotic for Ilse's friends who visited from the city. Her kindness had always been condescending, and she had always paid a bit extra for her berries with the air of doling out charity. And so, on this morning, Fujiko could not meet her eyes or acknowledge her despite the fact that Ilse Severensen had waved and called out her name in a friendly way – Fujiko studied the ground instead; she kept her eyes cast down.

At nine o'clock they were marched on board the *Kehloken*, with the white people gaping at them from the hill above, and Gordon Tanaka's daughter – she was eight years old – fell on the dock and began to cry. Soon other people were crying, too, and from the hill came the voice of Antonio Dangaran, a Filipino man who had married Eleanor Kitano just two months before. 'Eleanor!' he shouted, and when she looked up he let go a bouquet of red roses, which sailed gently toward the water in the wind and landed in the waves below the dock pilings.

They were taken from Anacortes on a train to a transit camp – the horse stables at the Puyallup fairgrounds. They lived in the horse stalls

---

11 **condescending** [ˌkɑːndɪˈsendɪŋ]: behaving as though you are more important and more intelligent than other people   12 **dole out charity**: Almosen verteilen
18 **gape at sb./sth.**: (here) stare at sb./sth. intensely and disrespectfully, usu. with your mouth open

and slept on canvas army cots; at nine P.M. they were confined to their stalls; at ten P.M. they were made to turn out their lights, one bare bulb for each family. The cold in the stalls worked into their bones, and when it rained that night they moved their cots because of the leaks in the roof. The next morning, at six A.M., they slogged through mud to the transit camp mess hall and ate canned figs and white bread from pie tins and drank coffee out of tin cups. Through all of it Fujiko maintained her dignity, though she'd felt herself beginning to crack while relieving herself in front of other women. The contortions of her face as she moved her bowels deeply humiliated her. She hung her head as she sat on the toilet, ashamed of the noises her body made. The roof leaked in the latrine, too.

After three days they boarded another train and began a languid crawl toward California. At night the MPs who roamed from car to car came through telling them to pull down their window shades, and they passed the dark hours twisting in their seats and exerting themselves not to complain. The train stopped and started and jolted them toward wakefulness, and there was a constant line at the door to the toilet. Many people had lost control of their bowels altogether as a result of eating in the Puyallup transit camp, including Fujiko. Her rectum burned as she sat in her train seat, her brain felt light and unmoored inside her skull, and a cold sweat beaded on her forehead. Fujiko did her best not to give in to her discomfort by speaking of it to her daughters. She did not want them to know that she was suffering inwardly and needed to lie down comfortably somewhere and sleep for a long time. For when she slept at all it was with her hearing tuned to the bluebottle flies always pestering her and to the crying of the Takami baby, who was three weeks old and had a fever. The wailing of this baby ate at her, and she rode with her fingers stuffed inside her ears, but this did not seem to change things. Her sympathy for the baby and for all of the Takamis began to slip as sleep evaded her, and she secretly began to wish for the baby's death if such a thing could mean silence. And at the same time she hated herself for thinking this and fought against it while her anger grew at the fact that the baby could not just be flung from the window so that the rest of them might have some peace. Then, long past the point when she had told herself that she could not endure another moment, the baby would stop its tortured shrieking, Fujiko would calm herself and close her eyes, retreat with enormous relief toward sleep, and then the Takami baby would once again wail and shriek inconsolably.

The train stopped at a place called Mojave in the middle of an interminable, still desert. They were herded onto buses at eight-thirty in the morning, and the buses took them north over dusty roads for four hours to a place called Manzanar. Fujiko had imagined, shutting her eyes, that the sandstorm battering the bus was the rain of home. She'd dozed and awakened in time to see the barbed wire and the rows of dark barracks blurred by blowing dust. It was twelve-thirty, by her watch; they were just in time to stand in line for lunch. They ate standing up, from army mess kits, with their backs turned against the wind. Peanut butter, white bread, canned figs, and string beans; she could taste the dust in all of it.

They were given typhoid shots that first afternoon; they stood in line for them. They waited in the dust beside their luggage and then stood in line for dinner. In the evening the Imadas were assigned to Block 11, Barrack 4, and given a sixteen-by-twenty-foot room furnished with a bare lightbulb, a small Coleman oil heater, six CCC camp cots, six straw mattresses, and a dozen army blankets. Fujiko sat on the edge of a cot with cramps from the camp food and the typhoid shot gathering to a knot in her stomach. She sat with her coat on, holding herself, while her daughters beat flat the straw in the mattresses and lit the oil heater. Even

---

1 **confine sb./sth. to sth.**: keep sb./sth. inside the limits of sth.   5 **slog**: walk steadily, with great effort or difficulty   8 **crack** (v): (of a person) no longer be able to function normally because of pressure   9 **contortion**: state of the face or body being twisted out of its natural shape   13 **languid**: (hier) schleppend
14 **crawl** (n): (here) very slow journey   **MP**: officer of the military police   17 **jolt sb. toward sth.**: give sb. a sudden shock so that they start or continue an activity
18 **wakefulness**: sleeplessness   20 **rectum**: Enddarm   21 **unmoor sth.**: separate sth. from its ties or restrictions   22 **bead on sth.** [bi:d]: cover sth. with small drops
26–27 **bluebottle fly**: Schmeißfliege   27 **pester sb.**: annoy sb. / bother sb.
39–40 **inconsolable** [,--'--]: untröstlich   42 **interminable**: endless   46 **barbed wire**: Stacheldraht   48–49 **mess kit**: Essgeschirr   50 **string bean** (AE): grüne Bohne   51 **typhoid shot**: Injektion zur Impfung gegen Typhus   53 **assign sb. to sth.**: jdn. zu etwas zuweisen   54 **sixteen by twenty foot**: ca. 4,9 x 6,1 Meter
55 **CCC** = Civilian Conservation Corps: government program in the US in the 1930s for unemployed young men who helped construct buildings, powerlines, etc. and who lived in work camps

with the heater she shivered beneath her blankets, still fully dressed in her clothes. By midnight she couldn't wait any longer and, with three of her daughters who were feeling distressed too, stumbled out into the darkness of the desert in the direction of the block latrine. There was, astonishingly, a long line at midnight, fifty or more women and girls in heavy coats with their backs braced against the wind. A woman up the line vomited heavily, and the smell was of the canned figs they'd all eaten. The woman apologized profusely in Japanese, and then another in the line vomited, and they were all silent again.

Inside they found a film of excrement on the floor and damp, stained tissue paper everywhere. All twelve toilets, six back-to-back pairs, were filled up near to overflowing. Women were using these toilets anyway, squatting over them in the semidarkness while a line of strangers watched and held their noses. Fujiko, when it was her turn, hung her head and emptied her bowels with her arms wrapped around her stomach. There was a trough to wash her hands in, but no soap.

That night dust and yellow sand blew through the knotholes in the walls and floor. By morning their blankets were covered with it. Fujiko's pillow lay white where her head had been, but around it a layer of fine yellow grains had gathered. She felt it against her face and in her hair and on the inside of her mouth, too. It had been a cold night, and in the adjacent room a baby screamed behind a quarter-inch wall of pine board.

On their second day at Manzanar they were given a mop, a broom, and a bucket. The leader of their block – a man from Los Angeles dressed in a dusty overcoat who claimed to have been an attorney in his former life but who now stood unshaven with one shoe untied and with his wire-rimmed glasses skewed on his face – showed them the outdoor water tap. Fujiko and her daughters cleaned out the dust and did laundry in a gallon-size soup tin. While they were cleaning more dust and sand blew in to settle on the newly mopped pine boards. Hatsue went out into the desert wind and returned with a few scraps of tar paper she'd found blown up against a roll of barbed wire along a firebreak. They stuffed this around the doorjamb and fixed it over the knotholes with thumbtacks borrowed from the Fujitas.

There was no sense in talking to anyone about things. Everyone was in the same position. Everyone wandered like ghosts beneath the guard

towers with the mountains looming on either side of them. The bitter wind came down off the mountains and through the barbed wire and
40 hurled the desert sand in their faces. The camp was only half-finished; there were not enough barracks to go around. Some people, on arriving, had to build their own in order to have a place to sleep. There were crowds everywhere, thousands of people in a square mile of desert scoured to dust by army bulldozers, and there was nowhere for a person
45 to find solitude. The barracks all looked the same: on the second night, at one-thirty A.M., a drunk man stood in the doorway of the Imadas' room apologizing endlessly while the dust blew in; he'd lost his way, he said. Their room had no ceiling either, and it was possible to hear people squabbling in other barracks. There was a man who distilled his own
50 wine three rooms down – he used mess hall rice and canned apricot juice – they heard him weeping late on their third night while his wife threatened him. On that same night the searchlights went on in the guard towers and swept across their single window. In the morning it turned out that one of the guards had become convinced of an escape in
55 progress and had alerted the tower machine gunners. On the fourth night a young man in Barrack 17 shot his wife and then himself while they lay in bed together – somehow he had smuggled in a gun. 'Shikata ga nai,' people said. 'It cannot be helped, it has to be.'

There was nowhere to put any clothing. They lived out of their
60 suitcases and packing crates. The floor was cold beneath their feet, and they wore their dusty shoes until bedtime. By the end of the first week Fujiko had lost track of her daughters' whereabouts altogether. Everybody had begun to look alike, dressed in surplus War Department clothing – pea coats, knit caps, canvas leggings, army earmuffs, and
65 wool khaki pants. Only her two youngest ate with her; the other three

---

3 **distress sb.**: make sb. suffer physical or mental pain 6 **brace yourself against sth.**: press your body firmly against sth. 16 **trough** [trɔːf]: Trog 17 **knothole**: Ast-loch 28 **skewed** [skjuːd]: schief 34 **doorjamb** ['dɔːdʒæm]: vertical post at the side of a door 35 **thumbtack** ['θʌmtæk]: Reißzwecke 41 **go around** (infml): be enough for everyone to have one 44 **scour sth.**: (hier) etwas zermahlen 49 **squabble**: argue about sth. that is not very important 62 **lose track of sth.**: have not enough information about sth. **sb.'s whereabouts** ['- - -] (pl): place where sb. is 63 **surplus** (adj): überschüssig 64 **pea coat**: short, warm coat, worn esp. by sailors **earmuff**: Ohrenschützer

ran with packs of young people and ate at other tables. She scolded them, and they listened politely and then went out again. The older girls left early and came back late, their clothes and hair full of dust. The camp was an enormous promenade of young people milling and walking in the fire lanes and huddling in the lee of barracks. On her way to the washhouse one morning after breakfast Fujiko had seen her middle daughter – she was only fourteen – standing in a group that included four boys dressed nattily in Eisenhower coats. They were, she knew, Los Angeles boys; most people in the camp were from Los Angeles. The Los Angeles people were not very cordial and looked down on her for some inexplicable reason; she could not get a word in with them edgewise. Fujiko fell silent about everything, collapsed in on herself. She waited for a letter from Hisao to come, but a different letter came instead.

When Hatsue's sister Sumiko saw the envelope with Ishmael's false return address – *Journalism Class, San Piedro High School* – she did not resist her urge to tear it open. Sumiko had been a sophomore before her exile, and although she knew the envelope was Hatsue's this mail remained irresistible. This mail was word from home.

Sumiko read the letter from Ishmael Chambers in front of the tarpaper YMCA building; she read it again, savoring the more astonishing phrases, out by the camp hog pens.

April 4, 1942

My Love,

I still go to our cedar tree in the afternoons every day. I shut my eyes, waiting. I smell your smell and I dream of you and I ache for you to come home. Every moment I think of you and long to hold and feel you. Missing you is killing me. It's like a part of me has gone away.

I'm lonely and miserable and think of you always and hope you will write me right away. Remember to use Kenny Yamashita's name for a return address on the envelope so my parents won't get too curious.

Everything here is horrible and sad and life is not worth living. I can only hope that you find some happiness during the time we have to be apart – some happiness of some kind, Hatsue. Myself, I can only be miserable until you are in my arms again. I can't live without you,

35 *I know that now. After all these years that we've been together, I find you're a part of me. Without you, I have nothing.*

All My Love Forever,
Ishmael

After a half hour of walking and thinking and of reading Ishmael's letter
40 four more times, she took it regretfully to her mother. 'Here,' she said. 'I feel like a creep. But I have to show this to you.'

Her mother read Ishmael Chambers's letter standing in the middle of the tar-paper hut with one hand on her forehead. While she read her lips moved rapidly, her eyes blinked severely and often. Finished, she
45 sat down on the edge of a chair, dangled the letter in her hand for a moment, then sighed and took off her glasses. 'Surely not,' she said in Japanese.

She set the glasses in her lap wearily, placed the letter on top of them, and pressed against her eyes with both palms.

50 'The neighborhood boy,' she said to Sumiko. 'The one who taught her how to swim.'

'Ishmael Chambers,' answered Sumiko. 'You know who he is.'

'Your sister has made a terrible mistake,' said Fujiko. 'One I hope you will never make.'

55 'I never would,' said Sumiko. 'Anyway, it isn't a mistake I could make in a place like this, is it?'

Fujiko picked up her glasses again and held them between her thumb and forefinger. 'Sumi,' she said. 'Have you told anyone? Have you shown this letter to anyone?'

60 'No,' said Sumi. 'Just you.'

---

1 **scold sb.**: speak angrily to sb., esp. because they have done sth. wrong
4 **mill** (v): move around an area without seeming to be going anywhere in particular
5 **huddle** [,hʌdl]: (of a group of people) gather or stand closely together **in the lee of sth.**: at the side or part of sth., esp. a building, that provides shelter from the wind   8 **natty**: neat and fashionable   11 **inexplicable**: unerklärlich   **not get a word in with sb. edgewise** ['edʒwaɪz] (AE): bei jdm. nicht zu Wort kommen; nicht mit jdm. ins Gespräch kommen   16 **sophomore** ['sɑːfəmɔːr] (AE): high school student in the 10th grade   20 **savor sth.**: enjoy sth. thoroughly   21 **hog**: pig
41 **creep** (n): person that you dislike very much and find very unpleasant

'You must promise something,' said Fujiko. 'You must promise not to tell this to anyone – don't tell anyone about it. There's enough gossip here without something like this. You must promise to keep your mouth closed and never tell this again. Do you understand me?'

'All right. I promise,' said Sumiko.

'I'll tell Hatsue I found the letter. You don't have to take the blame.'

'Okay,' answered Sumiko. 'Good.'

'Go out now,' said her mother. 'Go and leave me alone.'

The girl went out to wander aimlessly. Fujiko perched her glasses on her nose once more and began to reread the letter. It was clear to her from the words in it that her daughter had been deeply entangled with this boy for a long time, for many years. It was evident that he had touched her body, that the two of them had been sexually intimate inside a hollow tree they'd used as a trysting place in the forest. Hatsue's walks had been a ruse, just as Fujiko had suspected. Her daughter had returned with *fuki* tendrils in her hands and a wetness between her thighs. *Deceitful girl*, thought Fujiko.

She thought for a moment of her own romantic life, how she'd been wed to a man she'd never seen before and passed the first night of her life with him in a boardinghouse where the pages of *hakujin* magazines had been substituted for wallpaper. She had refused, on that first night, to let her husband touch her – Hisao was unclean, his hands were rough, he had no money but a few coins. He'd spent those first hours apologizing to Fujiko and explaining in detail his financial desperation, pleading with her to work beside him and underscoring his talents and better traits – he was ambitious, hardworking, didn't gamble or drink, he had no bad habits and saved his money, but times were so hard, he needed someone at his side. He could understand, he said, having to earn her love, and he was willing to prove himself to her with time if she would agree to be patient. 'Don't even speak to me,' she'd replied.

He'd slept in a chair that first night, and Fujiko had stayed awake pondering ways to extricate herself from this situation. She did not have enough money to buy a return ticket, and at any rate, she knew in her bones, she could not return to her family in Japan – her parents had sold her and paid a percentage to the deceitful *baishakunin* who had assured them that Hisao had amassed great wealth during his years in

America. She stayed awake growing angrier about this; by dawn she had begun to feel murderous.

In the morning Hisao stood at the foot of the bed and asked Fujiko if she'd slept well. 'I'm not talking to you,' she answered. 'I'm going to write home for the money I need and go back as soon as I can.'

'We'll save together,' pleaded Hisao. 'We'll go back together, if that's what you want. We'll – '

'What about your twelve acres of mountain land?' Fujiko said to him angrily. 'The *baishakunin* took me to see it – peach trees, persimmons, weeping willows, rock gardens. None of that turns out to be true.'

'You're right, it isn't true,' confessed Hisao. 'I don't have money – that's correct. I'm a pauper and I work my fingers to the bone. The *baishakunin* lied to you, I'm sorry for that, but – '

'Don't talk to me, please,' said Fujiko. 'I don't want to be married to you.'

It had taken her three months to learn how to sleep with him. When she did she found that she had learned to love him, if love was the proper word to use, and it occurred to her then, sleeping in his arms, that love was nothing close to what she'd imagined as a girl growing up near Kure. It was less dramatic and far more practical than her girlhood had led her to believe. Fujiko had cried when her hymen broke, in part because sacrificing her virginity to Hisao's need had not been what she had hoped for. But she was married now, and he was a steady sort of a man, and she grew, gradually, close to him. They'd been, already, through much hardship together, and he had never once complained.

Now she stood with this letter in her hand – a letter a *hakujin* boy had sent to her daughter about love inside a cedar tree, about his loneliness and misery and how horribly he missed her and how she should write to him with a false return address – '*use Kenny Yamashita's name*,' he'd written. She wondered if her daughter loved this boy or if she knew the first thing about love. It made sense to her now that Hatsue

---

2 **gossip**: Klatsch, Gerede 11 **become entangled with sb.**: sich auf jdn. einlassen
14 **trysting place** ['trɪstɪŋ]: secret place where lovers meet 15 **ruse**: trick
25 **underscore sth.** [ˌʌndər'skɔːr]: underline sth., emphasize sth. 32 **extricate yourself from sth.** ['ekstrɪkeɪt]: escape from sth., esp. a difficult situation
57 **hymen** ['haɪmən]: Jungfernhäutchen

had been so silent and morose – more silent and morose than her other daughters – since the day they left San Piedro. Everybody had been unhappy and Hatsue had used this, the general unhappiness had been convenient, but still she had sulked more than anyone; she'd been listless and had gone about her chores with the sluggishness of someone grieving. She missed her father, she said when asked; she missed San Piedro Island. But she did not say to anyone that she missed the *hakujin* boyfriend who had been her secret lover. The depth of her deceit became vivid to Fujiko, and she felt in herself a mother's rage at the weight of this betrayal. The rage mingled with the general melancholy that had been growing in her steadily since the bombing of Pearl Harbor; it was one of the rare times in Fujiko's adult life when she felt inconsolable.

She reminded herself to behave with dignity no matter what the circumstances. It was a lesson she'd forgotten in her early days in America, but with time she had rediscovered it as something worthy passed down from her grandmother in Kure. *Giri* was her grandmother's word for it – it could not be precisely translated into English – and it meant doing what one had to do quietly and with an entirely stoic demeanor. Fujiko sat back and cultivated in herself the spirit of quiet dignity that would be necessary in confronting Hatsue. She breathed deeply and shut her eyes.

Well, she told herself, she would have a talk with Hatsue when the girl came back from wandering aimlessly around the camp. She would put an end to this business.

Three hours before dinner a group of San Piedro boys knocked on the door of her room. They had with them tools and scraps of lumber, and they were prepared, they said, to build for the Imadas whatever was wanted: shelves, a chest of drawers, chairs. She recognized all of them as the sons of island families – the Tanakas, the Kados, the Matsuis, the Miyamotos – and she told them yes, she could use all of those things, and the boys set about working in the lee of the barrack, measuring and cutting and sawing while the wind blew. Kabuo Miyamoto came inside and nailed up brackets while Fujiko sat on a cot with her arms crossed and the letter from the *hakujin* boy behind her back. 'There are some scraps of tin at the side of the block kitchen,' Kabuo Miyamoto said to her. 'We can nail them over those knotholes in the floor – they'll do a better job than tar paper.'

'Tar paper tears like *that*,' answered Fujiko in the English Kabuo used. 'And it not help keep cold out.'

Kabuo nodded and went back to work, his hammer striking efficiently. 'How is your family?' Fujiko said. 'Your mother? Your father? How everybody?'

'My father is ill,' Kabuo answered. 'The camp food is bad for his stomach.' He paused to slip another nail from his pocket. 'And you?' he said. 'How are all of the Imada women?'

'Dusty,' said Fujiko. 'We eat dust.'

At this moment Hatsue came through the door, her face reddened by the cold outside, and tugged the scarf from her head. Kabuo Miyamoto stopped his work for a moment to gaze at her while she shook her hair free. 'Hello,' he said. 'It's good to see you.'

Hatsue tossed her hair once more, gathered it in her hands swiftly, and smoothed it down the back of her head. Then she stuffed her hands in her overcoat and sat down beside her mother. 'Hello,' she said, but nothing more.

They sat for a moment watching in silence while Kabuo Miyamoto went about his work. He sat on his shins with his back to them, tapping carefully with a hammer. Another of the carpenters came through the door with a stack of freshly sawed pine boards. Kabuo Miyamoto laid each on the brackets and tested each with a level. 'They're straight,' he announced. 'They should work out well. I'm sorry we couldn't do better.'

'They're very nice,' said Fujiko. 'It's kind of you. Our thanks.'

'We're going to build you six chairs,' said Kabuo, looking at Hatsue now. 'We're going to build you two chests of drawers and a table you can eat on. We'll have them to you in a few days' time. As soon as we can get them built.'

'Thank you,' said Fujiko. 'You're very kind.'

'We're glad to do it for you,' said Kabuo Miyamoto. 'It isn't any trouble at all.'

Still holding his hammer, he smiled at Hatsue, and she dropped her eyes to her lap. He slipped the hammer into a cloth ring on his pants,

---

4 **sulk**: schmollen   5 **sluggishness**: Trägheit   33 **bracket**: (here) piece of wood that is fixed to a wall in order to support a shelf   56 **shin**: Schienbein
70 **cloth ring**: Tuchöse

then picked up his level and measuring tape. 'Good-bye, Mrs. Imada,' he said. 'Good-bye, Hatsue. It's good to see you.'

'Our thanks again,' said Fujiko. 'Your help is greatly appreciated.'

When the door had shut she reached behind her and handed Hatsue the letter. 'Here,' she spat. 'Your mail. I don't know how you could have been so deceitful. I'll never understand it, Hatsue.'

She had planned to discuss the matter right there and then, but she understood suddenly that the strength of her bitterness might prevent her from saying what she really meant. 'You will not write again to this boy or accept his letters,' she said sternly from the doorway.

The girl sat with the letter in her hand, tears gathering in her eyes. 'I'm sorry,' Hatsue said. 'Forgive me, Mother. I've deceived you and I've always known it.'

'Deceiving me,' said Fujiko in Japanese, 'is only half of it, daughter. You have deceived yourself, too.'

Then Fujiko went out into the wind. She walked to the post office and told the clerk there to hold all mail for the Imada family. From now on, she herself would come for it. It should be handed to her only.

That afternoon she sat in the mess hall and wrote her own letter addressed to the parents of the boy Ishmael Chambers. She told them about the hollow tree in the woods and how Ishmael and Hatsue had deceived the world for a number of years successfully. She revealed to them the contents of the letter their son had written to her daughter. Her daughter, she said, would not be writing back, now or at any time in the future. Whatever had been between them was over, and she apologized for her daughter's role in it; she hoped that the boy would see his future in a new light and give no more thought to Hatsue. She understood, she wrote, that they were only children; she knew children were often foolish. Still, both of these young people were culpable and must look to themselves now, examine their souls, consider this a matter of conscience. It was no crime to find oneself attracted to another, she wrote, or to believe what one felt was love. The dishonor lay instead in concealing from one's family the nature of one's affections. She hoped that the parents of Ishmael Chambers would understand her position. She did not wish for any further communication to pass between her daughter and their son. She had expressed her feelings clearly to her daughter and asked her not to write to the boy or accept his letters in the future. She added that she admired the Chambers family and had great respect for the *San Piedro Review*. She wished them well, all of them.

She showed this letter to Hatsue when it was folded and ready to go in its envelope. The girl read it over twice, slowly, with her left cheek resting on her left hand. When she was done she held it tightly in her lap and looked blandly at her mother. Her face, strangely, was drained of emotion; she had the look of one exhausted from the inside, too tired to feel. Fujiko saw that she had gotten older in the three weeks since they'd left San Piedro. Her daughter was suddenly grown up, a woman, weary from the inside. Her daughter had suddenly grown hardened.

'You don't have to send this,' she said now to Fujiko. 'I wasn't going to write him again anyway. I was on the train, coming down here, and all I could think about was Ishmael Chambers and whether I should write him a letter. Whether I loved him anymore.'

'Love,' spat Fujiko. 'You not know about love. You – '

'I'm eighteen,' replied Hatsue. 'I'm old enough. Stop thinking of me as a little girl. You have to understand – I've grown up.'

Fujiko removed her glasses carefully and, as was her habit, rubbed her eyes. 'On the train,' she said. 'What you decide?'

'Nothing, at first,' said Hatsue. 'I couldn't think very clearly. There were too many things to think about, Mother. I was too depressed to think.'

'And now?' said Fujiko. 'What now?'

'I'm done with him,' said Hatsue. 'We were children together, we played on the beach, and it turned out to be something bigger. But he isn't the husband for me, Mother. I've known that all along. Anyway I wrote him, I said that whenever we were together it seemed like something was wrong. I always knew, deep inside, it was wrong, I felt it down inside somewhere – this feeling like I loved him and at the same time couldn't love him – I was always confused, every day, ever since we

---

1 **level** (n): Wasserwaage   **measuring tape**: Maßband   5 **spit**: (here) speak in an angry or aggressive way   10 **stern** (adj): serious and disapproving   29 **culpable** ['kʌlpəbl]: responsible and deserving blame for having done sth. wrong   43 **bland**: showing no strong emotions or excitement   **drain sb./sth. of sth. else**: empty sb./sth. of sth. else   61 **be done with sb.**: have finished dealing with sb.; break off any contact with sb.

met. He's a good person, Mother, you know his family, he's really a very good person. But none of that matters, does it? I wanted to tell him it was over, Mother, but I was *leaving* … it was all *confused*, I couldn't get the words out, and, besides, I didn't really know what I felt. I was confused. There was too much to think about. I needed to straighten it all out.'

'And is it straighten out now, Hatsue? Is it straighten?'

The girl was silent for a moment. She ran a hand through her hair and let it fall, then the other hand, too. 'It's straight,' she said. 'I have to tell him. I have to put an end to it.'

Fujiko took her letter from her daughter's lap and ripped it neatly down the middle. 'Write your own letter,' she said in Japanese. 'Tell him the truth about things. Put all of this in your history. Tell him the truth so you can move forward. Put this *hakujin* boy away now.'

In the morning Sumiko was reminded of the importance of revealing nothing about this episode. She promised her mother she would keep silent. Fujiko took Hatsue's letter to the post office and paid the postage on it. She licked the envelope shut herself and, because the notion took hold of her suddenly – a kind of caprice and nothing more – she pressed the stamp on upside down before putting the letter in the mailbox.

When Kabuo Miyamoto brought his chests of drawers, Fujiko asked him to stay for tea, and he sat with them for more than two hours, and again on the next night when he delivered the table, and on the following night when he delivered the chairs. Then on the fourth night he came to their door with his hat in his hand and asked Hatsue if she would go for a walk with him underneath the stars. She said no on that occasion and did not speak to him for another three weeks, and yet she saw that he was polite and handsome, the clear-eyed son of strawberry farmers, and anyway she couldn't grieve over Ishmael Chambers until the end of her days.

When the time came, a few months later, that Ishmael was mostly a persistent ache buried beneath the surface of her daily life, she spoke to Kabuo Miyamoto in the mess hall and sat beside him to eat lunch. She admired his impeccable table manners and the graciousness of his smile. He spoke softly to her, asked her about her dreams, and when she said she wanted an island strawberry farm he said he wanted the same thing precisely and told her about how his family's seven acres would soon be transferred to his name. When the war was over he planned to farm strawberries back home on San Piedro Island.

When she kissed him for the first time, she felt the grip of her sadness, how it seized more tightly around her, and how different his mouth was from Ishmael's. He smelled of earth and his body's strength was far greater than her own. She found she couldn't move within the circle of his arms and struggled against him, breathless. 'You'll have to be more gentle,' she'd whispered. 'I'll try,' Kabuo had answered.

---

17 **notion**: (here) idea   18 **caprice** [kə'priːs]: sudden change in attitude or behavior for no obvious reason   28 **grieve over sb.**: feel very sad about losing sb.
32 **graciousness** ['greɪʃəsnəs]: Eleganz

Chapter 16

Ishmael Chambers trained as a marine rifleman with seven hundred and fifty other recruits at Fort Benning, Georgia, in the late summer of 1942. In October he fell ill with fever and dysentery and was hospitalized for eleven days, during which he lost considerable weight and passed his time reading Atlanta newspapers and playing chess with other boys. Sprawled in his bed with his knees up and his hands behind his head, he listened to radio news accounts of the war and studied the diagrams of troop movements in the papers with a lazy, unruffled fascination. He grew a mustache for six days, then shaved it, then let it grow again. Through almost every afternoon he slept, waking in time to feel dusk settle in and to watch the light die beyond the window three beds away to his right. Other boys came and went, but he stayed. The war wounded came to the hospital but convalesced on two other floors he had no access to. He lived in his T-shirt and underwear, and the smell from the open window was of dying leaves and of rain in the dirt and turned fields, and it began to seem to him strangely apt that he lay so many thousand miles from home and was so alone in his sickness. It was the kind of suffering, after all, he'd yearned for during the last five months, since receiving Hatsue's letter. It was an easy, sleepy kind of languid fever, and so long as he did not try to move too much or exert himself unnecessarily he could live this way indefinitely. He surrounded himself with his illness thoroughly and embedded himself in it.

In October he trained a second time, as a radioman, and was sent to a staging area on the North Island of New Zealand as part of the Second Marine Division. They assigned him to B Company in the Second Marine Regiment, Third Battalion, and he soon met men who'd been at Guadalcanal, and he replaced a radio operator who'd been shot during the fighting in the Solomons. One night a lieutenant named Jim Kent recollected how the former radioman had taken an interest in a dead Japanese boy with his pants turned inside out around his muddy ankles. The radioman, a Private Gerald Willis, had propped the boy's penis up by

placing a stone under it, then had lain down carefully in the dirt and
shot carbine rounds until he'd blown the head of it off. He'd been proud
of himself afterward and had bragged about his aim for a half hour or
35 more, describing for others how the boy's penis had looked with the
head of it severed and how the head itself had looked lying on the
ground. Private Willis had been killed two days later on patrol, by
friendly mortar fire he'd called for at the direction of Lieutenant Kent
himself, who'd given the correct coordinates. Seven men in the platoon
40 had died on that occasion, and Kent had lowered himself into a foxhole
and watched a Private Wiesner toss a grenade unsuccessfully toward a
pillbox while at the same moment a stream of machine-gun fire caught
Wiesner at the waist and forced his viscera out. A piece of it had landed
on Kent's forearm, blue, fresh, and glistening.

45 They trained incessantly and practiced landing maneuvers at Hawkes
Bay, where the tides were bad. Men died during these exercises. Ishmael
tried to take maneuvers seriously, but the veterans in his squad went
through them hung over or bored or both simultaneously, and their
attitude of indifference had its influence. On liberty he drank ale and at
50 other times gin with boys who like him were new to the war, and they
played pool in Wellington together. Even at those times, drunk at one
o'clock in the morning, leaning against his pool cue in the smoky light
while another boy lined up a shot and a Wellington band played dance

---

1 **marine**: member of the US Marine Corps, a branch of the US military that specializes in amphibious warfare, i.e. transports troups and material by sea but also fights on land   3 **dysentery** ['dɪsənteri]: illness that involves severe diarrhea (= Durchfall)   13 **convalesce** [ˌkɑːnvə'les]: spend time getting your health and strength back after an illness   16 **apt**: appropriate in the circumstances   24 **staging area**: (here) area where troups and equipment are gathered in order to be transported to the place of an attack   26–27 **Guadalcanal**: largest of the Solomon islands in the western Pacific Ocean that was occupied by the Japanese in World War II   33 **carbine**: short light rifle   **round** (n): single bullet or shot from a gun   34 **brag about sth.**: mit etwas angeben   37–38 **be killed by friendly fire**: be killed in a battle by soldiers of the same side   38 **mortar**: Mörser, Granatwerfer   39 **platoon**: small unit in a company of soldiers   40 **foxhole** (sl): (in military battle) defensive fighting position that is dug into the ground, usu. large enough for one soldier   42 **pillbox**: small shelter for soldiers, often partly underground   43 **viscera**: Einge-weide   45 **incessant** [ɪn'sesnt]: never stopping   48 **hung over**: tired because of having drunk alcohol   52 **pool cue**: Billardqueue

tunes he didn't recognize, Ishmael felt a peculiar detachment from everybody. He was numb to it all, uninterested in drinking and pool and other people, and the more drunk he became the more lucid his mind was and the colder he felt toward everyone. He did not understand the laughter of his compatriots or their ease or anything else about them. What were they doing here, drinking and shouting at one o'clock in the morning in a country so far from the homes they knew; what were they so feverishly happy about? One morning, in a heavy downpour, he wandered back to his Wellington hotel at four-thirty and lay down heavily with his writing tablet to compose a letter to his parents. After he'd written to them he wrote one to Hatsue, and then he took both letters and ripped them up and fell asleep with some of the pieces jammed into his coat pocket and the rest scattered across the floor. He slept with his shoes on and at six-fifteen awoke to vomit in the toilet closet down the hall.

On the first day of November the Second Division left Wellington, presumably on maneuvers at Hawkes Bay again, but ending up instead at Nouméa on the French island of New Caledonia. By the thirteenth Ishmael's regiment was on board the *Heywood*, a transport ship traveling with more than half of the Third Fleet – frigates, destroyers, light and heavy cruisers, half a dozen battleships – all headed for an unknown destination. On the second day his company was assembled on the top deck and told that they were moving toward Tarawa atoll, where they would go ashore at Betio, a strongly defended island. A major stood in front of them sucking on his pipe stem, with his right elbow tucked into his left palm. The idea, he explained, was to let the navy obliterate the place – it was less than two square miles of coral sand – then wade in and mop up the leftovers. The Jap commander, he said, had boasted that Betio could not be successfully invaded by even a force of a million soldiers with a thousand years to do battle. The major pulled his pipe from his mouth and proclaimed the Japanese commander laughable in this regard. He predicted a battle lasting two days at most, with few if any marine casualties. It was a matter the navy guns would take care of, he repeated, a tailor-made place for shipboard artillery to do the dirty work.

On the night of the nineteenth a quarter moon rose over the sea while the fleet stood seven miles off Tarawa. Ishmael ate a last meal on the *Heywood*'s messing deck with Ernest Testaverde, a boy he liked, an anti-tank gunner from Delaware. They ate steak and eggs, fried potatoes and coffee, and then Testaverde put down his plate and took a pad of paper and a pen from his pocket. He began to write a letter home.

'You better write one yourself,' he said to Ishmael. 'Last chance you're going to get, you know.'

'Last chance?' answered Ishmael. 'There's no one I really want to write to in that case. I – '

'It isn't up to you,' said Testaverde. 'So just in case – write a letter.'

Ishmael went below and got his pad of paper. He sat on the top deck with his back against a stanchion and composed a letter to Hatsue. From where he sat he could see twenty other men, all of them writing intently. It was warm for so late at night, and the men all looked comfortable with their collars open and the sleeves of their uniform shirts rolled up. Ishmael told Hatsue how he was about to go ashore on an island in the South Pacific and that his job was to kill people who looked like her – as many of them as he could. What did she think about that? he wrote. How did that make her feel? He said that his numbness was a terrible thing, he didn't feel anything except that he looked forward to killing as many Japs as possible, he was angry at them and wanted their deaths – all of them, he wrote; he felt hatred. He explained to her the nature of his hatred and told her she was as responsible for it as anyone in the world. In fact, he hated her now. He didn't want to hate her, but since this was a last letter he felt bound to tell the truth as completely as he could – he hated her with everything in his heart, he wrote, and it felt good to him to write it in just that way. *'I hate you with all my heart,'* he wrote. *'I hate you, Hatsue, I hate you always.'* It was at this point that he ripped the sheet from his writing pad, crumpled it, and threw it into the sea. He watched it floating on the water for a few seconds, then threw his pad in after it.

---

3 **lucid**: clear   8 **downpour**: heavy rain   17 **presumably** [prɪˈzuːməbli]: vermutlich   26 **obliterate sth.**: remove all signs of sth., (here) by destroying it completely   28 **mop sth. up**: etwas aufwischen, (hier: fig) etwas beseitigen   33 **casualty**: person who is killed or injured in war or in an accident   34 **tailor-made**: made for a particular person or purpose   37 **messing deck**: Messe, Speisedeck   38 **anti-tank gunner**: Panzerabwehrschütze   60 **be bound to do sth.**: verpflichtet sein etwas zu tun

At 3:20 in the morning, wide awake in his bunk, Ishmael heard the order delivered to the troop hold: 'All marines lay topside to your debarkation stations!' He sat up and watched Ernest Testaverde lace his boots and then began to lace his own, stopping once to drink from his canteen – 'Dry mouth,' he said to Ernest. 'You want some water before we die?'

'Lace up,' said Ernest. 'Get topside.'

They went up, dragging their gear along with them, and Ishmael felt wide awake now. There were already more than three hundred men squatting and kneeling on the top deck of the *Heywood*, rearranging their equipment in the dark – C rations, canteens, entrenching tools, gas masks, rounds of ammunition, steel helmets. There had been no firing yet, and it did not feel so much like war – another nighttime exercise in tropical waters. Ishmael heard the whine of the landing craft plummeting over the sheaves of the boat blocks; then men were going overboard into them, snaking their way down the cargo nets with packs on their backs and their helmets strapped on and timing their lunges to coincide with the bobbing of the boats below.

Ishmael watched a half-dozen navy corpsmen busily packing medical field kits and stacking ambulatory litters. This was something he hadn't seen on maneuvers, and he pointed it out to Testaverde, who shrugged and went back to counting antitank rounds. Ishmael turned on his TBX, listened for a moment to the static in the headphones, then switched it off and waited. He did not want to strap it to his back too early, then have to stand around with its weight burdening him until his turn came to crawl down the cargo net. Sitting beside his gear, peering out to sea, he tried to make out Betio, but the island could not be seen. Each of the LCP landing craft that had left the *Heywood* in the past half hour appeared as a dark spot against the water, though – Ishmael counted three dozen of them.

The three squads of Third Platoon were briefed on the top deck by a First Lieutenant Pavelman from San Antonio, who explained in detail the role of B Company in the larger scheme of things. He had before him a relief model of the island made out of three square sections of rubber and with a pointer began to point out its topographical features, doing so with no flourishes. Amtracs, he said, were going in first, followed by waves of Higgins boats. There was going to be air cover – dive-bombers and Hellcats on strafing runs, then B-24s from out of Ellice Island, right up to the point of attack. B Company would go ashore at a place called Beach Red Two, he said, and the mortar section would place itself at the disposal of the weapons platoon leader, a Second Lieutenant Pratt, for the purpose of establishing a base of fire. Second Platoon would come in simultaneously on Pratt's right and advance over the seawall behind its light machine guns, then collect on higher ground and move inland. There were bunkers and pillboxes, said Lieutenant Pavelman, directly south of Beach Red Two; marine intelligence was furthermore of the opinion that the Jap command bunker was perhaps located in this area, possibly at the eastern end of the airfield. Second Platoon should look for it and fix the location of air vents for the demolitions teams, who would come in directly behind. Three minutes after Second went ashore, Third Platoon – Ishmael's – would beach and come in close or, according to the judgment of Lieutenant Bellows, go to the support of whichever platoon appeared to have made a solid advance. The platoon could expect support from K Company, which was scheduled to come in with the headquarters group and a heavy machine-gun platoon just behind the Third. They would land from more amtracs, which could be used against the seawall; the theory, said Lieutenant Pavelman, was to come in fast

2 **topside**: (hier) an Deck   2–3 **debarkation station**: place where people leave a ship to go ashore or aboard another ship   3 **lace sth.**: etwas zubinden
10 **C ration** = combat (individual) ration: packed food supply for one soldier to provide him with energy in a battle situation   **entrenching tool**: tool that is used to dig trenches   13 **plummet**: fall suddenly and quickly from a high level or position
14 **sheave**: Teil eines Flaschenzugs   **block** = pulley block: Flaschenzug   15 **snake** (v): move like a snake in long twisting curves   16 **strap sth. on**: etwas festschnallen
lunge (n): (hier) Absprung   19 **ambulatory litter**: Ambulanztrage   21 **TBX**: Sprechfunkgerät (Markenname)   22 **static** (n): Rauschen   27 **LCP** = Landing Craft Personnel: Landungsbootstyp der US-Navy   30 **brief sb.**: give sb. information about sth. so that they are prepared to deal with it   33 **relief model** [rɪˈliːf]: three-dimensional model of an area of land   35 **amtrac** = amphibious tractor: landing vehicle used by the US forces that can operate in the water as well as on land   36 **air cover**: Deckung aus der Luft   **dive-bomber**: Sturzbomber   37 **Hellcat**: US fighter plane starting from aircraft carriers (= Flugzeugträger)   **strafe sth.**: attack a place with bullets or bombs from a low-flying aircraft   **B-24**: short name of a heavy bomber aircraft used by the US forces in World War II   39–40 **place yourself at the disposal of sb./sth.**: sich jdm./etwas zur Verfügung stellen   42 **seawall**: defense construction built along a coast line on a beach (here: in order to prevent an attack or invasion)   48 **air vent**: Belüftungsschacht

and hard with full support behind the initial wave of riflemen. 'Another name for it is suckers first,' someone in Third Platoon called out bitterly, but no one laughed at this. Pavelman pushed on mechanically with his briefing: rifle platoons, he explained, would cut a careful but persistent advance, followed by reinforcements in the second wave, command and support in the third tractor wave, then more rifle companies and more support and command, until the beachhead was well established. Then, with his hands at his belt, Lieutenant Pavelman called on a Chaplain Thomas to lead them in a recitation of the twenty-third psalm and in the singing of 'What a Friend We Have in Jesus.' When they were done, everyone fell silent on the deck and the chaplain called on the men to contemplate their relationship to God and Jesus. 'That's fine,' a soldier called out in the darkness. 'But, look here, I'm an atheist, sir, the exception to the rule that there ain't no atheists in foxholes or firefights, and I'm gonna stay a goddamn atheist to the goddamn end, goddamn it!'

'So be it,' Chaplain Thomas answered softly. 'And may God bless you just the same, my friend.'

Ishmael began to wonder how any of this would direct him once he hit the beach. He had listened to Lieutenant Pavelman as closely as he could but had not discerned the relationship between his words and the specific direction in which his own feet should move once he landed on Betio. Why was he going there? To do what exactly? The chaplain was passing out pieces of lucky candy and rolls of military toilet paper, and Ishmael took one of each from him chiefly because everyone else had done so. The chaplain, a Colt .45 strapped to his belt, encouraged him to take more of the candy – 'It's good stuff,' he said. 'Come on.' They were peppermints, and Ishmael popped one in his mouth, then strapped his radio onto his back and pulled himself into a standing position. The entire weight of his equipment, he guessed, was more than eighty-five pounds.

It was not easy to crawl down the cargo net so loaded, but Ishmael had been able to practice on maneuvers and had taught himself to relax. Halfway down he spit out the peppermint and leaned out over the water. A whistling had begun to sound in his ears, growing louder by the second. He turned to look, and at the same moment a shell plunged into the sea seventy-five feet to stern. A spray of salt water broke across the boat, dousing the soldiers there; the phosphorescence boiled up green and luminous against the darkness. The boy next to Ishmael, a Private

Jim Harvey from Carson City, Nevada, swore softly under his breath twice, then leaned in against the net. 'Shit,' he said. 'A goddamn shell. I don't believe this shit.'

'Me neither,' said Ishmael.

'I thought they blew the shit out of this place,' Jim Harvey complained. 'I thought they dusted all the big guns off before we had to go in. Jesus fucking Christ,' he added.

'The big boys are still coming out from Ellice,' Walter Bennett down the net pointed out. 'They're gonna dust the Japs with daisy cutters before we ever hit the sand.'

'That's bullshit,' said another voice. 'There aren't going to be no daisy cutters coming. You're a motherfucking dreamer, Walter.'

'A fucking Jap shell,' Jim Harvey said. 'Goddamn it to shit, I – '

But another shell came whistling down and slammed into the water a hundred yards in front of them, sending up a momentary geyser.

'Fuckers!' Private Harvey yelled. 'I thought they softened the bastards up! Thought we was just mopping up!'

'They been fucking up for days, lobbing 'em long,' a boy named Larry Jackson explained calmly. 'All that softening-up bullshit don't mean a rat's ass. They fucked it all up, and now we're going in, and there's all sorts of fucking Jap fire.'

'Jesus,' said Jim Harvey. 'I can't *believe* this bullshit. What the fuck is going on here?'

The LCP pushed on toward Betio with Third Platoon aboard. Ishmael could hear the whistling of shells now distantly across the water. He sat low beneath a plywood gunnel a navy crew had jury-rigged during down time

2 **sucker** (infml): (here) person who is easily tricked or persuaded to do sth.
5 **reinforcement**: Verstärkung   7 **beachhead**: strong position on a beach from which an army that has just landed prepares to attack   34 **shell**: (hier) Granate
38 **swear under your breath**: use rude or offensive language, usu. because you are angry, but so quietly that nobody can hear you   43 **dust sb./sth. off** (infml): (here) kill sb. / destroy sth. completely so that not even their dust is left behind   45 **big boys** = B-24 bombers   46 **daisy cutter** (sl): very powerful bomb dropped from an aircraft that explodes close to the ground and causes a lot of destruction over a large area   53–54 **soften sb. up** (infml): make sb., esp. an enemy weaker and easier to attack   55 **lob sb./sth.** (infml): throw sb./sth. hard, so that they are sent flying high through the air   63 **jury-rig sth.**: etwas provisorisch anbringen   **down time** (also downtime) ['--]: Pause, Freizeit

in Nouméa. He was weighted down now heavily by his pack, with his helmet pulled to his brow. He could hear Jim Harvey chattering hopefully: 'The fuckers been pounding 'em up for days, right? There ain't nothing left there but sand and bullshit and a whole lot of little Jap pieces. That's what *everyone's* been hearing. Madsen read it off the radio and Bledsoe was right there in the room with him, it's no bullshit, they fucking dusted 'em ...'

The seas, as it turned out, contrary to all plans, were running high and choppy. Ishmael did not stand up well on high seas and had become addicted to Dramamine. He swallowed two with water from his belt canteen and peered out over the plywood gunnel with his helmet on but not strapped. The boat thrummed under him, and he saw that they were running alongside three other transports immediately off to the left. He could see the men in the boat next to his; one of them had lit a cigarette and the glow of its tip was visible, though he'd tucked it down inside his cradled palm. Ishmael lowered himself against his pack again, shut his eyes, and put his fingers in his ears. He tried not to think about any of it.

For three hours they pushed toward Betio, the waves coming in constantly over the gunnels and soaking everybody on board. The island became visible as a low black line almost on the horizon. Ishmael stood to stretch his legs now. There were fires glowing all up and down Betio, and a man beside him with a waterproof watch was attempting to time the battleship salvos being fired on the island. On the other side two men were complaining bitterly about an Admiral Hill who was in charge of things and who had timed matters such that they were going in at daylight instead of under cover of darkness. They could see that the navy was firing heavily — black smoke rose from the island in great billows — and this began to have a positive influence on the disposition of Third Platoon. 'There ain't gonna be nothing left of the fuckers,' Private Harvey asserted. 'Them five-inch guns'll do the trick. They're pounding the shit out of them.'

Fifteen minutes later they ran the big current at the entrance to Tarawa lagoon. They bobbed past two destroyers, the *Dashiell* and the *Ringgold*, both of which were firing in waves at the beach; the noise of it was deafening, louder than anything Ishmael had ever heard. Strapping his helmet on now, he decided he was done looking over the gunnel. He had peered up once and seen three amphibious tractors going up on the beach far ahead. They were taking a lot of machine-gun fire; one fell down into a shell hole; another caught fire and halted. There were no more divebombers coming in at all, and the B-24s had not appeared. The best thing to do was to tuck down, strap up, and keep well out of the line of fire. Ishmael had somehow arrived at the war moment little boys are prone to dream about. He was storming a beach, he was a marine radioman, and he felt like shitting his pants, literally. He could feel his rectum puckering.

'Holy shit,' Jim Harvey was saying. 'Goddamn it to hell, the motherfuckers, goddamn those assholes, the fucking shitheads, goddamn it, this ain't *right*!'

The squad leader, a man named Rich Hinkle from Yreka, California, who had made Ishmael an excellent chess partner in New Zealand, was the first among them to die. The transport ground up suddenly on the reef – they were still more than five hundred yards from the beach – and the men sat looking at one another for thirty seconds or more while artillery pinged off the LCP's port side. 'There's bigger stuff coming,' Hinkle yelled above the din. 'We'd better get the hell out of here. Let's move it! Move! Let's go!' 'You first,' somebody answered.

Hinkle went over the starboard gunnel and dropped down into the water. Men began to follow him, including Ishmael Chambers, who was manuevering his eighty-five-pound pack over the side when Hinkle was shot in the face and went down, and then the man just behind him was shot, too, and the top of his head came off. Ishmael wrestled his pack into the lagoon and splashed in hard behind it. He submerged himself for as long as he could, came up only for a single breath – he could see small-arms fire flashing along the shore – then went deep again. When he came up he saw that everybody – the ammo carriers, the demolitions guys, the machine gunners, *everybody* – they were all dropping everything into the water and going under like Ishmael.

---

3 **pound sb./sth. up**: attack sb./sth. with bombs   5 **read sth. off the radio** (infml): get information by listening to the radio   8 **choppy**: (of the sea) with a lot of small waves, not calm   11 **thrum** [θrʌm]: make a low sound like the sound of an engine   22 **salvo** ['sælvoʊ]: Salve   26 **billow**: Rauchschwaden   27 **disposition**: (hier) Laune, Verfassung   31 **bob** (v): move quickly up and down, esp. in water   33 **deafening**: ohrenbetäubend   40 **be prone to do sth.**: veranlagt sein, etwas zu tun   42 **pucker**: sich zusammenziehen   48 **grind up on sth.**: auf etwas auflaufen   51 **ping off sth.**: hit sth. hard, rebound off it (= abprallen) and make a short, high ringing sound when doing so   **port side**: Backbordseite   52 **din**: loud, unpleasant noise that lasts for a long time   62 **ammo** (infml) = ammunition

He swam back behind the LCP with three dozen other soldiers. The navy coxswain was still exerting himself, cursing and ramming the throttle back and forth, to free the landing craft from the reef. Lieutenant Bellows was screaming at the men on board who had refused to go over the gunnels. 'Fuck you, Bellows,' somebody kept saying. 'You go first!' screamed someone else. Ishmael recognized the voice of Private Harvey, now at a hysterical pitch.

The LCP took more small-arms fire, and the crowd of men who had crouched behind it began to wade toward shore. Ishmael kept to the middle of the group, swimming and keeping low, breaststroking, and tried to think of himself as a dead marine floating harmlessly in Betio's lagoon, a corpse borne by the current. The men were in chest-high water now, some of them carrying rifles above their heads, and they were dropping into seas already tinged pink by the blood of other men in front of them. Ishmael saw men go lurching down, saw the machine-gun fire whipping the water's surface, and lowered himself even farther. In the shallows ahead of him a Private Newland stood up to run for the seawall, and then another man he didn't know made a run for it and was shot dead in the surf, and then a third man ran for it. The fourth, Eric Bledsoe, was shot in the knee and lay down again in the shallows. Ishmael stopped and watched the fifth and sixth men draw fire, then gathered himself and thrashed out of the water while the men ahead of him ran for it. All three of them made the seawall unharmed and crouched there watching Eric Bledsoe; his knee had been shot away.

Ishmael saw Eric Bledsoe bleed to death. Fifty yards away he lay in the surf pleading in a soft voice for help. 'Oh, shit,' he said. 'Help me, you guys, come on, you guys, fucking help me, please.' Eric had grown up in Delaware with Ernest Testaverde; they'd gotten drunk together a lot in Wellington. Robert Newland wanted to run out to save him, but Lieutenant Bellows held him back; there was nothing to be done about it, Bellows pointed out, there was far too much gunfire for something like that, the upshot of it all would be two dead men, and everyone silently agreed. Ishmael pushed his body up against the seawall; he was not going to run down the beach again to drag a wounded man to safety, though a part of him wanted to try. What could he have done about it anyway? His equipment was floating in the lagoon. He could not even offer Eric Bledsoe a bandage, much less save his life. He sat there and watched Eric roll over in the surf so that his face was pointing toward the sun. His legs were only partly in the water, and Ishmael could see plainly where one of them had come off and was moving with the undulations of the surf. The boy bled to death and then his leg floated away a few feet on the waves while Ishmael crouched behind the seawall.

At ten o'clock he was still there, unarmed and without a job to do, hunkered down with hundreds of other men who had come ashore and been shot at. There were plenty more dead marines on the beach now, and plenty more of the wounded, too, and the men behind the seawall tried not to listen when they moaned or called out for help. Then a sergeant from J Company, from out of nowhere, it seemed, was suddenly standing above them on the seawall with a cigarette hanging from the corner of his mouth, calling them 'a bunch of chickenshits.' He berated them relentlessly, a stream of invective, characterizing them as 'the sorts of cowards who ought to have your balls chewed off real slow and painful like when this goddamn battle is over,' men who'd let 'other men do the dirty work to save your own sorry asses,' men who 'aren't men at all but cornhole-fuckers and jack-off artists with half-inch hard-ons on those days once a year when you can get your sorry dicks to stand at half-mast,' and so on and so forth, while the men below pleaded with him to take cover and save himself. He refused and was shot through the spine with a shell that ripped open his shirt front and dropped some of his guts onto the beach. The sergeant had no time to be surprised and simply fell over face first into the sand and squarely on top of his own intestines. Nobody said anything.

A tractor at last breached a hole in the seawall, and a few men began to go through. All of them were shot immediately. Ishmael was commandeered

---

2 **coxswain** ['kɑːksn]: person who is in charge of a small boat, esp. a lifeboat and who controls its direction   7 **pitch** (n): Ton, Stimmlage   14 **tinge sth.**: add a shade of a color to sth.   15 **lurch**: make a sudden, unsteady movement in a direction   22 **thrash**: move violently   32 **upshot of sth.**: outcome/result of sth.   40 **undulation**: (here) up-and-down movement of the waves   50 **chickenshit** (sl): (hier) Angsthase   50–51 **berate sb.**: criticize or speak angrily to sb.   51 **relentless**: not stopping or becoming less fierce   **invective**: rude language and unpleasant remarks, usu. shouted at sb.   55 **jack-off artists** (sl): Wichser   **hard-on**: erect penis   56 **sorry**: (hier) armselig   **dick** (sl): penis   62 **intestines** (pl): Gedärme

to help dig free a half-track that had been deposited on Betio by a tank lighter and had promptly buried itself. He dug on his knees with an entrenching tool while the man beside him threw up in the sand before lying down with his helmet across his face and fainting. A radioman from K Company had set up against the seawall and was railing loudly about interference; every time battleship guns were fired offshore even the static died out, he complained. He couldn't raise anybody.

Ishmael realized, in the early afternoon, that the sweetish smell coming at him from off the beach was the odor of dead marines. He, too, vomited, then drank the last of his water. As far as he knew, no one else in his squad was even alive anymore. He had not seen any of them in over three hours, but he had been given a carbine, an ammo pack, and a field machete by a crew of cargo handlers moving down the wall with resupply orders. He fieldstripped the carbine – it was full of sand – and cleaned it as carefully as he could under the conditions, sitting against the base of the seawall with his steel helmet unstrapped. He was sitting there like that with the trigger assembly in hand, dabbing at it with the tail of his shirt, when a new wave of amtracs came up on the beach and began drawing mortar fire. Ishmael watched them with interest for a while, men spilling out and falling to the sand – some dead, some wounded, some screaming as they ran – then lowered his head and, refusing to look, went back to cleaning his carbine. He was still there, huddled in the same place with his carbine in hand, his machete in a sheath that hung from his belt, when darkness fell four hours later.

A colonel came down the beach with his entourage, exhorting the noncoms and junior officers to re-form and improvise squads. At 1900 hours, he said – less than twenty minutes from now – every man there was going over the top; anyone who stayed behind would be court-martialed; it was time, he added, to act like marines. The colonel moved on, and a Lieutenant Doerper from K Company asked Ishmael where his squad was and what the hell he thought he was doing dug in by himself against the seawall. Ishmael explained how he had lost his equipment going over the gunnel of an LCP and how everyone around him had died or been wounded; he didn't know where anyone was. Lieutenant Doerper listened impatiently, then told Ishmael to pick out a man along the wall, and then pick out another, and then some more, until he had himself a squad formed, and then to report to the command post Colonel Freeman had set up beside the buried half-track. He had, he said, no time for bullshit.

Ishmael explained matters to two dozen boys before he'd gathered enough of a squad. One boy told him to go fuck himself; another claimed to have an incapacitating leg wound; a third said he'd be along in a minute but never moved. There was gunfire coming from off the water suddenly, and Ishmael surmised that a Jap sniper had swum out and was manning the machine gun left behind on an amtrac destroyed in the lagoon. The seawall was no longer safe.

Moving down the wall, staying low and talking rapidly to people, he came at last on Ernest Testaverde, who was returning fire over the coconut logs with his gun held high and his head down. 'Hey,' said Ishmael. 'Jesus.'

'Chambers,' said Ernest. 'Jesus fucking Christ.'

'Where is everybody?' asked Ishmael. 'What about Jackson and those guys?'

'I saw Jackson get hit,' Ernest answered. 'All the demolitions guys and the mine detector guys got hit coming up onto the beach. And Walter,' he added. 'And Jim Harvey. And that guy Hedges, I saw him go down. And Murray and Behring got hit, too. They all got hit in the water.'

'So did Hinkle,' said Ishmael. 'And Eric Bledsoe – his leg came off. And Fitz – he got hit on the beach, I saw him go down. Bellows made it, but I don't know where he is. Newland, too. Where are those guys?'

Ernest Testaverde didn't answer. He pulled at his helmet strap and set his carbine down. 'Bledsoe?' he said. 'You sure?'

Ishmael nodded. 'He's dead.'

---

1 **half-track**: Halbkettenfahrzeug   1–2 **tank lighter**: vehicle transporting tanks
5 **rail about sth.**: complain about sth. in a very angry way   6 **interference** [ˌɪntərˈfɪrəns]: Frequenzstörung   7 **raise sb.**: (here) contact sb. and speak to them by radio   13 **crew of cargo handlers**: Versorgungstrupp   14 **resupply**: Nachschub   **fieldstrip sth.**: etwas zerlegen (bes. Waffen)   17 **trigger assembly**: Abzugsmechanismus   25 **entourage**: group of people who accompany an important person   **exhort sb. to do sth.**: try hard to persuade sb. to do sth.   26 **noncom** = non-commissioned officer (AE): Unteroffizier   28 **court martial sb.**: jdn. vor das Kriegsgericht stellen   43 **surmise sth.** [sərˈmaɪz]: etwas annehmen   **sniper**: person who shoots at sb. from a hidden position

'His leg came off?' said Ernest.

Ishmael sat down with his back to the seawall. He did not want to talk about Eric Bledsoe or remember how he had died. It was difficult to know what the point would be of talking about such a thing. There was no point to anything, that was clear. He couldn't think straight about anything that had happened since the landing craft had ground onto the coral reef. The situation he found himself in now had the sodden quality of a dream in which events repeated themselves. He was dug in against the seawall, and then he found himself there again, and again he was still dug in beneath the seawall. Occasionally a flare lit things well enough so that he saw the details of his own hands. He was weary and thirsty, and he could not really focus, and the adrenalin had died inside of him. He wanted to live, he knew that now, but everything else was unclear. He could not recollect his reason for being there – why he had enlisted to fight in the marines, what the point of it was. 'Yeah,' he said. 'Bledsoe's dead.'

'Goddamn it,' answered Ernest Testaverde. He kicked the first log in the seawall twice, then a third time, then a fourth. Ishmael Chambers turned away from him.

At 1900 hours they went over the seawall along with three hundred other men. They were met by mortar and machine-gun fire from straight ahead in the palm trees. Ishmael never saw Ernest Testaverde get hit; later he found out, on making inquiries, that Ernest had been found with a hole in his head roughly the size of a man's fist. Ishmael himself was hit in the left arm, squarely in the middle of his biceps. The muscle tore when the round entered – a single round from a Nambu machine gun – and the bone cracked jaggedly into a hundred splinters that were driven up against his nerves and veins and lodged into the meat of his arm.

Four hours later, when the light came up, he became aware of two medical corpsmen kneeling beside the man next to him. The man had been hit in the head, it seemed, and his brains were leaking out around his helmet. Ishmael had maneuvered behind this dead man and taken the sulfa pills and a roll of bandages from the medical kit at his belt. He'd wrapped his arm and had used the weight of his body to keep his blood from spilling out. 'It's okay,' one of the corpsmen told Ishmael. 'We're bringing up a litter team and a squad of bearers. The beach is secured. Everything's fine. We're going to get you shipboard pronto.'

'Fucking Japs,' said Ishmael.

Later he lay on the deck of some ship or other, seven miles out to sea from Betio, one boy in the middle of rows and rows of wounded, and the boy on the litter to his left died from the shrapnel that had pierced his liver. On the other side was a boy with buckteeth who'd been shot squarely in the thighs and groin; the blood had soaked his khaki pants. The boy could not speak and lay with his back arched; every few seconds he groaned mechanically between forced, shallow breaths. Ishmael asked him once if he was all right, but the boy only went on with his groaning. He died ten minutes before the bearers came around to take him down to surgery.

Ishmael lost his arm on a shipboard operating table to a pharmacist's mate who had done only four amputations in his career, all of them in the past few hours. The mate used a handsaw to square up the bone and cauterized the stump unevenly, so that the wound healed more slowly than it would have otherwise and the scar tissue left behind was thick and coarse. Ishmael had not been fully anesthetized and awoke to see his arm where it had been dropped in a corner on top of a pile of blood-soaked dressings. Ten years later he would still dream of that, the way his own fingers curled against the wall, how white and distant his arm looked, though nevertheless he recognized it there, a piece of trash on the floor. Somebody saw him staring at it and gave an order, and the arm was scooped up inside a towel and dumped into a canvas bin. Somebody else pricked him once again with morphine, and Ishmael told whoever it was that 'the Japs are ... the fucking Japs ...' but he didn't quite know how to finish his words, he didn't quite know what he meant to utter, *'that fucking goddamn Jap bitch'* was all he could think to say.

---

10 **flare** (n): Leuchtrakete   27 **jagged**: with rough, pointed, often sharp edges
33 **sulfa** = sulfonamid: antibacterial drug   36 **bearer**: person whose job it is to carry sth.   42 **buckteeth**: top teeth that stick forward   50 **square sth. up**: make sth. have straight edges   51 **cauterize sth.**: burn a wound, using a chemical or heat, in order to stop the loss of blood or to prevent infection   52 **scar tissue**: Narbengewebe   55 **dressing**: Verband   59 **scoop sth. up**: lift sth. up quickly, esp. by putting it inside a container

Chapter 17

By two o'clock on the first afternoon of the trial, snow had covered all the island roads. A car pirouetted silently while skating on its tires, emerged from this on a transverse angle, and slid to a stop with one headlight thrust into the door of Petersen's Grocery, which somebody opened at just the right moment – miraculously – so that no damage was done to car or store. Behind the Amity Harbor Elementary School, a girl of seven bending over to pack a snowball was rammed from behind by a boy skidding down a hill on a piece of cardboard box. She broke her right arm – a greenstick fracture. The principal, Erik Karlsen, wrapped a blanket around her shoulders and sat her down next to a steam radiator before going out to run his car engine. Then, gingerly, peering out through the crescents of glass his defroster had carved from the icy windshield, he drove her down First Hill into town.

On Mill Run Road Mrs. Larsen of Skiff Point ran her husband's DeSoto into a ditch. Arne Stolbaad overloaded his wood-burning stove and ended up with a chimney fire. The volunteer fire department was called out by a neighbor, but the pumper truck driver, Edgar Paulsen, lost traction on Indian Knob Hill and had to halt to put on tire chains. In the meantime Arne Stolbaad's chimney fire expired; when the firemen showed up at last he expressed to them his delight at having burned clean the flue creosote.

At three o'clock five school buses left Amity Harbor with their windshield wipers batting ice from the windshields and their headlights casting into the snowfall. High school students walking home hurled snowballs at them; the South Beach bus slid off the road shoulder just beyond Island Center. The schoolchildren climbed out and walked home in the snow-storm with Johnny Katayama, the bus driver, escorting them from behind. As each child turned off toward home, Johnny handed him or her a half stick of spearmint gum.

A boy on a sled that afternoon broke his ankle against the base of a cedar tree. He had not quite understood how to make the thing turn,

David Guterson: **Snow Falling on Cedars** 221

and the tree had come up on him suddenly. He'd put his foot out to ward it off.

A retired dentist, old Doc Cable, slipped hard on the way to his
35 firewood shed. Something in his tailbone twisted when he went down, so that Doc Cable winced and curled fetally in the snow. After a while he hauled himself up, lurched inside, and reported to his wife through clenched teeth that he'd injured himself. Sarah put him on the couch with a hot-water bottle, where he took two aspirins and fell asleep.

40 Two teenagers engaged in a snowball-throwing contest from the dock at Port Jefferson Harbor. The point was to hit a mooring buoy at first, then a piling on the next dock. One of the teenagers, Dan Daniels's son Scott, took a three-step running start, threw out to sea, then pitched headlong into the salt water. He was out again in five seconds, steam
45 rising off his clothes. Running home, racing through the snowfall, his hair froze into icy tufts.

The citizens of San Piedro made their run on Petersen's and cleared the shelves of canned goods. They brought so much snow into the store on their boots that one of the box boys, Earl Camp, stayed busy all afternoon
50 with a mop and a towel, cleaning up after them. Einar Petersen took a box of salt from his shelf and spread its contents outside the door, but two customers slipped despite this. Einar decided to offer free coffee to shoppers and asked one of his checkers, Jessica Porter – who was twenty-two and cheerful looking – to stand behind a folding table and serve.

55 At Fisk's Hardware Center the citizens of San Piedro bought snow shovels, candles, kerosene, kitchen matches, lined gloves, and flashlight batteries. The Torgerson brothers sold out their supply of tire chains by three o'clock, as well as most of their ice scrapers and antifreeze. Tom pulled ditched cars free with his freshly painted two-ton wrecker; Dave

---

3 **transverse**: diagonal   9 **greenstick fracture**: way of breaking a limb in which one side of the bone is broken and the other only bent   11 **gingerly**: in a careful way, esp. because you are afraid of being hurt   15 **ditch**: Graben   18 **traction** ['trækʃn]: Bodenhaftung   21 **flue**: Rauchabzug   33 **ward sb./sth. off**: protect or defend yourself against sb./sth.   35 **tailbone**: Steißbein   36 **fetally**: like a foetus   43–44 **pitch into sth.**: fall heavily into sth.   44 **headlong**: kopfüber   46 **tuft**: Büschel   49 **box boy**: person working at a supermarket, packing up the goods into boxes for the customers to take them home in   53 **checker**: Kassierer/~in   56 **lined**: gefüttert   59 **wrecker** ['rekər]: Abschleppwagen

sold gasoline, batteries, and motor oil and advised his customers to go home and *stay* home. Dozens of islanders stopped in to listen while Dave pumped their gas or put on their tire chains and made grim predictions about the weather. 'Three-day blow,' he'd say. 'Folks'd better be ready.'

By three o'clock the branches of the cedars were loaded down with snow. When the wind came up it blew right through them, whirling flurries to the ground. San Piedro's strawberry fields became fields of white, as untouched and flawless as desert. The noise of living things was not so much muted as halted – even the seagulls were silenced. Instead there was the wind and the collapse of waves and the withdrawing of the water down the beaches.

Everywhere on San Piedro Island a grimness set in, accompanied by a strained anticipation. Who knew what might happen now that a December storm had started? The homes of these islanders might soon lie in drifts so that only the sloped roofs of the beach cabins would show and only the upper stories of the larger houses. The power might fizzle when the wind blew hard and leave them all in darkness. Their toilets might not flush, their well pumps might not draw, they would live close to their stoves and lanterns. Yet on the other hand the snowstorm might mean a respite, a happy wintertime vacation. Schools would shut down, roads would close, no one would go off to their jobs. Families would eat large breakfasts late, then dress for snow and go out in the knowledge that they'd return to warm, snug houses. Smoke would curl from chimneys; at dusk lights would come on. Lopsided snowmen would stand sentinel in yards. There would be enough to eat, no reason for worry.

Still, those who had lived on the island a long time knew that the storm's outcome was beyond their control. This storm might well be like others past that had caused them to suffer, had *killed* even – or perhaps it might dwindle beneath tonight's stars and give their children snow-bound happiness. Who knew? Who could predict? If disaster, so be it, they said to themselves. There was nothing to be done except what could be done. The rest – like the salt water around them, which swallowed the snow without any effort, remaining what it was implacably – was out of their hands, beyond.

When the afternoon recess was over that day, Alvin Hooks called Art Moran again. The sheriff had left the courtroom for two and a half hours in order to contact the volunteer fire department and to call out his volunteer deputies, men who could be counted on in times of trouble. Generally their role was to keep order at the Strawberry Festival and other public occasions; now they would divide up the island terrain according to the locations of their homes and businesses and assist those stranded on the roads.

Art fidgeted in the witness stand for the second time that day. The snowstorm, just now, preoccupied him. He understood that Alvin's case necessitated his appearing twice at the trial, but on the other hand he wasn't glad about it. He'd eaten a sandwich during the fifteen-minute recess, sat in Alvin's office with a piece of wax paper laid across his knees and an apple on the edge of the desk. Hooks had reminded him to tell his story methodically, to pay attention to those minor details that might seem to him irrelevant. Now, on the witness stand, pinching the knot of his tie together and checking the corners of his lips for crumbs, Art waited impatiently while Alvin asked the judge to admit four pieces of rope into evidence. 'Sheriff Moran,' Hooks said at last. 'I have in my hand four lengths of rope of the sort fishermen use for mooring lines. May I ask you to inspect them, please?'

Art took the pieces of rope in his hand and made a show of looking at them carefully. 'Okay,' he said after a moment.

'Do you recognize them?'

'Yes, I do.'

'Did you refer to these pieces of mooring line in your report, Sheriff Moran? Are they the same four referred to in your report?'

'Yes, they are. They're the ones I wrote about in my report, Mr. Hooks. These are them.'

The judge admitted the lines as evidence, and Ed Soames put a tag on each. Alvin Hooks put them back in Art's hands and asked him to explain where he'd found them.

3 **prediction** [prɪ'dɪkʃn]: Vorhersage   7 **flurry**: Wirbel   8 **flawless**: makellos
13 **strained**: angespannt   14 **drift**: Schneewehe   16 **story**: Stockwerk   **fizzle**: become less   18 **well** (n): hole made in the ground to obtain water   19 **respite** ['respɪt]: short break or escape from sth. difficult or unpleasant   23 **snug** [snʌg]: warm and comfortable   24 **stand sentinel** ['sentɪnl]: Wache stehen   43 **fidget**: keep moving your body, esp. your hands or feet because you are nervous or excited   45 **necessitate sth.** [nə'sesɪteɪt]: make sth. necessary

'Well,' said the sheriff. 'This one here, marked with an A, came from the defendant's boat. It came off the port side cleat, to be exact, *third* cleat up from the stern. It matches all his other mooring lines, you see? Matches 'em all except the one on the port side cleat *second* up from the stern. That's this one here, the one marked B – that one was new, Mr. Hooks, but the rest were worn. They were all three-strand manila lines with a bowline knotted into one end, pretty well worn down, too. That's how Mr. Miyamoto kept his mooring lines – bowlined and pretty well worn out, except the one. It was brand-new but had the bowline in it.'

'And the other two?' asked Alvin Hooks. 'Where did you find them, sheriff?'

'I found them on Carl Heine's boat, Mr. Hooks. This one here – the one marked C' – the sheriff held the line up for the benefit of the jury – 'is exactly the same as every other line I found on Mr. Heine's, the deceased's, boat. You see here? It's a three-strand manila rope in new condition with a fancy eye braided in at one end – braided in by hand, Mr. Hooks, the way Carl Heine was known to do them. All his lines were braided up in loops, none of them had bowlines.'

'The fourth line you have there,' Alvin Hooks pushed on. 'Where did you find it, sheriff?'

'Found it on Carl Heine's boat, too, but it doesn't match up with the rest of them. Found it on the starboard side, second cleat back from the stern. Peculiar thing is, it *does* match up with the lines I found on board the defendant's boat. It's pretty well worn, and it's got the bowline in it just like the other one I showed you, just like *all* his mooring lines except the new one. It looks so much like all the others, it's clear it came from the same set. Worn down just the same.'

'This line looks like the ones on the defendant's boat?'

'Exactly.'

'But you found it on the deceased's boat?'

'That's right.'

'On the starboard side, second cleat from the stern?'

'Yes.'

'And the defendant's boat – do I understand this right? – had a new line on the port side, sheriff – again the second cleat from the stern?'

'That's right, Mr. Hooks. There was a new line there.'

'Sheriff,' Alvin Hooks said. 'If the defendant had tied up to Carl Heine's boat would these two cleats in question line up?'

'You bet they'd line up. And if he – Miyamoto there – had gotten in a hurry to cast off from the deceased's boat, he could have left a line behind tied off to that second cleat.'

'I see,' said Alvin Hooks. 'Your inference is that he left a line behind, then replaced it with that new one – exhibit B, right there in your hand – replaced it when he got back to the docks.'

'It is,' said Art Moran. 'Exactly. He tied up to Carl's boat and left a line on it. That seems to me pretty clear.'

'But sheriff,' said Alvin Hooks. 'What led you to investigate the defendant in the first place? Why did you think to look around his boat and to notice something like a new mooring line?'

Art pointed out that his investigation into the death of Carl Heine had led him, quite naturally, to ask questions of Carl's relatives. He'd gone to see Etta Heine, he said, and explained to her that even in the case of a fishing accident there was a formal investigation to proceed with. Did Carl have any enemies?

After Etta, he said, the path to Ole Jurgensen was clear, and from Ole to Judge Lew Fielding's chambers: Art had needed a search warrant. He intended to search Kabuo Miyamoto's boat, the *Islander*, before it left that night for the salmon grounds.

---

2 **cleat**: small bar on a boat to which ropes are fastened   6 **manila**: fibers (= Fasern) of a plant which are used to make textiles, paper and ropes   7 **bowline**: kind of knot esp. used on boats, which produces a hole, with which a rope can be fastened to a cleat but which is not fixed   16 **fancy eye**: kind of knot with a fixed hole which can be used to fasten a rope to a cleat   **braid sth. in sth. else**: etwas in etwas anderes hineinknüpfen

Chapter 18

It had been the judge's bailiff, Ed Soames, who'd answered the door when Art Moran knocked at five after five on the evening of the sixteenth and asked to see Lew Fielding. The bailiff wore his coat and held his lunchbox in his hand; he'd been on his way out, he explained; the judge was still working at his desk.

'This about Carl Heine?' inquired Ed.

'I guess you heard,' the sheriff answered. 'But, no, this isn't about him. And if you go down to the cafe and say it is, you know what? You'll be wrong, Ed.'

'I'm not that way,' said the bailiff. 'Maybe others are, but I'm not.'

"Course you're not,' said Art Moran.

The bailiff knocked at the door to the judge's chambers, then opened it and said that the sheriff was present on business he wished to keep private. 'All right,' answered the judge. 'Send him in.'

The bailiff held the door open for Art Moran and stood aside to let him pass. 'Good night, judge,' he said. 'See you in the morning.'

'Good night, Ed,' the judge replied. 'Could you lock up on your way out, please? The sheriff here is my last visitor.'

'Will do,' said Ed Soames, and shut the door.

The sheriff sat and adjusted his legs. He set his hat on the floor. The judge waited patiently until he heard the lock click. Then he looked the sheriff in the eye for the first time. 'Carl Heine,' he said.

'Carl Heine,' the sheriff answered.

Lew Fielding put his pen down. 'A man with kids, with a wife,' he said.

'I know,' Art answered. 'I went out this morning and told Susan Marie about it. Christ,' he added bitterly.

Lew Fielding nodded. He sat morosely with his elbows on his desk, cradling his chin in his hands. As always he looked to be on the verge of sleep; his eyes were those of a basset hound. His cheeks were creviced, his forehead furrowed, his silver eyebrows grew in fat tufts. Art remembered when he had been more spry, remembered him pitching horseshoes at the Strawberry Festival. The judge in his suspenders with his sleeves rolled up, squinting and half bent over.

'How is she?' the judge asked. 'Susan Marie?'

'Not good,' Art Moran replied.

Lew Fielding looked at him and waited. Art picked his hat up, set it in his lap, and began fiddling with its brim. 'Anyway, I came down to get you to sign a warrant. I want to search Kabuo Miyamoto's boat, maybe his house, too – I'm not sure yet.'

'Kabuo Miyamoto,' the judge said. 'What are you looking for?'

'Well,' the sheriff answered, leaning forward. 'I've got these *concerns*, judge. Five of 'em altogether. Number one, I've got men telling me Miyamoto worked the same waters Carl did last night when this thing happened. Number two, I've got Etta Heine saying Miyamoto and her son were enemies from way back – an old dispute over land. Three, I've got a piece of mooring line somebody left on Carl's boat wrapped around one of the cleats; seems like he could have been boarded, maybe, and I want to take a look at Miyamoto's mooring lines. Four, I've got Ole Jurgensen claiming both Carl and Miyamoto were out to see him recently 'bout buying his property, which Ole sold to Carl. 'Cording to Ole, Miyamoto went away hopping mad. Said he was going to have a talk with Carl. And, well, maybe he did. At sea. And things ... got out of hand.'

'And what's the fifth?' asked Lew Fielding.

'Fifth?'

'You claimed to have five categories of cause. I've heard four. What's the fifth?'

'Oh,' said Art Moran. 'Horace did a ... pretty thorough autopsy. There's a bad wound in the side of Carl's head. And Horace said something interesting about it that fits in with what I'm hearing from Ole. And from Etta, too, for that matter. Said he'd seen wounds like this one during the war. Said the Japs made 'em with their gun butts. Said they were trained to fight with sticks from the time they were kids. They were trained in *kendo*, Horace called it. And one of these *kendo* blows, I guess, would leave the kind of wound Carl has. Now at the time I didn't

---

28 **be on the verge of sth.**: be very near to sth. in time   29 **creviced**: eingefallen
31 **spry** (adj): (esp. of older people) full of life and energy   45 **way back**: long time ago   52 **get out of hand**: become difficult to control

make nothing of it. I didn't even think of it when some of the guys down at the docks said Miyamoto'd been out on Ship Channel Bank last night – same place as Carl. Didn't even occur to me then. But I did think of it this afternoon when Etta told 'bout all the problems she'd had with Miyamoto, and I thought about it even more after Ole Jurgensen said his piece. And I decided I'd better follow this lead through and search Miyamoto's boat, Judge. Just in case. See what signs there are, if any.'

Judge Lew Fielding pinched the tip of his nose. 'I don't know, Art,' he said. 'First of all, you've got Horace's off-the-cuff-statement regarding a coincidental resemblance between this wound in Carl Heine's head and ones he saw inflicted by Japanese soldiers – now does *that* really point us toward Miyamoto? You've got Etta Heine, who I won't go into, but suffice it to say I don't trust that woman. She's hateful, Art; I don't trust her. And you've got at least fifty gill-netters out in the fog last night – any one of them as contentious as the next when he figures some other guy is cutting into his fish – and then you've got Ole Jurgensen. And I admit Ole is interesting. I admit you've got something worth thinking about with Ole. But – '

'Judge,' Art Moran cut in, 'can I say something? If you think about it *too* long we'll lose our chance altogether. The boats'll be going out soon.'

The judge pulled his sleeve back and squinted at his watch. 'Five-twenty,' he said. 'You're right.'

'I've got an affidavit here,' the sheriff pressed on, pulling it free of his shirt pocket. 'I did it up fast, but it's right, Judge. Lays it all out plain and simple. What I want to look for is a murder weapon, that's all, if there's a chance of that.'

'Well,' replied Lew Fielding. 'No harm, I suppose, if you do it properly, Art.' He leaned across his desk toward the sheriff. 'And for technicality's sake let's make *this* move, too: do you swear that the facts in this affidavit are true, so help you God – do you *swear*?'

The sheriff did.

'All right. You bring a warrant?'

The sheriff produced one from the opposite shirt pocket; the judge unfolded it beneath his desk lamp and picked up his fountain pen. 'I'm going to put this down,' he said. 'I'm going to allow you to search the boat but not Miyamoto's house. No intruding on his wife and children, I don't see there's any hurry to do something like that. And remember, now, this is a *limited* search. The murder weapon, Art, and nothing else. I won't have you running roughshod over this man's privacy.'

'Got it,' Art Moran said. 'The murder weapon.'

'You don't find anything on the boat, come see me in the morning. We'll talk about his house at that point.'

'All right,' said Art Moran. 'Thanks.'

He asked, then, if he might use the telephone. He dialed his office and spoke with Eleanor Dokes. 'Have Abel meet me down to the docks,' he said. 'And tell him to bring along his flashlight.'

San Piedro fishermen, in 1954, were apt to pay attention to signs and portents other men had no inkling of. For them the web of cause and effect was invisible and simultaneously everywhere, which was why a man could sink his net with salmon one night and catch only kelp the next. Tides, currents, and winds were one thing, the force of luck another. A fisherman didn't utter the words horse, pig, or hog on the deck of a gill-netter, for to do so was to bring bad weather down around his head or cause a line to foul in his propeller. Turning a hatch cover upside down brought a southwest storm, and bringing a black suitcase on board meant snarled gear and twisted webbing. Those who harmed seagulls risked the wrath of ship ghosts, for gulls were inhabited by the spirits of men who had been lost at sea in accidents. Umbrellas, too, were bad business, as were broken mirrors and the gift of a pair of scissors. On board a purse seiner only a greenhorn would ever think to trim his fingernails while sitting on a seine pile, or hand a shipmate a bar of soap as opposed to dropping it into his washbasin, or cut the bottom end off a can of fruit. Bad fishing and bad weather could result from any of these.

Kabuo Miyamoto, as he came up the south dock toward his boat that evening – carrying a battery for the *Islander* – saw a flock of seagulls perched on his net drum and stabilizer bars and sitting atop his cabin. When he moved to board they lofted themselves skyward, thirty or forty birds, it appeared at first, a clamor of wings, more of them than he imagined possible, half a hundred seagulls rising from the *Islander*, exploding out of her cockpit. They circled overhead a half-dozen times in arcs that took in the entire breadth of the docks, then settled on the swells to seaward.

Kabuo's heart worked hard in his chest. He was not particularly given to omens, but on the other hand he had never seen this before.

He went in and pried up the battery well cover. He slid his new battery into place and bolted the cables to it. Finally he started his boat engine. He let it run, then flicked the toggle for the number-one pump in order to run his deck hose. Kabuo stood on the edge of the hatch cover and washed gull droppings out the scupper holes. The gulls had disturbed his equilibrium, put him ill at ease. Other boats were pulling out, he saw, motoring past the buoys in Amity Harbor on their way to the salmon grounds. He looked at his watch; five-forty already. It occurred to him to try his luck at Ship Channel that evening; the good sets would be taken at Elliot Head.

When he looked up a lone gull had perched arrogantly on the port gunnel ten feet away and to stern. It was pearl gray and white winged, a young herring gull with a wide, flaring breast, and it seemed to be watching him, too.

Kabuo reached back delicately and turned the hose valve full open. The water shot harder against the aft deck and ricocheted to stern. When he had fixed in on the gull again he watched it for a moment out of the corners of his eyes, then shifted his weight to the left swiftly and aimed his hose at it. The stream caught the surprised bird broadside in the breast, and while it struggled to escape from the force of the water its head smashed against the gunnel of the *Channel Star*, which was moored in the adjacent berth.

Kabuo, the hose still in his hand, was standing beside the port gunnel staring at the dying gull when Art Moran and Abel Martinson appeared beside his boat, both carrying flashlights.

The sheriff, twice, slashed a hand across his throat. 'Cut your engine,' he called.

'What for?' asked Kabuo Miyamoto.

'I've got a warrant,' replied the sheriff, and took it out of his shirt pocket. 'We're going to search your boat tonight.'

Kabuo blinked at him, and then his face hardened. He shut the nozzle off and looked the sheriff in the eye. 'How long will it take?' he asked.

'I don't have any idea,' said the sheriff. 'It might take quite a while.'

'Well, what are you looking for?' asked Kabuo Miyamoto.

'A murder weapon,' answered Art Moran. 'We think you might be responsible for the death of Carl Heine.'

Kabuo blinked a second time and dropped the hose to the deck. 'I didn't kill Carl Heine,' he insisted. 'It wasn't me, sheriff.'

'Then you won't mind us searching, will you?' Art Moran said, and stepped up onto the boat.

He and Abel Martinson rounded the cabin and stepped down into the cockpit. 'You'll want to take a peek at this,' the sheriff said, and handed Kabuo the warrant. 'Meanwhile we're going to start looking around. We don't find anything, you're on your way.'

'Then I'm on my way,' Kabuo answered. 'Because there isn't anything to find.'

'Good,' answered Art. 'Now cut your engine.'

The three of them went into the cabin. Kabuo hit the kill switch beside the wheel. It was quiet now without the engine running. 'Have at it,' Kabuo said.

---

6 **loft yourself skyward**: fly high up in the air   7 **clamor** ['klæmər]: loud noise, esp. one made by a lot of animals   15 **bolt sth. to sth. else**: etwas mit etwas anderem verschrauben   16 **flick a toggle**: einen Schalter umlegen   17 **hose**: Schlauch   18 **scupper hole** ['skʌpər]: opening in the side of a ship at deck level that allows water to run off   19 **equilibrium** [ˌiːkwɪˈlɪbriəm]: calm state of mind   **put sb. ill at ease**: make sb. feel uncomfortable   24 **perch on sth.**: (of a bird) land and sit on sth.   28 **valve** [vælv]: Ventil   29 **ricochet** ['rɪkəʃeɪ]: (von etwas) abprallen   35 **berth**: Liegeplatz   44 **nozzle** ['nɑːzl]: Düse   55 **take a peek at sth.**: einen Blick auf etwas werfen   61 **kill switch**: switch with which an engine can be turned off at once, esp. in an emergency   62–63 **Have at it!**: etwa: 'Legen Sie los! / Bedienen Sie sich!'

'Why don't you just take a load off?' replied Art. 'Have a seat on your bunk.'

Kabuo sat. He read the search warrant. He watched while the deputy, Abel Martinson, went through the tools in his toolbox. Abel picked up each wrench and examined it in the beam of his flashlight. He ran his beam along the galley floor, then knelt with a flathead screwdriver in his hand and pried ajar the battery well cover. His flashlight beam ran over the batteries and down into the recesses of the well. 'D-6s,' he said.

When Kabuo did not reply to this, Abel slid the cover back into place and put the screwdriver away. He turned his flashlight off.

'Engine under the bunk?' he said.

'That's right,' Kabuo answered.

'Stand up and haul the mattress,' said Abel. 'I'll have a look, if you don't mind.'

Kabuo stood, rolled the bedding aside, and opened the engine compartment hatch. 'There you go,' he said.

Abel flicked his flashlight on again and poked his head into the engine compartment. 'Clean,' he said after a while. 'Go ahead and put your mattress back.'

They went out onto the aft deck, Abel Martinson leading. The sheriff was laying hands on things – rain gear, rubber gloves, floats, lines, hose, life ring, deck broom, buckets. He moved slowly, pondering each. He circumnavigated the boat carefully, checking the mooring lines on each cleat as he went, kneeling to look at them closely. For a moment he went forward and knelt beside the anchor, brooding in silence over something. Then he made his way back to the stern and tucked his flashlight into his pants waist.

'I see you replaced a mooring line lately,' he said to Kabuo Miyamoto. 'One right there on that second cleat to port. It's a brand-new line, isn't it.'

'I've had that one around for a while,' Kabuo Miyamoto explained.

The sheriff stared at him. 'Right,' he said. 'Sure you have. Help me with this hold cover, Abel.'

They slid it to one side and peered in together. The stink of salmon flew up at them. 'Nothing,' said Abel. 'Now what?'

'Jump down in there,' urged the sheriff. 'Poke around a little.'

The deputy lowered himself into the hold. He knelt and flicked on his flashlight. He went through the motions of looking. 'Well,' he said. 'I don't see nothing.'

'There's nothing to see,' said Kabuo Miyamoto. 'You guys are wasting your time and mine. I need to get out there fishing.'

'Come on out,' said Art Moran.

Abel turned to starboard, his hands on the hatch combing. Kabuo watched while he peered up under the starboard gunnel at the long-handled gaff wedged against the wall. 'Look at this,' Abel said.

He pulled himself out of the hold and grabbed it – a stout three-and-a-half-foot gaff with a barbed steel hook on one end. He gave it to Art Moran.

'There's blood on it,' he pointed out.

'Fish blood,' said Kabuo. 'I gaff fish with that.'

'What's fish blood doing on the butt end?' Art asked. 'I'd expect maybe to see blood on the hook, but on the *butt* end? Where your hand goes? *Fish* blood?'

'Sure,' said Kabuo. 'It gets on your hands, sheriff. Ask any of these fishermen about that.'

The sheriff took a handkerchief from the rear pocket of his trousers and held the gaff with it. 'I'm going to take and have this tested,' he said, and handed it to Abel Martinson. 'The warrant allows me to do that. I wonder if I could get you to stay in tonight, stay off the water until you hear from me. I know you want to go out and fish, but I wonder if you shouldn't stay in tonight. Go home. Wait and see. Wait there until you hear from me. Because otherwise I'm going to have to arrest you now. Hold you in connection with all this.'

'I didn't kill him,' repeated Kabuo Miyamoto. 'And I can't afford not to fish. I can't let the boat sit idle on a night like this and – '

'Then you're under arrest,' cut in Art Moran. 'Because there's no way I'm letting you go out there. In a half hour you might be in Canada.'

5 **wrench** [rentʃ]: Schraubenschlüssel   6 **galley**: kitchen on a ship or plane
21 **float** (n): (here) light object that floats in the water like a cork that is used to hold a fishing net at water surface   42 **comb** (v): search sth. carefully   44 **gaff** [gæf]: Fischhaken   **wedge sth.**: put sth. into a narrow space, so that it cannot move or fall over   46 **barbed steel hook** (adj): Widerhaken aus Stahl   50 **butt end**: Griffende
64 **let sth. sit idle**: not use sth., not make sth. run or work

'No, I wouldn't,' replied Kabuo. 'I'd fish and then I'd come home. And by the time I did, you'd know that gaff of mine has fish blood on it, not Heine's. I could go out and get my salmon, check with you in the morning.'

The sheriff shook his head and slipped his hands to his belt, where he hooked his thumbs over the buckle. 'No,' he said. 'You're under arrest. Sorry, but we're going to have to hold you.'

The investigation, it occurred to the sheriff, had thus far taken five hours. *Sherlock Holmes*, he remembered. Horace Whaley had laughed at his queasiness about the corpse, the peeled-back head, the bone splinters in Carl's brain. There was that diaper spread over Susan Marie's shoulder, and her gloved index finger pointing out the church cake, that white finger inviting him to slide a mint between his lips. She'd collapsed on the stairs with her feet splayed out, the baby bottle beside her toes. All right, in the end he had played Sherlock Holmes, yes: it had been a sort of game. He had not really expected to find anything other than that Carl Heine had drowned. Fallen into the sea like other men before him and died because that was the nature of things. Art Moran was a believer in circumstances. To him the occasional misfortunes of life were simply part of things. The misfortunes he'd seen in the course of his work remained painful and vivid in his memory, and because he had seen them for so many years he knew that more would come his way; that was how things went. Island life was like life anywhere in this regard: bad things now and then happened.

Now he began to believe, for the first time, that he had a murder on his hands. He should have expected that sooner or later the course of things would bring him to this pass. He was satisfied to have conducted himself, in the face of it, professionally; he had pursued his investigation as well as anyone could have. Horace Whaley would not ridicule him now about playing Sherlock Holmes.

It occurred to him, too, that for all his arrogance Horace Whaley had been right. For here was the Jap with the bloody gun butt Horace had suggested he look for. Here was the Jap he'd been led to inexorably by every islander he'd spoken with.

Art Moran looked into the Jap's still eyes to see if he could discern the truth there. But they were hard eyes set in a proud, still face, and there was nothing to be read in them either way. They were the eyes of a man with concealed emotions, the eyes of a man hiding something.

'You're under arrest,' repeated Art Moran, 'in connection with the death of Carl Heine.'

9 **queasiness**: nausea, feeling of sickness 13 **splay sth. out**: spread sth. out and wide apart 24–25 **have sb./sth. on your hands**: be responsible for sb./sth., have to deal with sb./sth. 26 **pass** (n): (here) point in life, esp. in a serious and trying situation 28 **ridicule sb.** ['rɪdɪkjuːl]: make fun of sb. 32 **inexorable** [ɪn'eksərəbl]: unvermeidlich

Chapter 19

By eight-thirty on the morning of December 7, Judge Fielding's courtroom was filled with citizens who were thankful for the heat from the boilers. They'd left damp overcoats hanging in the cloakroom but still carried the smell of snow in their hair and on their pants, boots, and sweaters. Ed Soames had again turned the heat up; he did so because the foreman of the jury had reported that certain of the jurors had passed a cold night in the Amity Harbor Hotel. Groans from the hapless radiators, coupled with the slamming of the wind against their windows, had kept them awake through the dark hours. They had been sequestered on the second floor and had speculated before going to bed, said the foreman, that the snowstorm would interrupt the trial. They'd been sleepless, most of them, and had shivered in their beds while the storm rattled the hotel.

Ed Soames apologized to the members of the jury for the inferior nature of their accommodations and pointed out to them the urn of coffee in the anteroom, which they were welcome to serve themselves from – the coffee was hot – at any time during the day's recesses. He showed them, as he had the day before, a cabinet inside which fourteen coffee cups hung on angles from brass hooks. He pointed out the sugar dispenser and apologized to them for the fact that there was no way to make cream available: Petersen's had run out. He hoped they could make do despite this.

The foreman indicated that the jurors were ready, so Ed Soames led them to the courtroom. The reporters found their places, the defendant was brought in, Eleanor Dokes took her seat at the stenograph. Ed Soames asked all of them to rise, and as they did so Lew Fielding emerged from his chambers and strode to the bench as if no one were present. As always he looked disinterested. He propped the weight of his head against his left fist and nodded at Alvin Hooks. 'A new day,' he told him, 'but still your day in court, Mr. Prosecutor. Have at it. Call your witness.'

Alvin Hooks rose and thanked Judge Fielding. He was fresh looking and clean shaven, neat in his serge suit with its exaggerated shoulders. 'The state calls Dr. Sterling Whitman,' he announced, and then a man

stood up in the gallery whom nobody had seen before, passed through the low gate, and approached the witness box, where he was sworn in by Ed Soames. He was tall, six foot five at least, and seemed too large for
35 the suit he wore; a large portion of each shirt cuff showed; the coat bunched at the armpits.

'Dr. Whitman,' said Alvin Hooks. 'We thank you for battling the elements this morning in order to give your testimony. I understand that only a handful of mainlanders were brave enough to travel the waters to San
40 Piedro on the 6:25 ferry run – is that correct, sir?'

'That's right,' said Dr. Whitman. 'There were six of us.'

'A thrilling ride through a blinding snowstorm,' added Alvin Hooks.

'That's right,' repeated Dr. Whitman.

He was entirely too large for the witness box and had the appearance
45 of a stork or crane packed into a crate.

'Dr. Whitman,' said the prosecutor. 'You are a specialist in hematology employed by the Anacortes General Hospital – is that correct? Do I have that right?'

'That's correct.'

50 'And you have been employed there for how long?'

'Seven years.'

'And during this time, doctor, what precisely has been the nature and content of your work?'

'I've been a hematologist for the past six and a half years. Strictly a
55 hematologist.'

'A hematologist,' said Alvin Hooks. 'A hematologist does what exactly?'

Dr. Whitman scratched the back of his head, then above and below the left stem of his glasses. 'I specialize in the pathology and therapeutics

---

5 **foreman**: person who acts as the leader of a jury in court   7 **hapless**: (hier) marode   9 **sequester sb.** [sɪˈkwestər]: keep a group of people, esp. a jury, together in a place away from other people   20 **make do**: manage or be content with a lack of sth.   30 **serge**: type of strong cloth made of wool   36 **bunch** (v): become tight   45 **stork**: Storch   **crane** (n): (hier) Kranich   46 **hematology** [ˌhiːməˈtɑːlədʒi]: scientific study of the blood and its diseases   59 **pathology** [pəˈθɑːlədʒi]: scientific study of diseases   **therapeutics** [ˌθerəˈpjuːtɪks]: branch of medicine concerned with the treatment of diseases

of the blood,' he said. 'Mostly blood testing and analysis. I consult with attending physicians.'

'I see,' said Alvin Hooks. 'So for six and a half years it has been your profession – let me find a way to put this simply – to perform blood tests? And to analyze the results of those tests, doctor? Is that correct?'

'In a nutshell,' said Sterling Whitman.

'Very good then,' said Alvin Hooks. 'Now, Dr. Whitman, could we accurately characterize you as an expert in the matter of blood testing? Given your six and a half years of experience? Would you say you have gained a degree of expertise in, for example, determining human blood type?'

'By all means,' said Sterling Whitman. 'Blood type is a ... standard matter. A standard procedure for any hematologist – typing blood.'

'All right,' said Alvin Hooks. 'On the evening – the late evening – of September 16 of this year, the sheriff of this county brought you a fishing gaff, did he not, and asked you to test a bloodstain he found on it. Is that correct, Dr. Whitman?'

'It is.'

Alvin Hooks swiveled and looked at Ed Soames; Ed handed him the fishing gaff.

'Now, Dr. Whitman,' said the prosecutor. 'I'm showing you what has already been admitted into evidence as state's exhibit 4-B. I'm going to hand it to you and ask you to look it over.'

'All right,' said Sterling Whitman.

He took the gaff and examined it – a long-handled gaff with a barbed hook at one end, tagged as admitted around the butt.

'Okay,' he said. 'I've looked at it.'

'Very good,' said Alvin Hooks. 'Do you recognize this fishing gaff, Dr. Whitman?'

'I do. It's the one Sheriff Moran brought in on the evening of September 16. It was bloodstained, and he asked me to do some tests on it.'

Alvin Hooks took the gaff and placed it on the evidence table in full view of the jurors. Then he selected a folder from among his papers and returned to the witness stand.

'Dr. Whitman,' he said. 'I'm now handing you what has been marked as state proposed exhibit 5-A. Would you please tell me whether you recognize it, whether you can identify it for the court?'

'I can,' said Sterling Whitman. 'It's my investigative report. The one I wrote after Sheriff Moran brought me the fishing gaff.'

'Examine it for a moment,' said Alvin Hooks. 'Is it in the same condition as it was when you prepared it?'

Sterling Whitman went through the motions of turning pages. 'It is,' he said after a moment. 'It seems to be. Yes.'

'And do you recognize your signature thereon?'

'I do.'

'Thank you, doctor,' Alvin Hooks said, and took the folder in his hand again. 'The state moves the introduction of exhibit 5-A, Your Honor.'

Nels Gudmundsson cleared his throat. 'No objection,' he said.

Lew Fielding admitted the exhibit. Ed Soames, with a flourish, stamped it. Then Alvin Hooks returned it to Sterling Whitman.

'All right,' he said. 'Now, Dr. Whitman. I'm returning to you what is now in evidence as exhibit 5-A: your investigative report concerning this fishing gaff, among other things. Would you please summarize for the court your findings?'

'Certainly,' Sterling Whitman said, pulling uncomfortably at a cuff. 'Number one was that the blood on the fishing gaff I received from Sheriff Moran was human blood, it reacted immediately to human antibodies. Number two was that the blood was of a sort we can describe as B positive, Mr. Hooks. I obtained a clear identification in this regard, without any difficulties, under a microscope.'

'Anything else significant?' asked Alvin Hooks.

'Yes,' said Sterling Whitman. 'The sheriff asked me to check our hospital records as to the blood type of a fisherman named Carl Heine, Jr. I did so. We had the records on file. Mr. Heine had been admitted after the war at our hospital for a series of physicals, and we had obtained his medical records. I looked these over and have included them in my investigative report. Mr. Heine's blood type was B positive.'

---

1 **consult with sb**: (hier) jdn. beraten   2 **attending physician**: behandelnder Arzt   16 **bloodstain**: mark or spot of blood on sth.   36 **state proposed**: von der Staatsanwaltschaft eingebracht   47 **move sth.**: (here) suggest sth. formally, esp. in court or at parliament, so that it can be discussed and decided officially   58–59 **antibody** ['æntibɑːdi]: Antikörper   66 **physical** (n): medical examination of the body, usually to check up on its condition of health

'B positive,' said Alvin Hooks. 'Do you mean to say that the blood of the deceased *matched* the blood found on the fishing gaff?'

'Yes,' said Sterling Whitman. 'It did.'

'But, Dr. Whitman,' said Alvin Hooks. 'Many people must have this type of B positive blood. Can you say with any certainty that it was Carl Heine's?'

'No,' said Dr. Whitman. 'I can't say that. But let me add that B positive is a relatively rare blood type. Statistically rare. Ten percent of Caucasian males, at best.'

'One out of every ten Caucasian males? No more?'

'That's right.'

'I see,' said Alvin Hooks. 'One out of ten.'

'That's right,' said Sterling Whitman.

Alvin Hooks crossed in front of the jurors and approached the defendant's table. 'Dr. Whitman,' he said. 'The defendant's name here is Kabuo Miyamoto. I am wondering if his name appears in your report.'

'It does.'

'In what regard?' asked Alvin Hooks.

'Well, the sheriff asked me to check his records, too. As long as I was checking on Carl Heine, he asked, could I bring out Miyamoto's records? I did so and examined them at his request. Again, service medical records were available. Kabuo Miyamoto had been typed upon entering the service as O negative: he has an O negative blood type.'

'O negative?' said Alvin Hooks.

'That's right. Yes.'

'And the blood on the fishing gaff that Sheriff Moran brought you, the one he found while searching the defendant's boat – the one you held in your hands a moment ago – was B positive, doctor?'

'Yes. B positive.'

'So the blood on the gaff was not the defendant's?'

'No.'

'It was not salmon blood?'

'No.'

'It was not fish blood or animal blood of any kind?'

'No.'

'It was of the same type as the deceased's? As Carl Heine, Jr.?'

'Yes.'

'A blood type that you would characterize as rare?'

'Yes.'

'Thank you, Dr. Whitman. That's all.'

Nels Gudmundsson now tottered to his feet in order to cross-examine Sterling Whitman. By the morning of this second day he had become an amusement to the newspapermen, who smiled to themselves each time he cleared his throat and at his awkward attempts to stand or sit. He was an old man in suspenders, one useless eye wandering loose in its socket, poorly shaven wattles of skin at his throat – raw, chafed, and pinkish folds with sparse silver bristles poking out of them. Yet, though Nels Gudmundsson was at times vaguely laughable, the reporters fell serious when he passed in front of them and allowed them to see up close how his temples pulsed, the depth of the light in his good eye.

'All right,' said Nels. 'Dr Whitman, sir. Do you mind if I ask you a few questions?'

Sterling Whitman said he didn't mind at all; that was what he'd come to San Piedro for.

'Well, then,' said Nels. 'About this fishing gaff. You say you found blood on it?'

'Yes,' said Sterling Whitman. 'I've testified to that effect. Yes, I did.'

'This blood,' said Nels. 'Where *exactly* did you find it?' He picked up the gaff and brought it to the witness. 'On what part, Dr. Whitman? The butt end? The hook?'

'The butt,' the doctor answered. 'This end' – he pointed – '*opposite* the hook.'

'Right here?' said Nels, and put his hand on it. 'You found blood on this wooden handle?'

'Yes.'

'It hadn't soaked in?' Nels Gudmundsson asked. 'Wouldn't wood of this sort absorb blood, doctor?'

'Some soaking had occurred, yes,' said Sterling Whitman. 'But I was still able to obtain a blood sample.'

'How?' said Nels, still holding the gaff.

---

7 **Caucasian** [kɔːˈkeɪʒn] (adj): being member of any of the races of people who have pale skin   40 **totter**: move unsteadily   44 **socket**: Augen-höhle   46 **sparse** [spɑːrs]: spread over a surface in small amounts   56 **to that effect**: saying exactly that   65 **soak in**: (of a liquid) slowly enter into a material

'By scraping. It's the procedure with dried blood. You have to scrape.'

'I see,' said Nels. 'You used a blade, doctor?'

'Yes.'

'You scraped it onto a microscope slide? You placed the slide under a microscope?'

'Yes.'

'And you saw what? Blood and wood scrapings?'

'Yes.'

'Anything else?'

'No.'

'Nothing. Only blood and wood scrapings?'

'That's right.'

'Doctor,' said Nels Gudmundsson. 'Were there no bits of bone, or strands of hair, or particles of scalp, on this fishing gaff?'

Sterling Whitman shook his head firmly. 'None,' he said. 'It was just as I have said. As I testified. As I wrote in my investigative report. Blood and wood scrapings only.'

'Doctor,' said Nels. 'Does this seem odd to you? If this fishing gaff were in fact used to inflict a head wound, would you not expect to see evidence of that? In the shape of, say, strands of hair? Or bits of skull bone? Or particles of scalp? The sort of things we might normally associate with a head wound, Dr. Whitman? As evidence that the instrument in question had been used to inflict such a wound?'

'Sheriff Moran asked me to perform two blood tests,' said the witness. 'I did so. We determined that – '

'Yes, yes,' Nels Gudmundsson cut in. 'As you have testified previously. The blood on the gaff was of the type known as B positive: no one is contesting *that*, doctor. What I want to know is, to the best of your knowledge as a man who has for six and a half years made his living looking at blood under a microscope, would you not expect to see hair or bone or scalp particles as *well* as blood if this gaff were used to inflict a head wound? Would you not, doctor? Would it seem logical?'

'I don't know,' said Sterling Whitman.

'You don't know?' asked Nels Gudmundsson. He still carried the gaff in his hand, but now he perched it on the ledge of the witness box between himself and the expert hematologist.

'Doctor,' he said. 'The coroner who examined the deceased in question included mention in his report of, if I remember it correctly, a "secondary and minor laceration of the right hand extending laterally from the fold between the thumb and forefinger to the outside of the wrist." A cut on the palm, in other words. An ordinary cut on Carl Heine's right palm. Would it be possible, Dr. Whitman, that a cut like this – if the hand were wrapped around the butt end of this gaff here – that a cut like this might have caused the B positive blood you spoke of to soak into the wood? Would that be possible, doctor? *Possible?*'

'Possible, yes,' said Sterling Whitman. 'But I don't know anything about that. My only job was to perform the blood tests that Sheriff Moran asked me to perform. I found B positive blood on this fishing gaff. How it got there, I have no idea.'

'Well,' said Nels Gudmundsson. 'It's good of you to say so. Because, as you've said, one of every ten Caucasian males has blood of the B positive type, don't they? And on an island like this one that means, probably, two hundred men, doctor? Would that be about right?'

'Yes. I suppose. Ten percent of the island's Caucasian male population. It – '

'And isn't the percentage even higher, doctor, for males of Japanese descent? A higher percentage of B positives among the island's Japanese – Americans?'

'Yes, it is. Somewhere around twenty percent. But – '

'Twenty percent – thank you, doctor. That's quite a large number of island men we're talking about who have B positive blood. But let's suppose, for purposes of argument, that the blood on the fishing gaff was in fact Carl Heine's, even though it might have come from hundreds of other men – let's just suppose that hypothetically for a moment. It might have gotten there, it seems to me, in at least one of two ways. It might have come from the deceased man's head, or it might have come from this ordinary cut on his hand – his head or his hand, doctor, either one. Now, given the fact that

---

1 **scrape**: (ab)kratzen   5 **slide** (n): small piece of glass that small pieces of material or drops of liquid are placed on so that they can be looked at under a microscope
15 **scalp** [skælp]: the skin that covers the part of the head where the hair grows
36 **ledge**: (hier) Rahmen, Umrandung   39 **mention of sth.** (n, fml): act of referring to sb./sth. in speech or writing

the blood is on the *butt* end of this gaff where a person would normally place their *hand*, and given the fact that you found only blood there and no bone or skin or hair, doctor – the probable evidence of a head wound, I would think – what seems to you to be likely? That the blood on the gaff, if it came from Carl Heine at all, came from his head or his hand?'

'I have no idea,' said Sterling Whitman. 'I'm a hematologist, not a detective.'

'I'm not asking you to be a detective,' Nels said. 'I just want to know which is more *probable*.'

'The hand, I suppose,' Sterling Whitman confessed. 'The hand, I guess, would be more probable than the head.'

'Thank you,' answered Nels Gudmundsson. 'I appreciate your having battled the elements to come here and tell us so.' He turned away from the witness, made his way to Ed Soames, and handed him the fishing gaff. 'You can put that away, Mr. Soames,' he said. 'Thank you very much. We're done with that.'

Three fishermen – Dale Middleton, Vance Cope, and Leonard George – all testified for the court that on the evening of September 15 they'd seen Carl Heine's boat, the *Susan Marie*, with her net set on the fishing grounds at Ship Channel Bank; furthermore they'd seen Kabuo Miyamoto's boat, the *Islander*, in the same vicinity at approximately the same time. Ship Channel, Leonard George explained, was like many other places island men netted salmon: a narrow and limited seafloor topography which forced you to fish within sight of other men and to move about with care lest, in the night fog general to Island County in early autumn, you motor across a set net and destroy it by winding it up in your propeller. That was why, even in the fog, Leonard had made out both the *Susan Marie* and the *Islander* between eight and eight-thirty at Ship Channel Bank: he recalled that as he cruised past he'd seen the *Islander* come about, that ten minutes later he'd come across the *Susan Marie* and seen that Carl Heine was backing net off his drum by motoring away from his jacklight. They'd been fishing, in short, the same waters, with Carl a bit farther toward the north and down current: a thousand yards closer to the shipping lanes that gave Ship Channel Bank its name.

Nels Gudmundsson asked Leonard George if it was common among gill-netters to board another's boat at sea. 'Absolutely not,' replied

Leonard. 'There aren't many reasons why a guy'd do that. If you're stalled out and somebody's bringing you a part maybe – that's about it, no other reason. Maybe if you was hurt or broke down or somethin'. Otherwise you don't tie up to nobody. You do your job, keep to yourself.'

'Do men argue at sea?' said Nels. 'I've heard they do. That gill-netters do. Are there arguments out there, Mr. George?'

'You bet there are,' said Leonard. 'A guy gets corked off he – '

'Corked off?' interrupted Nels. 'Can you explain that for us briefly?'

Leonard George answered that a gill net was constructed to have a top and a bottom; that the bottom of the net was called the lead line – bits of lead were crimped onto it in order to weight it down – and that the top was known as the cork line: cork floats allowed it to stay on the surface, so that from a distance a gill net appeared as a line of cork with the stern of the boat at one end and a warning jacklight at the other. When a man set his wall of net up current from your own he'd 'corked you off,' stolen your fish by getting to them before they could get to you. It meant trouble, said Leonard: you had to pick up, motor past him, and set your net somewhere up current, in which case the other guy might decide to play leapfrog and force both of you to waste your fishing time. Still, in all of this, Leonard pointed out, no man ever boarded another's boat. It wasn't done; he'd never heard of it. You kept to yourself unless you had some kind of emergency and needed another man's help.

Alvin Hooks called Army First Sergeant Victor Maples to the stand after that morning's recess. Sergeant Maples wore his green dress uniform and the insignia of the Fourth Infantry Division. He wore his expert marksmanship and combat infantryman's badges. The brass buttons on Sergeant Maples's coat, the insignia on his collar, and the badges on his chest all caught the meager courtroom light and held it. Sergeant Maples was overweight by thirty-five pounds but still looked distinguished in

---

21 **vicinity**: area close to a particular place   25 **lest sth. happens** (fml): in order to prevent sth. from happening   33–34 **shipping lane**: Wasserstraße   47 **crimp sth. onto sth. else**: (hier) etwas in etwas anderes hineinknüpfen   55 **play leapfrog with sb.**: mit jdm. Bockspringen spielen   61 **insignia** [ɪn'sɪɡniə]: badge or sign that shows sb.'s rank or membership in a group   61–62 **marksmanship**: skill in shooting   64 **meager**: poor, (here) dim

his dress uniform. The extra weight was nicely distributed; Maples was a powerful man. He had short, thick arms, no neck, and a pudgy, adolescent face. His hair stood up in a razor cut.

First Sergeant Maples explained to the court that since 1946 he had been assigned to Fort Sheridan, Illinois, where he specialized in the training of combat troops. Prior to that he'd trained troops at Camp Shelby, Mississippi, before taking part in the Italian campaign in 1944 and '45. Sergeant Maples had been wounded in fighting on the Arno River – he'd taken a German round in the small of his back which narrowly missed his spine – and had been awarded the Silver Star on account of it. He'd also, he said, been at Livorno and Luciana and seen the 442nd – the Nisei regiment to which the defendant had been attached – in action along the Gothic Line.

Sergeant Maples had in his time trained thousands of men in hand-to-hand combat. Hand-to-hand was his specialty, he said; he'd worked in other areas of basic training but generally found his way back to it. Sergeant Maples recollected for the court his astonishment in early 1943 when the 442nd – composed of Nisei boys – began training at Camp Shelby. These were boys from the internment camps, enlistees headed for the European theater, and among them, Sergeant Maples recalled, was the defendant, Kabuo Miyamoto.

He remembered Kabuo from among the thousands who'd come his way because of a ... peculiar episode. Ten squads of trainees had surrounded Sergeant Maples on the drill field at Camp Shelby one February afternoon – ten squads composed of Nisei boys, so that he found himself in the midst of a hundred Japanese faces while he explained the particulars of the bayonet. Sergeant Maples informed his trainees that it was the policy of the United States Army to preserve their lives until they reached the battlefield; that was why a wooden staff would be substituted for an actual weapon during drill sessions. Helmets would be worn as well.

The sergeant began to demonstrate bayonet thrusts, then asked for a volunteer. It was at this point, he told the court, that he came face to face with the defendant. A young man stepped forward into the ring of trainees and presented himself to the sergeant, bowing slightly before saluting and calling out loudly, 'Sir!' 'First off,' Sergeant Maples scolded him, 'you don't have to salute me or call me sir. I'm an enlisted man, just like you – a sergeant, not a warrant officer or a major. Second, nobody in this army bows to nobody. There's plenty of officers who'll expect a salute, but a bow? It isn't *military*. Not *American* military. It isn't done.'

Sergeant Maples gave Miyamoto a wooden staff and tossed him a sparring helmet. There was something aggressive in the way the boy had spoken, and Sergeant Maples had heard it. He was vaguely aware of this particular young man, who had built a reputation during basic training as a thoroughly eager warrior, ready to kill and businesslike every bit of the time. Maples had seen many such boys come his way and was never cowed by their youthful swagger; he was only on rare occasions impressed or prepared to view them as his equal. 'In combat your enemy won't be stationary,' he said now, looking the boy in the eye. 'It's one thing to work out on a dummy or a bag, another to spar with a trained human being who represents more accurately live movement. In this case,' he told the gathered recruits, 'our volunteer will seek to avoid the model bayonet thrusts put to him this afternoon.'

'Yes, sir,' said Kabuo Miyamoto.

'No more "sir," ' Sergeant Maples replied. 'That's the last time with that.'

He explained to the court how astonished he was – how thoroughly astonished – to find he couldn't hit the defendant. Kabuo Miyamoto hardly moved, and yet he slipped every thrust. The one hundred Nisei trainees looked on in silence and gave no indication that they approved of either man. Sergeant Maples fought on with his wooden staff until Kabuo Miyamoto knocked it from his hands.

'Excuse me,' said Miyamoto. He knelt, picked up the staff, and handed it to the sergeant. Once again, he bowed.

---

2 **pudgy** (infml): slightly fat   3 **razor cut**: very short hair clipped with a razor blade so that it stands up   8–9 **Arno River**: river in Tuscany (Italy) passing through Florence and Pisa   10 **Silver Star**: military decoration   12 **Nisei** [niseɪ]: Japanese for 'Second Generation'; used for people of Japanese origin born in the USA, esp. the generation that had just reached adulthood when World War II broke out
13 **Gothic Line**: Teil der Westfront im 2. Weltkrieg   19 **enlistee**: (hier) Freiwilliger   31 **thrust** (n): sudden strong movement that pushes sth./sb. forward   35 **first off**: zuerst einmal   37 **warrant officer**: (Ober)feldwebel   41 **sparring** (adj): (here) used for training fights only   46 **cow sb.**: frighten sb. in order to make them respect or obey you   **swagger** (n): way of behaving that seems too confident   58 **slip sth.**: (hier) einer Sache ausweichen

'There's no need to bow,' the sergeant repeated. 'I already told you about that.'

'I do it out of habit,' said Kabuo Miyamoto. 'I'm used to bowing when I'm sparring somebody.' Then, suddenly, he brought his wooden staff up. He looked Sergeant Maples in the eye and smiled.

Sergeant Maples acquiesced to the inevitable and did combat with the defendant that afternoon. It lasted all of three seconds. On his first rush the sergeant was swept off his feet, then felt his head pinned to the ground with the point of the staff, then the staff was withdrawn, the defendant bowed and picked him up. 'Excuse me, sergeant,' he'd said afterward. 'Your staff, sergeant.' He'd handed it to him.

After that Sergeant Maples availed himself of the opportunity to study *kendo* with an expert. Sergeant Maples wasn't stupid – he told the court this about himself without a trace of irony – and so he learned all he could from Miyamoto, including the importance of bowing. Sergeant Maples became a master with time and after the war taught *kendo* techniques to the army rangers at Fort Sheridan. From his point of view as an expert in the ancient Japanese art of stick fighting, Sergeant Maples could say with certainty that the defendant was eminently capable of killing a man far larger than himself with a fishing gaff. In fact, there were few men known to him who could ably defend themselves against such an attack by Kabuo Miyamoto – certainly a man with no training in *kendo* had little chance of warding him off. He was, in Sergeant Maples's experience, a man both technically proficient at stick fighting and willing to inflict violence on another man. He had made, the record showed, an excellent soldier. No, it would not surprise Sergeant Victor Maples to hear that Kabuo Miyamoto had killed a man with a fishing gaff. He was highly capable of such a deed.

---

6 **acquiesce to sth.** [ˌækwi'es]: accept sth. without arguing   8 **rush** (n): (here) attack   12 **avail yourself of sth.**: make use of sth., esp. an opportunity (= Gelegenheit)   19 **eminently**: extremely   24 **be proficient at doing sth.** [prə'fɪʃnt]: be able to do sth. well because of training and practice

Chapter 20

Susan Marie Heine had been a widow for nearly three months by the time of Kabuo Miyamoto's murder trial but had not grown very much accustomed to it yet and still passed long hours – especially at night – during which she could think of nothing but Carl and the fact that he had gone out of her existence. In the gallery, with her sister on one side and her mother on the other, dressed in black from head to foot and with her eyes shrouded behind a chenille-dot veil, Susan Marie looked mournfully attractive: she exuded a blond, woeful distress that caused the reporters to turn in her direction and ponder the propriety of speaking intimately with her under the guise of professional necessity. The young widow's thick hair had been plaited and pinned up beneath her hat so that the alabaster neck Art Moran so much admired when Susan Marie poured coffee at church socials lay exposed to the crowded courtroom. The neck and the plaits of hair and the white hands folded decorously in her lap all stood in sharp contrast to her black mourning outfit and gave Susan Marie the air of an unostentatious young German baroness who had perhaps just recently lost her husband but had not in the face of it forgotten how to dress well, even when she dressed to suggest grief. And it was grief, foremost, that Susan Marie suggested. Those who had known her for a long while recognized that even her face had changed. The superficial among them attributed this to the fact that she'd neglected to eat heartily since Carl died – shadows had formed just under her cheekbones – but others recognized it as a deeper alteration, one that involved her spirit. The pastor at the First Hill Lutheran

---

7 **chenille-dot veil**: getupfter Chenille-Schleier   8 **mournful**: full of grief and sorrow   **exude sth.** [ɪgˈzuːd]: having an aura of sth.   **woeful**: very sad
9 **propriety** [prəˈpraɪəti]: Schicklichkeit   10 **under the guise of sth.** [gaɪz]: unter dem Vorwand von etwas   15 **decorous**: schicklich, anständig   16 **unostentatious** [ˌʌnɑːstenˈteɪʃəs]: not meaning to impress people by your appearance deliberately

Church had on four successive Sundays asked his congregation to pray not only for Carl Heine's soul but for Susan Marie's 'deliverance from grief in the course of time' as well. In pursuit of this latter end, the church women's auxiliary had provided Susan Marie and her children with a straight month's worth of hot suppers in casserole dishes, and Einar Petersen had seen to it that groceries were delivered to her kitchen door. It was through food that the island expressed its compassion for Susan Marie in her widowhood.

Alvin Hooks, the prosecutor, knew well the value of a Susan Marie Heine. He had called to the witness box the county sheriff and the county coroner, the murdered man's mother and the bent-over Swede from whom the murdered man had planned to buy his father's old farm. He had proceeded to a variety of secondary witnesses – Sterling Whitman, Dale Middleton, Vance Cope, Leonard George, Sergeant Victor Maples – and now he would finish matters by presenting the wife of the murdered man, a woman who had already done much good merely sitting in the gallery where the jurors could view her. The men especially would not wish to betray such a woman with a not-guilty verdict at the end of things. She would persuade them not precisely with what she had to say but with the entirety of who she was.

On the afternoon of Thursday, September 9, Kabuo Miyamoto had stood at her doorstep and asked to speak with her husband. It was a cloudless day of the sort San Piedro rarely saw in September – this year there'd been an early string of them, though – a day of deep heat but with an onshore breeze that tossed the leaves in the alders and even ripped a few loose to fall earthward. One minute it was silent, the next a rush of wind came up from off the water smelling of salt and seaweed, and the roar of the leaves in the trees was as loud as waves breaking on a beach. A gust caught Kabuo Miyamoto's shirt as he stood on the porch so that the collar of it brushed his neck for a moment and the shoulders ballooned out, filled with air. Then the wind died and his shirt settled, and she asked him to come in and sit in the front room; she would go, she said, to find her husband.

The Japanese man had seemed uncertain about entering her house that afternoon. 'I can wait on the porch, Mrs. Heine,' he suggested. 'It's a nice afternoon. I'll wait outside.'

'Nonsense,' she replied, and stepped aside from the door. She gestured in the direction of the living room. 'You come in and make yourself comfortable. Get out of the sun and sit, why don't you? It's nice and cool inside.'

He looked at her, blinked, but took only one step. 'Thank you,' he said. 'It's a beautiful house.'

'Carl built it,' Susan Marie answered. 'Please come in now. Sit.'

The Japanese man passed her, turned to his left, and perched on the edge of the bench sofa. His back was straight, his demeanor formal. It was as if he considered making himself comfortable an insult of some kind. With a deliberation that bordered, to her thinking, on something stylized, he folded his hands together and waited at attention. 'I'll go after Carl,' said Susan Marie. 'It'll only take me a minute.'

'Fine,' said the Japanese man. 'Thank you.'

She left him there. Carl and the boys were out culling raspberry canes, and she found them down among the southward trellises, Carl cutting free the older stock, the boys filling the wheelbarrow. She stood at the end of the row and called to them. 'Carl!' she said. 'There's someone to see you. It's Kabuo Miyamoto. He's waiting.'

They all turned to look at her, the boys shirtless and small against the walls of raspberries, Carl bent at the knees, his knife in hand. He, a giant with a russet beard, closed the knife, and slipped it into the sheath at his belt. 'Where?' he said. 'Kabuo?'

'In the living room. He's waiting.'

'Tell him I'm coming,' said Carl. And he swung both boys into the wheelbarrow and planted them on top of the culled canes. 'Watch out for thorns,' he said. 'Here we go.'

She went back to the house and informed the Japanese man that her husband would be with him shortly; he'd been out among the raspberry canes working. 'Would you care for coffee?' she added.

'No, thank you,' replied Kabuo Miyamoto.

'It's no trouble,' she urged. 'Please have some.'

---

2 **deliverance** [-'---]: state of being rescued from danger, evil or pain
3 **in pursuit of sth.** [pər'suːt]: trying to achieve sth.   4 **auxiliary**: (here) group of volunteers who help people in need   18 **betray sb.**: (hier) jdn. im Stich lassen
29 **gust**: Windstoß   48 **stylized** ['staɪlaɪzd]: done in a way that is not natural

'It's very nice of you,' he said. 'You're very kind.'

'Will you have some, then?' Susan Marie asked. 'Carl and I were planning on a cup.'

'All right, then,' said Kabuo. 'Thank you. I will. Thank you.'

He was still seated in the same position, perched on the edge of the worn bench sofa precisely as she'd left him minutes before. Susan Marie found his immobility disquieting and was about to suggest that he sit back and relax, make himself at home, get comfortable, when Carl came through the front door. Kabuo Miyamoto stood up.

'Hey,' Carl said. 'Kabuo.'

'Carl,' said the Japanese man.

They came together and locked hands, her husband half a foot taller than his visitor, bearded and heavy through the shoulders and chest and wearing a sweat-stained T-shirt. 'What do you say we go out,' he suggested. 'Take a walk 'round the property or something? Get out of the house, go outside?'

'That sounds fine,' said Kabuo Miyamoto. 'I hope this is a good time,' he added.

Carl turned and looked at Susan Marie. 'Kabuo and me are going out,' he said. 'Be back after a while. Going to walk.'

'All right,' she said. 'I'll put coffee on.'

When they were gone she went upstairs to check her baby. She leaned over the side of the crib and smelled the girl's warm breath and let her nose brush against the girl's cheek. From the window she could see her boys in the yard, the tops of their heads as they sat in the grass beside the overturned wheelbarrow. They were tying knots in the culled raspberry canes.

Susan Marie knew Carl had spoken with Ole Jurgensen and had put down earnest money on Ole's farm; she knew how Carl felt about the old place at Island Center and his passion for growing strawberries. Still, she didn't want to leave the house on Mill Run Road with its bronze light, varnished pine boards, and exposed roof rafters in the upstairs room, its view of the sea beyond the raspberry canes. From the window of her baby's room, looking out across the fields, it was more clear to her than ever that she didn't want to move. She'd grown up the daughter of a hay farmer and shake cutter, a man who couldn't get ends to meet; she'd cut thousands of shakes, had hunched over a cedar block with a froe and a mallet, her blond hair hanging in her eyes. She was the second of three daughters and remembered how her younger sister had died of tuberculosis one winter; they'd buried her on Indian Knob Hill in the Lutheran part of the cemetery. The ground had been frozen, and the men had difficulty digging Ellen's grave. It had taken the better part of a December morning.

She'd met Carl Heine because she'd wanted to meet him. On San Piedro a woman with her looks could do such a thing if she did it with the proper innocence. She'd been twenty and employed at Larsen's Pharmacy, where she clerked from behind an oak sales counter. One Saturday evening at eleven-thirty, on a hill above the dance pavilion at West Port Jensen, she stood beneath the branches of a cedar tree while Carl ran his hands up under her blouse and caressed her breasts with his fisherman's fingers. The woods were lit with lanterns, and far below in the bay, through the interstices of trees, she could make out the deck lights of moored pleasure boats. Some of the light came to where they stood so that his face was visible to her. This was their third dance together. By now she knew definitely that she admired his face, which was large, weathered, and durable. She held his face between her hands and looked at it from a distance of six inches. It was an island boy's face and at the same time mysterious. He'd been to the war, after all.

Carl began to kiss her throat so that Susan Marie had to throw back her head to make room for him – him with his russet beard. She looked up into the branches of the cedars and breathed in their perfume, and he moved his lips over her collarbones and then down into the space between her breasts. She let him. She remembered clearly how she had let him, how it was not resignation as it had been with two other boys – one near the end of her senior year of high school, the other during the summer before this one – but instead intensely and deeply what she wanted, this bearded fisherman who had been to the war and

---

7 **disquieting** [dɪsˈkwaɪətɪŋ]: causing worries and distrust 36 **get ends to meet**: earn just enough money to be able to buy the things you need for a living
37 **hunch** (v): vornüber gebeugt stehen oder sitzen 38 **froe**: Spaltmesser **mallet**: hammer with a large wooden head 50 **caress sb./sth.**: touch sb./sth. gently
56 **weathered**: showing the effects of being exposed to sun, rain and wind **durable** [ˈdʊrəbl]: strong and likely to last for a long time

on occasion, if she pressed him, spoke about it without exaggerating. She stroked the top of his head with her fingers and felt the odd sensation of his beard against her breasts. 'Carl,' she whispered, but there was nothing to follow that with, she didn't know what other words she wanted to speak. After a while he stopped and pressed his hands against the bark of the cedar tree behind her so that his blunt muscled arms passed on either side of her head. He looked at her closely, with an intimacy and seriousness that did not seem to embarrass him – this somber man – then tucked a strand of blond hair in behind her ear. He kissed her and then, still looking into her eyes, unbuttoned two of the buttons on her blouse and kissed her again so that she was caught gently between Carl and the tree. She pushed back against him with the muscles of her pelvis, something she'd never done with a man before. It was an admission of her desire, a revealing of it, and it surprised her to the root of her being.

Yet in another way she was not surprised at all to find herself, at the age of twenty, pressing herself against Carl Heine beneath a cedar above the West Port Jensen dance pavilion. After all, she had brought this about, willed it into being. She had discovered when she was seventeen that she could shape the behavior of men with her behavior and that this ability was founded on her appearance. She was no longer astonished to look in the mirror and find she had developed the breasts and hips of an attractive, grown-up woman. Her astonishment gave way quickly to happiness about it. There was a roundness and firmness to her, a clean, strong roundness, and her heavy blond hair cast a glow over her shoulders when she wore a bathing suit. Her breasts turned just slightly away from one another and brushed against the insides of her arms when she walked. They were large, and when she got over her embarrassment about them she was able to take pleasure in the fact that boys became unnerved in their presence. Yet Susan Marie never flirted. She did not let on she knew she was attractive. She went out with two boys before meeting Carl and insisted on their politeness and reserve. Susan Marie did not want to be foremost a pair of breasts, but on the other hand she was proud of herself. This pride remained with her into her midtwenties, until she'd given birth to a second child and her breasts were no longer so important to her as the most visible locus of her sexuality. Two sons had tugged at them with their gums and lips, and her breasts appeared different to her now. She wore a bra with stiff wire along its base in order to lift them up.

Susan Marie knew within three months of marrying Carl that she'd made an excellent choice. In his grave, silent veteran's way he was dependable and gentle. He was gone nights fishing. He came home in the morning, ate and showered, and then they got into bed together. He kept his hands smooth with a pumice stone, so that even though they were fishermen's hands they felt good stroking her shoulders. The two of them moved from position to position, trying everything, the sunlight just behind the pulled shade, their bodies moving in morning shadow but plainly visible. She found she had married an attentive man whose pursuit as a lover was to ensure her satisfaction. He read all her movements as signs and when she was close to coming retreated just enough so that her excitement became more desperate. Then it was necessary for her to put him on his back and rock high with her spine arched while he, half-sitting now, his stomach muscles clenched, stroked her breasts and kissed them. She often came this way, in control of her sensations, guiding herself along Carl's body, and Carl timed matters so as to begin to come while she was and thus carry her back up so that when she was through she did not feel satisfied and was compelled to press on toward a second coming that the pastor at the First Hill Lutheran Church could neither approve nor disapprove of because – she felt certain of this – he had no idea that it was possible.

Carl would sleep until one o'clock in the afternoon, then eat again and go out to work on the property. He was happy when she told him she was pregnant. He did not stop making love to her until she asked him to stop at the beginning of the ninth month. Sometime after their first son was born Carl bought his own boat. When he named it for her she was pleased and came aboard, and they took the baby out into the bay and west until the island was nothing but a low black line on the

---

8 **intimacy** ['ɪntɪməsi]: state of having a close personal relationship with sb.
9 **somber**: (of a person) sad and serious   13 **pelvis**: Becken   14 **admission of sth.**: act of accepting that sth. is true   21 **founded on sth.**: based on sth.
31 **let sth. on**: sich etwas anmerken lassen   36 **locus** ['loʊkəs]: (here) center
37 **gum**: Zahnfleisch   42 **dependable**: reliable   44 **pumice stone**: Bimsstein
53 **clench sth.**: (hier) etwas anspannen

horizon. She sat on the short bunk nursing their son while Carl stood at the wheel. She sat there looking at the back of his head, his short, tousled hair, the broad muscles in his back and shoulders. They ate a can of sardines, two pears, a bag of filberts. The baby slept on the bunk, and Susan Marie stood on a pallet board piloting the boat while Carl, behind her, massaged her shoulders and the small of her back and then her buttocks. She gripped the wheel more tightly when he lifted her skirt and slid her under-pants out of the way, and then, leaning forward against the boat's wheel and reaching back to slide her hands along her husband's hips, she shut her eyes and rocked.

These were the things Susan Marie remembered. In her estimation of it, their sex life had been at the heart of their marriage. It had permeated everything else between them, a state of affairs she sometimes worried over. If it went bad, would they go bad? Somewhere down the road, when they were older and less passionate, when their desire for one another had staled and worn out – then where would they be? She didn't even want to think about that or to mull how one day they might have nothing except his silence and his obsession with whatever he was working on – his boat, their house, his gardens.

She could see her husband and Kabuo Miyamoto walking the border of the property. Then they went over a rise out of view, and she leaned downstairs again.

In twenty minutes' time Carl returned alone, changed into a fresh T-shirt, and hunkered down on the front porch with his head in his hands.

She came out with a cup of coffee in each hand and sat down next to him, on his right. 'What did he want?' she asked.

'Nothing,' answered Carl. 'We had some things to talk about. Nothing much. No big deal.'

Susan Marie handed him a coffee cup. 'It's hot,' she said. 'Be careful.'

'All right,' said Carl. 'Thanks.'

'I made him some,' said Susan Marie. 'I thought he was going to stay.'

'It was nothing,' said Carl. 'It's a long story.'

Susan Marie put her arm around his shoulder. 'What's the problem?' she said.

'I don't know,' sighed Carl. 'He wants seven of Ole's acres. He wants me to let Ole sell them to him. Or sell them to him myself. You know, step out of his way.'

'Seven acres?'

'The ones his family had. He wants them back. That thing my mother talks about.'

'That,' said Susan Marie. 'I had a feeling it was that when he showed up. *That*,' she added grimly.

Carl said nothing. It was like him at a moment like this not to say very much. He did not like to explain or elaborate, and there was a part of him she couldn't get to. She attributed this to his war experiences, and for the most part she let it be, this silence of his. But it irritated her at times.

'What did you tell him?' she asked now. 'Did he go off angry, Carl?'

Carl set down his coffee. He leaned his elbows against his knees. 'Damn,' he answered. 'What could I tell him? There's my mother to think about, you know her, I have to think about that business. If I let him get back in out there ...' He shrugged and seemed hapless for a moment. She saw the lines the sea wind had etched at the corners of his blue eyes. 'I told him I'd have to think it over, have a talk with you. Told him how upset my mother was with him – 'bout his dirty looks and mean faces. He froze when I brought that up. Real polite, but frozen. Wouldn't look at me no more. Wouldn't come back up to the house for coffee. I don't know, I guess it was my fault. We got into a scrap, I guess. I couldn't *talk* with him, Susan. I just ... didn't ... know how to do it. I didn't know what to say to him ...'

He trailed off. She recognized it as one of his *moments*, thought it over, and held her tongue. It had never been very clear to her if Carl and Kabuo were friends or enemies. This was the first time she had seen them together, and it seemed to her – it was her impression – that there remained some measure of kind feelings between them, that after all this time they held inside at least the memory of their friendship. But there

---

3 **tousle sth.** ['taʊzl]: make sth. untidy, esp. sb.'s hair   4 **filbert**: hazelnut
5 **pallet board**: wooden platform that can be used for moving or storing goods
11 **estimation**: judgement, opinion   12 **be at the heart of sth.**: be the most important part of sth.   16 **stale** (v): schal werden   46 **irritate sb.**: (here) annoy sb.
53 **etch sth. into sth. else**: cut sth., esp. lines, into sth. else   58 **scrap**: short fight or disagreement   61 **trail off**: become more and more quiet while speaking and then stop altogether

was no way, truly, of telling. It could be that their cordiality and handshaking had been nothing but stiff formality, that underneath they hated each other. She knew, anyway, that Carl's mother had nothing but ill feelings for all the Miyamotos; she sometimes spoke of them at the dinner table on Sundays, rattling on obsessively. Carl generally fell silent when she did, or agreed with her in a perfunctory fashion, afterward dismissing the subject. Susan Marie had grown accustomed to these dismissals and to Carl's reluctance to speak about the matter. She was accustomed to it, but it pained her, and she wished she could clear it all up right now, while they sat together on the porch.

The wind came up and tossed the tops of the alders, and she felt the odd fall warmth in it. Carl had told her more than once – he'd repeated it just the other day – how since the war he couldn't *speak*. Even his old friends were included in this, so that now Carl was a lonely man who understood land and work, boat and sea, his own hands, better than his mouth and heart. She felt sympathy for him and rubbed his shoulder gently and waited patiently beside him. 'Damn,' Carl said after a while. 'Anyway, I guess as far as you're concerned I could hand the whole business over to him and let him do what he wants with it. I guess you don't want to move out there anyway.'

'It's so beautiful here,' replied Susan Marie. 'Just look around for a minute, Carl.'

'Look around out *there*,' he said. 'That's sixty-five acres, Susan.'

She understood that. He was a man who needed plenty of space, a vast terrain in which to operate. It was what he'd grown up with, and the sea, despite its size, was no substitute for green fields. Carl *needed* room, far more room than his boat could offer, and anyway in order to put his war behind him – the *Canton* going down, men drowning while he watched – he would have to leave his boat for good and grow strawberries like his father. She knew this was the only way for her husband to grow sound; it was what made her willing, ultimately, to follow him out to Island Center.

'Supposing you sell him his seven acres,' Susan Marie said. 'What's the worst your mother can do?'

Carl shook his head emphatically. 'It doesn't really come down to her,' he said. 'It comes down to the fact that Kabuo's a *Jap*. And I don't hate Japs, but I don't like 'em neither. It's hard to explain. But he's a Jap.'

'He's not a Jap,' Susan Marie said. 'You don't mean that, Carl. I've heard you say nice things about him. You and he were friends.'

'Were,' said Carl. 'That's right. A long time ago. Before the war came along. But now I don't like him much anymore. Don't like how he acted when I told him I'd think it over, like he expected me to just hand those seven acres to him, like I owed it to him or – '

There was a boy's cry from the back of the house then, a cry of pain instead of argument or upset, and Carl was already moving toward it before Susan Marie could stand. They found their older boy sprawled on a flagstone with his left foot gripped in both his hands; he'd sliced it open against the sharp edge of a strut on the overturned wheelbarrow beside him. Susan Marie knelt and kissed his face and held him closely while his foot bled. She remembered how Carl had looked at the wound, tenderly, transformed. He was no longer a war veteran. They'd taken the boy in to Dr. Whaley, and then Carl had gone off fishing. The two of them hadn't discussed Kabuo Miyamoto again, and Susan Marie soon recognized that the subject was somehow forbidden. It was forbidden in her marriage to open up her husband's wounds and look at them unless he asked her to.

Their marriage, she understood after Carl was gone, had largely been about sex. It had been about sex right up to the end, until the day Carl went out of her life: that morning, while the children slept, they'd shut the bathroom door and pulled the latch and taken off their clothes. Carl showered, and Susan Marie joined him when the stink of salmon had been washed down the drain. She washed his large penis and felt it harden in her fingers. She put her arms around his neck, locked her feet at the small of his back. Carl held her up with his strong hands clenching the muscles in her legs and leaned the side of his face against her breasts and took to licking them. They moved that way, standing up in the bathtub with the water pouring over them and Susan Marie's blond hair

1 **cordiality** [ˌkɔːrdʒiˈæləti]: great politeness   5 **rattle on**: talk continuously about sth.   **obsessive**: thinking too much about one particular person or thing, in a way that is not normal   6 **perfunctory** [pərˈfʌŋktəri]: done as a duty or habit, without real interest   7 **dismiss sth.**: (here) decide that sth. is not important   31 **grow sound**: (here) recover from emotional wounds   35 **emphatic** [ɪmˈfætɪk]: with force, to show sth. is important   47 **flagstone**: Steinplatte   60 **pull the latch**: eine Tür verriegeln   66 **take to doing sth.**: (here) start doing sth.

pasted to her face and her hands clutched around her husband's head. They washed each other afterward, taking their time about it in the friendly way of certain married people, and then Carl got into bed and slept until one in the afternoon. At two, having eaten a lunch of fried eggs and Jerusalem artichokes, canned pears and bread spread with clover honey, he went out to change the oil in his tractor. She saw him from the kitchen window that afternoon gathering early windfall apples and dropping them in a burlap bag. At three forty-five he came up to the house again and said good-bye to the children, who were seated on the porch drinking apple juice and eating graham crackers and rolling pebbles back and forth. He came into the kitchen, wrapped himself around his wife, and explained that unless the fishing was excellent he was coming home early the next morning, would be home, he hoped, by four A.M.. Then he left for the Amity Harbor docks, and she never saw him again.

---

8 **burlap bag**: Tasche aus Sackleinen

Chapter 21

Nels Gudmundsson stood at a distance from the witness stand when it was his turn to question Susan Marie Heine: he did not want to appear lecherous by placing himself in close proximity to a woman of such tragic, sensual beauty. He was self-conscious about his age and felt that
5 the jurors would see him as disgusting if he did not distance himself from Susan Marie Heine and appear in general detached from the life of his body altogether. The month before, Nels had been told by a doctor in Anacortes that his prostate gland had become moderately enlarged. It would have to be removed surgically and he would no longer be able to
10 produce seminal fluid. The doctor had asked Nels embarrassing questions and he had been forced to reveal a truth about which he was ashamed: that he could no longer achieve an erection. He could achieve one briefly, but it would wither in his hand before he had a chance to take pleasure from it. The bad part was not really this so much as it was
15 that a woman like Susan Marie Heine inspired a deep frustration in him. He felt defeated as he appraised her on the witness stand. It was no longer possible for him to communicate to *any* woman – even those his own age he knew in town – his merit and value as a lover, for he no longer had this sort of worth and had to admit as much to himself – as a
20 lover he was entirely through.

Nels remembered as he watched Susan Marie Heine the finest years of his sex life, now more than a half a century behind him. He could not quite believe that this was so. He was seventy-nine and trapped inside a decaying body. It was difficult for him to sleep and to urinate. His body

---

3 **lecherous** ['letʃərəs]: lüstern   4 **self-conscious about sth.**: too aware of sth. to behave naturally   8 **prostrate gland**: Prostata   9 **surgical** ['sɜːrdʒɪkl]: chirurgisch
10 **seminal fluid**: Sperma   16 **appraise sb.**: (here) examine sb. by questioning them in order to form an opin-ion about them   19 **as much**: this fact, the same
20 **be through as sb./sth.** (infml): lose the quality of being sb./sth. forever

had betrayed him and most of the things he once took for granted were no longer even possible. A man might easily be embittered by such circumstances, but Nels made it a point not to struggle unnecessarily with life's unresolvable dilemmas. He had indeed achieved a kind of wisdom – if you wanted to call it that – though at the same time he knew that most elderly people were not wise at all but only wore a thin veneer of cheap wisdom as a sort of armor against the world. Anyway, the kind of wisdom younger people sought from old age was not to be acquired in this life no matter how many years they lived. He wished he could tell them this without inviting their mockery or their pity.

Nels's wife had died from cancer of the colon. They had not gotten along particularly well, but nevertheless he missed her. Occasionally he sat in his apartment and wept in order to empty himself of self-pity and remorse. Occasionally he attempted unsuccessfully to masturbate in the hope of rediscovering that lost part of himself he deeply, achingly missed. He was convinced at rare moments that he could succeed and that his youth was still buried inside of himself. The rest of the time he accepted this as untrue and went about the business of consoling himself in various unsatisfying ways. He liked to eat. He enjoyed chess. He did not mind his work and knew himself to be quite good at it. He was a reader and recognized his habit of reading as obsessive and neurotic, and told himself that if he read something less frivolous than newspapers and magazines he might indeed be better off. The problem was that he could not concentrate on 'literature,' however much he might admire it. It wasn't that *War and Peace* bored him exactly, but rather that his mind couldn't *focus* on it. Another loss: his eyes provided him with only half a view of the world, and reading caused his neurasthenia to flare up and made his temples throb. His mind, too, was failing him, he felt – although one could not be sure of such a thing. Certainly his memory was not as good as it had been when he was younger.

Nels Gudmundsson tucked his thumbs in behind his suspenders and looked with studied detachment at the witness. 'Mrs. Heine,' he said. 'The defendant here appeared on your doorstep on Thursday, September 9? Is that what I heard you say?'

'Yes, Mr. Gudmundsson. That's right.'

'He asked to speak to your husband?'

'He did.'

'They walked outside in order to talk? They didn't speak in the house?'

'Correct,' said Susan Marie. 'They spoke outside. They walked our property for thirty or forty minutes.'

'I see,' said Nels. 'And you didn't accompany them?'

'No,' said Susan Marie. 'I didn't.'

'Did you hear any part of their conversation?'

'No.'

'In other words, you have no firsthand knowledge of its content – is that correct, Mrs. Heine?'

'What I know is what Carl told me,' answered Susan Marie. 'I didn't hear their conversation, no.'

'Thank you,' Nels said. 'Because that concerns me. The fact that you've testified about this conversation without having heard any part of it.'

He pinched the wattles of skin at his throat and turned his good eye on Judge Fielding. The judge, his head resting on his hand, yawned and looked back with detachment.

'Well then,' Nels said. 'To summarize, Mrs. Heine. Your husband and the defendant walked and talked, and you stayed behind. Is that right?'

'Yes, it is.'

'And after thirty to forty minutes your husband returned. Is that also right, Mrs. Heine?'

'Yes, it is.'

'You asked him about the content of his conversation with the defendant?'

'Yes.'

'And he replied that the two of them had discussed the land in question? The land that your mother-in-law sold to Ole Jurgensen more

---

2 **embitter sb.**: make sb. feel angry or disappointed about sth.   4 **unresolvable** [ˌʌnrɪˈzɑːlvəbl]: incapable of being solved   6 **veneer of sth.** (fig, fml): outer appearance of sth., esp. a positive quality, that hides the true nature of your feelings or character   7 **armor** [ˈɑːrmər]: Rüstung   10 **mockery**: Spott   11 **colon**: Dickdarm   14 **remorse** [rɪˈmɔːrs]: feeling of being extremely sorry for sth. wrong or bad that you have done   27 **flare up**: suddenly become much stronger   28 **throb**: pulse regularly and painfully

than a decade ago? The land on which the defendant's childhood home sat? Is all of that right, Mrs. Heine?'

'Yes,' said Susan Marie. 'It is.'

'You and your husband had recently put down earnest money on this land. Is that correct, Mrs. Heine?'

'Yes. My husband did.'

'Let's see,' said Nels Gudmundsson. 'Monday, September 6, was Labor Day, Tuesday the seventh Mr. Jurgensen put his land up for sale … was it Wednesday, then – the eighth of September – that your husband signed the contract on Mr. Jurgensen's property?'

'It must have been,' said Susan Marie. 'Wednesday the eighth sounds right.'

'And the defendant visited the next day? On Thursday, the ninth of September?'

'Yes.'

'All right, then,' said Nels Gudmundsson. 'You've testified that on the afternoon of the ninth the defendant presented himself at your door and that he and your husband walked and talked, but that you were not present during their conversation. Do I have that right, Mrs. Heine?'

'Yes, you do.'

'And furthermore,' said Nels, 'after the defendant left that afternoon you and your husband sat on the porch and had your own conversation?'

'Yes.'

'Your husband indicated an unwillingness to talk about the content of his conversation with the defendant?'

'Correct.'

'You pressed him?'

'I did.'

'He reported to you that he had indicated to the defendant a willingness to think matters over? That he would ponder whether or not he might sell the seven acres to Mr. Miyamoto? Or allow Mr. Jurgensen to do so?'

'Yes.'

'He reported to you a concern about how his mother might react if he sold to the defendant? Did I hear you say that, Mrs. Heine?'

'You did.'

'But he was pondering such a sale anyway?'

'That's right.'

'And he had indicated as much to the defendant?'

'Yes.'

'So in other words Mr. Miyamoto left your residence on the ninth having heard from your husband there was at least a possibility your husband would sell the seven acres to him.'

'That's right.'

'Your husband reported to you that he had encouraged Mr. Miyamoto to believe in such a possibility?'

'Encouraged?' replied Susan Marie Heine. 'I don't know about that.'

'Let me put it this way,' Nels said. 'Your husband did not state an unequivocal no? He did not lead the defendant to believe that no hope existed for the reclaiming of his family's land?'

'He did not,' answered Susan Marie.

'In other words, he encouraged Mr. Miyamoto to believe that at the very least a possibility existed.'

'I guess so,' said Susan Marie.

'I guess you'd have to guess,' said Nels, 'having not been present at their conversation. Having to report to the court only, Mrs. Heine, what your husband reported to you. Words that might not be one hundred percent accurate, since your husband was aware of your disenchantment about the possibility of moving, as you've said, and may well have altered the tone and substance of his conversation with Mr. Miyamo – '

'Objection,' put in Alvin Hooks. 'Argumentative.'

'Sustained,' said the judge. 'Stop rambling, Mr. Gudmundsson. Your purpose here is to ask questions of the witness that refer directly to her testimony. You must refrain from doing anything else – but you know this. Get on with it.'

'Apologies,' Nels replied. 'All right, then. Mrs. Heine, forgive me. Your husband and the defendant – do I have this right? – had grown up together as boys?'

---

59 **disenchantment** [,dɪsɪn'tʃæntmənt]: state of not feeling that sth. is good or worth doing   62 **argumentative**: (here) arguing with the witness   63 **ramble**: talk about sth. for a long time without coming to the point   65 **refrain from doing sth.** [rɪ'freɪn]: stop yourself from doing sth., esp. sth. you would like to do

'As far as I know, yes.'

'Did your husband ever mention him as a neighbor, an acquaintance from his youth?'

'Yes.'

'Did he tell you how they'd gone fishing together as boys of ten or eleven? Or that they'd played on the same high school baseball and football teams? That they rode the same school bus for many years? Any of that, Mrs. Heine?'

'I suppose so,' Susan Marie said.

'Hmmm,' said Nels. He pulled the wattles of skin at his throat again and gazed at the ceiling for a moment. 'Mrs. Heine,' he said. 'You mentioned during the course of your testimony these "dirty looks" Mr. Miyamoto is supposed to have aimed at your mother-in-law. Do you remember mentioning that?'

'Yes.'

'You didn't mention that the defendant had aimed similar looks at you. Is that right? Do I remember right?'

'No, I didn't.'

'Or at your husband? Did I hear you say he aimed dirty looks at your husband? Or is it just something your mother-in-law reported as having occurred?'

'I can't speak for either of them,' answered Susan Marie. 'I don't know what they experienced.'

'Of course not,' said Nels. 'And I wouldn't want you to speak for them, either. It's just that earlier – when Mr. Hooks was questioning you? – you seemed happy to do so, Mrs. Heine. So I thought I'd take a flyer myself.' He smiled.

'All right,' Judge Fielding interrupted. 'That'll do, Mr. Gudmundsson. Get on with your questioning or sit down at once.'

'Judge,' replied Nels. 'There's been a lot of hearsay admitted as evidence. That bears pointing out.'

'Yes,' said the judge. 'A lot of hearsay – hearsay you didn't object to, Mr. Gudmundsson. Because you know that Mrs. Heine is entitled under statute to report the nature and content of a conversation held with her deceased husband. The unfortunate fact is that he cannot do it himself. Mrs. Heine is under oath to tell the truth. As a court of law, we have no choice but to trust that what she tells us is accurate.' He turned slowly toward the jurors. 'For want of a gentler title, the legal institution in question here is known as the Deadman's Statute,' he explained. 'Normally it prohibits evidence from being entered into the record – it allows me to rule it inadmissible as hearsay – because the individual in question is deceased. In criminal cases, however, the Deadman's Statute does *not* bar such evidence from being presented, as Mr. Gudmundsson well knows. Nevertheless, and quite frankly, the Deadman's Statute creates a ... shady legal area. This is, I believe, what Mr. Gudmundsson seeks to point out.'

'Yes,' said Mr. Gudmundsson. 'It is precisely what I seek to point out.' He bowed his head to the judge, glanced at the jurors, then turned and looked fully at Kabuo Miyamoto, who still sat erectly in his place at the defendant's table with his hands folded neatly in front of him. It was at this moment that the courtroom lights flickered in the storm, flickered again, and went out. A tree had fallen on Piersall Road and knocked the power wires down.

26–27 **take a flyer**: gewagt spekulieren   30 **hearsay**: things that you have heard but do not definitely know to be true   31 **bear doing sth.**: be suitable or necessary to do sth. in the present situation   33–34 **be entitled to do sth.**: officially have the right to do sth.   **under statute** ['stætʃuːt]: nach dem Gesetz   38 **for want of sth.**: because of the lack of sth.   **gentle**: (here) not formal but humane or sympathetic   41 **inadmissible** [ˌɪnəd'mɪsəbl]: (here) not allowed or accepted as testimony or evidence in court   43 **bar sth. from being presented**: ban or prevent sth. from being presented   45 **shady legal area**: juristische Grauzone

Chapter 22

Well timed,' Nels Gudmundsson said when the lights went out in the Island County Courthouse. 'I have no further questions for Mrs. Heine, Your Honor. As far as we're concerned, she may step down.'

The four tall windows, frosted with vapor from the steam radiators, allowed a gray snowfall light to descend into the courtroom. Its timbre replaced that of the overhead lights and cast a subtle pall across the citizens in the gallery, who sat looking at one another and at the ceiling.

'Very well,' Judge Fielding replied. 'One thing at a time now. Patience, patience. Let's proceed methodically, lights or no lights. Mr. Hooks, will you redirect?'

Alvin Hooks rose and told the court that the prosecution had no further questions. 'In fact,' he added, winking at Nels, 'the timing of this power outage is even more propitious than my colleague for the defense suspects. Mrs. Heine is our last witness. The state rests at the same moment the county's power supply does.'

The jurors – some of them – stirred and smiled. 'The state rests,' repeated Lew Fielding. 'Very well, then. Very good. I was at any rate going to call for a lunch recess. We will get a report from the power company and take matters from there. We shall see what we shall see. In the meantime, I would like to ask Mr. Hooks and Mr. Gudmundsson to visit with me in my chambers.'

The judge picked his gavel up and dropped it again listlessly against its walnut plate. 'Go have lunch,' he advised. 'If we begin again at all, we'll begin at one sharp – one P.M. according to *my* watch, which now reads' – he peered at it – 'eleven fifty-three. The electric clocks in this building are useless, incidentally. Pay no attention to them.'

Ed Soames held the door open for him, and Judge Fielding disappeared into his chambers. The citizens in the gallery filed out; the reporters picked up their notepads. Soames followed the judge with the intention of lighting a pair of candles he knew to be lodged in the back of a desk drawer. Judge Fielding would need them, after all. It was dark in his chambers, darker than dusk, with only a pale light seeping through the windows. Ed had the candles lit by the time Nels Gudmundsson and Alvin Hooks had arrived and situated themselves across the desk from Judge Fielding. The candles sat between them so that they looked like three men preparing for a séance – the judge in his silk robe, Nels in his bow tie with its touch of the theatrical, Alvin Hooks dapper and elegant, his legs crossed, one knee over the other. Ed made his way to the door and excused himself for interrupting; was there anything more the judge required? If not, he would see to the jurors.

'Oh, yes,' Judge Fielding answered. 'Go and check on the boiler room, won't you? Find out how it looks to keep the radiators perking. And ring the power company and get a report. And, let's see, scare up as many candles as you can find around.' He turned his attention to the attorneys in front of him. 'What am I forgetting?' he added.

'The hotel,' Alvin Hooks answered. 'You'd better ask about their boiler, too, or the jurors aren't going to make it. They didn't fare well last night, recollect, and with the power out things will be worse.'

'Right,' Ed Soames said. 'Will do.'

'Very well, Ed,' the judge returned. Then: 'Quite solicitous of you, Alvin.'

'I'm a solicitous man,' Alvin Hooks replied.

Soames went out, grimly. The courtroom was empty except for Ishmael Chambers, who sat in the gallery with the look on his face of a man willing to wait forever. Eleanor Dokes had tended to the jurors; they were gathered in the anteroom getting coats on. 'The judge will be

5 **timbre** ['tæmbər]: (here) shade of color   6 **pall**: (here) darkness or dimness causing a gloomy atmosphere   10 **redirect** [ˌriːdəˈrekt]: (bei Gericht) einen Zeugen abermals vernehmen   13 **power outage**: Stromausfall   **propitious** [prəˈpɪʃəs]: günstig   14 **the state rests** (fml): official statement saying that the prosecutor has finished his examination of witnesses in the course of a trial   22 **gavel**: Richterhammer   26 **incidentally**: by the way   28 **file out**: exit from a place in a line of people, one after the other   32–33 **seep through sth.**: (of light) only faintly shine through sth.   36 **séance** ['seɪɑːns]: meeting at which people try to make contact with the spirits of dead people   38 **dapper**: (of a man) small with a neat appearance and nice clothes   42 **keep sth. perking** (infml) [ˈpɜːrkɪŋ]: etwas in Gang halten   43–44 **scare up sth.**: find sth. by taking whatever is available   47 **fare** (v): sich befinden, ergehen   50 **solicitous** [səˈlɪsɪtəs]: attentive to the needs and wishes of other people

conferring throughout the lunch recess,' Ed told Ishmael Chambers. 'There's no point in waiting around to speak to him. An announcement will be made at one o'clock.'

The newspaperman stood and stuffed his notepad in his pocket. 'I'm not waiting,' he said softly. 'I was just thinking about things.'

'You'll have to think about them elsewhere,' said Ed. 'I'm going to lock up the courtroom.'

'All right,' said Ishmael. 'Excuse me.'

But he left slowly, preoccupied. Ed Soames watched him impatiently. A *strange bird*, he told himself. *'Bout half the man his father was.* Maybe the missing arm had something to do with it. Ed remembered Ishmael's father and shook his head, disconcerted. He and Arthur had been friendly enough, but the boy was not someone you could speak to.

Ishmael, with his shoulders hunched, his collar turned up, his pinned coat sleeve whipping in the wind, slogged through the snow to his office. The wind blew from off the water to the northwest and swept raucously down Hill Street. Ishmael had to keep his head lowered; when he raised it needles of snow lashed his eyes. He could see, nevertheless, that there were no lights anywhere in Amity Harbor; the power was out entirely. Four cars had been abandoned at haphazard angles along Hill Street, and one near the intersection of Hill and Ericksen had slid into a parked pickup truck, crumpling the driver's-side rear panel.

Ishmael pushed the door to his office open and shut it again with his shoulder. In his overcoat and snow-flecked hat he picked up the telephone to call his mother; she lived alone five miles from town, and he wanted to see how she was faring in the storm and find out if the south end was in as bad a state as Amity Harbor just now. If she stoked it up – and hung a curtain across the pantry door – the cookstove in the kitchen should keep her warm enough.

The phone in his office was dead, however, and gave him back only a hollow silence; so was his printing press dead, for that matter, he realized now with a start. The office, furthermore, was quickly going cold, giving up its electric heat, and he sat for a moment with his hand in his coat pocket and considered the snow whirling past his window. The stump of his amputated arm throbbed, or more precisely it was as if the arm were *there* again but half-numb, a phantom limb. His brain apparently did not fully grasp – or still disbelieved – that the arm was gone. At times past, just after the war, his missing arm had caused him a great deal of pain. A Seattle doctor had suggested sympathetic denervation of the limb – doing away with its ability to feel – but Ishmael had balked for unfathomable reasons. Whatever there was to feel in his arm, pain or anything else, he wanted to feel it, he didn't exactly know why. Now he reached up inside his coat, cupped the stump of his arm in his right hand, and thought of all he had to do on account of the power being out. He must see to his mother, first of all; he must use Tom Torgerson's ham radio set and put in a call to Anacortes about printing the paper there. He wanted to talk to Nels Gudmundsson and Alvin Hooks. He wanted to find out if the Anacortes ferry was running and if the power company would project a time for getting the wires up again. It would be good to find out where the lines were down and to go out to wherever it was for pictures. It would be good to drive out to the coast guard station, too, and get a full storm report, the speed of the wind, the height of the tides, the rate of snowfall. He should probably take his mother food from town and a can of kerosene. There was a kerosene heater in the shed she could use to keep her bedroom warm, but it needed a new wick. He'd have to stop in at Fisk's.

Ishmael slung his camera around his neck and shoved out into Hill Street to take pictures. Even in good conditions it was not easy for him, a one-armed man, to steady his camera in the way he would like. It was a large box camera with an accordion apparatus for the lens, unwieldy and as heavy as a stone around his neck, and he disliked it thoroughly. When he had a choice he bolted it to a tripod; when he didn't he propped it on the stump of his missing arm, turned his head to look over his left shoulder, and got his pictures as best he could. Doing this always embarrassed him. Twisted and turned, the camera perched precariously beside his ear, he felt like a circus grotesque.

1 **confer** [-'-]: be in a conference   12 **disconcerted**: disturbed, irritated
17 **raucous** ['rɔːkəs]: sounding loud and rough   32 **with a start**: with a sudden feeling of surprise, which also makes you move your head or body quickly
39 **sympathetic denervation**: Abtötung/Durchtrennung des Sympathikusnervs
40 **balk** [bɔːk]: be unwilling   **unfathomable** [ʌnˈfæðəməbl]: too strange or difficult to be understood   45 **ham radio set**: Amateurfunkgerät   48 **project sth.**: (hier) etwas ankündigen   55 **wick**: Docht   59 **unwieldy**: difficult to move or control because of its size, shape or weight   65 **precarious** [prɪˈkeəriəs]: likely to fall

Ishmael took three shots of the car that had plowed into the pickup truck. It was impossible to keep the snow off the lens, and after a time he gave up trying. He felt certain that he should carry his camera, though, since a blizzard like this one did not come along often – the last had hit in '36 – and was sure to do the sort of damage that constituted island news. Nonetheless, from Ishmael's perspective this inclement weather should not be allowed to overshadow the trial of Kabuo Miyamoto, which was an affair of a different sort entirely and of a greater magnitude. In the hearts of his fellow islanders, though, weather of this sort overwhelmed absolutely everything, so that even when a man stood trial for his life it was no doubt the destruction of docks and bulkheads, the trees fallen on homes, the burst pipes, the stranded cars, that would most interest San Piedro's citizens. Ishmael, a native, could not understand how such transitory and accidental occurrences gained the upper hand in their view of things. It was as if they had been waiting all along for something enormous to enter their lives and make them part of the news. On the other hand the trial of Kabuo Miyamoto was the first island murder trial in twenty-eight years – Ishmael had looked it up in back issues of the *Review* – and unlike the storm was a human affair, stood squarely in the arena of human responsibility, was no mere accident of wind and sea but instead a thing humans could make sense of. Its progress, its impact, its outcome, its meaning – these were in the hands of people. Ishmael intended to lead with it – with the trial of Kabuo Miyamoto – if somehow he could get Thursday's edition printed despite the storm.

He picked his way down to Tom Torgerson's filling station, where a half-dozen battered cars stood lined up along the fence, gathering snow on their hoods and roofs while Tom backed yet another into place – 'They're everywhere,' he told Ishmael from the wrecker's window. 'I've seen fifteen alone on Island Center Road and a dozen more up on Mill Run. It'll take me three days just to get to 'em.'

'Listen,' answered Ishmael. 'I know you're busy. But I need to get chains on my DeSoto. It's parked up on Hill Street and I can't bring it down to you. There are four stranded cars up there you'll need to move anyway. What do you say to heading up there next? I've got the chains sitting on the floor in the backseat. On top of that I've got to raise Anacortes on your radio, unless I can find a phone that's working. I've got no power to print my paper.'

'Whole island's down,' Tom Torgerson answered. 'Nobody's got power or phone anywhere. There's trees across lines in twenty different places. Crew's over on Piersall now trying to bring town back up – maybe by morning would be my guess. Anyway, okay, I'll get somebody on the DeSoto, but I just can't do it myself. We've got two high school kids working for us, I'll send one of 'em up, okay?'

'That's fine,' said Ishmael. 'The keys are in it. Any chance I can use your radio?'

'Took it home last week,' Tom answered. 'You want to head out to the house, that's fine. It's set up there – Lois'll show you.'

'I'm heading up to the coast guard station. Maybe I'll get them to put a call through for me if your radio isn't handy.'

'Either way,' Tom said. 'You're welcome to have at it, like I said. Just go on out to the house.'

Ishmael made his way down Main Street to Fisk's, where he bought a one-gallon can of kerosene and a wick for his mother's heater. Fisk had sold all of his size D batteries and all but one of his snow shovels. Three-quarters of his stock of candles had gone out the door and four-fifths of his supply of kerosene. Fisk, Kelton Fisk, had a highly developed sense of civic duty that had led him, at ten o'clock that morning, to refuse to sell more than a gallon of kerosene to any one island household. He stood with his feet planted wide beside the potbellied stove, polishing his glasses on the hem of his flannel shirt and, without having been prompted by Ishmael to do so, recited in detail an inventory of items that had gone out his door since eight o'clock. He also reminded Ishmael that the wick he had purchased would have to be cut after six uses.

Ishmael stopped in at the Amity Harbor Restaurant and asked Elena Bridges to put two cheese sandwiches in a paper sack for him; he didn't have time to stay and eat. The restaurant, though half-dark, was full and

---

1 **shot**: photograph   4 **blizzard**: snowstorm   8 **magnitude** ['mægnɪtjuːd]: importance   11 **bulkhead**: Schutzwand   13 **transitory** ['trænsətɔːri]: continuing for only a short time   19 **squarely**: directly   22 **lead with sth.**: choose sth. as the main topic in a newspaper, i.e. as an article on the first page   40 **bring town back up**: (here) repair the power lines, so the town has electricity again   55 **stock**: Vorrat   57 **civic duty**: Bürgerpflicht   61 **prompt sb.**: encourage sb. to speak

loud with conversation – people sat in booths and at the counter wrapped in coats and scarves, with bags of groceries underfoot, and turned their glances toward the snowfall beyond the windows. They were glad to have found a place to come in from the storm. Later, when they were done eating, it would be difficult for them to go outside again. Ishmael, waiting, listened to the conversation of two fishermen hunkered down at the counter. They were lapping up tomato soup that had been warmed on the gas stove and speculating on when the power might come on again. One wondered if high tide, with the wind behind it at fifty-five knots, might not swamp the town docks. The other said that a wind out of the northwest would bring down a lot of trees that were used to southerlies, including a white fir he feared mightily that grew on a bluff behind his cabin. He had gone out that morning and tied his boat off to a mooring buoy with tripled lines and through his binoculars could see it from his living room swinging about when the wind gusted down the bay. The first man cursed and said he wished he'd done the same with his boat, which would have to take its chances moored on slack lines with a dozen fenders out, six on either side; it was too tricky in these winds to move it.

At a quarter to one Ishmael stopped in at the office of the Island County Power & Light Company on the corner of Second Street and Main. He was loaded down now with the sack of sandwiches stuffed into one coat pocket and the new heater wick in the other, the camera dangling around his neck, and the can of kerosene carried in his hand. The report, which had been posted on the door for San Piedro's citizens to read, listed Piersall Road, Alder Valley Road, South Beach Drive, New Sweden Road, Mill Run Road, Woodhouse Cove Road, and at least a half-dozen others as blocked by fallen trees that had brought down power lines. It projected that power would be restored to Amity Harbor by eight o'clock the following morning and requested patience on the part of citizens. The repair crew had the help of the volunteer fire department and intended to work through the night, it said; all that could be done was being done as speedily as possible.

Ishmael returned to the courthouse. He ate one of his sandwiches in the second-floor corridor, sitting on a bench with his camera beside him and the can of kerosene on the floor. The corridor, he noticed, was slick with the snow that had melted from the shoes of passersby. Those who came down it did so carefully, treading their way like novice ice-skaters

– the only light was whatever passed through the windows of offices and from there through the translucent glass panels of doors. The same was true of the public cloakroom – a damp, slippery, dark place full of dripping coats, bags, hats, and gloves. Ishmael left his kerosene and his camera there on the shelf above his coat. He knew no one would steal the camera, and he hoped no one would steal the kerosene. With the power out, the latter, he supposed, was suddenly a possibility.

Judge Fielding's announcement to the gathered court was terse. The trial would adjourn until eight o'clock the following morning, at which time the power company expected to have the lights on. There were high seas between San Piedro and the mainland that were preventing the Anacortes ferry from running, so it was not possible to house the members of the jury anywhere but where they had been housed the previous evening – the cold, dark rooms of the Amity Harbor Hotel, where they would have to make the best of things, since circumstances were now beyond Judge Fielding's control and other accommodations were not available. He hoped that the elements would not divert the jurors from the crucial and difficult matters at hand. They had an obligation, Judge Fielding said, to brave the storm and power outage as best they could, in order to keep their minds fully on the facts of the trial and the testimony of its witnesses. The judge folded his arms in front of him and leaned from the bench so that the members of the jury could see, through the shadows, his shaggy, exhausted face. 'The thought of a retrial makes me weary,' he sighed. 'I think that with a little effort we can avoid one, can't we? I hope you will pass a relatively pleasant night at the Amity Harbor Hotel, but if you do not, then be brave about it and return tomorrow with your thoughts centered on the case at hand. This is a murder trial, after all,' the judge reminded them, 'and snow or no snow, we have got to keep that foremost in our hearts and minds.'

7 **lap sth. up**: drink sth. quickly, usually with great enjoyment 10 **swamp sth.**: fill or cover sth. with a lot of water 11 **southerly** (n): wind that blows from the south 28 **restore sth. to sb./sth.**: bring sth. back to sb./sth., esp. in the same condition it was in before 37 **novice** (adj) ['nɑːvɪs]: having little experience in sth.
45 **terse** [tɜːrs]: using few words 46 **adjourn** [əˈdʒɜːrn]: (of a trial) stop for a period of time 54–55 **divert sb. from sth.** [daɪˈvɜːrt]: take sb.'s thoughts or attention away from sth. 56 **brave sth.**: manage to deal with sth. difficult or unpleasant
61 **retrial**: new trial of sb. whose criminal offence has already been judged in court

At two thirty-five that afternoon, Ishmael Chambers put his can of kerosene, the heater wick, and two bags of groceries into the trunk of his DeSoto. Tom Torgerson's high school kid had gotten the chains on his tires, and Ishmael, bending low, checked now to see that they were tightly bound. He scraped ice from the DeSoto's windows and ran the defroster before inching out into the snow. The trick, he knew, was to stay off the brake and to keep his traveling speed low and steady, backing off the accelerator at the crests of hills and evenly gaining momentum in the dips. On First Hill he heard his chains, felt them biting, and made his way down cautiously, in first gear, leaning forward in his seat. He did not stop when he got to Main but turned immediately left instead, skidding a little, in the direction of Center Valley Road. He was less worried now. The snow had compacted under the wheels of other cars. The roads were passable if you were patient and paid attention. His chief concern was not the snow but other, more careless drivers. It would be important to watch his rearview mirror and to pull over, if that was possible, when he was being gained on.

Ishmael took Lundgren Road out of Amity Harbor because it made a steady ascent, without curves or coils, on a grade more reasonable than Mill Run's or Piersall's, and because it had not been listed on the power company door as blocked by fallen trees. He did see, at George Freeman's place, a Douglas fir that had toppled over so that its root wad now stood twelve feet high beside George's mailbox. The top section of the tree had crushed a piece of George's split-rail cedar fence. George was out there with a chisel-toothed bucksaw, his wool hat perched on top of his balding head, working on it in the storm.

Ishmael pushed on down the back side of Lundgren and turned onto Scatter Springs Drive. In the first curve a Hudson was nosed into a ditch; in the second a Packard Clipper sedan had flipped onto its roof and sat in the brambles beside the road with its undercarriage facing toward the sky. Ishmael stopped and took photographs of it, setting his tripod on the road verge. The straight lines of the alders and maples behind the Packard, blunt and clean against a sea of snow, the hard, grayish quality of the snowstorm light, the forlorn and helpless car itself with its upturned tires gathering soft mounds of white, its passenger compartment nuzzled into the frozen undergrowth so that only the bottom halves of the windows showed – this was a storm scene if ever there was one, and

Ishmael shot it with an eye toward its pathetic aspect and because it seemed to him to embody what the storm was about: a world in which a Packard Clipper lost its meaning and became unmoored from whatever purpose it originally had; it had no more practical value now than a ship on the bottom of the sea.

Ishmael was glad to see that the driver's side window had been rolled down and that no one was still in the car. He thought he recognized it as Charlie Torval's – Charlie lived on New Sweden Road and made his living building bulkheads and docks and anchoring mooring buoys. He owned a lot of driving equipment, a barge on which a crane had been mounted, and – if Ishmael remembered it right – this rust brown Packard. Perhaps it would be an embarrassment to him if an image of his upturned car appeared in the pages of the *Review*. Ishmael decided to talk to him about it before going ahead with the photograph.

In the third bend in Scatter Springs Drive – a hairpin turn where the road rolled down out of cedar woods and onto the breaks over Center Valley – Ishmael saw three men busying themselves with a snowbound Plymouth half in the road: one jumped up and down on its bumper, another squatted and kept an eye on its spinning tires, a third sat behind the wheel with his door thrown open and worked the accelerator. Ishmael threaded past without stopping and swiveled, skidding – a little gleefully, his stomach leaping – onto Center Valley Road. An odd enthusiasm for this drive and its dangers had been growing in him ever since he'd left First Hill.

The DeSoto, he knew, was a dubious snow car. Ishmael had mounted a cherry wood knob on its steering wheel in order to ease the difficulties

6 **inch out**: move slowly and carefully into a particular direction   8 **accelerator** [ək'seləreɪtər]: Gaspedal   **gain momentum**: an Fahrt gewinnen   10 **gear**: Gang (beim Auto)   12 **skid** (v): (hier) ins Schleudern geraten   16 **pull over**: an die Seite fahren   17 **gain on sb./sth.**: auf jdn./etwas auffahren   19 **ascent** [ə'sent]: upward path or slope   **coil** (n): Windung   **grade**: (hier) Steigung   24 **split-rail fence**: Lattenzaun   25 **chisel-toothed bucksaw**: handsaw that is used to cut logs for firewood   29 **sedan**: Limousine   30 **bramble**: Brom-beerstrauch   **undercarriage** ['ʌndərkærɪdʒ]: Fahrwerk   32 **road verge**: Seitenstrei-fen   34 **forlorn**: lonely and unfortunate   38 **pathetic** [pə'θetɪk]: making you feel pity and sadness   47 **barge** (n): Last-kahn   52 **hairpin turn**: very sharp bend in a road   53 **break**: (hier) Lichtung   55 **bumper**: Stoßstange   56 **spin**: turn round and round quickly   62 **dubious** ['duːbɪəs]: (here) probably not safe or reliable

driving presented to a man with only one arm. He had changed nothing else, though, and didn't intend to. The DeSoto, strictly an island car for more than a decade, had been purchased by Ishmael's father fifteen years before, a four-speed with a semiautomatic transmission, hypoid rear axle, and column shift. Arthur had traded in his Ford Model A plus five hundred dollars cash for it in 1939 at a lot in Bellingham. It was a modest vehicle, square and bulky in the manner of a Dodge, so long in front as to look out of balance and with its radiator grille low over the bumper. Ishmael had hung on to it in part from sheer inertia, in part because driving it reminded him of his father. Sitting behind the wheel he felt his father's contours in the way the seat molded under him.

Center Valley's strawberry fields lay under nine inches of powder and were as fuzzy through the snowfall as a landscape in a dream, with no discernible hard edges. On Scatter Springs Drive the trees had closed the road in so that the sky was little more than an indistinct, drab ribbon overhead, but down here the dramatic expanse of it was visible, chaotic and fierce. Looking out past the windshield wipers Ishmael saw billions of snowflakes falling in long tangents, driven southward, the sky shrouded and furious. The wind propelled the snow against the sides of barns and homes, and Ishmael could hear it whistling through the wing window's rubber molding, which had been loose now for many years: it had been loose back when his father was alive, one of the car's small idiosyncrasies, part of the reason he was loath to part with it.

He passed Ole Jurgensen's house, where white wood smoke furled from the chimney and disappeared on the wind – Ole, apparently, was keeping warm. The snowfall obliterated the borders between the fields and made Kabuo Miyamoto's long-cherished seven acres indistinguishable from the land that surrounded them. All human claims to the landscape were superseded, made null and void by the snow. The world was one world, and the notion that a man might kill another over some small patch of it did not make sense – though Ishmael knew that such things happened. He had been to war, after all.

At the intersection of Center Valley Road and South Beach Drive Ishmael spied, ahead of him in the bend, a car that had failed to negotiate the grade as it coiled around a grove of snow-hung cedars. Ishmael recognized it as the Willys station wagon that belonged to Fujiko and

Hisao Imada; in fact, Hisao was working with a shovel at its rear right wheel, which had dropped into the roadside drainage ditch.

Hisao Imada was small enough most of the time, but he looked even smaller bundled up in his winter clothes, his hat pulled low and his scarf across his chin so that only his mouth, nose, and eyes showed. Ishmael knew he would not ask for help, in part because San Piedro people never did, in part because such was his character. Ishmael decided to park at the bottom of the grade beside Gordon Ostrom's mailbox and walk the fifty yards up South Beach Drive, keeping his DeSoto well out of the road while he convinced Hisao Imada to accept a ride from him.

Ishmael had known Hisao a long time. When he was eight years old he'd seen the Japanese man trudging along behind his swaybacked white plow horse: a Japanese man who carried a machete at his belt in order to cut down vine maples. His family lived in two canvas tents while they cleared their newly purchased property. They drew water from a feeder creek and warmed themselves at a slash pile kept burning by his children – girls in rubber boots, including Hatsue – who dragged branches and brought armfuls of brush to it. Hisao was lean and tough and worked methodically, never altering his pace. He wore a shoulder strap T-shirt, and this, coupled with the sharp-honed weapon at his belt, put Ishmael in mind of the pirates he'd read about in illustrated books his father had brought him from the Amity Harbor Public Library. But all of this was more than twenty years ago now, so that as he approached Hisao Imada in the South Beach Drive, Ishmael saw the man in another

---

4 **four-speed**: Vierganggetriebe   4–5 **hypoid rear axle**: besondere Art des Hinterradantriebs   5 **column shift**: Lenkradschaltung   5–6 **trade sth. in for sth. else**: give sth. used as part of the payment for sth. new   6 **lot** (n): (hier) Autohof
8 **radiator grille**: Kühlergrill   9 **hang on to sth.** (infml): not sell sth. or give it away
inertia [ɪ'nɜːrʃə]: lack of energy   14 **discernible** [dɪ'sɜːrnɪbl]: noticeable
15 **indistinct**: not to be seen clearly   **drab**: blass   20–21 **wing window**: Seitenfenster   21 **rubber molding**: (hier) Gummidichtung   22–23 **idiosyncrasy** [ˌɪdiə'sɪŋkrəsi]: Eigenart   27 **cherish sth.**: (here) hope for sth.   29 **supersede sth.** [ˌsuːpər'siːd]: (hier) etwas als veraltet verwerfen   **null and void**: not valid   34 **spy sth.**: suddenly see or notice sth.   34–35 **negotiate the grade of sth.**: (here) manage to keep in line with the bend in a road   53 **feeder creek**: Nebenfluss   57 **sharp-honed**: scharf geschliffen

light: hapless, small in the storm, numb with the cold and ineffective with his shovel while the trees threatened to come down around him.

Ishmael saw something else, too. On the far side of the car, with her own shovel in hand, Hatsue worked without looking up. She was digging through the snow to the black earth of the cedar woods and throwing spadefuls of it underneath the tires.

Fifteen minutes later the three of them walked down the road toward his DeSoto. The Willys station wagon's rear right tire had been perforated by a fallen branch still wedged up under both axles. The rear length of exhaust pipe had been crushed, too. The car wasn't going anywhere – Ishmael could see that – but it took Hisao some time to accept this truth. With his shovel he'd struggled defiantly, as if the tool could indeed change the car's fate. After ten minutes of polite assistance Ishmael wondered aloud if his DeSoto wasn't the answer and persisted in this vein for five minutes more before Hisao yielded to it as an unavoidable evil. He opened his car door, put in his shovel, and came out with a bag of groceries and a gallon of kerosene. Hatsue, for her part, went on with her digging, saying nothing and keeping to the far side of the car, and throwing black earth beneath the tires.

At last her father rounded the Willys and spoke to her once in Japanese. She stopped her work and came into the road then, and Ishmael was granted a good look at her. He had spoken to her only the morning before in the second-floor hallway of the Island County Courthouse, where she'd sat on a bench with her back to an arched window just outside the assessor's office. Her hair had been woven then, as now, into a black knot against the nape of her neck. She'd told him four times to go away.

'Hello, Hatsue,' said Ishmael. 'I can give you a lift home, if you want.'

'My father says he's accepted,' Hatsue replied. 'He says he's grateful for your help.'

She followed her father and Ishmael down the hill, still carrying her shovel, to the DeSoto. When they were well on their way down South Beach Drive, easing through the flats along the salt water, Hisao explained in broken English that his daughter was staying with him during the trial; Ishmael could drop them at his house. Then he described how a branch had hurled down into the road in front of him; to avoid it he'd hit his brake pedal. The Willys had fishtailed while it climbed the snapped branch and nudged down into the drainage ditch.

Only once, driving and listening, nodding politely and inserting small exclamations of interest – '*I see, I see, yes, of course, I can understand*' – did Ishmael risk looking at Hatsue Miyamoto in the rectangle of his rear-view mirror: a risk that filled all of two seconds. He saw then that she was staring out the side window with enormous deliberation, with intense concentration on the world outside his car – she was making it a point to be absorbed by the storm – and that her black hair was wringing wet with snow. Two strands had escaped from their immaculate arrangement and lay pasted against her frozen cheek.

'I know it's caused you trouble,' Ishmael said. 'But don't you think the snow is beautiful? Isn't it beautiful coming down?'

The boughs in the fir trees hung heavy with it, the fence rails and mailboxes wore mantles of it, the road before him lay filled with it, and there was no sign, anywhere, of people. Hisao Imada agreed that it was so – *ah, yes, beautiful*, he commented softly – and at the same moment his daughter turned swiftly forward so that her eyes met Ishmael's in the mirror. It was the cryptic look, he recognized, that she'd aimed at him fleetingly on the second floor of the courthouse when he'd tried to speak to her before her husband's trial. Ishmael still could not read what her eyes meant – punishment, sorrow, perhaps buried anger, perhaps all three simultaneously. Perhaps some sort of disappointment.

For the life of him, after all these years, he couldn't read the expression on her face. If Hisao wasn't present, he told himself, he'd ask her flat out what she was trying to say by looking at him with such detached severity and saying nothing at all. What, after all, had he done to her? What had she to be angry about? The anger, he thought, ought to be his own; yet years ago now the anger about her had finished gradually bleeding out

---

8 **perforate sth.**: make a hole or holes through sth.   9 **wedge sth. up under sth. else**: (here) etwas unter etwas anderem verkeilen   14–15 **in this vein** [veɪn]: in this style or manner   22 **grant sb. sth.**: jdm. etwas gewähren   34 **ease through sth.**: move slowly and carefully through sth.   38 **fishtail** (v): (of a car) slide from side to side at the back end   39 **nudge down into sth.** [nʌdʒ]: push forward and down into sth.   42 **rectangle** ['rektæŋgl]: Rechteck   52 **mantle**: layer of sth. that covers a surface   57 **fleeting**: lasting only for a short period of time   61 **for the life of you** (infml): however hard you try   63 **severity** [sɪ'verəti]: Strenge

of him and had slowly dried up and blown away. Nothing had replaced it, either. He had not found anything to take its place. When he saw her, as he sometimes did, in the aisles of Petersen's Grocery or on the street in Amity Harbor, he turned away from seeing her with just a little less hurry than she turned away from seeing him; they avoided one another rigorously. It had come to him one day three years before how immersed she was in her own existence. She'd knelt in front of Fisk's Hardware Center tying her daughter's shoelaces in bows, her purse on the sidewalk beside her. She hadn't known he was watching. He'd seen her kneeling and working on her daughter's shoes, and it had come to him what her life was. She was a married woman with children. She slept in the same bed every night with Kabuo Miyamoto. He had taught himself to forget as best he could. The only thing left was a vague sense of waiting for Hatsue – a fantasy – to return to him. How, exactly, this might be achieved he could not begin to imagine, but he could not keep himself from feeling that he was waiting and that these years were only an interim between other years he had passed and would pass again with Hatsue.

She spoke now, from the backseat, having turned again to look out the window. 'Your newspaper,' she said. That was all.

'Yes,' answered Ishmael. 'I'm listening.'

'The trial, Kabuo's trial, is unfair,' said Hatsue. 'You should talk about that in your newspaper.'

'What's unfair?' asked Ishmael. 'What exactly is unfair? I'll be happy to write about it if you'll tell me.'

She was still staring out the window at the snow with strands of wet hair pasted against her cheek. 'It's all unfair,' she told him bitterly. 'Kabuo didn't kill anyone. It isn't in his heart to kill anyone. They brought in that sergeant to say he's a killer – that was just prejudice. Did you hear the things that man was saying? How Kabuo had it in his heart to kill? How horrible he is, a killer? Put it in your paper, about that man's testimony, how all of it was unfair. How the whole trial is unfair.'

'I understand what you mean,' answered Ishmael. 'But I'm not a legal expert. I don't know if the judge should have suppressed Sergeant Maples's testimony. But I hope the jury comes in with the right verdict. I could write a column about that, maybe. How we all hope the justice system does its job. How we hope for an honest result.'

'There shouldn't even *be* a trial,' said Hatsue. 'The whole thing is wrong, it's *wrong*.'

'I'm bothered, too, when things are unfair,' Ishmael said to her. 'But sometimes I wonder if unfairness isn't … part of things. I wonder if we should even expect fairness, if we should assume we have some sort of right to it. Or if – '

'I'm not talking about the whole universe,' cut in Hatsue. 'I'm talking about people – the sheriff, that prosecutor, the judge, you. People who can do things because they run newspapers or arrest people or convict them or decide about their lives. People don't have to be unfair, do they? That isn't just *part of things*, when people are unfair to somebody.'

'No, it isn't,' Ishmael replied coldly. 'You're right – people don't have to be unfair.'

When he let them out beside the Imadas' mailbox he felt that somehow he had gained the upper hand – he had an emotional advantage. He had spoken with her and she had spoken back, wanting something from him. She'd volunteered a desire. The strain between them, the hostility he felt – it was better than nothing, he decided. It was an emotion of some sort they shared. He sat in the DeSoto and watched Hatsue trudge away through the falling snow, carrying her shovel on her shoulder. It occurred to him that her husband was going out of her life in the same way he himself once had. There had been circumstances then and there were circumstances now; there were things beyond anyone's control. Neither he nor Hatsue had wanted the war to come – neither of them had wanted that intrusion. But now her husband was accused of murder, and that changed things between them.

---

3 **aisle** [aɪl]: (here) passage between two rows of sth., e.g. of shelves in a supermarket or of benches in a church or courtroom   6–7 **immerse sb. in sth.** [ɪˈmɜːrs]: make sb. become completely involved in sth.   17 **interim**: period of time between two events   46–47 **convict sb.** [-ˈ-]: officially decide and state in court that sb. is guilty of a crime   62 **intrusion** [ɪnˈtruːʒn]: sth. that affects people's lives in a way that they do not want

Chapter 23

The coast guard lighthouse on the rocks at Point White was a tower built out of reinforced concrete that rose a hundred feet above the sea. In the thirty years before it went up, eleven ships came aground at the point – two mail steamers, seven timber schooners, a Norwegian freighter, and a four-masted bark with a cargo of Newcastle coal on board, inbound for Seattle in a windstorm. There was no sign of them at all anymore – they'd broken up and, over the years, washed away into the ocean. There was only a jumble of barnacle-encrusted sea rock and a view of the water stretching to the horizon, unbroken, gray, and blurred in the distance at the place where the ocean and the sky met.

On occasions when the tide ran exceptionally high, waves washed perilously close to the lighthouse, dashing its base with salt-tinged algae, which clung to it now like sea moss. Underneath the lighthouse's copper dome lay sixteen reflecting prisms and four projecting lenses floating in a bath of mercury. The coast guard kept the clockworks greased, and the lenses revolved twice each minute. And yet there were still accidents, despite everything. There seemed no way to prevent them. In a thick fog the light could not be seen and boats continued to come aground. The coast guard installed sounding boards along island beaches and anchored numbered buoys at intervals in the shipping channel, and these measures seemed sufficient to islanders until the next accident came along. A tug towing a diesel ferry from San Francisco broke up on the rocks a mile to the north; then a tug towing a barge full of peeler logs; then a salvage steamer working out of Victoria. News of such wrecks was received by islanders with a grim brand of determinism; it seemed to many that such things were ordained by God, or at any rate unavoidable. They came out in large numbers in the aftermath of a shipwreck to stand on the beach and stare in awe at the latest foundering vessel; some brought binoculars and cameras. Old fishermen with time on their hands built bonfires out of driftwood and warmed themselves while the sea made breaches in the hulls of ships that had come hard aground. There was much discussion and finger pointing. Working without a single hard fact, islanders drew a variety of conclusions: pilot error, pilot inexperience, misread charts, crossed signals, fog, wind, tide, ineptitude. When after days a ship broke apart, or the pieces of it sank, or a salvage company gave up in despair after off-loading one twenty-fifth of its cargo, islanders watched blankly with their mouths hard-set and shook their heads once or twice. For a week or so they spoke cautiously of what they'd seen, and then it faded out of the realm of the discourse they shared together. They thought of it only at private moments.

Ishmael Chambers, in the last light of day, found himself seated in the office of the lighthouse chief petty officer, a large man named Evan Powell. The place was lit by kerosene lanterns and heated by a cast-iron wood stove. Outside a generator powered the lighthouse, so that each thirty seconds the beacon flashed against the glass of the office window. Petty Officer Powell kept an immaculate desk – a calendar blotter, twin upright pen stands, a nearly full ashtray, a telephone. He sat back in a reclining desk chair with a lit cigarette between his fingers, scratching his face and coughing. 'I've got a cold,' he explained to Ishmael hoarsely. 'I'm not firing on every cylinder right now. But I'll help you out if I can, Mr. Chambers. You need something for your newspaper?'

'I do,' said Ishmael. 'I'm putting an article together on this storm. I'm wondering if you have archives of some kind, weather records from way back, maybe, something I could take a look at. Go through old logs, something like that, try to make some comparisons. I can't remember a storm like this one, but that doesn't mean it never happened.'

'We do a *lot* of record keeping,' Petty Officer Powell replied. 'The lighthouse has been here longer than the coast guard – I don't know

2 **reinforced concrete** [riːɪnˌfɔːst ˈkɑːŋkriːt]: Stahlbeton   3 **come aground**: (of a ship) touch the ground   6 **inbound for sth.** ['--]: traveling towards a place   8 **jumble of sth.** (n): untidy or confused mixture of sth.   12 **perilous** (fml) [ˈperələs]: very dangerous   13 **copper**: soft reddish-brown metal   15 **grease sth.**: etwas einfetten   16 **revolve**: go in a circle around a central point   19 **sounding board**: (hier) Reflektortonne/~boje   21 **tug** (n): Schlepper   22 **tow sth.** [toʊ]: pull sth., esp. a car or boat behind another vehicle using a chain or rope   23 **peeler logs**: Bauholz   23–24 **salvage steamer** [ˈsælvɪdʒ]: Bergungsschiff   28 **founder** (v): (of a ship) fill with water and sink   31 **hull**: Rumpf   34 **ineptitude** [ɪˈneptɪtuːd]: lack of skill   39 **realm** [relm]: area   42 **chief petty officer**: officer of middle rank in the navy   45 **beacon** [ˈbiːkən]: Leuchtfeuer   46 **blotter**: Schreibtischunterlage

how far back there's reliable information – anyway you can have a look, if you want. There's more stuff around than you'd ever want to get into. I'd be interested in seeing what you find out.'

Petty Officer Powell fell forward in his chair and carefully snubbed out his cigarette. He picked up the telephone and, dialing a single number, drew a handkerchief out of his pocket. 'Who's this?' he said gruffly into the receiver. 'I want you to see if you can find Levant. Find Levant and tell him to come down here. Tell him to bring a couple kerosene lanterns. Tell him I need him right away.'

He put his hand over the receiver mouth, blew his nose, and looked at Ishmael. 'How much time you got?' he said. 'I can spare Levant to help you out for a couple of hours, tops.'

'That's all right,' said Ishmael. 'I don't want to trouble anybody here. Just point me in the right direction.'

Evan Powell slipped his hand from the receiver. 'Smoltz,' he said. 'Get Levant. Tell him I need him right away. Find Levant for this.'

He hung up and blew his nose one more time. 'There's no shipping in this weather,' he said. 'We raised Neah Bay an hour ago. We figure the snow isn't going to let up until tomorrow afternoon.'

The radioman named Levant arrived. Levant was tall enough to be a basketball player, six five or six six, with a large Adam's apple and tightly curled black hair, and he carried a lantern and a flashlight. 'This man here is Ishmael Chambers,' Petty Officer Powell explained. 'He runs the newspaper down in town and needs to take a look into our weather records. I want you to set things up for him, get him squared away, help him out. Give him what he needs, set him up a couple lanterns.'

'Anything else?' Levant said.

'Don't miss your radio watch over it,' Powell said. 'There's two hours before you're on.'

'Listen,' said Ishmael. 'Just point me in the right direction. I don't want to take anybody's time.'

Levant led the way to the records room on the second floor, which was stacked floor to ceiling with wooden crates, file cabinets, and stacked duffel bags. It smelled of brittle paper and of mimeograph ink and had not been dusted recently. 'Everything's dated,' Levant pointed out, finding a place for a lantern. 'That's how we do things – by dates, mainly. Radio transmissions, shipping log, weather reports, maintenance – everything's in here by date, I guess. There's a date on everything.'

'You have a radio watch?' Ishmael asked. 'Are you the radioman?'

'I am now,' Levant said. 'I have been for the last couple months or so – last guys got transferred, I moved up.'

'Is there a lot of record keeping with your job? Does a radioman contribute to all of this?'

'There's a guy shorthands all the radio transmissions,' Levant explained to him. 'He writes 'em up, files 'em, they end up here in a cabinet. And that's all they're good for, seems like. They just take up space, is all. No one pays any attention.'

Ishmael picked up a manila folder and turned it toward the lantern light. 'Looks like I'm going to be awhile,' he said. 'Why don't you go about your business? If I need something I can find you.'

'I'll bring another lantern,' Levant replied.

He was alone then with the fog of his breath in the lantern light and the crates of maritime records. The room smelled of salt water and snow and of the past – it was full of the scent of lost days. Ishmael tried to concentrate on his work, but the image of Hatsue in the backseat of his car – her eyes meeting his in the rearview mirror – carried him away into his memories.

The first time he'd seen her after the war she'd tried, he recalled, to be amiable, but he had not been capable of accepting this. He'd stood behind her with his milk and crackers, waiting in line at Petersen's. He'd stood in silence, hating her, and she'd turned toward him with a baby on her shoulder and said with a detached formality that she was very sorry to have heard about his arm, how he had lost it in the war. She was, he remembered, as beautiful as ever, a little older and harder around the eyes, and it hurt him to look at her face and at her hair, which she wore in a braid down her back. Ishmael stood there looking pale and ill – he had a cold and a mild fever – with the sleeve of his

12 **tops** (infml): (hier) höchstens   25 **square sb. away**: (here) help sb. to find what they are looking for   28 **radio watch**: Funkbereitschaft   33 **file cabinet**: piece of office furniture with deep drawers for storing files   34 **brittle**: (of paper) old and likely to fall apart   **mimeograph ink**: Kopiertinte   37 **log**: Logbuch   **maintenance** ['meɪntənəns]: Wartung   44 **shorthand sth.**: etwas stenografieren

mackinaw coat pinned up, his milk and crackers clutched in his hand, and stared long and hard at Hatsue's baby while the grocery checker, Eleanor Hill, pretended not to notice that Hatsue had spoken of what others, including Eleanor, would not acknowledge – that Ishmael was missing an arm. 'The Japs did it,' Ishmael said flatly, still staring hard at the baby. 'They shot my arm off. *Japs.*'

Hatsue looked at him a moment longer, then turned toward Eleanor Hill again and opened up her coin purse. 'I'm sorry,' said Ishmael immediately. 'I didn't mean that. I didn't mean what I said.' But she showed no sign of having heard, and so he put down the crackers and milk and put his hand on her shoulder. 'I'm sorry,' he said a second time, but she still didn't turn to look at him, and she moved away from his hand. 'I'm more than sorry. I'm miserable. Do you understand? I don't mean what I say. You can't trust me when I speak anymore. I just say things. I – '

Eleanor Hill was pretending, busily, that Ishmael, a war veteran, wasn't standing in her presence speaking the words he was speaking. It was what he'd gotten when he spoke about himself, when he'd tried to say what he had to say; there was nothing he could easily explain to anyone, and nobody who wanted to listen. There were other boys who had been to the war, and he found that on occasion he could speak to them, but that didn't mean anything. 'I'm sorry, Hatsue,' he said one more time. 'I'm sorry about everything. All of it.'

He'd left without buying the milk and crackers. He went home and wrote an apologetic letter, explaining at length that he was not himself, that he sometimes said what he did not mean, that he wished he had never said *Jap* in front of her, that he would never do so again. The letter sat in his desk drawer for two weeks before he threw it away.

Despite himself he knew where she lived and which car she drove and when he saw her husband, Kabuo Miyamoto, he felt something tighten around his heart. He felt himself grow tight inside, and for a long time he could not sleep at night. He would lie awake until two o'clock in the morning, then turn a light on and attempt to read from a book or magazine. Gradually dawn came and he would not have slept. He would go out to wander the island's trails in the early morning, at a slow pace. Once, so doing, he came across her. She was down on the beach at Fletcher's Bay, raking for steamer clams busily. Her baby slept on a blanket beside her, underneath an umbrella. Ishmael had come up the beach deliberately, and squatted beside Hatsue while she raked clams free and dropped them into a bucket. 'Hatsue,' he'd pleaded. 'Can I talk to you?'

'I'm married,' she'd said, without looking at him. 'It isn't right for us to be alone. It will look bad, Ishmael. People will talk.'

'There's no one here,' answered Ishmael. '*I've got* to talk to you, Hatsue. You owe me that much, don't you? Don't you think you do?'

'Yes,' said Hatsue. 'I do.'

She turned away from him and looked at her baby. The sun had crept up onto the child's face; Hatsue adjusted the beach umbrella.

'I'm like a dying person,' Ishmael said to her. 'I haven't been happy for a single moment since the day you left for Manzanar. It's like carrying a weight around in my gut, a ball of lead or something. Do you know how that feels, Hatsue? Sometimes I think I'm going to go crazy, end up in the hospital in Bellingham. I'm crazy, I don't sleep, I'm up all night. It never leaves me alone, this feeling. Sometimes I don't think I can stand it. I tell myself this can't go on, but it goes on anyway. There isn't anything I can do.'

Hatsue pushed the hair from her eyes with the back of her left wrist. 'I'm sorry for you,' she said softly. 'I don't want your unhappiness. I never meant for you to suffer. But I don't know what I can do for you now. I don't know how I can help you.'

'You'll think this is crazy,' Ishmael said. 'But all I want is to hold you. All I want is just to hold you once and smell your hair, Hatsue. I think after that I'll be better.'

Hatsue had looked at him, hard, for a long moment, the clamming rake clutched in her hand. 'Look,' she said. 'You know I can't. I can never touch you, Ishmael. Everything has to be over between us. We both have to put it all behind us and go on, live our lives. There's no halfway, from my point of view. I'm married, I have a baby, and I can't let you hold me. So what I want you to do right now is get up and walk away from here and forget about me forever. You have to let go of me, Ishmael.'

'I know you're married,' Ishmael had said. 'I want to forget about you, I do. I think if you hold me I can start, Hatsue. Hold me once, and I'll walk away and never speak to you again.'

'No,' she'd said. 'It can't be. You'll have to find some other way. I'm not going to hold you, ever.'

'I'm not talking about love,' he said. 'I'm not asking you to try to love me. But just as one human being to another, just because I'm miserable and don't know where to turn, I just need to be in your arms.'

Hatsue sighed and turned her eyes from his. 'Go away,' she'd said. 'I hurt for you, I honestly do, I feel terrible for your misery, but I'm not going to hold you, Ishmael. You're going to have to live without holding me. Now get up and leave me alone, please.'

The years had passed, and now her husband was on trial for the murder of a man at sea. It dawned on Ishmael, in the coast guard record room, that perhaps something pertinent to Kabuo's case could be found right here among these files. And suddenly he put aside his weather records and began to search the cabinets, and a strange excitement grew in him.

It took Ishmael all of fifteen minutes to find what it was he wanted. It was in a file cabinet to the right of the door, near the front of the third drawer down — records for September 15 and 16 of 1954. No wind, moderate tides, thick fog, balmy. One ship through at 0120 hours, the S.S. *West Corona*, Greek owned, Liberian flag; she'd called in her position from out to the west, headed southbound toward Seattle. The radio transmissions were in shorthand: the *Corona* had put in a call from northwest of sounding board 56, looking for a fix from the lighthouse radio signal. She'd come down the strait plotting soundings as she went, but the pilot would not put his faith in this, and at 0126 hours that morning, in heavy fog, had radioed the lighthouse for assistance. There was interference and the signal was weak, so the radioman on duty had advised the *Corona*'s navigator to take a reading off sounding board 56, which lay on the north shore of Lanheedron Island, and to plot his position accordingly. The *Corona*'s navigator had ordered a whistle blast and timed the interval of the echo. He did his division and his multiplication and relayed his position to the radioman. The *Corona* was out of the lane, he reported, somewhere south of buoy 56, and would have to dogleg to the northeast, bisecting Ship Channel Bank.

Ship Channel Bank. Where Dale Middleton, Vance Cope, and Leonard George had all seen Carl Heine with his net out on the night he went into the sea. On that night an enormous freighter had plowed right through the fishing grounds, throwing before it a wake large enough to knock even a big man overboard.

At 0142, on pilot's orders, the *Corona* made its corrective dogleg while the navigator fixed twice more on the sounding board. Later the navigator took three more insurance readings – boards 58, 59, and 60. It seemed to the *Corona*'s radioman that they were safely back in the shipping lane. In the vicinity of White Sand Bay he picked up the lighthouse's radio beacon and, gaining confidence by the moment, made the big swing to the south. The *Corona* locked onto the lighthouse radio signal and made headway for Seattle.

Everything was in triplicate – military standard carbon copies. They were signed by the radioman's assistant, a Seaman Philip Milholland – he'd transcribed the radio transmissions. Ishmael slipped three center pages of Seaman Milholland's notes free and folded them into quarters. The pages fit neatly into his coat pocket, and he let them sit there, feeling them, composing himself a little. Then he grabbed one of the lanterns and went out.

At the bottom of the stairs, in an anteroom, he found Levant slowly paging through the *Saturday Evening Post* beside a kerosene floor heater. 'I'm done,' he pointed out. 'There's just one more thing. Is Philip Milholland around somewhere? I want to talk to him.'

Levant shook his head and put the magazine on the floor. 'You know Milholland?' he said.

'Sort of,' said Ishmael. 'An acquaintance.'

'Milholland's gone. He got transferred out to Cape Flattery, Milholland and Robert Miller. That's when we moved up.'

---

11 **dawn on sb.**: jdm. dämmern   12 **pertinent to sth.**: relevant to sth.   20 **call in your position**: seine Position durchgeben   22 **put in a call**: einen Funkspruch absetzen   23 **fix** (n): (hier) Standort, Position   24 **strait**: narrow passage of water that connects two large areas of the sea   **plot soundings:** measure the depth of the water at certain points and locate these points on a sea map in order to determine the course of a ship   28 **take a reading off sth.**: (hier) etwas anpeilen   30 **blast**: (hier) Signalton   32 **relay sth. to sb.**: receive and send sth., esp. a piece of information, to sb.   34 **dogleg** (v): (hier) abdrehen, den Kurs ändern   **bisect sth.** [baɪˈsekt]: divide sth. into two equal parts   38 **wake** (n): track that a ship leaves behind on the surface of the water   42 **take insurance readings**: (hier) eine Peilung überprüfen   46 **swing** (n): (here) movement of changing your position quickly and completely   **lock onto sth.**: etwas erfassen und verfolgen

'We?' asked Ishmael. 'Who's we?'

'Me and Smoltz, the two of us, we started in together. Smoltz.'

'When was that? When did Milholland leave?'

'That was back in September,' said Levant. 'Me and Smoltz started in September 16 as dogwatch radio team.'

'Dogwatch? Like at night?'

'Night shift, yes,' Levant said. 'Me and Smoltz work the night shift.'

'So Milholland's gone,' said Ishmael. 'He left September 15?'

'He couldn't have left the fifteenth,' said Levant. "Cause he worked the night of the fifteenth. So he must have left on the sixteenth – that's it. He and Miller went out to Flattery the sixteenth of September.'

Nobody knows, thought Ishmael. The men who'd heard the *Corona*'s radio transmissions had gone somewhere else the next day. They'd done their watch on the night of the fifteenth, slept through the morning of the sixteenth, and then they'd left San Piedro. The transcribed transmissions had gone into a manila folder, and the folder had gone into a file cabinet in a room stuffed full of coast guard records. And who would find them there? They were as good as lost forever, it seemed to Ishmael, and no one knew the truth of the matter: that on the night Carl Heine had drowned, stopping his watch at 1:47, a freighter plowed through Ship Channel Bank at 1:42 – just five minutes earlier – no doubt throwing before it a wall of water big enough to founder a small gillnetting boat and toss even a big man overboard. Or rather one person, he himself, knew this truth. That was the heart of it.

Chapter 24

Ishmael's mother had the woodstove in the kitchen going – he could see the smoke rising thick from the chimney, a ghostly white against the hard-falling snow – and was standing at the sink in her overcoat and scarf when Ishmael passed in front of her window carrying his can of
5   kerosene. A fog of condensation had formed on the inside of the pane, so that her image appeared to him as a kind of silhouette, a vague impression of his mother at the sink, refracted and fragmented, a wash of color. As he passed by, peering through the window mist and snowfall, he saw her hand work with sudden clarity to wipe a circle of the pane
10 dry, and then her eye met his and she waved. Ishmael held up the can of kerosene, still moving steadily toward the kitchen door. His mother had shoveled clear a path to the woodshed, but the snowfall was already covering it. Her shovel stood propped against the fence railing.

He stood in the kitchen doorway, set the kerosene down, and felt the
15 place in his coat pocket where Philip Milholland's coast guard notes lay folded against his leg. He took his hand out and then returned it and touched the notes again. Then he picked up the kerosene and went in.

His mother had on rubber boots, unbuckled, and had used small finishing nails to tack a wool blanket across the entry to the living room.
20 The light in the kitchen came opaquely through the wet windows; the room was warm, and on the table, neatly arranged, lay a collection of candles, a kerosene lantern, two flashlights, and a box of wooden matches. His mother had set a soup kettle full of snow on the woodstove; it hissed and snapped as Ishmael shut the door behind him. 'I've got
25 some food in the car,' he said, setting the can of kerosene against the wall, 'and a new wick for the heater.' He put it on the table beside the candles. 'Did you freeze last night?' he asked.

---

7 **refracted**: in gebrochenem Licht   7–8 **wash of sth.**: (here) mixture of sth.
18 **unbuckled**: nicht zugeschnürt   19 **tack sth. to sth. else**: etwas mit Nägeln/
Reißzwecken an etwas anderem befestigen   24 **hiss**: make a sound like a long 's'

'Not at all,' replied his mother. 'I'm really glad to see you, Ishmael. I tried to call, but the phone is out. The lines must all be down.'

'They are,' said Ishmael. 'Everywhere.'

She finished pouring snowmelt water from a second kettle into jugs in the sink, then dried her hands and turned to him. 'Are people stranded?' she said.

'I must have seen fifty cars along the roads between here and town,' said Ishmael. 'I saw Charlie Torval's car upside down in the blackberry stickers up on Scatter Springs. Trees are down all over the place; there's no power anywhere. They're trying to get town back up by morning – they're doing town first, like always. If they do get it lit again you should come stay with me; we'll shut this place up and move to town, there's no need to stay out here and freeze to death. I – '

'I'm not freezing,' his mother said, pulling the scarf from her head. 'In fact, it's a little *too* hot just now. I just got done shoveling and bringing stove wood around. I'm perfectly comfortable except for my worry about what's going to happen when the plumbing thaws out. The last thing I need is a burst pipe.'

'We'll open the taps,' answered Ishmael. 'You shouldn't have any problems. There's a pressure valve in the line on the east wall in the cellar – Dad put it in, remember?' He sat down at the table and cupped the stump of his amputated arm in his hand, then rubbed and squeezed it gently. 'Thing aches when it gets this cold,' he said.

'It's twelve degrees,' said his mother. 'Are those groceries up in your car going to freeze? Maybe we should go for them.'

'All right,' said Ishmael. 'Let's.'

'When your arm is ready,' said his mother.

They brought the two bags of groceries down, as well as Ishmael's camera. His mother's flower beds were all covered over, and the snow was lining up on her holly trees and mulberry and frosting the tops of her rhododendrons. She was, she said, worried about her flowers, whether the less hardy of them would survive the freeze – she'd lost flowers in lesser weather, she pointed out. Ishmael saw where she had worked with the wheelbarrow at bringing cordwood from the shed to the kitchen door; there were splinters around the wood block where she'd cut kindling.

His mother, at fifty-six, was the sort of country widow who lives alone quite capably; he knew that she rose at a quarter after five every morning, made her bed, fed her chickens, showered, dressed, cooked herself a poached egg and toast, steeped strong tea and sipped it at the table, then got immediately at her breakfast dishes and whatever housework needed doing. By nine o'clock, he speculated, there was nothing left she felt obligated to do, and so she read or tended her flowers or drove in to Petersen's Grocery. It was unclear to him, though, exactly how she passed her time. He knew she read incessantly – Shakespeare, Henry James, Dickens, Thomas Hardy – but he did not think this could fill her days. On Wednesday evenings twice a month she attended a meeting of her book circle, five other women who enjoyed discussing *Benito Cereno*, *Flowers of Evil*, *The Importance of Being Earnest*, and *Jane Eyre*. She was on friendly terms with Lillian Taylor, with whom she shared a passion for flowers and for *The Magic Mountain* and *Mrs. Dalloway*. The two of them would stoop or stand in the garden picking the seeds from the feathery spires of astilbes a few weeks past their prime, then sit at a garden table shaking the seeds clean and collecting them in small manila packets. They drank lemon-scented water and ate sandwiches with the crusts cut off at three o'clock in the afternoon. 'We're dainty old ladies,' he heard Lillian exclaim once. 'We'll wear painters' smocks and blue berets and do watercolors next – what do you say to that, Helen? Are you ready to be an old biddy with her paints?'

Helen Chambers was homely and dignified in the manner of Eleanor Roosevelt. Her homeliness composed a form of beauty; she was quite impressive to look at. Her nose was broad and her forehead stately. For

9 **sticker**: (here) thorny bush   17 **plumbing** [ˈplʌmɪŋ]: Rohrleitungen
20 **pressure valve**: Druckventil   30 **mulberry**: Maulbeerbaum   32 **hardy**: (of a plant) able to live outside through the winter   34 **cordwood**: Klafterholz
40 **steep tea**: Tee aufbrühen   53 **spire**: (hier) Spitze   **astilbe** [əsˈtɪlbe]: family of plants with colorful flowers arranged in panicles (= Rispen)   56 **dainty**: small and delicate (= zart)   57 **smock**: Kittel   **beret** [bəˈreɪ]: round flat cap made out of soft cloth   59 **biddy**: disrespectful term to describe an old woman   60 **homely**: (here) warm-hearted and enjoying the pleasures of home and family   60–61 **Eleanor Roosevelt** (1884–1962): wife of US President Franklin D. Roosevelt known for supporting the rights of women and minority groups; she helped to write the Universal Declaration of Human Rights (1948) as a US representative to the United Nations
62 **stately**: impressive in size or appearance

her shopping trips to town she wore a camel's-hair coat and a boater festooned with ribbon and striped lace. Her husband's death had inspired in her a greater attentiveness to her books and flowers and a greater need for people. Ishmael had stood beside her at church while she greeted her friends and acquaintances with the sort of cordiality and genuine feeling he couldn't muster in himself. Often he ate lunch with her afterward. He had explained to his mother, when she asked him to say grace, that like his father before him he was an incorrigible agnostic and suspected God was a hoax. 'Suppose you had to choose right now,' his mother had once replied. 'Supposing somebody put a gun to your head and forced you to choose, Ishmael. Is there a God or isn't there?'

'Nobody has a gun to my head,' Ishmael had answered her. 'I don't have to choose, do I? That's the whole point. I don't *have* to know for certain one way or the other if – '

'Nobody *knows*, Ishmael. What do you *believe*'

'I don't believe anything. It isn't in me. Besides, I don't know what you mean by God. If you tell me what he is, Mom, I'll tell you if I think he exists.'

'Everybody knows what God is,' said his mother. 'You feel what God is, don't you?'

'I don't feel what God is,' answered Ishmael. 'I don't feel anything either way. No feeling about it comes to me – it's not something I have a choice about. Isn't a feeling like that supposed to *happen*? Isn't it just supposed to happen? I can't make a feeling like that up, can I? Maybe God just chooses certain people, and the rest of us – we can't feel Him.'

'You felt Him as a child,' his mother said. 'I remember, Ishmael. You felt Him.'

'That was a long time ago,' Ishmael answered. 'What a child feels – that's different.'

Now, in the twilight, he sat in the kitchen of his mother's house with Philip Milholland's notes in his coat pocket and tried to feel that intimation of God he had felt as a younger person. It was not something he could conjure up again. After the war he had tried to feel God, to take solace in Him. It hadn't worked, and he had dismissed the attempt when he could no longer ignore that it felt like a pathetic falsehood.

The wind shuddered against the window behind him and the snow outside fell fast. His mother had a soup they could eat, she said: five kinds of beans, onions and celery, a ham shank, two small turnips. Was he hungry now or did he want to wait? She was happy either way, she could eat or not eat, it didn't matter to her. Ishmael pushed two slabs of fir heartwood into the fire in the cook stove. He put a kettle of water on, then sat down again at the table. 'It's plenty warm in here,' he pointed out. 'You don't have to worry about getting cold.'

'Stay,' replied his mother. 'Spend the night. I've got three extra comforters. Your room will be cold, but your bed should be fine. Don't go back out into all of that snow. Stay and be comfortable.'

He agreed to stay and she put the soup on. In the morning he would see about printing his newspaper; for now he was warm where he was. Ishmael sat with his hand in his coat pocket and wondered if he shouldn't just tell his mother about the Coast Guard notes he had stolen from the lighthouse and then drive carefully back into town to hand the notes over to Judge Fielding. But he did nothing. He sat watching the twilight fade beyond the kitchen windows.

'That murder trial,' his mother said finally. 'I suppose you've been busy with that.'

'It's all I think about,' said Ishmael.

'It's a shame,' said his mother. 'I have to think it's a travesty. That they arrested him because he's Japanese.'

Ishmael made no reply to this. His mother lit one of the candles on the table and placed a saucer under it. 'What do you think?' she asked him. 'I haven't been there listening, so I'm interested in what you have to say.'

'I've covered every minute,' Ishmael answered. And he felt himself growing cold now, and the depth of his coldness was not a surprise, and he closed his hand around Milholland's notes.

---

1 **boater**: hard straw hat with a flat top   2 **lace** (n): Spitze   8 **incorrigible** [ɪnˈkɔːrɪdʒəbl]: unverbesserlich **agnostic**: person who believes that it is not possible to know whether God exists or not   9 **hoax**: Schwindel   33 **conjure sth. up** [ˈkʌndʒər]: make sth. appear as a picture in your mind   34 **take solace in sb.** [ˈsɑːləs]: find comfort in sb.   35 **pathetic** (infml): (hier) erbärmlich, jämmerlich   36 **shudder against sth.**: shake sth. hard   38 **shank** (AE): lower part of the leg **turnip**: Rübe   45 **comforter**: type of thick cover for a bed   57 **travesty**: (here) grotesque show, i.e. sth. that cannot really be taken seriously, but unfortunately is accepted as valid by many people

'I have to think he's guilty,' lied Ishmael. 'The evidence is very solidly against him – the prosecutor has a good case.'

He explained to her about the blood on the fishing gaff, the wound on the left side of Carl Heine's head, the sergeant who had testified that Kabuo Miyamoto was an expert when it came to killing with a stick. He told her about Ole Jurgensen's testimony and the long dispute over land. He told her how three different fishermen had reported seeing Kabuo Miyamoto fishing near Carl Heine on the night the murder happened, and he told her about the length of mooring rope. The accused man sat so rigorously in his chair, so unmovable and stolid. He did not appear remorseful. He did not turn his head or move his eyes, nor did he change his expression. He seemed to Ishmael proud and defiant and detached from the possibility of his own death by hanging. It reminded him, he told his mother, of a training lecture he'd listened to at Fort Benning. The Japanese soldier, a colonel had explained, would die fighting before he would surrender. His allegiance to his country and his pride in being Japanese prevented him from giving in. He was not averse to dying at war in the way Americans were. He did not have the same feeling about death on the battlefield that American soldiers felt. To the Japanese soldier a life in defeat was not for a moment worth living; he knew he could not return to his people having suffered the humiliation of losing. He could not meet his Maker afterward, either – his religion demanded he die with honor. Understand, the colonel added: the Jap preferred to die with honor intact, and in this the infantryman should indulge him. In other words, take no prisoners: shoot first and ask questions later. The enemy, you see, has no respect for life, his own or anyone else's. He doesn't play by the rules. He'll put up his hands, pretend to surrender, and all the while he's rigged himself to booby-trap as you approach. It's characteristic of the Jap to be sly and treacherous. He won't show what he's thinking in his face.

'It was all propaganda,' added Ishmael. 'They wanted us to be able to kill them with no remorse, to make them less than people. None of it is fair or true, but at the same time I find myself thinking about it whenever I look at Miyamoto sitting there staring straight ahead. They could have used his face for one of their propaganda films – he's that inscrutable.'

'I know who he is,' said Ishmael's mother. 'He's a striking man, his face is powerful. Like you, Ishmael, he served in the war. Have you forgotten – that – that he fought in the war? That he risked his life for this country?'

'All right,' said Ishmael, 'he served. Is that a fact pertinent to the murder of Carl Heine? Is it relevant to the case at hand? I grant you the man is "striking", as you say, and that he served in the war – are those things relevant? I don't understand what makes them relevant.'

'They're at least as relevant as your propaganda lecture,' Ishmael's mother replied. 'If you're going to remember something like that and connect it in some way to the defendant's expression – well then, you'd better be remembering other things, too, just to keep yourself fair. Otherwise you're being subjective in a way that is not at all fair to the accused. You're allowing yourself an imbalance.'

'The defendant's expression isn't part of it,' said Ishmael. 'Impressions aren't part of it; feelings aren't part of it. The facts are all that matter,' said Ishmael, 'and the facts weigh in against him.'

'You said yourself the trial isn't over,' Ishmael's mother pointed out. 'The defense hasn't made its case yet, but you're all ready to convict. You've got the prosecutor's set of facts, but that might not be the whole story – it never is, Ishmael. And besides, really, facts are so cold, so horribly cold – can we depend on facts by themselves?'

'What else do we have?' replied Ishmael. 'Everything else is ambiguous. Everything else is emotions and hunches. At least the facts you can cling to; the emotions just float away.'

'Float away with them,' said his mother. 'If you can remember how, Ishmael. If you can find them again. If you haven't gone cold forever.'

She got up and went to the woodstove. He sat in silence with his forehead in his hand, breathing through his nose and suddenly empty

---

10 **stolid**: not showing much emotion or interest   16 **surrender** [səˈrendər]: admit that you have lost a fight, give up   **allegiance** [əˈliːdʒəns]: loyalty   17–18 **be not averse to doing sth.**: be not opposed to doing sth.   24–25 **indulge sb. in sth.**: allow sb. to have or do sth. they would like to have or do   28 **rig yourself to do sth.** (old-fashioned): (here) prepare yourself to do sth.   **booby trap** (v): (here) suddenly start attacking like a hidden bomb that explodes when the object to which it is connected is touched   29 **sly**: listig   **treacherous**: not to be trusted
35 **inscrutable** [ɪnˈskruːtəbl]: unergründlich   52 **the facts weigh in against him**: die Fakten/Beweise sprechen gegen ihn   59 **hunch** (n): intuition, feeling that sth. is true even though you do not have any evidence to prove it

– a great, airy space had blown up inside of him, a bubble of ether expanding against his rib cage – he was empty now, emptier than he had been just a moment earlier, before his mother had spoken. What did she know about the vast region of emptiness that inhabited him all of the time? What did she know about him anyway? It was one thing for her to have known him as a child; it was another for her to come to terms with the nature of his adult wounds. She didn't know, finally; he couldn't explain himself. He did not want to explain to her his coldness or reveal himself in any way. He had watched her, after all, mourn her husband's death and it had been for her in part the discovery that grief could attach itself with permanence – something Ishmael had already discovered. It attached itself and then it burrowed inside and made a nest and stayed. It ate whatever was warm nearby, and then the coldness settled in permanently. You learned to live with it.

His mother had gone cold when Arthur died; her grief for him was fixed. But this had not stopped her from taking pleasure in life, it now occurred to Ishmael. There she stood at the stove ladling soup with the calm ease of one who feels there is certainly such a thing as grace. She took pleasure in the soup's smell, in the heat of the woodstove, in the shadow of herself the candlelight now cast against the kitchen wall. The room had gone dark and tranquil now, the one warm place in all the world, and he felt empty in it.

'I'm unhappy,' he said. 'Tell me what to do.'

His mother made no reply at first. Instead she came to the table with his bowl of soup and set it down in front of him. She brought her own bowl to the table, too, and then a loaf of bread on a cutting board and a dish of creamery butter and spoons. 'You're unhappy,' she said, seating herself. She put her elbows down on the table and rested her chin against her palms. 'That you are unhappy, I have to say, is the most obvious thing in the world.'

'Tell me what to do,' repeated Ishmael.

'Tell you what to do?' his mother said. 'I can't tell you what to do, Ishmael. I've tried to understand what it's been like for you – having gone to war, having lost your arm, not having married or had children. I've tried to make sense of it all, believe me, I have – how it must feel to be you. But I must confess that, no matter how I try, I can't really understand you. There are other boys, after all, who went to war and came back home and pushed on with their lives. They found girls and married and had children and raised families despite whatever was behind them. But you – you went numb, Ishmael. And you've stayed numb all these years. And I haven't known what to do or say about it or how I might help you in some way. I've prayed and I've talked to Pastor – '

'There were guys who prayed at Tarawa,' said Ishmael. 'They still got killed, Mother. Just like the guys who didn't pray. It didn't matter either way.'

'But just the same I've prayed for you. I've wanted you to be happy, Ishmael. But I haven't known what to do.'

They ate their soup and bread in silence while the kettle on the woodstove hissed. The candle on the table cast an arc of light across their food, and outside, through the misty windowpane, the snow on the ground caught the moonlight beyond the clouds and held it so that it suffused everything. Ishmael tried to enjoy the small pleasures of warmth and light and bread. He did not want to tell his mother about Hatsue Miyamoto and how he had, many years ago, felt certain they would be married. He did not want to tell her about the hollow cedar tree where they'd met so many times. He had never told anybody about those days; he had worked hard to forget them. Now the trial had brought all of that back.

'Your father fought at Belleau Wood,' his mother told him suddenly. 'It took him years to get over it. He had nightmares and he suffered just as you do. But it didn't stop him from living.'

'He didn't get over it,' said Ishmael. 'Getting over it isn't possible.'

'It didn't stop him from living,' his mother insisted. 'He went right on with his life. He didn't let self-pity overwhelm him – he just kept on with things.'

'I've kept on,' said Ishmael. 'I've kept his newspaper going, haven't I? I – '

'That isn't what I mean,' his mother said. 'That isn't what I'm getting at. You know as well as I do what I'm trying to say. Why on earth don't you go out with someone? How can you stand your loneliness? You're an attractive man, there are a lot of women who – '

---

1 **ether**: (here) air   12 **burrow** ['bɜːroʊ] (v): dig   17 **ladle sth.**: put sth., esp. food, on a plate with a large spoon   51–52 **suffuse sth.**: spread all over or through sth.

'Let's not go over all of this again,' said Ishmael, putting down his spoon. 'Let's talk about something else.'

'For you, what else is there?' said his mother. 'When it comes down to it – to answer your question – here's what you should do about being unhappy: you should get married and have some children.'

'That isn't going to happen,' said Ishmael. 'That's not the answer to the question.'

'Yes, it is,' said his mother. 'It genuinely, surely is.'

After dinner he lit the kerosene heater and put it in her bedroom. His parents' grandfather clock still ticked away after all these years with a maniacal endurance. It reminded him now of Saturday mornings when his father would read to him under the sheets with the clock thundering in the background. They'd read *Ivanhoe* together, taking turns, and then *David Copperfield*. Now, he saw in his flashlight beam, his mother slept under eiderdown quilts that were just beginning to yellow. He was surprised to find beside her bed the antique RCA turntable that had, until recently, resided in his father's old study. She'd been listening to Mozart's *Jupiter* Symphony as performed by the Vienna Symphony Orchestra in 1947, and Ishmael, seeing it on the turntable, imagined her in bed with that melancholy music playing and a cup of tea beside her. He imagined her with the Mozart on at nine o'clock at night.

He opened the taps in the sink and bathtub and went out to check on her chickens. There were twelve of them, all Rhode Island Reds, huddled into a ball at one end of the chicken house his father had built years before. For a moment Ishmael caught them in the beam of his flashlight; then he reached in and took up a nearby egg left untended in the cold. It was hard to the touch and he knew that inside the embryo was solidly frozen. He warmed it for a moment in the palm of his hand, then rolled it gently in the direction of the chickens. They rearranged themselves in the face of this, panicking and fluttering just a little.

He went back in and, still wearing his coat and hat, wandered through the rooms of the cold house. His breath came forth in jets of fog and disappeared into the darkness. Ishmael put his hand on the newel post at the bottom of the stairway, then removed it and shone the flashlight beam upward. Shallow moons had been worn into the risers; the bannister, he saw, had lost its luster. Upstairs, the room he'd slept in as a boy had been

converted by his mother into a place to sew and iron and to store her clothes. Ishmael went up and, sitting on his old bed, tried to remember how it had once been. He recollected that on a good day in winter, when
40 the maple trees stood bare, he could look through his dormer window out beyond the trees and see the green salt water to the southwest.

He'd had a button and a pennant collection, a thousand pennies in a large mason jar, a fishbowl, and a model tin lizzie hung from a strand of wire in one corner. They were all gone now, he didn't know where. He'd
45 kept his glass underwater box in the corner of the closet, his mitt on top of it. On certain nights the moonlight had flooded through his dormer window and bathed everything in blue, beguiling shadows that prevented him from sleeping. He'd sit up listening to crickets and frogs and on some nights to the radio at his bedside. He'd listened mostly to baseball
50 games – the Seattle Rainiers of the Pacific Coast League – and he could still remember the voice of Leo Lassen barely audible beyond a field of static: 'White leads off first, dancing, dancing, ready to break, he's driving Gittelsohn ab-so-lute-ly crazy. ... Strange is at the plate now after taking his practice cuts ... hum, baby, hear this fine crowd on hand at Sick's Stadium
55 greet Strange as he digs in, he's a real favorite, isn't he? Oh, you should be here tonight! Mount Rainier is out beyond the rightfield fence looming up like a great big ice cream cone. Gittelsohn is into his windup now and ... there goes White no time for a throw White is standing up safe at second base hoooo boy! White is safe! He's stolen second base! White is safe at second base!'

11 **maniacal** [məˈnaɪəkl]: wild or violent   **endurance** [ɪnˈdʊrəns]: Ausdauer
15 **eiderdown**: Eiderdaune   16 **RCA** = Radio Corporation of America: large US company producing electronic equipment   **turntable**: record player
26 **untended**: unbehütet, unbeaufsichtigt   32 **jet**: (hier) Schwaden   33 **newel post**: post at the top or bottom of a set of stairs   35 **riser**: (hier) Stufe
bannister: Geländer   36 **luster**: shining quality of a surface   37 **sew** [soʊ]: nähen
42 **pennant**: Wimpel, Fähnchen   43 **mason jar**: Steingutkrug   **Tin Lizzie** (also 'tin lizzie'): popular name for the Model T car, produced between 1908 and 1927, the first car that was built on an assembly line (= Fließband)   45 **mitt**: (in baseball) large thick leather glove worn for catching the ball   47 **beguiling** [bɪˈgaɪlɪŋ]: attractive and interesting but sometimes mysterious   51 **audible**: able to be heard
53 **plate**: (in baseball) home base, i.e. place where the person hitting the ball stands and where they must return after running around all the bases   54 **cut**: (here) swing   57 **windup**: (in baseball) movements of the pitcher (= Werfer) before throwing the ball

His father, too, had liked baseball. Ishmael had sat with him by the Bendix in the living room, and they had both been mesmerized by the urgency Leo Lassen imparted to a battle so many miles away in Seattle, Portland, or Sacramento. The voice from the radio – it had dropped an octave, altered pitch, slowed and lengthened measurably – was now that of someone's wayward uncle confiding the secrets of his golf game; now it miraculously glided through a tongue twister; now it suddenly sensed great depths of meaning in an ordinary double play. Arthur would slam the armrest of his chair in satisfaction at a fortunate turn of events; he was saddened when errors in judgment or carelessness cast the team into a hole. At lulls in the game he would stretch his legs out, twine his hands across his lap, and stare at the radio as it spoke to him. Eventually he slept with his head lolled forward and stayed that way until Leo Lassen went shrill again in ecstasy about the game. Freddy Mueller had hit a double.

Ishmael remembered his father half-asleep, the crescent of warm light thrown by the table lamp containing only his figure, that of the radio, and the turned-back pages of a magazine in his lap – *Harper's or Scientific Agriculture*. By the late innings of the game the rest of the room – a few laggard coals glowed orange beneath the fireplace grate – lay sleeping in soft, quiescent shadows. Coats hung from polished brass hooks in the foyer, and his father's books, arranged by size, stood neatly along the glassed-in shelves of two vaultlike oak bookcases. When something momentous came to pass – a home run, a stolen base, a double play, a run batted in – his father would stir, blink two or three times, and by dint of habit bring his hand to rest on the spectacles sitting atop his magazine. His hair lay close to his skull in gray twists, and his chin tilted slightly heavenward. Gray hairs sprouted from his ears and nostrils, and more straggled forth from his eyebrows. When the game was over he would shut off the radio and fix his spectacles carefully in place by curling their stems behind his ears. They were antique steel full moons, and when he put them on he invariably underwent a quiet transformation, becoming suddenly professorial, handsome in the way that some outdoorsmen are yet scholarly at the same time. He would pick up his magazine and begin to read as if the game had never happened.

Ishmael's father had died in Seattle at the Veterans Administration Hospital. He'd had cancer of the pancreas and in the end of the liver, and Ishmael had not been there at the final moment. One hundred and seventy islanders turned out for Arthur's funeral, which was held on a warm, cloudless day in June at the San Piedro Memorial Cemetery. Masato Nagaishi, Ishmael recalled, had presented himself in the funeral's aftermath to offer condolences on behalf of the Japanese-American Citizens' League and the Japanese Community Center. 'I wish to say,' said Masato Nagaishi, 'that the Japanese people of San Piedro Island are saddened by the death of your father. We have always had great respect for him as a newspaperman and as a neighbor, a man of great fairness and compassion for others, a friend to us and to all people.' Masato Nagaishi took Ishmael's hand and gripped it in his own tightly. He was a large man with a broad face and no hair on his head, and he blinked often behind his spectacles. 'We know you will follow in your father's footsteps,' Mr. Nagaishi said forcefully, shaking Ishmael's hand. 'We are certain you will honor his legacy. For now, like you, we are all sad. We mourn with you and honor your father. We think of you in your grief.'

Ishmael opened the closet door and looked in at the boxes stacked there. He had not gone through the things he'd packed in them in more than eight years' time. He was no longer very interested in what they contained – his books, his arrowheads, his essays from high school, his pennant collection, his penny jar, his buttons and sea glass and beach stones; they were the things of another time. He had it in mind, though, to dig out the letter Hatsue had written him from Manzanar and read it again after all these years in the spirit of an indulgence. Ever since he'd stopped to pick her up in the snowstorm he'd been indulging himself

---

2 **mesmerize sb.**: fascinate sb.   3 **impart sth.**: give a particular quality to sth.
6 **confide sth.**: give secret or personal information   8 **double play**: (in baseball) act of getting two players back to the home base in one play, i.e. with the batting of one ball only   11 **lull** (n): quiet period between times of activity   **twine sth.**: wind or twist around sth.   13 **loll forward**: (here) move forward or hang down in a relaxed way   18 **inning**: one of the nine parts of a baseball game   19 **laggard**: (hier) verbleibend, übrig geblieben   20 **quiescent** [kwi'esnt] (fml): quiet, not active
22 **vaultlike** ['vɔ:ltlaɪk]: gewölbeartig   23 **momentous**: very important, esp. because of the results of an activity   25 **by dint of habit**: aus Gewohnheit
28 **straggle forth**: (here) grow longer or in different directions so that they stick out   30 **full moons**: (hier) Brille mit runden Gläsern   33 **scholarly**: (here) having the outside appearance of sb. who has a lot of knowledge   36 **pancreas**: Bauchspeicheldrüse   51 **legacy** ['legəsi]: Vermächtnis   60 **indulgence** [ɪn'dʌldʒəns]: sth. that you allow yourself to have although you do not really need it

foolishly. Beneath the surface of everything else he'd been thinking about her with pleasure.

It was buried in a box, just where he'd left it, between the pages of a book on boatmanship he'd been given on his thirteenth birthday. The return address on the envelope was Kenny Yamashita's, and the stamp, curiously, was upside down. The envelope, now brittle with age, felt dry and cold to the touch. Ishmael tucked the flashlight under his armpit and sat down again on the edge of the bed with the envelope held between his fingers. The letter inside had been written on rice paper that after all these years was fast deteriorating, and he held it with the care he felt it deserved, moving it now into the flashlight beam, where he saw her delicate handwriting.

Dear Ishmael,

These things are very difficult to say – I can't think of anything more painful to me than writing this letter to you. I am now more than five hundred miles away, and everything appears to me different from what it was when I was with you last on San Piedro. I have been trying to think clearly about everything and to use all this distance to advantage. And here is what I've discovered.

I don't love you, Ishmael. I can think of no more honest way to say it. From the very beginning, when we were little children, it seemed to me something was wrong. Whenever we were together I knew it. I felt it inside of me. I loved you and I didn't love you at the very same moment, and I felt troubled and confused. Now, everything is obvious to me and I feel I have to tell you the truth. When we met that last time in the cedar tree and I felt your body move against mine, I knew with certainty that everything was wrong. I knew we could never be right together and that soon I would have to tell you so. And now, with this letter, I'm telling you. This is the last time I will write to you. I am not yours anymore.

I wish you the very best, Ishmael. Your heart is large and you are gentle and kind, and I know you will do great things in this world, but now I must say good-bye to you. I am going to move on with my life as best I can, and I hope that you will too.

Sincerely,
Hatsue Imada

He read it over a second time, and then a third, and then he turned off the flashlight. He thought of how she'd had her revelation at the very moment he'd entered her, how the invasion of his penis had brought with it a truth she could discover in no other way. Ishmael shut his eyes and thought back to that moment in the cedar tree when he had moved, briefly, inside of her and how he had not been able to predict how pleasurable that would feel. He had no way of knowing what it would feel like to be inside, all the way in where he could feel the heat of her, and his surprise at the sensation had been overwhelming, and then she had suddenly pulled away. He had not come, he had been there for less than three seconds altogether, and in that time – if her letter was right – she'd discovered she didn't love him anymore while he'd come to love her even more. Wasn't that the strangest part? That by entering her he'd granted her the means to understand the truth? He'd wanted to be inside of her again, and he'd wanted her to ask him to be there again, and on the next day she'd gone away.

In his Seattle years he'd slept with three different women, two of whom he felt briefly hopeful about, wondering if he might in fact fall in love with them, but this had never happened. The women he slept with asked often about his arm, and he told them about his war experiences, and he decided before long that he didn't respect them and a kind of disgust developed. He was a war veteran with a missing arm, and this fascinated a certain type of woman in her early twenties who fancied herself mature beyond her years and was serious about herself. He slept with each for a few more weeks after deciding he wanted nothing to do with them – he slept with them angrily and unhappily and because he was lonely and selfish. He came inside them hard and often, keeping each up until the middle of the night, and in the late afternoons, too, before dinner. He knew that when he asked them to walk out of his life he would be even lonelier than he'd been before, and so he waited for a few weeks, both times, just to have someone around at night, just to come inside someone, just to hear someone breathing under him while

10 **deteriorate** [dɪˈtɪriəreɪt]: (of paper) become worse in quality   38 **revelation**: Enthüllung, Offenbarung   57 **before long**: soon   58 **disgust**: strong feeling of dislike   59–60 **fancy yourself mature**: think that you are mature yourself, esp. when you are not yet so

he moved his hips with his eyes shut. Then his father came down to the city because he was dying, and Ishmael forgot about women. His father died one afternoon while Ishmael was in the newsroom at the *Seattle Times* banging away with his five fingers at a typewriter. Ishmael went back to San Piedro for the funeral and to tie up his father's business affairs; he stayed to run his father's paper. He lived in an apartment in Amity Harbor and kept to himself insofar as that was possible for a newspaperman on a small island. Once every two weeks or so he masturbated into the folds of his handkerchief, and that was the extent of his sex life.

Yes, he decided, he would write the article Hatsue wanted him to write in the pages of the *San Piedro Review*. It was perhaps not the manner in which his father would proceed, but so be it: he was not his father. His father, of course, would have gone hours earlier directly to Lew Fielding in order to show him the coast guard shipping lane records for the night of September 15. But not Ishmael, not now – no. Those records would stay in his pocket. Tomorrow he would write the article she wanted him to write, in order to make her beholden to him, and then in the trial's aftermath he would speak with her as one who had taken her side and she would have no choice but to listen. That was the way, that was the method. Sitting by himself in the cold of his old bedroom, her letter held uneasily in his hand, he began to imagine it.

---

5 **tie sth. up**: (here) deal with all the remaining details of sth.   18 **make sb. beholden to you**: (here) make sb. feel that they owe you for sth. you have done for them

Chapter 25

At eight in the morning on the third day of the trial – a dozen tall candles now lighting the courtroom in the manner of a chapel or sanctuary – Nels Gudmundsson called his first witness. The wife of the accused man, Hatsue Miyamoto, came forward from the last row of seats in the gallery with her hair tightly bound to the back of her head and tucked up under an unadorned hat that threw a shadow over her eyes. As she passed through the swinging gate Nels Gudmundsson held open for her she stopped to look for a moment at her husband, who sat at the defendant's table immediately to her left with his hands folded neatly in front of him. She nodded without altering her calm expression, and her husband nodded back in silence. He unclasped his hands, laid them on the table, and watched her eyes intently. The wife of the accused man appeared, briefly, as if she might turn in his direction and go to him, but instead she proceeded without hurry toward Ed Soames, who stood in front of the witness stand proffering the Old Testament patiently.

When Hatsue Miyamoto had seated herself, Nels Gudmundsson coughed three times into his fist and cleared the phlegm from his throat. Then he passed in front of the jury box with his thumbs once again hooked inside of his suspenders and his one good eye leaking tears. The arteries in his temples had begun to pulse, as they often did when he'd been sleepless. Like others there he'd passed a difficult night with no electricity or heat. At two-thirty, bitter with cold, he'd struck a match and held it close to the face of his pocket watch; he'd padded in his socks to the unlit bathroom and found the toilet water frozen in its bowl. Nels, flailing, his breath issuing forth in vaporous grunts, had broken out the ice with the handle of his toilet plunger, propped himself against the wall – his lumbago plagued him mercilessly – and dribbled night water unsteadily. Then he'd climbed into bed again, curled up like an

6 **unadorned**: without any decoration   25 **flail**: move your arms and legs around without control   27 **lumbago**: Hexenschuss

autumn leaf, every blanket in the house thrown over him, and lain without sleeping until dawn came. Now, in the courtroom, the jurors could see that he had not shaved or combed his hair; he looked at least ten years older. His blind left pupil seemed especially transient and beyond his control this morning. It traveled in its own eccentric orbit.

The gallery was as crowded as it had been throughout the trial. Many of the citizens gathered there wore overcoats, shoe rubbers, and woolen scarfs, having elected not to leave these things in the cloakroom: there'd been a rush to find a place to sit. They'd carried the smell of wet snow into the room – it had melted against the wool in their coats – and were grateful to be in a warm place where something of interest was going forward. Stuffing their mittens and wool caps into their pockets, they settled in conscious of their extraordinary good fortune in having escaped temporarily from the snowstorm. As always their demeanor was formally respectful; they took the law seriously and felt its majesty emanating toward them from the bench where Lew Fielding sat with his eyes halfshut, inscrutable and meditative, and from the way in which the jurors sat ruminating in rows on their elevated podium. The reporters, for their part, had focused their attention on the wife of the accused man, who wore a knife-pleated skirt on this day and a blouse with long darts through the shoulders. Her hand where it lay atop the Bible was graceful, and the planes of her face were smooth. One of the reporters – he'd lived in Japan just after the war, training automotive engineers to write manuals – was reminded of the calm of a geisha he'd witnessed performing the tea ceremony at Nara. The sight of Hatsue's face in profile elicited in him the smell of pine needles strewn in the courtyard outside the tearoom.

But inwardly Hatsue felt no serenity; her calm was a practiced disguise. For her husband, she knew, was a mystery to her, and had been ever since he'd returned from his days as a soldier nine years before. He'd come home to San Piedro, and they'd rented a cottage out on Bender's Spring Road. It was a dead-end road overhung with alders; they could see no other homes. At night Kabuo was subject to disturbing dreams that sent him to the kitchen table in his slippers and bathrobe, where he sat drinking tea and staring. Hatsue found that she was married to a war veteran and that this was the crucial fact of her marriage; the war had elicited in him a persistent guilt that lay over his soul like a shadow. For her this meant loving him in a manner she hadn't anticipated before he'd left for the war. There was nothing of charity in it and she did not step lightly around his heart or indulge his sorrow or his whims. Instead she brought herself to his sorrow completely, not to console him but to give him time to become himself again. Without regrets she honored the obligation she felt to him and was happy to efface herself. This gave her life a shape and meaning that were larger than her dream of farming strawberries from island soil, and at the same time giving herself over to his wounds was both disturbing and rewarding. She sat across from him at the kitchen table at three o'clock in the morning, while he stared in silence or talked or wept, and she took when she could a piece of his sorrow and stored it for him in her own heart.

The advent of her pregnancy had been good for Kabuo; he'd taken a job at the cannery, where he packed salmon beside his brother Kenji. He began to talk about buying a farm and drove her up and down island roads where property was for sale. Something was wrong with each, however – drainage, sunlight, clay soil. Kabuo pulled into a turnout one rainy afternoon and explained to her in grave tones that he intended to repurchase his parents' property as soon as the chance arose. He told the story, once again, of how they had been within one last payment of owning the seven acres outright. How Etta Heine had pulled out from under them and sold their land to Ole Jurgensen. How the land was to have gone over into his name, because he was the eldest son and the first of the Miyamotos to become a citizen. They'd lost everything because of Manzanar. His father had died of stomach cancer; his mother had gone to live in Fresno, where Kabuo's sister had married a furniture merchant. Kabuo struck the steering wheel with the side of his fist and cursed the injustice of the world. 'They stole from us,' he said angrily, 'and they got away with it.'

---

12 **mitten**: (Faust)Handschuh 15–16 **emanate from somewhere**: come from somewhere 18 **ruminate**: think deeply about sth. 20 **knife-pleated skirt**: Plisseerock **dart** (n): (hier) Abnäher 26 **strew sth.** [struː]: cover a surface with sth. 27 **serenity** [səˈrenəti]: state of inner calm 39 **whim**: Laune 42 **efface yourself**: attract no attention to yourself 49 **advent** ['--]: the coming of an important event 53 **turnout**: (hier) Ausweichstelle 55 **repurchase sth.**: buy sth. again that you once owned 65 **get away with sth.**: do sth. wrong without being punished for it

One night six months after his return from the war she woke up to find him gone from their bed and nowhere to be found in the house. Hatsue sat in the dark of the kitchen, where she waited for seventy-five minutes uneasily; it was raining outside, a windy night, and the car was gone from the garage.

She waited. She ran her hands across her belly, imagining the shape of the baby inside, hoping to feel it move. There was a leak in the shed roof over the pantry, and she got up to empty the pan she'd placed under it. Sometime after four A.M. Kabuo came in with two burlap sacks; he was rain soaked, there was mud on his knees. He turned on the light to find her there, sitting motionless at the kitchen table, staring at him in silence. Kabuo, staring back, set one sack on the floor, hauled the other up onto a chair, and took the hat from his head. 'After Pearl Harbor,' he said to her, 'my father buried all of this.' Then he began to pull things out – wooden swords, *hakama* pants, a *bokken*, a *naginata*, scrolls written in Japanese – and placed each carefully on the kitchen table. 'These are my family's,' he said to her, wiping the rain from his brow. 'My father hid them in our strawberry fields. Look at this,' he added.

It was a photograph of Kabuo dressed like a *bugeisha* and wielding a *kendo* stick in both hands. In the photograph he was only sixteen years old, but he already looked wrathful and fierce. Hatsue studied the photograph for a long time, particularly Kabuo's eyes and mouth, to see what she might discern there. 'My great-grandfather,' said Kabuo, pulling off his coat, 'was a samurai and a magnificent soldier. He killed himself on the battlefield at Kumamoto – killed himself with his own sword, *seppukku*' – Kabuo pantomimed disemboweling himself, the imaginary sword plunged deep into his left side and drawn steadily to the right. 'He came to battle wielding a samurai's sword against the rifles of an imperial garrison. Try to imagine that, Hatsue,' said Kabuo. 'Going to battle with a sword against rifles. Knowing you are going to die.'

He'd knelt beside the wet sack on the floor then and took a strawberry plant from it. The rain bellowed against the roof and struck against the side of their house. Kabuo took out another strawberry plant and brought them both into the light over the table where she could look at them closely if she wanted to. He held them out to her, and she saw how the veins and arteries in his arms flowed in ridges just beneath his skin and how strong his wrists and fingers were.

'My father planted the fathers of these plants,' Kabuo said to her angrily. 'We lived as children by the fruit they produced. Do you understand what I am saying?'

'Come to bed,' answered Hatsue. 'Take a bath, dry yourself, and come back to bed,' she said.

She got up and left the kitchen table. She knew that he could see in profile the new shape their baby was making. 'You're going to be a father soon,' she reminded him, halting in the doorway. 'I hope that will make you happy, Kabuo. I hope it will help you to bury all of this. I don't know how else I can help you.'

'I'll get the farm back,' Kabuo had answered over the din of the rain. 'We'll live there. We'll grow strawberries. It will be all right. I'm going to get my farm back.'

That had been many years ago – nine years, or nearly. They'd saved their money insofar as that was possible, putting away as much as they could, until they had enough to buy their own house. Hatsue wanted to move from the dilapidated cottage they rented at the end of Bender's Spring Road, but Kabuo had convinced her the better move was to purchase a gill-netting boat. Within a year or two, he said, they would double their money, own the boat outright, and have enough left over for a land payment. Ole Jurgensen was getting old, he said. He would want to sell before long.

Kabuo had fished as well as he could but he was not really born to fish. There was money in fishing and he wanted the money, he was ambitious, strong, and a zealous worker, but the sea, in the end, made no sense to him. They had not doubled their money or even come close, and they did not own the *Islander* outright. Kabuo only pressed himself harder and measured his life according to his success at bringing salmon home. On every night that he did not catch fish he felt his dream recede before him and the strawberry farm he coveted moved further into the

---

26 *seppukku'*: Japanese word for the ritual suicide of the samurai, also called 'hara-kiri'   **disembowel yourself** [ˌdɪsɪmˈbaʊəl]: (here) kill yourself by wounding your inner organs with a knife or sword   32 **bellow against sth.**: (here) fall heavily on sth. and make a loud deep sound   57 **outright**: completely   62 **zealous**: showing great energy and enthusiasm, fanatical   66 **recede**: (here) become gradually weaker or smaller

distance. He blamed himself and grew short with her, and this deepened the wounds in their marriage. Hatsue felt she did him no favors by indulging his self-pity, and he resented her for this. It was difficult for her to distinguish these moments from the deeper anguish of his war wounds. Besides, she had three children now, and it was necessary to turn her attention toward them and to give to them a part of what she had once given to her husband. The children, she hoped, would soften him. She hoped that through them he might become less obsessed with the dream of a different life. She knew that had happened in her own heart.

Yes, it would be nice to live in a nicer house and to walk out into the perfume of berries on a June morning, to stand in the wind and smell them. But this house and this life were what she had, and there was no point in perpetually grasping for something other. Gently she tried to tell him so, but Kabuo insisted that just around the corner lay a different life and a better one, that it was simply a matter of catching more salmon, of waiting for Ole Jurgensen to slow down, of saving their money, of waiting.

Now Hatsue sat upright with her hands in her lap in order to give her testimony. 'I'm going to ask you to think back,' said Nels, 'to events that occurred about three months ago, in early September of this year. Would it be fair to say that at that time your husband became interested in purchasing land that was for sale at Island Center? Do you recollect, Mrs. Miyamoto?'

'Oh, yes,' answered Hatsue. 'He was very interested in buying land out there. He had always been interested in buying land out there. It had been his family's land – strawberry land – and he badly wanted to farm it again. His family had worked very hard to buy it, and then, during the war, they lost everything, their land was taken from them.'

'Mrs. Miyamoto,' said Nels. 'Think back specifically now to Tuesday, September 7, if you will do that for me. A Mr. Ole Jurgensen, you might recall, a retired strawberry farmer from out at Island Center, has testified that your husband came to see him on that date to inquire about purchasing seven acres of his land, the strawberry land you mentioned. Does this ring a bell with you?'

'It does,' said Hatsue. 'I know about it.'

Nels nodded and began to knead his forehead; he sat down on the edge of the defendant's table. 'Did your husband mention he'd gone out there? Did he tell you about his conversation with Mr. Jurgensen regarding the purchase of these seven acres?'

'Yes,' said Hatsue. 'He did.'

'Did he say anything about this conversation? Anything you can remember?'

'He did,' said Hatsue. 'Yes.'

Hatsue recounted that on the afternoon of September 7 she'd driven with her children past the old farm at Island Center and seen Ole Jurgensen's sign. She'd turned the car around and driven over Mill Run into Amity Harbor, where she used the public telephone booth beside Petersen's to call her husband and tell him. Then she'd gone home and waited for an hour until Kabuo returned with the unhappy news that Carl Heine had purchased Ole's farm.

'I see,' said Nels. 'This unhappy news – this was on the evening of September 7 that your husband told you about this?'

'Afternoon,' said Hatsue. 'We talked about it in the late afternoon, I remember, before he went out fishing.'

'Late afternoon,' Nels repeated. 'Did your husband seem disappointed, Mrs. Miyamoto, that he had not succeeded in purchasing his seven acres? Did he seem to you disappointed?'

'No,' said Hatsue. 'He was not disappointed. He was hopeful, Mr. Gudmundsson, as hopeful as I'd seen him. To his way of thinking the important thing was that Ole Jurgensen had decided to retire from farming strawberries and sell off all his holdings. Something, he said, had been set in motion – there'd been no opportunity, now there was one. He'd waited many years for this moment to arrive – now the opportunity was at hand. He was very eager, very hopeful?'

'Let's skip forward one day,' said Nels, raising his head from his hand. 'On the next day, September 8, did he talk about it? Was he still feeling, as you say, hopeful?'

'Oh, yes,' answered Hatsue. 'Very much so. We talked about it again the following day. He'd decided to go have a talk with Carl Heine, to see him about purchasing the seven acres.'

'But he didn't go. Until the next day. He waited a day, is that right?'

1 **grow short with sb.**: speak to sb. using only few words in a way that seems rude
35 **knead sth.**: rub and squeeze sth.

'He waited,' said Hatsue. 'He was nervous about it. He wanted to plan what he would say.'

'It's now Thursday, September 9,' Nels Gudmundsson said to her. 'It's two days since your husband spoke with Ole Jurgensen; two long days have passed. What, as you recall it, happened?'

'What happened?'

'He went to talk to Carl Heine – am I correct? – as Susan Marie Heine testified yesterday. According to Susan Marie Heine's testimony your husband showed up at their residence on the afternoon of Thursday, September 9, asking to talk to Carl. According to Susan Marie Heine they spoke for thirty or forty minutes as they walked about the property. She did not accompany them or overhear their words, but she has testified as to the content of a conversation she held with her husband after your husband left that day. She said that the two of them had discussed the seven acres and the possibility that your husband might purchase them. Susan Marie Heine has testified under cross-examination that Carl did not give your husband an unequivocal no answer regarding the purchase of these seven acres. Carl did not lead your husband to believe no hope existed for reclaiming his family's property. It was her understanding that Carl had encouraged your husband to believe that a possibility existed. Now, does that seem accurate to you, Mrs. Miyamoto? On the afternoon of September 9, in the aftermath of his talk with Carl Heine, did your husband still seem hopeful?'

'More hopeful than ever,' said Hatsue. 'He came home from his conversation with Carl Heine more hopeful and more eager than ever. He told me that he felt closer to getting the family land back than he had in a long, long time. I felt hopeful, too, at that point. I was hopeful it would all work out.'

Nels pushed himself upright again and began, slowly, to pace before the jurors, brooding in silence for a moment. In the quiet the wind pushed against the window sashes; steam hissed and boiled through the radiators. With no overhead lights the courtroom, always pallid, seemed grayer and duller than ever. The smell of snow was in the air.

'You say, Mrs. Miyamoto, that you felt hopeful. And yet, as you well know, the deceased man's mother and your husband over there were not on the best of terms. There had been, shall we say, words between them.

So on what grounds did you hold out hope, if I might ask? What made you optimistic?'

Yes, said Hatsue, she understood this question. She'd brought it up with Kabuo herself: would such people agree to sell him the land they'd once stolen so eagerly? 'Etta and Carl are two different people,' Kabuo had replied to this. It was up to Carl, not his mother, this time. And Carl had been his friend long ago. Carl would do what was right.

'Mrs. Miyamoto,' Nels continued. 'Your husband had his conversation with Carl Heine on the afternoon of Thursday, September 9. On the following Thursday, September 16, Carl Heine was found drowned in his fishing net out in White Sand Bay. A week intervened between the two events – six full days passed, and seven nights. A full week, or nearly a week anyway. My question is whether during this week your husband spoke to you about Carl Heine or the seven acres in question. If he said anything to you about the seven acres or about his attempts to reacquire them. Do you recall your husband having spoken about this or having done anything pertinent to reacquiring his family's land during the week between the ninth and the sixteenth?'

Well, explained Hatsue, Kabuo felt there was nothing to do, that the next move was Carl's, that it was Carl who had to come forward. It was Carl who had to think about things and come to some conclusion. It was Carl's heart that was now in question, whether he wanted to redress a wrong his own mother had perpetrated. Did Carl feel responsible for the actions of his family? Did he understand his obligations? It was dishonorable, anyway, added Kabuo, to approach Carl once again with the same tired question; he did not wish to beg, to place himself at Carl's mercy. He did not wish to appear weak in Carl's presence or reveal a humiliating eagerness. No, it was best to be patient in such a matter. There was nothing to be gained by putting oneself forward or revealing oneself too fully. He would wait instead. He would wait one week, he explained to Hatsue, and then he would decide what to do.

---

12 **overhear sth.** [,- - '-]: hear a conversation in which you are not involved, esp. by accident   31 **sash**: (here) upper or lower part of a particular kind of window that is opened by sliding the lower part up inside the frame   32 **pallid**: (here) dark, not lit   58 **redress sth.**: correct sth. that is unfair or wrong   59 **perpetrate sth.** ['pɜːrpətreɪt]: do sth., esp. sth. that is illegal

On the morning of the sixteenth, while she boiled tea water, he pushed through the door in his rubber boots and rubber bib overalls and explained how he had seen Carl out at sea, helped Carl with a dead battery in the fog, and the two of them had shaken about the matter. They'd come to an agreement about the seven acres. Eighty-four hundred dollars, eight hundred down. The Miyamotos' land was Kabuo's again, after all these years.

But later that day, at one o'clock in the afternoon, a clerk at Petersen's – it was Jessica Porter – told Hatsue about the terrible accident that had befallen Carl Heine while he fished the preceding evening. He'd been found tangled in his net, dead, out in White Sand Bay.

---

4 **shake about sth.**: (here) shake hands in order to show that you agree on sth.

Chapter 26

Alvin Hooks began his cross-examination by perching himself on the edge of the prosecutor's table and crossing his well-shined shoes in front of him as though he were relaxing on a street corner. His hands in his lap, his fingers intertwined, he cocked his head to the right for a moment and studied Hatsue Miyamoto. 'You know,' he said, 'it's been interesting hearing from you. On this matter of the morning of the sixteenth in particular. This story you've just told us about boiling tea water when the defendant burst through your kitchen door, just terribly excited, and told you about his conversation at sea, how he and Carl Heine came to some sort of agreement? I found this all quite interesting.'

He stopped and studied her for another moment. Then he began to nod. He scratched his head and turned his eyes toward the ceiling. 'Mrs. Miyamoto,' he sighed. 'Was I fair just now in describing your husband's state of mind as "terribly excited" on the morning of the sixteenth – the morning Carl Heine was murdered? Have I by any chance misinterpreted your testimony? Did he come home on that morning "terribly excited"?'

'I would use that phrase, yes,' said Hatsue. 'He was terribly excited, certainly.'

'He didn't seem himself? His state of mind was – agitated? He seemed to you somehow ... different?'

'Excited,' answered Hatsue. 'Not agitated. He was excited about getting his family's land back.'

'All right, so he was "excited",' Alvin Hooks said. 'And he told you this story about stopping at sea to help Carl Heine with a ... dead battery or something. Is that correct, Mrs. Miyamoto?'

'That's correct.'

'He said that he tied up to Carl Heine's boat and came aboard to loan Carl a battery?'

'That's right.'

2 **well-shined**: polished   19 **agitated** ['ædʒɪteɪtɪd]: aufgeregt, erregt

'And that in the course of this charitable maneuver on his part he and Carl discussed the seven acres they'd been arguing about until that point? Is that right? And that somehow Carl agreed to sell it to him? For eighty-four hundred dollars or something? Is that all correct? Do I have it right?'

'You do,' said Hatsue. 'That's what happened.'

'Mrs. Miyamoto,' said Alvin Hooks. 'Did you, by any chance, repeat this story to anyone? Did you, for example, call a friend or a relative to deliver the happy news? Did you let your friends and family know that your husband had come to terms with Carl Heine in the middle of the night on his fishing boat – that you would soon be moving to seven acres of strawberry land, starting a new life, anything like that?'

'No,' said Hatsue. 'I didn't.'

'Why not?' asked Alvin Hooks. 'Why didn't you tell anyone? It seems like the sort of thing that would constitute news. It would seem you might tell your mother, for example, or your sisters, perhaps – someone.'

Hatsue adjusted herself in her chair and brushed uneasily at her blouse front. 'Well,' she said. 'We heard about how Carl Heine had ... passed away just a few hours after Kabuo came home. Carl's accident – that changed how we thought. It meant there was nothing to tell anyone. Everything was up in the air again.'

'Everything was up in the air,' said Alvin Hooks, settling his arms across his chest. 'When you heard that Carl Heine had died, you decided not to talk about the matter? Is that what you're saying, am I correct?'

'You're misinterpreting,' complained Hatsue. 'We just – '

'I'm not interpreting or misinterpreting,' Alvin Hooks cut in. 'I merely want to know what the facts are – we all want to know what the facts are, Mrs. Miyamoto, that's what we're doing here. You're under oath to give us the facts, so please, ma'am, if I might ask again, did you decide not to talk about your husband's night at sea, his encounter with Carl Heine? Did you decide not to talk about this matter?'

'There was nothing to talk about,' said Hatsue. 'What news could I announce to my family? Everything was up in the air.'

'Worse than up in the air,' said Alvin Hooks. 'On top of your husband's real estate deal going sour, a man, we might note, had died. A man had died, let us understand, the side of his skull bashed in. Did it occur to you, Mrs. Miyamoto, to come forward with the information you had about this and notify the sheriff? Did you ever think it might be proper to share what you knew, your husband's night at sea, this battery business, and so on and so forth, with the sheriff of Island County?'

'We thought about it, yes,' said Hatsue. 'We talked about it all afternoon that day, if we should go to the sheriff and tell him, if we should talk about things. But in the end we decided not to, you see – it looked very bad, it looked like murder, Kabuo and I understood that. We understood that he could end up here, on trial, and that's exactly what has happened. That's exactly how it has turned out, you see. You've charged my husband with murder.'

'Well, of course,' said Alvin Hooks. 'I can see how you felt. I can see how you might be very concerned that your husband would be charged with murder. But if, as you imply, the truth was on your side, what in the world were you worried about? Why, if the truth was really with you – why on earth, Mrs. Miyamoto – why not go immediately to the sheriff and tell him everything you know?'

'We were afraid,' said Hatsue. 'Silence seemed better. To come forward seemed like a mistake.'

'Well,' said Alvin Hooks, 'that's an irony. Because the mistake, it seems to me, was in *not* coming forward. The mistake was in your having been deceitful. In having deliberately concealed information during the course of a sheriff's investigation.'

'Maybe,' said Hatsue. 'I don't know.'

'But it *was* a mistake,' said Alvin Hooks, pointing a forefinger at her. 'A very serious error in judgment, don't you think, in retrospect? Here we have a death under suspicious circumstances, the sheriff is out and about gathering information, and you're not coming forward to help. You're in a position to be of assistance and you're not coming forth or being honest. Frankly, it makes you suspect, Mrs. Miyamoto, I'm sorry to say it but it's true. If you can't be trusted to come forward at such a time with what you know, with vital information, how can we trust you now – you see? How on earth can we trust you?'

---

22 **up in the air**: not yet decided   35 **go sour**: (here) not work out as planned
38 **notify sb.**: inform sb.   50 **imply sth.**: etwas andeuten   62 **in retrospect**: im Rückblick   63–64 **out and about**: auf den Beinen, unterwegs

'But,' said Hatsue, leaning forward in her chair, 'there wasn't time to come forward. We heard about Carl's accident in the afternoon. Within hours of that, my husband was arrested. There just wasn't very much time.'

'But Mrs. Miyamoto,' Alvin Hooks replied. 'If in fact you felt it was an accident, why not come forward immediately? Why not come forward that very afternoon and tell the good sheriff what you know about this *accident*? Why not help him with the details of his investigation? Why not lend him a hand? Why not tell him your husband had boarded Carl Heine's boat to help him with – what was it now? – a dead battery, was that it? I hope you can understand how I just have to say that I just don't understand this at all. I'm stumped, I'm confused, I'm completely at a loss. I don't know what to believe and what not to believe. I'm at a loss with all of this, I really am.'

Alvin Hooks tugged at the seams of his pants, rose and swiveled around the edge of the table, then settled in his chair and pressed his palms together. 'No more questions, Your Honor,' he said abruptly. 'The witness is through. She may step down.'

'Wait a minute,' answered Hatsue Miyamoto. 'I – '

'That's enough, you'll stop right there,' Judge Fielding cut in sternly. He glared without wavering at the wife of the accused man, and she glared at him in return. 'You've answered the questions put to you, Mrs. Miyamoto. I understand that you must be upset, but your state of mind, your emotional condition, these are not considerations I can legally contemplate under the rules governing these proceedings. The fact that you wish to speak, that you would like to give Mr. Hooks over there a piece of your mind just now – I don't blame you for having strong feelings – this just isn't allowed. You've answered the questions put to you and now, I'm afraid, you must step down. I'm afraid you have no other choice.'

Hatsue turned toward her husband. He nodded at her, and she nodded back, and in the next moment she composed herself deliberately. She stood up without saying another word and went to her seat at the rear of the courthouse where, adjusting her hat, she sat down. A few citizens in the gallery – including Ishmael Chambers – turned impulsively to look at her, but she made no move to acknowledge them. She stared straight ahead and said nothing.

Nels Gudmundsson called Josiah Gillanders, the president of the San Piedro Gill-Netters Association, a man of forty-nine with a walrus mustache and the watery, dull eyes of an alcoholic. Short, broad, and powerful, Josiah had fished alone for thirty years from the cockpit of his boat, the *Cape Eliza*. Islanders knew him as a nautical sot who affected the gait and mannerisms of a sea captain: he tipped his captain's hard-billed blue cap wherever he went on San Piedro. He wore wool dungarees and shetland sweaters and often got *dead mucked* – his term – with Captain Jon Soderland at the San Piedro Tavern. The two of them would trade stories in voices that grew louder with each pint of beer they hoisted. Captain Soderland would stroke his beard; Josiah would wipe the froth from his mustache and clap the captain on the shoulder blade.

Now, on the witness stand, he held his hard-billed captain's hat between his fingers, crossed his arms over his barrel chest, and pointed his cleft chin at Nels Gudmundsson, who wavered unsteadily before him, blinking.

'Mr. Gillanders,' Nels said. 'How long have you been president of the San Piedro Gill-Netters Association?'

'Eleven years,' Josiah answered. 'Been fishing thirty, though.'

'Fishing for salmon?'

'Yes. Mostly.'

'On board a gill-netter, Mr. Gillanders? Thirty years an island gill-netter?'

'That's correct. Thirty years.'

'Your boat,' said Nels. 'The *Cape Eliza*. Ever had a hand aboard?'

Josiah shook his head. 'Never,' he said. 'I work alone. Always have, always will. I fish by myself, like it.'

'Mr. Gillanders,' Nels said. 'In your thirty years of fishing have you ever had occasion to board another man's boat, sir? Have you ever, while at sea, tied up to another gill-netter and come aboard for any reason?'

---

12 **stumped**: (here) not knowing what to say   21 **waver** ['weɪvər]: hesitate
25 **contemplate sth.**: (here) consider sth., take sth. into account   26–27 **give sb. a piece of your mind** (infml): tell sb. that you do not like their behavior or are angry with them   42 **sot** (infml): drunkard   43 **mannerism**: (hier) Eigenart   43 **hard-billed**: (hier) mit hartem Schirm   44 **dungarees** (pl., AE): heavy trousers that are worn for work   46 **trade sth.**: (here) exchange sth.   47 **hoist sth.** (infml): sich etwas einverleiben   48 **froth**: Schaum

'Just about never,' said Josiah Gillanders, primping his mustache as he spoke. 'Maybe, at best, a half-dozen times in all my years – half-dozen times, no more 'n that. Five or six – that's all.'

'Five or six times,' Nels said. 'Can you recall for us, Mr. Gillanders, what occasioned these at-sea boardings? Do you remember what your purpose might have been, on each of these occasions, for tying up to another man's boat? Can you recollect for the benefit of the court?'

Josiah worked on his mustache again; it was a habit of his when he was thinking. ''Thout going into too much detail, I guess it was always some fellow was broke down. Some fellow had engine problems or couldn't run and needed help. Or – all right now – there was one fellow needed a hand with things on account of he'd broke his hip, I believe it was. I tied up and boarded on that one, too. Helped him out, got things squared away. But 'thout going into too much detail, you board, see, in an emergency. You board if a fellow needs a hand.'

'You board if a fellow needs a hand,' said Nels. 'In your thirty years of gill-netting, Mr. Gillanders, have you ever boarded another man's boat for some reason other than an emergency? For some reason other than the fact that the fellow on the other boat, as you say, needs a hand?'

'Never,' said Josiah. 'Fishing's fishing. Let 'em fish and don't bother me neither. We all got work to do.'

'Yes,' said Nels. 'And in your thirty years of gill-netting, sir, and in your capacity as president of the association – as a man who reviews, I would presume, various incidents between gill-netters at sea – have you ever heard of a boarding for a reason other than an emergency? Can you recall any such thing?'

'Doesn't happen,' said Josiah. 'Unwritten rule of the sea, Mr. Gudmundsson. Code of honor among fishermen. You keep to yourself and I'll keep to myself. We got nothing to say to one another out there. We're busy working, got no time for jawing, can't sit on the deck drinking rum and telling stories while someone else hauls fish. No, you don't board for no other reason than a good one – other guy's in need, he's got an emergency, his engine ain't running, his leg's broke. Then, go on ahead and board.'

'You don't suppose, then,' Nels asked, 'that the defendant here, Mr. Miyamoto, would have boarded Carl Heine's boat on September 16 for any reason other than to help him in an emergency? Does that make sense to you?'

'I never heard of no boarding for no other reason, if that's what you're asking, Mr. Gudmundsson. Only kind I know about is what I said – a man's got engine problems, his leg's broke.'

Nels set himself down precariously against the edge of the defendant's table. With a forefinger he attempted to check the erratic movement of his bad eye, but to no avail; it continued. 'Mr. Gillanders,' he said. 'Isn't it tricky to tie up at sea? Even in calm weather, in good light?'

'A bit,' said Josiah. 'It can be.'

'A night tie-up on open water? Can this be done speedily, in the manner of an attack? Could a man who wanted to make a boarding against another's will even do so? Is it possible?'

'Never heard of it,' replied Josiah, throwing up his hands. 'Two willing skippers helps mightily, yes. Takes a bit of maneuvering, you see. Tying up against another man's will – I'd think that impossible, Mr. Gudmundsson. I never heard of no such thing.'

'You've never heard of one gill-netter boarding another's boat against his will, sir? You see such an act as physically impossible? Is that an accurate summary of what you've told us? Am I getting all of this right?'

'You're getting it right,' Josiah Gillanders said. 'Can't be done. The other man'd throw you off. Wouldn't let you line up, tie off.'

'Only in an emergency,' said Nels. 'There'd be no other logical reason for boarding. Is that correct, Mr. Gillanders?'

'That's correct. Emergency boardings. I never heard of no other kind.'

'Supposing you wanted to kill a man,' Nels said emphatically. 'Do you think you'd try boarding his boat against his will and hitting him with your fishing gaff? You're a man with many years of experience at sea, so I'm asking you to imagine this. Would that plan be a sensible one, a good one, in your estimation, sir? Would you think it workable to tie up to his boat and board him for the purpose of committing murder? Or would

---

1 **primp sth.**: make yourself look attractive by arranging sth., e.g. your hair, make-up, etc.   43 **erratic** [ɪˈrætɪk]: irregular   44 **to no avail**: unsuccessfully

you try something else, some other approach, something other than a forced boarding in the fog on the open sea, in the middle of the night, against the other man's will – what do you think, Mr. Gillanders?'

'You couldn't board him if he didn't want you to,' Josiah answered. 'I just don't see that happening. Carl Heine in particular. He wouldn't be an easy man to board against – darn tough, big, and strong. There's just no way, Mr. Gudmundsson, that Miyamoto here could have made a forced boarding. It just isn't possible. He didn't do that.'

'It isn't possible,' Nels said. 'In your estimation, as a veteran gillnetter, as president of the San Piedro Gill – Netters Association, it isn't possible that the defendant boarded Carl Heine's boat for the purpose of committing murder? The problem of a forced boarding precludes that – makes it impossible?'

'Miyamoto there didn't board Carl Heine against his will,' Josiah Gillanders said. 'Tie-up's too tricky, and Carl was no slouch. Had to be, if he boarded at all, some kind of emergency, engine problem or something. Battery, that's what his missus said. Carl had battery problems.'

'All right,' said Nels. 'Battery problems. Let's say you had a battery problem. You couldn't run. No lights. You're dead in the water. What would you do about it, Mr. Gillanders? Would you, say, put a spare in?'

'Don't carry a spare,' Josiah answered. 'Be like carrying a spare in your car. Just doesn't happen much, does it?'

'But, Mr. Gillanders,' said Nels Gudmundsson. 'If you will recall from the county sheriff's testimony, as well as from his written report, there was, in fact, a spare on board Carl Heine's boat when it was found adrift in White Sand Bay. There was a D-8 and a D-6 in his battery well, in use, and a D-8 sitting on the floor of his cabin – a third battery, albeit dead, which might presumably be thought of as a spare.'

'Well,' said Josiah. 'All of that's mighty strange. Three batteries – that's mighty strange. A dead spare – that's mighty strange, too. Everybody I know runs off two batteries, a main and the other, an auxiliary. One goes bad you can run off the other 'til you get to the docks again. And something else here, a D-8 and a D-6 side by side in the well – I never heard of that before neither, in all my time on the water. I never heard of no such arrangement – a guy'd use just one size battery – and I don't think Carl Heine would've run that way, you see, so irregular and all. I think Mrs. Miyamoto there had it true – Carl had battery problems, probably pulled his D-8, set it on his cabin floor dead, and borrowed a D-6 from Miyamoto, who ran off his other the rest of the night – that's the most likely explanation.'

'I see,' said Nels. 'Say you're dead in the water and in need of help. What would be your next move?'

'I'd get on the radio,' said Josiah. 'Or I'd hail somebody in sight distance. Or if my net was set and I was doing all right I'd wait for somebody to come into sight distance and hail them at that point.'

'Your first choice would be the radio?' Nels asked. 'You'd call for help on your radio? But if your battery's dead do you even *have* a radio? What's powering it, Mr. Gillanders, sir, what's powering your radio if you have no battery? Can you really put a call out on your radio?'

'You're right,' said Josiah Gillanders. 'Radio's dead. I can't call. You're dead to rights.'

'So what do you do?' Nels asked. 'You hail someone, if it isn't too foggy. But if it is foggy, as it was on the night Carl Heine drowned – sometime on the morning of September 16, a very foggy morning, you might recall – well then, you have to hope – don't you? – that someone passes closely by, and you have to hail whoever it is, because the chances of your seeing another boat are not too good, are they? You have to take whatever help comes along because otherwise you're in big trouble.'

'You're straight all the way,' said Josiah Gillanders. 'Spot like that, you'd better get some help, drifting along in the fog and all, right up next to the shipping lanes out there at Ship Channel Bank. Dangerous spot to be dead in the water. Big freighters come right through all the time. You'd better get yourself some help if you can – whoever, like you say, shows up out of the fog when you start blowing on your horn. All right, I'm ahead of you on this one,' Josiah added. 'Carl'd have aboard a compressed-air horn, see. He didn't need no battery to give his emergency blow. He'd be out there with his hand horn blowing away. He didn't need no battery to blow his horn.'

---

12 **preclude sth.**: make sth. impossible   15 **be no slouch** (infml): be very good at sth. or quick to do sth.   19 **dead**: (here) motionless due to a lack of power
45 **hail sb.**: (here) call to sb. in order to attract their attention   51 **dead to rights** (AE, infml): (here) definitely right, right without any doubts   66–67 **emergency blow**: akustisches Notsignal

'Well,' said Nels. 'All right then. He's drifting in the fog near the shipping lanes, no engine, no lights, no radio, no spare battery – do you think he would welcome it if help came along? Do you think he'd be thankful if another gill-netter came along and offered to tie up to him, help him out?'

'Of course,' said Josiah. 'Sure he'd welcome it. He's stranded at sea, he can't get under way, he can't even bring his net in, pick fish. He'd better be pretty damn thankful, you bet. If he isn't, he's off his rocker.'

'Mr. Gillanders.' Nels coughed into his hand. 'I want you to think back to a question I asked you just a few moments ago, sir. I want you to ponder this matter of murder – of first-degree murder, premeditated. Of planning to kill someone in advance of the fact, then executing the following strategy: approaching your victim while he fished at sea, tying up to his boat against his will, leaping aboard, and hitting him in the head with the butt of a fishing gaff. I want to ask you – I'm asking you again – from the perspective of a man who has been fishing for thirty years, from the perspective of the gill-netters association president – a man who presumably hears about almost everything that happens out there on the sea at night – would you, sir, consider this a good plan? Is this the plan a fisherman would make if he wanted to kill someone?'

Josiah Gillanders shook his head as if offended. 'That, Mr. Gudmundsson,' he said emphatically, 'would be the most cockeyed procedure imaginable. Absolutely the most cockeyed, see. If one fellow wanted to kill another he could find a way less foolhardy and dangerous, I guess you'd have to say. Boardin' another man's boat against his will – that, I've told you, isn't possible. Leapin' at him with a fishing gaff? That's just laughable, sir. That's pirates and stories and such like. I guess if you could get close enough to tie up – you couldn't – you'd also be close enough to shoot him, wouldn't you? Just shoot him, you see, then tie up to him real easy, then toss him overboard and wash your hands. He's going down hard to the bottom of the sea and twon't be seen again. I'd shoot him, I would, and skip being the first gill-netter in the history of the profession to make a successful forced boarding. No, sir, if there's anyone in this court thinks Kabuo Miyamoto there boarded Carl Heine's boat against his will, bashed him in the head with a fishing gaff, and tossed him over-board – well, they're just daft, that's all. You'd have to be daft to believe that.'

'All right, then,' Nels said. 'I have no further questions for you, Mr. Gillanders. I thank you, however, for coming down here this morning. It's snowing hard outside.'

'It's snowing hard, yes,' said Josiah. 'But it sure is warm in here, Mr. Gudmundsson. It's mighty warm for Mr. Hooks there, in fact. It – '

'Your witness,' interrupted Nels Gudmundsson. He sat down next to Kabuo Miyamoto and put his hand on Kabuo's shoulder. 'I'm all through, Mr. Hooks,' he said.

'Well then, I suppose it's my turn,' Alvin Hooks answered calmly. 'I have just a few questions, Mr. Gillanders. Just a few things we need to turn about in all this heat – is that all right with you sir?'

Josiah shrugged and clasped his hands over his belly. 'Turn 'em then,' he advised. 'I'm all ears, cap'n.'

Alvin Hooks stood and strolled casually to the witness box with his hands deep in his trousers pockets. 'Well,' he said. 'Mr. Gillanders. You've been fishing for thirty years.'

'That's right, sir. Thirty. Count 'em.'

'Thirty years is a long time,' said Alvin Hooks. 'A lot of lonely nights at sea, yes? Plenty of time to think.'

'Landlubber might see it as lonely, I s'pose. A man like you might get lonely out there – a man who talks for a living. I – '

'Oh, yes,' said Alvin Hooks. 'I'm a landlubber, Mr. Gillanders. I'm the sort of man who would feel lonely at sea – all of that's true, yes. Fine, fine, perfectly fine – my personal life is out of the way, then. So let's talk about the case instead and skip these other matters for just right now – would that be all right with you, sir?'

'You're calling the shots here,' said Josiah Gillanders. 'Ask me whatever you want to ask me and let's be done with it.'

---

7 **get under way**: (here) start the ship's engine   8 **be off your rocker** (infml): be crazy   11 **first-degree murder** = murder in the first degree   **premeditated** [ˌpriːˈmedɪteɪtɪd]: (of a crime) planned in advance   22 **cockeyed**: (hier) blödsinnig   24 **foolhardy**: taking unnecessary risks   36 **daft** [dɑːft] (infml): silly, esp. in a way that is amusing   44 **be all through**: have finished sth. completely   47–48 **turn sth. about**: (here) examine sth. (again) in detail   51 **stroll** (v): walk somewhere in a slow and relaxed way   57 **landlubber** (sl): Landratte   64 **call the shots** (infml): be the person who controls a situation

Alvin Hooks passed in front of the jurors with his hands clasped at the small of his back neatly. 'Mr. Gillanders,' he said. 'I understood you to say earlier that no gill-netter would board another's boat except in the case of an emergency. Is this correct, sir? Did I hear you right?'

'Correct,' said Josiah Gillanders. 'You got me.'

'Is it a matter of principle among gill-netters, then, to help out another in distress? That is, Mr. Gillanders, would you consider yourself duty bound to assist a fellow fisherman in an emergency at sea of some sort? Is that about the size of it?'

'We're men of honor,' said Josiah Gillanders. 'We fish alone but we work together. There's times at sea when we need each other, see? Any man worth his salt out there is going to come to the aid of his neighbor. It's the law of the sea – you bet it is – to put away whatever you're doin' and answer any distress call. I can't think of a single fisherman on this island who wouldn't make it his business to help another man in an emergency out there on the water. It's a law, see – not written anywhere exactly, but just as good as something written. Gill-netters help each other.'

'But Mr. Gillanders,' said Alvin Hooks. 'We've heard here in previous testimony, sir, that gill-netters don't always get along very well, they're silent men who fish alone, they argue about the placement of their boats at sea, about who is stealing fish from who, and so forth, et cetera, et cetera. They're not known to be particularly friendly men, and they prefer to fish alone, keep their distance. Now, sir, even with all of this – with this atmosphere of isolation, of competition, of disregard for the company of others – is it fair to say that a gill-netting man will always help another in an emergency? Even if he doesn't like the other man, even if they have argued in the past, even if they are enemies? Does all of that get pushed aside, become suddenly irrelevant, in the face of distress at sea? Or do men harbor grudges and ignore one another, even take pleasure in the difficulties of a stranded enemy – illuminate us, sir.'

'Bah,' said Josiah. 'We're good men through and through. Don't matter what sort of scrap there's been, we help each other, that's the way we do things – why, a man'll even help his enemy. We all know that someday we could need a hand, too; we all know we're subject to grief, see. Much as you get fried with someone else, much as he gets under your skin, you don't just let him drift away – that'd be plain sour, wouldn't it? We help each other in an emergency, it don't matter what else is going on.'

'Well then,' said Alvin Hooks. 'We'll take you at your word, Mr. Gillanders, and move on to other matters. We'll take you at your word that even enemies help each other in an emergency at sea. Now, did I understand you to say earlier that a forced boarding at sea was impossible? That conditions prevent a gill-netting man from boarding the boat of another gill-netter unless there is mutual consent? Unless the two of them agree and work together? Is that, sir, also correct? Did I understand you clearly on this?'

'You got me plain,' said Josiah Gillanders. 'That's exactly what I said – you won't see no forced boardings.'

'Well,' said Alvin Hooks. 'Mr. Gudmundsson here, my esteemed colleague for the defense, asked you earlier to imagine a scenario at sea in which one man seeks to kill another in a premeditated fashion. He asked you to imagine a forced boarding, a leap, a thrust of a fishing gaff. You, sir, said it wasn't possible. You said such a murder couldn't happen.'

'It's a sea yarn if it includes a forced boarding, and that's that. It's a pirate story and that's all.'

'All right, then,' said Alvin Hooks. 'I'll ask you to imagine another scenario – you tell me if it sounds plausible. If this sort of thing could have happened, sir, or if it's just another sea yarn.'

Alvin Hooks began to pace again, and as he paced he looked at each juror. 'Number one,' he began. 'The defendant here, Mr. Miyamoto, decides he wishes to kill Carl Heine. Is that part plausible – so far?'

'Sure,' Josiah answered. 'If you say so.'

'Number two,' said Alvin Hooks. 'He goes out to fish on September 15. There's a bit of mist but no real fog yet, so he has no trouble motoring out within sight distance of his intended victim, Carl Heine. He follows him out to Ship Channel Bank – how's all of that, so far?'

'I guess,' said Josiah Gillanders.

12 **be worth one's salt** (old-fashioned): etwas taugen 30 **harbor** (v) **grudges**: keep negative feelings for sb. in your mind for a long time 35 **grief**: (here) problems and worry 36 **get fried with sb.**: jdn. zur Weißglut bringen **get under sb.'s skin**: jdm. auf die Nerven gehen 37 **sour**: (hier) übel, bösartig 44 **consent** [-'-]: (here) agreement 55 **sea yarn**: Seemannsgarn

'Number three then,' continued Alvin Hooks. 'He watches Carl Heine set his net. He sets his own not too far off, deliberately up current, and fishes until late in the evening. Now the fog comes in thick and strong, a big fog, obscuring everything from sight. He can't see anything or anybody, but he knows where Carl Heine is, two hundred yards off, down current in the fog. It's late now, two A.M. The water is very quiet. He has listened over his radio while other men have motored off to fish at Elliot Head. He is not sure how many are still in the area, but he knows it can't be more than a handful. And so Mr. Miyamoto at last makes his move. He hauls in his net, cuts his motor, makes sure his trusty fishing gaff is handy, and drifts down current toward Carl Heine, perhaps even blowing his foghorn. He drifts nearly right into Carl, it seems, and lies to him, says his engine is dead. Now you tell me – you told us earlier – wouldn't Carl Heine feel bound to help him?'

'Sea yarn,' Josiah Gillanders spat. 'But a ripping good one. Go ahead.'

'Wouldn't Carl Heine feel bound to help him? As you said earlier – men help their enemies? Wouldn't Carl Heine have helped?'

'Yes, he'd have helped. Go ahead.'

'Wouldn't the two men have tied their boats together? Wouldn't you have the mutual consent necessary – an emergency situation, even if feigned – for a successful tie-up at sea? Wouldn't you, Mr. Gillanders?'

Josiah nodded. 'You would,' he answered. 'Yes.'

'And at this point, sir, in the scenario, could the defendant not – a trained *kendo* master, remember, a man proficient at killing with a stick, lethal and experienced at stick fighting – could the defendant not have leapt aboard and killed Carl Heine with a hard blow to the skull, hard enough to crack it open? As opposed to doing the job with a gunshot? Which potentially – which might – be heard across the water by somebody else out there fishing? Am I, sir, still plausible? Does my scenario sound plausible to a man of your expertise? Is all of that, sir, plausible?'

'It could have happened,' said Josiah Gillanders. 'But I don't much think it did.'

'You don't much think it did,' said Alvin Hooks. 'Your opinion is otherwise, it appears. But on what do you base your opinion, sir? You have not denied that my scenario is plausible. You have not denied that this premeditated murder might have happened in precisely the fashion I have just described, have you, Mr. Gillanders – *have* you?'

'No, I haven't,' Josiah said. 'But – '

'No further questions,' said Alvin Hooks. 'The witness can sit down. The witness can sit in the pleasant warmth of the gallery. I have no further questions.'

'Bah,' said Josiah Gillanders. But the judge held his hand up, and Josiah, seeing this, left the stand carrying his hat between his fingers.

---

4 **obscure sth. from sight**: hide sth., make it difficult to see sth.   11 **trusty**: reliable
15 **ripping** (old-fashioned): wonderful

Chapter 27

The storm winds battered the courtroom windows and rattled them in their casements so vigorously it seemed the glass would break. For three days and nights the citizens in the gallery had listened to the wind beat against their houses and echo violently inside their ears as they struggled against it to make their way to and from the courthouse. They had not at all grown accustomed to it. They were habituated to the sea winds that blew across the island each spring when the mud was up and the rain fell steadily, but a wind of this magnitude, so frigid and elemental, remained foreign to them. It seemed improbable that a wind should blow so consistently for days on end. It made them irritable and impatient. The snow was one thing, falling as it did, but the whine of the storm, the stinging force of it against their faces – everyone wished unconsciously that it would come to an end and grant them peace. They were tired of listening to it.

Kabuo Miyamoto, the accused man, had not heard the wind at all from his cell, not even a murmur of it. He had no inkling of the storm outside except when Abel Martinson led him up the stairs – handcuffed for his journey to Judge Fielding's courtroom – so that emerging into the twilight of the courthouse's ground floor he felt the wind shaking the building. And he saw through the windows in each of the stairwells how the snow fell hard out of a glowering sky and boiled, borne by the wind. The cold, cottony light of a winter storm was something he gave thanks for after living without windows for seventy-seven days. Kabuo had passed the preceding night wrapped in blankets – his concrete cell was especially cold – and pacing and shivering endlessly. The deputy appointed to watch him through the dark hours – a retired sawyer named William Stenesen – had shone a flashlight on him just before midnight and inquired if he was faring well. Kabuo had asked for extra blankets and a glass of tea, if possible. 'I'll see about that,' William Stenesen had answered. 'But Jesus, man, if you hadn't gotten yourself into this mess, neither of us would be here in the first place.'

And so Kabuo had pondered the mess he'd indeed gotten himself into. For when Nels Gudmundsson had asked for his side of the story after their chess game two and a half months ago he'd stuck with the lie he'd told Sheriff Moran: he didn't know anything about it, he'd insisted, and this had deepened his problems. Yes, he'd spoken with Carl about the seven acres, yes, he'd had an argument with Etta Heine, yes, he'd gone to see Ole. No, he hadn't seen Carl out at Ship Channel Bank on the night of September 15. He had no idea what had happened to Carl and could offer no explanation to anyone, no information about Carl's drowning. He, Kabuo, had fished through the night, then gone home and gone to bed, that was all there was to it. That was all he'd had to say.

Nels Gudmundsson, in the beginning, had been satisfied with this and seemed to take him at his word. But then he came again on the following morning with a yellow legal pad tucked beneath his arm and, a cigar between his teeth, settled down on Kabuo's bed. The cigar ashes fell into the lap of his pants, but he did not seem to mind or notice, and Kabuo felt sorry for him. His back was bent and his hands trembled. 'The sheriff's report,' he said with a sigh. 'I read it, Kabuo. The whole thing.'

'What does it say?' Kabuo asked.

'It contains a few facts I'm concerned about,' said Nels, pulling a pen from his coat pocket. 'I hope you won't mind if I ask you, once more, to give me your side of the story. Can you do that for me, Kabuo? Tell me everything all over again? Your story about the seven acres, et cetera? Everything that happened?'

Kabuo moved to the door of his cell and put his eye to the opening. 'You don't believe what I've told you,' he said softly. 'You think I'm lying, don't you.'

'The blood on your fishing gaff,' Nels Gudmundsson replied. 'They had it tested in Anacortes. It matches Carl Heine's blood type.'

'I don't know anything about it,' said Kabuo. 'I told that to the sheriff and I'm telling it to you. I don't know anything about it.'

---

6 **habituated to sth.**: familiar with sth. 8 **frigid** [ˈfrɪdʒɪd]: very cold 20 **stairwell** (AE): space in a building in which the stairs are built 21 **glower** [ˈɡlaʊər] (v): (here) look dark and dangerous **boil**: (here) be moved around in wisps, swirl 26 **sawyer**: Sägewerksarbeiter 34 **stick with sth.**: (here) continue telling sth.

'Another thing,' insisted Nels, pointing his pen at Kabuo. 'They found one of your mooring lines on Carl's boat. Wrapped around a cleat on the *Susan Marie*. One of your lines, clearly, they say. Matched all your other lines with the exception of a new one. That's in the report, too.'

'Oh,' said Kabuo, but nothing more.

'Look,' said Nels Gudmundsson. 'I can't help you with this unless I know the truth. I can't build a case around an answer like "oh" when I've brought to your attention such damning evidence as your mooring line being found by the sheriff of Island County on the boat of a suspiciously dead fisherman. What good can I do you if all I get is "oh"? How am I going to help you, Kabuo? You've got to level with me, that's all there is to it. Otherwise, I can't help you.'

'I've told you the truth,' said Kabuo. He turned around and faced his attorney, an old man with one eye and trembling hands, appointed to his case because he, Kabuo, had refused to honor the prosecutor's point of view by purchasing his own defense. 'We talked about my family's land, I argued with his mother years ago, I went to see Ole, I went to see Carl, and that was the end of it. I've said what I have to say.'

'The mooring line,' Nels Gudmundsson repeated. 'The mooring line and the blood on the fishing gaff. I – '

'I can't explain those things,' insisted Kabuo. 'I don't know anything about them.'

Nels nodded and stared at him, and Kabuo held his gaze. 'You could hang, you know,' Nels said bluntly. 'There's no attorney in the world who can help you with this if you're not going to tell the truth.'

And the next morning Nels had come yet again, carrying a manila folder. He smoked his cigar and paced the length of the cell with the folder tucked beneath his arm. 'I've brought you the sheriffs report,' he said, 'so you can see exactly what we're up against. Problem is, once you read the thing, you may decide to concoct a *new* story – you may pretend you want to level with me by concocting a more defensible lie. Once you've read this report, Kabuo, you can make something up that's consistent with it and I'll go ahead and work with that, mainly because I'll have no choice. I don't like that. I'd rather it didn't turn out that way. I'd rather know I can trust you. So before you read what's in that thing, tell me a story that squares with its details and exonerate yourself in my eyes. Tell me the story you should have told the sheriff right off the bat, when it wasn't too late, when the truth might still have given you your freedom. When the truth might have done you some good.'

Kabuo, at first, said nothing. But then Nels dropped the manila folder on the mattress, dropped it and stood directly over him. 'It's because you're from Japanese folks,' he said softly; it was more a question than a statement. 'You figure because you're from Japanese folks nobody will believe you anyway.'

'I've got a right to think that way. Or maybe you've forgotten that a few years back the government decided it couldn't trust any of us and shipped us out of here.'

'That's true,' said Nels. 'But – '

'We're sly and treacherous,' Kabuo said. 'You can't trust a Jap, can you? This island's full of strong feelings, Mr. Gudmundsson, people who don't often speak their minds but hate on the inside all the same. They don't buy their berries from our farms, they won't do business with us. You remember when somebody pitched rocks through all the windows at Sumida's greenhouses last summer? Well, now there's a fisherman everybody liked well enough who's dead and drowned in his net. They're going to figure it makes sense a Jap killed him. They're going to want to see me hang no matter what the truth is.'

'There are laws,' said Nels. 'They apply equally to everyone. You're entitled to a fair trial.'

'There are men,' said Kabuo, 'who hate me. They hate anyone who looks like the soldiers they fought. That's what I'm doing here.'

'Tell the truth,' Nels said. 'Decide to tell the truth before it's too late.'

Kabuo lay down on his bed with a sigh and twined his fingers behind his head. 'The truth,' he said. 'The truth isn't easy.'

---

7 **build a case**: (here) prepare for defending sb.   11 **level with sb.** (infml) : tell sb. the truth and not hide any unpleasant facts from them   24 **blunt**: (here) very direct, not trying to be polite   29 **be up against sth.** (infml): have to face sth., esp. sth. unpleasant   30 **concoct sth.**: invent sth., esp. a story or an excuse   31 **defensible**: (here) plausible and therefore easy to present as part of the defense at court
36 **square with sth.**: mit etwas übereinstimmen / in Einklang sein   **exonerate sb.**: (here) prove that sb. is not responsible for sth. that they have been blamed for
37 **off the bat** (infml): immediately, without delay

'Just the same,' Nels said. 'I understand how you feel. There are the things that happened, though, and the things that did not happen. That's all we're talking about.'

It seemed to Kabuo a lushly textured dream, fogbound, still, and silent. He thought about it often in his darkened cell, and the smallest details were large for him and every word was audible.

On the night in question he'd checked the *Islander*'s engine oil and quickly greased the net drum's reel drive before putting out for Ship Channel Bank in the hour just before dusk. Ship Channel, he'd understood, had been fished hard and happily on two consecutive evenings. He'd spoken to Lars Hansen and Jan Sorensen about it and made the decision to fish at Ship Channel on account of their information. The silvers were running in immense schools, they said, mostly on the flood tide. There were fish to be had on the ebb tide, too, though nowhere near as many. It would be possible to take two hundred or more working the flood alone, Kabuo hoped, and perhaps a hundred more on the ebb if he was lucky – and luck, he knew, was what he needed. Elliot Head, on the previous night, had barely covered his costs. He'd come away with eighteen fish and had furthermore set his net in the dark beside a large and labyrinthine kelp island. The tide drift had taken him down into the kelp, and he'd wasted four hours extricating himself so as not to rip his gill net. Now, tonight, he would have to do better. He would need to have fortune on his side.

In the blue light of dusk he'd made the turn out of the harbor and run for open water. From his vantage point at the wheel of the *Islander* he saw the soft cedars of San Piedro Island, its high, rolling hills, the low mist that lay in long streamers against its beaches, the whitecaps riffling its shoreline. The moon had risen already behind the island and hung just over the big bluff at Skiff Point – a quarter moon, pale and indefinite, as ethereal and translucent as the wisps of clouds that traveled the skies, obscuring it. Kabuo, his radio on, checked his barometer; it still held steady despite talk of rough weather, cold squalls of sleet reported to the north, out of the Strait of Georgia. When he looked up again a raft of seabirds was scattering, gray silhouettes off the chop a hundred yards out, rising and then skimming over the surface of the waves in the manner of surf scoters, though there were too many to be surf scoters –

he didn't know what they might be, maybe murres, he couldn't tell. Steering wide of Harbor Rocks, bucking the sea wind head-on at seven knots, he ran with the tide race pushing hard behind him and fell in with the *Kasilof*, the *Antarctic*, and the *Providence*, all of which were making for Ship Channel, too: half the fleet was headed there. Half the fleet was spread out before him, running hard for the fishing grounds at dusk and throwing wide silver wakes.

Kabuo drank the green tea in his thermos and ran through the radio channels. It was his habit to listen but not to speak, to gather what he could about men by the manner in which they expressed themselves, and to discern what he could about the fishing.

At full dusk or thereabouts he ate three rice balls, a slab of rock cod, and two windfall apples from a wild tree behind Bender's Spring. The night mist hovered on the water already, so he backed the throttle down and ran with his spotlight broadcasting over the waves. The prospect of a blind fog, as always, concerned him. A fisherman could become so lost in a blind fog he'd set his own net in a circle without knowing it or end up working the middle of the shipping lane where the big freighters ran toward Seattle. It was better in such conditions to fish Elliot Head, since the head lay far from the shipping lane and well to the lee side of Elliot Island, out of the big water breezes.

But by eight-thirty he'd idled his engine at the bank and stood in the cockpit beside the net drum, listening, with the fog settling all around him. From the lighthouse station far to the east he could hear the low, steady intonation of the fog signal diaphone. It was the sound he associated with blind nights at sea – lonely, familiar, hushed, and so melancholy he could never listen without emptiness. Tonight, he knew, was what old-timers called *ghost time*, with fog as immobile and dense as

4 **lushly textured**: (hier) vielschichtig   8 **reel drive**: (hier) Antrieb der Netzwinde
10 **consecutive** [kən'sekjətɪv]: aufeinander folgend   13 **school**: (bei Fischen) Schwarm   20 **tide drift**: Gezeitenströmung   27 **streamer**: (here) strip, shred
27–28 **riffle sth.**: (hier) auf etwas auflaufen   32 **squall** [skwɔːl]: sudden, strong and violent wind   **sleet**: mixture of rain and snow   34 **off the chop**: (here) just above the movement of the sea   36 **surf scoter**: Brillenente   37 **murre**: black-and-white sea bird that dives for its food   38 **buck sth.**: (here) brace yourself against sth., oppose sth.   39 **tide race** = tide drift   39–40 **fall in with sb./sth.**: (here) have the same course as sb./sth.   50 **hover** ['hʌvər]: stay in the air in one place
61 **diaphone**: Nebelhorn

buttermilk. A man could run his hands through such a fog, separating it into tendrils and streamers that gathered themselves languidly once more into the whole and disappeared seamlessly, without a trace. Drifting on the tide, a gill-netter moved through it as though it composed its own netherworld medium halfway between air and water. It was possible on such a night to become as disoriented as a man without a torch in a cave. Kabuo knew that other fishermen were out there, drifting as he was and peering into the fog, blindly gliding across the bank in the hope of establishing their locations. The shipping lane boundaries were marked by numbered buoys, and the hope was to stumble across one fortuitously so as to orient oneself.

Kabuo, giving up, propped a buoy bag between the stern fairleads and lit a kerosene lantern with a wooden kitchen match. He waited until the wick held strong, pumped in some air, adjusted the fuel, then set the lantern carefully in its life ring and bent down over the *Islander*'s transom to place the buoy bag on the water. With his face so close to the surface of the sea he imagined he could smell the salmon running. He shut his eyes, put a hand in the water, and in his own manner he prayed to the gods of the sea to assist him by bringing fish his way. He asked for good luck, for a respite from the fog; he prayed that the gods would clear the fog away and keep him safe from the freighters in the shipping lane. Then he stood again in the stern of the *Islander*, square-knotted his buoy bag line to his net line, and released the brake on the net drum.

Kabuo laid his net out north to south by motoring away from it on a true blind heading as slowly as was possible. It seemed to him the lane lay to the north, though he couldn't be certain about that. The tidal drift, running east, would keep his net taut, but only if he laid it on the right bearing; if he quartered to the current, even slightly, on the other hand, he'd end up having to tow all night just to keep his net from collapsing. There was no way of knowing in dense fog how true a net lay; he couldn't see twenty corks down his line and would have to run it every hour or so with his spotlight seeking it out. Kabuo could not see the surface of the sea more than five yards beyond the bow of his boat from his place at the wheel in his cabin. The *Islander*, in fact, divided the fog, the bow literally peeling it open. The fog was dense enough to make him ponder running for Elliot Head before long; for all he knew he was setting his net in the Seattle-bound shipping lane. Besides, he had to hope no one had set due south, particularly at an angle to his own set. In this fog he'd no doubt miss the man's jacklight and twist his net up in the *Islander*'s prop, a long diversion from the night's fishing. Any number of things could go amiss.

In the stern the net slipped free from the drum and rolled over the fairleads easily toward the sea until at last the whole of it was out of the boat, three hundred fathoms long. Kabuo went back and hosed the net gurry out the scupper holes. When he was done he shut the engine down and stood on the hatch with his back against the cabin, listening for the blasts of passing freighters. Nothing, though – there was no sound now but lapping water and the distant sound from the lighthouse. The tidal current carried him gently east, just as he'd predicted. He felt better about things with his net in. He could not be certain he was not in the shipping lane, but he knew he was drifting at the same speed as every other gill-netter fishing these fogbound waters. He imagined there were thirty or more boats out there, all hidden and silent in the dense sea fog, moving to the same tidal rhythm that moved under him, keeping everyone equi-distant. Kabuo went in and flicked his mast light on: red over white, the sign of a man night fishing, not that it did any good. Not that the light was worth anything. But on the other hand he'd done all he could about matters. He'd set his net as well as possible. There was nothing to do now but be patient.

Kabuo brought his thermos into the cockpit, then sat on the port gunnel and sipped green tea, listening into the fog uneasily. Farther south he could hear someone idling, the sound of net unraveling from a drum, a boat under way at a crawl. There was an occasional dim crackle from his radio set, but other than that nothing. In the silence he sipped

---

3 **seamless**: (here) with no spaces between one part and the next   5 **netherworld**: Unterwelt   11 **fortuitous** [fɔːrˈtuːɪtəs]: by lucky chance   12 **bouy bag**: Schwimmkissenboje   25 **blind heading**: (hier) Blindfahrt   28 **bearing**: (here) direction measured from a fixed point   **quarter to sth.**: (here) move into a position that is at right angles to sth.   30 **true**: (here) straight and accurate   32 **seek sb./sth. out**: look for and find sb./sth.   38 **due** (adv): (of directions) exactly, in a straight line   40 **prop**: (here) propeller   41 **amiss** [-ˈ-]: wrong   44 **fathom** [ˈfæðəm](n): unit for measuring the depth of water (about 1.8 m)   44–45 **net gurry**: (here) remaining fish parts from the last set   55 **equi-distant** [,--ˈ--]: at the same distance

tea and waited for the salmon: as on other nights he imagined them in motion, swift in pursuit of the waters they'd sprung from, waters that held both past and future for them, their children and their children's children and their deaths. When he picked his net and held them pinched at the gills he felt in their silence how desperate their sojourn was, and he was moved in the manner a fisherman is moved, quietly, without words. Their rich silver flanks would feed his dreams and for this he was thankful and sorrowful. There was something tragic in the wall of invisible mesh he'd hung to choke the life from them while they traveled to the rhythm of an urging they could not deny. He imagined them slamming against his net in astonishment at this invisible thing that finished their lives in the last days of an urgent journey. Sometimes, hauling net, he came across a fish thrashing hard enough to elicit a cracking *thump* when it banged off the *Islander*'s transom. Like all the others, it went into the hold to die over the course of hours.

Kabuo put his thermos together and took it into the cabin. Once again he flipped through the radio channels, and this time he caught a voice – Dale Middleton's – chattering away in a slow island drawl: 'I done just got the bug out of my squelch,' it said, and then someone answered, 'What for?' Dale replied he'd had just about enough of setting by the shipping lane in soup fog for a dozen silvers, a few dogfish, a couple of hake, and what's more taking flack off his radio. 'I near can't see my own hands,' he said. 'I near can't see the nose on my own face.' Somebody, a third party, agreed the fishing had gone sour, the bank seemed all dried up real sudden, he'd been thinking on fishing at Elliot Head, couldn't tell but maybe things was better there. 'Leastwise off this shipping lane,' replied Dale. 'One good swing I got laid out now, that'll do it for me here. Hey, Leonard, your net coming up clear? Mine here's lookin' like a oil rag. Damn thing's darker 'n burnt toast.'

The fishermen on the radio discussed this for a while, Leonard saying his net was fairly clean, Dale asking him if he'd greased it lately, Leonard claiming to have seen a buoy marker, number 57, off to port. He'd worked off it for a half hour or so but never came on to 58 or 56, never fixed himself properly. Far as he was concerned he was lost in the fog and intended to stay that way – leastwise 'til his net was up, then he'd think about matters. Dale asked him if he'd picked once yet, and Leonard sounded disappointed. Dale described the fog again and said he guessed it was as thick as it gets, and Leonard, agreeing, said he remembered one last year at Elliot Head in rougher seas – a bad scene, he'd added. 'The Head'd be good about now,' replied Dale. 'Let's fog-run our way on down there.'

Kabuo left his radio on; he wanted to hear about it if a freighter came down the strait and put in a call to the lighthouse. He slid the cabin door open and stood listening, and in time came the air blasts, both muted and melancholy, of boats moving off the fishing grounds, the fog whistles of gill-netters running blindly east, farther off all the time and so less audible. It was time to pick, he decided, and then if necessary to make his own fog run to the fishing grounds off Elliot Head – a run he preferred to make alone. The boats out there now were moving on blind bearings, and he didn't necessarily trust their skippers. He'd wait an hour more, then pick and run if he came up short on fish.

At ten-thirty he stood on the beaver paddle in the cockpit, picking his net and stopping now and then to throw strands of kelp into the water. The net, under tension, rained seawater onto the deck along with sticks and kelp. He was happy to find there were salmon coming up as well, big silvers mostly over ten and eleven pounds, a half-dozen ten-pound chums, too, even three resident black-mouth. Some dropped to the deck coming over the transom, others he deftly maneuvered free. He was good at this part of things. His hands found their way through the folds of the net to the long flanks of dead and dying salmon. Kabuo lofted them into the hold along with three hake and three pale dogfish he intended to take home to his family. There were fifty-eight salmon, he counted, for this first set, and he felt grateful about them. Kneeling for a

---

5 **gill** [gɪl]: one of the openings on the side of a fish's head that it breathes through
sojourn ['soʊdʒɜːrn]: temporary stay in a place away from your home   9 **mesh**: (here) material that nets are made of, consisting of threads of rope   10 **urging**: (hier) Trieb   13 **elicit sth.**: (of sound) make, give   18 **drawl** (n): slow way of speaking in which the vowel sounds are longer than usual   18–19 **I done ... squelch.**: Ich habe das Netz aus der Suppe geholt.   22 **take flack** (fig): (here) be ridiculed for being out at sea in the fog   25 **all dried up**: (here) emptied of fish   26 **leastwise** (AE, infml): wenigstens   27 **swing** (n): (here) setting of the net   29 **oil rag**: Öllappen   33 **work off sth.**: (here) move away from sth.   34 **fix yourself**: (here) know your ship's position   40 **fog-run** (v): move through the fog   57 **resident**: (here) living off the West Coast all year

moment beside the hold, he looked down at them with satisfaction and calculated their worth at the cannery. He thought of the journey they'd made to him and how their lives, perhaps, would buy his farm back.

Kabuo watched for one long moment – an occasional fish flaring at the gills or jerking – then pulled the hatch cover over them and sprayed sea slime out the scupper holes. It was a good haul for a first set, enough to keep him fishing the bank – there was no reason for him to go elsewhere. Chances were that, fog and all, he'd made his drift dead center by happenstance; he'd had the luck he'd prayed for earlier. So far everything had gone right.

It was close to eleven-thirty, if his watch was right, the last of the flood still carrying him east, and he decided to motor west again in order to fish the tide turn. On the turn the salmon would pile up, milling on the bank by the hundreds, in schools, and some to the east would back in on the ebb so that his net would load up going both ways. He hoped for another hundred fish from his next set; it seemed a reasonable prospect. He was glad to have stuck it out in the fog and felt vindicated somehow. He'd made his drift successfully. There were fish in his hold, more to be had, and small competition to get them. He guessed more than two-thirds of the fishermen in the area had made the fog run for Elliot Head with their horns sounding across the water.

Kabuo stood at the wheel in his cabin with a cup of green tea on the table behind him and flipped once more through the radio channels. There was no talk now. All the men who couldn't help talking had moved on, it appeared. Out of habit he checked his engine gauges and took a reading from his compass. Then he throttled up, turned tight, and motored west, adjusting to the north less than five degrees in the hope of stumbling across a buoy marker.

The bow of the *Islander* cut through the fog for ten minutes or more. One eye on the binnacle, the other on the spotlighted water before his bow, Kabuo inched forward on blind faith. He was, he knew, motoring against the grain of boats drifting down the bank. The protocol among gill-netters in such conditions was to lay on one's foghorn at one-minute intervals and to keep a sharp ear turned toward the fog on the chance of receiving a reply. Kabuo, moving into the tidal drift, had signaled his position a half-dozen times when an air horn replied off his port bow. Whoever it was, he was close.

Kabuo backed into neutral and drifted, his heart beating hard in his chest. The other man was too near, seventy-five yards, a hundred at best, out there in the fog, his motor cut. Kabuo laid on his horn again. In the silence that followed came a reply to port – this time a man's voice, calm and factual, a voice he recognized. 'I'm over here,' it called across the water. 'I'm dead in the water, drifting.'

And this was how he had found Carl Heine, his batteries dead, adrift at midnight, in need of another man's assistance. There Carl stood in the *Islander*'s spotlight, a big man in bib overalls poised in his boat's bow, a kerosene lantern clutched in one hand and an air horn dangling from the other. He'd raised his lantern and stood there like that, his bearded chin set, expressionless. 'I'm dead in the water,' he'd said again, when Kabuo pulled up against his starboard side and tossed him a mooring line. 'My batteries are drawed down. Both of them.'

'All right,' said Kabuo. 'Let's tie up. I've got plenty of juice.'

'Thank God for that,' answered Carl. 'It's good luck to have run across you.'

'Kick your fenders out,' Kabuo said. 'I'll drift right up in close.'

They tied their boats together in the fog, underneath the *Islander*'s spotlight. Kabuo shut his engine down while Carl stepped across both gunnels and came aboard his boat. He stood in the doorway shaking his head; 'I drawed 'em both down,' he repeated. 'Volt meter's down around nine somewhere. Alternator belts were loose, I guess. I got 'em tightened up better now, but meanwhile I'm dead in the water.'

'Hope we're not in the lane,' said Kabuo, peering up at the *Susan Marie*'s mast. 'Looks like you put a lantern up.'

'Lashed it up there just a bit ago,' said Carl. 'Best I could do, seems like. Lost my radio when the juice ran out, couldn't call anyone. Couldn't do anything to help myself, just drifting along this last hour. Lantern's probably useless in this fog, but anyway I've got it up there. It's all the

---

6 **sea slime**: Seeschlamm   8–9 **dead center**: exactly towards the center   17 **stick sth. out** (infml): continue doing sth. to the end, even when it is difficult or boring   **vindicate sb.**: prove that sb. was right in having done sth.   25 **gauge** [geɪdʒ]: instrument for measuring the amount or level of sth., esp. of fuel or electric power   26 **throttle up**: die Maschine anlassen   32 **against the grain of sb./sth.**: (here) into the opposite direction from sb./sth.   51 **drawed (= drawn) down**: empty   60 **alternator belt**: Keilriemen   64 **lash sth.**: etwas festbinden

lights I got just now, that and the one I've been carrying. Probably isn't worth nothing to nobody.'

'I've got two batteries,' Kabuo answered. 'We'll pull one and get you started.'

''Preciate that,' said Carl. 'Thing is I run D-8s, you see. S'pose you run off 6s.'

'I do,' said Kabuo. 'But it'll work if you've got room. Anyway, we can refit your well. Or rig up some longer cables? It should go in just fine.'

'I'll measure,' said Carl. 'Then we'll know.'

He crossed back over the boat gunnels then, and Kabuo hoped that underneath his facade there was part of him wanting to discuss the land that lay between them silently. Carl would *have* to say something one way or the other simply because the two of them were at sea together, moored boat to boat but to nothing else, adrift and battling the same problem.

Kabuo had known Carl for many years; he knew that Carl avoided circumstances in which he had to speak. He spoke mostly of the world of tools and objects when he had to speak at all. Kabuo remembered trolling for cutthroat with Carl – they were twelve years old, long before the war – in a borrowed, weathered rowboat. It was just after sunset and the phosphorescence in the water boiling underneath Carl's rowing oars inspired him to comment – a boy so moved by the beauty of the world he could not keep himself from utterance: 'Look at those colors,' he'd said. And even at twelve Kabuo had understood that such a statement was out of character. What Carl felt he kept inside, showing nothing to anyone – as Kabuo himself did, for other reasons. They were more similar in their deepest places than Kabuo cared to admit.

Kabuo pried the cover from his battery well and loosened the cables from the terminals. He lifted one of his batteries out – twice as large as a car battery and twice as heavy as well – and carried it out to where he could rest it on his gunnel and pass it to Carl Heine. They stood each on his own boat, and the battery passed between them. 'It'll fit,' said Carl. 'There's a flange in the way. It's soft. I can bang it back.'

Kabuo reached down and took his gaff in his hand. 'I'll bring this,' he said. 'We can hammer with it.'

They passed into Carl's tidy cabin together, Kabuo carrying a lantern and the gaff, Carl in front with the battery. A cased sausage hung from a wire beside the binnacle; the cot was neatly made up. Kabuo recognized

Carl's neat hand in things, his way of establishing a rigid order, the force that had driven him, years before, to keep his tackle box shipshape. Even his clothes, no matter how worn-out, were conspicuously neat and well kept.

'Give me that gaff,' Carl said now.

He knelt on one knee beside his battery hold and banged with the gaff at the metal flange. Kabuo, beside him, was aware of his strength and of the facility with which he approached this problem; he made each stroke count, put his shoulders into each, and did not hurry his blows. Once his right hand slipped, though, and grazing the soft metal came away bloody, but Carl did not halt. He gripped Kabuo's fishing gaff harder and only afterward, when the battery was in the well, did he put his palm to his mouth and hold it there, taking back his blood in silence. 'Let's try starting up,' he said.

'You sure,' asked Kabuo, 'you got those belts tight? No point in starting up otherwise, you know. You'll just run this battery down, too, and we'll have another problem.'

'They're tight now,' said Carl, working on his palm. 'I put a wrench on 'em good.'

He pulled out the choke and threw his toggle switches. The *Susan Marie*'s engine wheezed twice below the floorboards, then coughed, rattled, and fired up when Carl backed down the choke.

'Tell you what,' said Kabuo. 'You keep that battery for the rest of the night. I can't wait around 'til you draw back up, so I'll just run off the one I've got and catch you back at the docks.'

Carl slid the dead battery out of the way, tucked it in to the right of the wheel, then snapped on the cabin light and took a volt meter reading with his handkerchief pressed against his hand. 'You're right,' he said. 'I'm charging now, but this'll take awhile. Maybe I'll find you later.'

---

8 **rig sth. up** (AE): make or build sth. quickly, using whatever materials are available   20 **oar**: Ruder   24 **out of character**: (here) not typical or appropriate   39 **tackle box**: Werkzeugkiste   **shipshape**: clean and neat   40 **conspicuous** [kən'spɪkjuəs]: easy to see or notice   45 **facility**: natural ability to do sth. easily   45–46 **make a stroke count**: (here) hit sth. in exactly the right place with the right force   47 **graze sth.**: (here) break the surface of your skin by rubbing it against sth. rough or sharp   57 **toggle switch**: Kippschalter   66 **charge sth.**: pass electricity through sth. so that it is stored there

'Catch fish,' said Kabuo. 'Don't worry about it. I'll see you back at the docks.'

He worked the battery hold cover into place. He picked up his gaff and waited there. 'I'm off,' he said finally. 'I'll see you.'

'Hold on,' answered Carl, still working on his hand – looking at it and not Kabuo. 'You know as well as I do we both got something to talk about.'

'All right,' replied Kabuo, his gaff in his hand. And then he stood and waited.

'Seven acres,' said Carl Heine. 'I'm wonderin' what you'd pay for 'em, Kabuo. Just curious, that's all.'

'What are you selling them for?' Kabuo asked. 'Why don't we start with what you want for them? I guess I'd rather start there.'

'Did I say I was selling?' Carl asked. 'Didn't say one way or the other, did I? But if I was, I guess I'd have to figure they're mine and you want 'em pretty bad. Guess I'd ought to charge you a small fortune, but then maybe you'd want your battery back, leave me out here stranded.'

'The battery's in,' Kabuo answered, smiling. 'That's separate from the rest of things. Besides, you'd do the same for me.'

'I *might* do the same for you,' said Carl. 'I have to warn you about that, chief. I'm not screwed together like I used to be. It isn't like it was before.'

'All right,' said Kabuo. 'If you say so.'

'Hell,' said Carl. 'I'm not saying what I mean. Look, goddamn it, I'm sorry, okay? I'm sorry over this whole damn business. I'd a been around, it wouldn't have happened how it did. My mother pulled it off, I was out at sea, fighting you goddamn Jap sons a – '

'I'm an American,' Kabuo cut in. 'Just like you or anybody. Am I calling you a Nazi, you big Nazi bastard? I killed men who looked just like you – pig-fed German bastards. I've got their blood on my soul, Carl, and it doesn't wash off very easily. So don't you talk to me about Japs, you big Nazi son of a bitch.'

He still held the gaff gripped tightly in one hand, and he became aware of it now. Carl put one boot on the *Susan Marie*'s port gunnel and spat hard into the water. 'I am a bastard,' he said finally, and stared out into the fog. 'I'm a big Hun Nazi son of a bitch, and you know what else, Kabuo? I still got your bamboo fishing rod. I kept it all these years. I hid it in the barn after my mother tried to make me go and return it over to your house. You went off to prison camp, I caught a mess of sea runs. Damn thing's still in my closet.'

'Leave it there,' said Kabuo Miyamoto. 'I forgot all about that fishing rod. You can have it. To hell with it.'

'To hell with that,' said Carl. 'It's been driving me crazy all these years. I open up my closet and there it is, your goddamn bamboo rod.'

'Give it back, if you want,' said Kabuo. 'But I'm telling you you can keep it, Carl. That's why I gave it to you.'

'All right,' said Carl. 'Then that settles it. Twelve hundred an acre and that's final. That's what I'm paying Ole, see. That's the going price on strawberry land, go and have a look around.'

'That's eighty-four hundred for the lot,' answered Kabuo. 'How much are you going to want down?'

Carl Heine spat into the water one more time, then turned and put out his hand. Kabuo put the gaff down and took it. They did not shake so much as grip like fishermen who know they can go no further with words and must communicate in another fashion. So they stood there at sea in the fog, floating, and locked their hands together. Their grip was solid, and there was the blood from Carl's cut palm in it. They did not mean for it to say too much overtly, and at the same time they wished for it to say everything. They moved away from this more quickly than they desired but before embarrassment overtook them. 'A thousand down,' said Carl Heine. 'We can sign papers tomorrow.'

'Eight hundred,' said Kabuo, 'and it's a deal.'

---

26 **pull sth. off** (infml): (here) succeed in doing sth. against the will of other people   36 **Hun**: Hunne, Schimpfname für einen Deutschen   39 **a mess of sth.** (AE): a lot of sth.   **sea run** = sea-run cutthroat: kind of fish   58 **overtly**: in an open way, not secretly

Chapter 28

When Kabuo had finished telling his story on the witness stand, Alvin Hooks rose and stood before him insistently working on a hangnail. Studying his fingers as he delivered his words, he attended in particular to his cuticles. 'Mr. Miyamoto,' he began. 'For the life of me I can't understand why you didn't tell this story from the start. After all, don't you think it might have been your citizenly duty to come forward with all of this information? Don't you think you should have gone to the sheriff and told him about this battery business you claim occurred on the high seas? I would think you would, Mr. Miyamoto. I would think you would go to Sheriff Moran and tell him all of this just as soon as you heard that Carl Heine had died so horribly.'

The accused man looked at the jurors now, ignoring Alvin Hooks entirely, and answered quietly and evenly in their direction, as if there were no one else present. 'You must understand,' he said to them, 'that I heard nothing about the death of Carl Heine until one o'clock on the afternoon of September 16 and that within just a few hours of my having heard of it Sheriff Moran arrested me. There was no time for me to voluntarily come forward with the events as I have just delivered them. I – '

'But,' Alvin Hooks intervened, placing himself between Kabuo and the jurors, 'as you've just said yourself, Mr. Miyamoto, you had in fact – what did you say? – a few *hours* in which to seek out the sheriff. You heard about this death, an afternoon passed, and then you went down to the Amity Harbor docks with the intent of putting out to sea. You intended to fish until the morning of the seventeenth, at which time, if you'd decided to come forward, at least *sixteen* hours would have passed since you'd heard of the death of Carl Heine. So let me put this another way, a bit more consistent with reality – did you, Mr. Miyamoto, *intend* to come forward? Were you about to come forward with your battery story at the time of your arrest?'

'I was thinking about it,' said Kabuo Miyamoto. 'I was trying to decide just what I should do. The situation was difficult.'

'Oh,' answered Alvin Hooks. 'You were thinking about it. You were weighing whether or not to come forward and tell Sheriff Moran, in a voluntary way, about this battery incident.'

'That's right,' said Kabuo Miyamoto. 'I was.'

'But then, as you say, Sheriff Moran came to you. He appeared at your boat on the evening of the sixteenth with a search warrant, is that correct?'

'He did.'

'And you were still considering, at that point in time, whether or not you should tell him your battery story?'

'I was.'

'But you didn't tell him your battery story.'

'I guess not. No, I didn't.'

'You didn't tell him your battery story,' Alvin Hooks repeated. 'Not even in the face of imminent arrest did you offer any sort of explanation. Here stood Sheriff Moran with your fishing gaff in hand, telling you he intended to have the blood on it tested, and you didn't tell him about Carl Heine's cut palm – wasn't that what you told the court, that Carl cut his palm using your fishing gaff? And that this is the explanation for the blood on it?'

'That's what happened,' said Kabuo Miyamoto. 'He cut his palm, yes.'

'But you didn't offer that as an explanation to the sheriff. You said nothing about having seen Carl Heine. Now why was this, Mr. Miyamoto? Why did you claim complete ignorance?'

'You must understand,' said Kabuo. 'The sheriff had appeared with a warrant in hand. I found myself under suspicion of murder. It seemed to me best not to say anything. To wait until I … had a lawyer.'

'So you didn't tell the sheriff your battery story,' Alvin Hooks said again. 'Nor did you tell it after your arrest, even when you *had* an attorney. Instead you claimed – am I correct about this? – you claimed to know nothing about the death of Carl Heine, you claimed not to have seen him on the night of the fifteenth at the Ship Channel Bank fishing grounds. These claims of yours, these claims of ignorance, were all recorded in the

---

2 **hangnail**: piece of skin near the bottom or at the side of your fingernail that is loose and hurting you   4 **cuticle** ['kjuːtɪkl]: area of hard skin at the base of the nails on the fingers and toes

sheriff's investigative report, which has been admitted as evidence in this trial. Your story, then, immediately *after* your arrest, differs from the one you've told today, Mr. Miyamoto. So I ask you – where lies the truth?'

Kabuo blinked; his lips tightened. 'The truth,' he said, 'is as I have just described it. The truth is that I loaned Carl a battery, helped him get his boat started, made arrangements for my family's seven acres with him, then motored away and fished.'

'I see,' said Alvin Hooks. 'You wish to retract the story of complete ignorance you told Sheriff Moran in the wake of your arrest and replace it with this new one you've just now told us? You wish us to believe this new story?'

'Yes, I do. Because it's true.'

'I see,' said Alvin Hooks. 'Well, then. On the morning of September 16 you returned from a night's fishing and informed your wife of your at-sea conversation with Carl Heine. Is that correct, Mr. Miyamoto?'

'It is.'

'And then?' asked the prosecutor. 'What next?'

'I slept,' said Kabuo. 'Until one-thirty. My wife woke me up at one-thirty or thereabouts with the news about Carl's death.'

'I see,' said Alvin Hooks. 'And then what?'

'We sat and talked,' said Kabuo. 'I ate lunch and took care of some bills I had to pay. About five I headed down to the docks.'

'About five,' said Alvin Hooks. 'And did you stop anywhere along the way? Errands, perhaps? Did you visit anyone or go anywhere? Speak to anybody about anything?'

'No,' said Kabuo. 'I left around five and went straight to my boat. That was all there was to it.'

'You didn't, say, stop at the store to stock up on supplies? Nothing of that sort, Mr. Miyamoto?'

'No.'

'At the docks,' said Alvin Hooks. 'Did you see anyone? Did you stop at another boat for any reason, speak to any other fishermen?'

'Straight to my boat,' said Kabuo Miyamoto. 'I didn't stop for anything, no.'

'Straight to your boat,' Alvin Hooks repeated. 'And there you were, preparing for a night of fishing, when the sheriff came along with his warrant.'

'That's right,' said Kabuo. 'He searched my boat.'

Alvin Hooks crossed over to the evidence table and selected a folder from it. 'The sheriff indeed searched your boat,' he agreed. 'And the details of his search, Mr. Miyamoto, are recorded in this investigative report I'm holding right here in my hand. In fact, in the course of cross-examining the sheriff, your counsel – Mr. Gudmundsson – made reference to this report, including an item on page twenty-seven which says –' Alvin Hooks shuffled through the pages, then stopped and tapped his forefinger against it, tapped it three times, emphatically. Once again he turned toward the jurors, swiveling the sheriff's report in their direction as if to suggest they read along with him despite their distance across the courtroom.

'Now this is highly problematic,' Alvin Hooks said. 'Because the sheriff's report states that in your battery well there were two D-6 batteries. "Two D-6 batteries in well. Each six celled" – that's what it says, right here.'

'My boat runs on D-6s,' answered Kabuo. 'There are many boats that do so.'

'Oh, yes,' said Alvin Hooks. 'I know about that. But what about the fact that there were *two* batteries? *Two* batteries, Mr. Miyamoto. If your story is true, if you loaned one to Carl Heine as you say you did – if you pulled one out of your own battery well in order to loan it to Carl Heine – shouldn't there have been just *one* present when the sheriff made his search? I've asked you about the course of your day, how you spent your afternoon, and at no point did you tell us that you stopped at the chandlery to purchase yourself a new battery, at no point did you say anything suggestive of time spent purchasing or finding a new battery. You didn't tell us that you spent any time getting another battery down in your well – so why, Mr. Miyamoto, why did the sheriff find *two* batteries on your boat if you'd loaned one to Carl Heine?'

The accused man looked once again at the jurors and let a moment of silence pass. Once again his face showed nothing; it was impossible to know what he was thinking. 'I had a spare battery in my shed,' he

---

8 **retract sth.**: say that sth. you have said earlier is not true or correct   9 **in the wake of sth.**: coming after or following sth.   24 **errand**: Erledigung, Besorgung
45 **shuffle through sth.**: (hier) etwas durchblättern   63 **suggestive of sth.**: suggesting sth. without directly pointing to it

said evenly. 'I brought it down and put it in before the sheriff showed up with his warrant. That's why he found two batteries when he searched. One of them had just gone in.'

Alvin Hooks put the sheriff's report in its place on the evidence table. With his hands behind his back, as though contemplating this answer, he made his way toward the jurors' platform, where he stopped and turned to face the accused man, nodding at him slowly.

'Mr. Miyamoto,' he said, and his tone suggested admonition. 'You are under oath here to tell the truth. You're under oath to be honest with the court, to be forthcoming with the truth about your role in the death of Carl Heine. And now it seems to me that once again you wish to change your story. You wish to say that you brought a battery from home and inserted it in your battery well during the hour before your boat was searched, or something of that sort – you're adding this now to what you said before. Well then, all right, that's all well and good, but why didn't you tell us this earlier? Why do you change your battery story every time a new question is raised?'

'These things happened almost three months ago,' said Kabuo. 'I don't remember every detail.'

Alvin Hooks held his chin in his fingers. 'You're a hard man to trust, Mr. Miyamoto,' he sighed. 'You sit before us with no expression, keeping a poker face through – '

'Objection!' cut in Nels Gudmundsson, but Judge Lew Fielding was already sitting upright and looking sternly at Alvin. 'You know better than that, Mr. Hooks,' he said. 'Either ask questions that count for something or have a seat and be done with it. Shame on you,' he added.

Alvin Hooks crossed the courtroom one more time and sat down at the prosecutor's table. He picked up his pen and, revolving it in his fingers, looked out the window at the falling snow, which seemed to be slowing finally. 'I can't think of anything more,' he said. 'The witness is free to step down.'

Kabuo Miyamoto rose in the witness box so that the citizens in the gallery saw him fully – a Japanese man standing proudly before them, thick and strong through the torso. They noted his bearing and the strength in his chest; they saw the sinews in his throat. While they watched he turned his dark eyes to the snowfall and gazed at it for a long moment. The citizens in the gallery were reminded of photographs they had seen of Japanese soldiers. The man before them was noble in appearance, and the shadows played across the planes of his face in a way that made their angles harden; his aspect connoted dignity. And there was nothing akin to softness in him anywhere, no part of him that was vulnerable. He was, they decided, not like them at all, and the detached and aloof manner in which he watched the snowfall made this palpable and self-evident.

---

8 **admonition** [ˌædməˈnɪʃn]: warning to sb. about their behavior   26 **shame on you** = you should be ashamed   40 **aspect**: (here) appearance   **connote sth.** [-ˈ-]: suggest sth.   41 **akin to sth.**: similar to sth.   43 **aloof**: detached, not showing any interest in the situation you are in

Chapter 29

Alvin Hooks, in his final words to the court, characterized the accused man as a murderer in cold blood, one who had decided to kill another man and had executed his plan faithfully. He told the court that Kabuo Miyamoto had been driven by hatred and cold desperation; that after so many years of coveting his lost strawberry fields he had found himself, in early September, in a position to lose them for good. And so he'd gone to Ole Jurgensen and heard from Ole that the land was sold, and then he'd gone to Carl Heine and Carl had turned him away. He'd pondered this crisis during his hours at sea and come to the conclusion that unless he acted, his family's land – for from his point of view it *was* his family's land – would slip from his grasp forever. Like the man he was – a strong man of bold character, trained from an early age at the art of stick fighting; a man Sergeant Victor Maples had described for the court as not only capable of committing murder but willing to commit it as well – this strong, cold, unfeeling man decided to solve his problem. He decided to end the life of another man who stood between him and the land he coveted. He decided that if Carl Heine was dead, Ole would sell him the seven acres.

So it was that he trailed Carl to the fishing grounds at Ship Channel Bank. He followed him out, set his net above him, and watched while the fog concealed everything. Kabuo Miyamoto was a patient man and waited until the deepest part of the night to do what he had in mind. He knew that Carl was not far off, a hundred and fifty yards at best; he could hear his engine in the fog. He listened and then finally, at about one-thirty, he laid hard on his foghorn. In this way he attracted his victim.

Carl, Alvin Hooks explained, came out of the fog towing his net behind – he'd been nearly ready to pick salmon from it – to find the accused man, Kabuo Miyamoto, 'adrift' and 'in need of help'. It was here, he said, that the treachery of the defendant was surely most horrible – for he relied on the code among fishermen to assist one another in times of trouble and on the residue of friendship he knew

David Guterson: **Snow Falling on Cedars** 357

remained from the youth he and Carl had passed together. Carl, he must have said, I am sorry for what has come between us, but here on the water, adrift in the fog, I plead with you for your help. I beg you to tie up and help me, Carl. Please don't leave me like this.

Imagine, Alvin Hooks implored the jurors, leaning toward them with his hands outstretched like a man petitioning God – imagine this good man stopping to help his enemy in the middle of the night at sea. He moors his boat to his enemy's boat, and while he is busy making fast a line – you will note there is no sign, anywhere, of struggle, such was the treachery of the defendant over there – his enemy leaps aboard with a fishing gaff and strikes a blow to his head. And so this good man falls dead – or nearly dead, that is. He is unconscious and mortally wounded.

Let us imagine, too, said Alvin Hooks, the defendant rolling Carl Heine over a gunnel and the splash on the black night water. The sea closes over Carl Heine – it seeps into his pocket watch, stopping it at 1:47, recording the time of his death – and the defendant stands watching the place where it seals up, leaving no trace behind. But just under the surface the tidal current is working – stronger than the defendant had imagined it – and carries Carl into the folds of his own net, which still trails out behind. The buckle of his bib overalls catches in the webbing and Carl hangs there, under the sea, the evidence of Kabuo Miyamoto's crime waiting to be discovered. It is one of three things the defendant hasn't counted on – the body itself, the bloody fishing gaff, and the mooring line he'd left behind in his haste to leave this scene of murder.

Now he sits in this court before you, Alvin Hooks told the jurors. Here he is in a court of law with the evidence displayed and the testimony given, the facts all aired and the arguments made and the truth of the matter manifest. There was no uncertainty any more and the jurors were bound to do their duty to the people of Island County. 'This is not a happy occasion,' Alvin Hooks reminded them. 'We are talking about

2 **in cold blood**: kaltblütig   8 **turn sb. away**: (here) make sb. go away without granting them what they wanted from you   19 **trail sb./sth.**: follow sb./sth. by looking for signs that show you where they have been   36 **implore sb.** (fml): jdn. inständig bitten   37 **petition sb.**: make a formal request to sb. in authority
49 **seal up**: close tightly   52 **trail out behind sth.**: (here) be pulled along behind sth.   59 **air sth.**: (here) express sth. publicly

convicting a man of murder in the first degree. We're talking about *justice*, finally. We're talking about looking clearly at the defendant and seeing the truth self-evident in him and in the facts present in this case. Take a good look, ladies and gentlemen, at the defendant sitting over there. Look into his eyes, consider his face, and ask yourselves what your duty is as citizens of this community.'

Just as he had throughout the trial, Nels Gudmundsson rose with a geriatric awkwardness that was painful for the citizens in the gallery to observe. By now they had learned to be patient with him as he cleared his throat and wheezed into his handkerchief. They had learned to anticipate how he would hook his thumbs behind the tiny black catch buttons of his suspenders. The jurors had noted how his left eye floated and how the light winked against its dull, glassy surface as it orbited eccentrically in its socket. They watched him now as he gathered himself up and cleared his throat to speak.

In measured tones, as soberly as he could, Nels recited the facts as he understood them: Kabuo Miyamoto had gone to Ole Jurgensen to inquire about his land. Mr. Jurgensen had directed him to Carl Heine, and Kabuo had sought out Carl. They had spoken and Kabuo had come to believe that Carl was pondering the matter. And so, believing this, he waited. He waited and on the evening of September 15 a circumstance of fate, a coincidence, brought him through the fog at Ship Channel Bank to where Carl was stranded at sea. Kabuo had done what he could in these circumstances to assist the friend he had known since childhood, a boy he'd fished with years earlier. And finally, said Nels, they spoke of the land and resolved this matter between them. Then Kabuo Miyamoto went his way again and fished on into the dawn. And the next day he found himself arrested.

There was no evidence presented, Nels Gudmundsson told the jurors, to suggest that the accused man had planned a murder or that he'd gone to sea in search of blood. The state had not produced a shred of evidence to suggest premeditation. Not a single witness had been brought forward to testify about the defendant's state of mind in the days prior to Carl's death. No one had sat beside Kabuo at a tavern and listened to him rail against Carl Heine or announce his intent to kill him. There were no receipts from any sort of shop where a murder weapon had been newly purchased; there were no journal entries or overheard phone calls or late-night conversations. The state had not proved beyond a reasonable doubt that the crime the defendant had been charged with had in fact occurred. There was more than reasonable doubt, added Nels, but reasonable doubt was all that was needed. There was reasonable doubt, he emphasized, so the jury could not convict.

'The counsel for the state,' added Nels Gudmundsson, 'has proceeded on the assumption that you will be open, ladies and gentlemen, to an argument based on prejudice. He has asked you to look closely at the face of the defendant, presuming that because the accused man is of Japanese descent you will see an enemy there. After all, it is not so long since our country was at war with the Empire of the Rising Sun and its formidable, well-trained soldiers. You all remember the newsreels and war films. You all recall the horrors of those years; Mr. Hooks is counting on that. He is counting on you to act on passions best left to a war of ten years ago. He is counting on you to remember this war and to see Kabuo Miyamoto as somehow connected with it. And, ladies and gentlemen,' Nels Gudmundsson pleaded, 'let us recall that Kabuo Miyamoto *is* connected with it. He is a much-decorated first lieutenant of the United States Army who fought for his country – the United States – in the European theater. If you see in his face a lack of emotion, if you see in him a silent pride, it is the pride and hollowness of a veteran of war who has returned home to *this*. He has returned to find himself the victim of prejudice – make no mistake about it, this trial is about prejudice – in the country he fought to defend.

'Ladies and gentlemen,' Nels pressed on, 'perhaps there is such a thing as fate. Perhaps for inscrutable reasons God has looked down and allowed the accused man to come to this pass, where his very life lies in your hands. An accident of some kind befell Carl Heine at a moment that could not be less propitious or less fortunate for the accused. And yet it happened. It happened and Kabuo Miyamoto has been accused. And here he sits awaiting your verdict, in the hope that although fate

---

16 **measured** (adj): controlled 36 **receipt** [rɪˈsiːt]: piece of paper that shows that goods or services have been paid for 40–41 **reasonable doubt** (fml): begründeter Zweifel 43 **counsel for the state**: prosecutor 49 **newsreel**: short film of news that was shown in cinemas in the past

has acted against him, human beings will be reasonable. There are things in this universe that we cannot control, and then there are the things we can. Your task as you deliberate together on these proceedings is to ensure that you do nothing to yield to a universe in which things go awry by happen-stance. Let fate, coincidence, and accident conspire; human beings must act on *reason*. And so the shape of Kabuo Miyamoto's eyes, the country of his parents' birth – these things must not influence your decision. You must sentence him simply as an American, equal in the eyes of our legal system to every other American. This is what you've been called here to do. This is what you must do.

'I am an old man,' Nels Gudmundsson continued. 'I do not walk so well anymore, and one of my eyes is useless. I suffer from headaches and from arthritis in my knees. On top of all this I nearly froze to death last night, and today I am weary, having slept not a wink. And so, like you, I hope for warmth tonight and for an end to this storm we are enduring. I would wish for my life to continue pleasantly for many years to come. This final wish, I must admit to myself, is not something I can readily count on, for if I do not pass on in the next ten years I will certainly do so in the next twenty. My life is drawing to a close.

'Why do I say this?' Nels Gudmundsson asked, moving nearer to the jurors now and leaning toward them, too. 'I say this because as an older man I am prone to ponder matters in the light of death in a way that you are not. I am like a traveler descended from Mars who looks down in astonishment at what passes here. And what I see is the same human frailty passed from generation to generation. What I see is again and again the same sad human frailty. We hate one another; we are the victims of irrational fears. And there is nothing in the stream of human history to suggest we are going to change this. But – I digress, I confess that. I merely wish to point out that in the face of such a world you have only yourselves to rely on. You have only the decision you must make, each of you, alone. And will you contribute to the indifferent forces that ceaselessly conspire toward injustice? Or will you stand up against this endless tide and in the face of it be truly human? In God's name, in the name of humanity, do your duty as jurors. Find Kabuo Miyamoto innocent as charged and let him go home to his family. Return this man to his wife and children. Set him free, as you must.'

Judge Lew Fielding looked down from the bench with the tip of his left forefinger set against his nose and his chin propped against his thumb. As always he had the air of a weary man; he looked reluctantly awake. He appeared to be half-alert at best – his eyelids drooped, his mouth hung open. The judge had been uncomfortable throughout the morning, annoyed by the sensation that he had not performed well, had not conducted the proceedings adroitly. He was a man of high professional standards, a careful and deliberate, exacting judge who held himself to the letter of the law, however soporifically. Having never presided over a trial of murder in the first degree before, he felt himself in a precarious position: if the jury returned a guilty verdict the decision would be his alone as to whether the accused man should hang.

Judge Lew Fielding roused himself and, pulling at his robe, turned his gaze toward the jurors. 'This case,' he announced, 'now draws to a close, and it will be your duty in just a few moments to retire to the room reserved for you and deliberate together toward a verdict. Toward that end, ladies and gentlemen, the court charges you to take into account the following considerations.

'First of all, in order to find the defendant guilty you must be convinced of every element of the charge beyond a reasonable doubt. *Beyond a reasonable doubt*, understand. If a reasonable doubt exists in your minds, you cannot convict the accused man. If there is in your minds a reasonable uncertainty regarding the truth of the charge made here, you must find the defendant not guilty. This is a duty you are bound to by law. No matter how strongly you feel yourselves compelled to act in any other manner, you can convict only if you are certain it is correct to do so beyond a reasonable doubt.

---

3 **deliberate** [dɪ'lɪbəreɪt] (v): (here) have a discussion before making a decision 4 **go awry** [ə'raɪ]: go wrong 5 **conspire**: (here) seem to work together to make sth. bad happen 14 **sleep not a wink**: kein Auge zutun 25 **frailty** ['freɪlti]: weakness 28 **digress** [daɪ'grés]: abschweifen 31 **indifferent**: (here) uncaring 32 **ceaseless**: not stopping 34–35 **innocent as charged** (fml): unschuldig im Sinne der Anklage 39 **reluctant** [rɪ'lʌktənt]: widerwillig 40 **alert**: able to think quickly **droop**: herabhängen 43 **conduct sth.**: (here) be in charge of sth. **adroit** [ə'drɔɪt]: skilful and clever, esp. in dealing with people 51 **retire**: sich zurückziehen

'Second,' said the judge, 'you must keep in mind the specificity of the charge and address that charge exclusively. You have only to determine one thing here: whether or not the defendant is guilty of murder in the first degree, and nothing else. If you determine that he is guilty of something else – of hatred, of assault, of manslaughter, of murder in self-defense, of coldness, of passion, of second-degree murder – none of that will be relevant. The question is whether the man brought before you is guilty of first-degree murder. And *first-degree* murder, ladies and gentlemen, implies a question of *planned intent*. It is a charge that suggests a state of mind in which the guilty party *premeditates a murder in cold blood*. That he thinks about it ahead of time and makes a conscious decision. And here,' said the judge, 'is a difficult matter for jurors in cases of this sort. For premeditation is a condition of the mind and cannot be seen directly. Premeditation must be inferred from the evidence – it must be seen in the acts and words of the human beings who have testified before you, in their conduct and conversation, and in the evidence brought to your attention. In order to find the defendant guilty, you must find that he *planned and intended* to commit the acts for which he has been charged. That he premeditated murder, understand. That he went forth in search of his victim with the conscious intent of committing a premeditated murder. That it did not happen in the heat of the moment or as the accidental result of escalating violence but was rather an act planned and executed by a man with murder on his mind. So once again the court charges you to consider only first-degree murder and absolutely nothing else. You must be convinced beyond a reasonable doubt of one thing and one thing exclusively: that the defendant in this case is guilty of murder in the first degree, premeditated.

'You were selected as jurors in this case,' Judge Lew Fielding continued, 'in the belief that each of you could, without fear, favor, prejudice, or sympathy, in sound judgment and clear conscience, render a just verdict on evidence presented in conformity with these instructions. The very object of our jury system is to secure a verdict by comparison of views and discussion among jurors – provided this can be done reasonably and in a way consistent with the conscientious convictions of each. Each juror should listen, with a disposition to be convinced, to the opinions and arguments of the other jurors. It is not intended under the law that a juror should go into the jury room with a fixed determination that the verdict shall represent his opinion of the case at that moment. Nor is it intended that he should close his ears to the discussions and arguments of his fellow jurors, who are assumed to be equally honest and intelligent. You must, in short, *listen* to one another. Stay objective, be reasonable.'

The judge paused and let his words sink in. He let his eyes meet the eyes of each juror, holding the gaze, momentarily, of each. 'Ladies and gentlemen,' he sighed. 'Since these are criminal proceedings, understand, your verdict – whether guilty or not so – must be a unanimous one. There is no call for haste or for anyone to feel that they are holding up the rest of us as you deliberate. The court thanks you in advance for having served in this trial. The power has gone out and you have passed difficult nights at the Amity Harbor Hotel. It has not been easy for you to concentrate on these proceedings while you are worried about the conditions of your homes and the welfare of your families and loved ones. The storm,' said the judge, 'is beyond our control, but the outcome of this trial is not. The outcome of this trial is up to you now. You may adjourn and begin your deliberations.'

---

30 **sound** (adj): (here) sensible, reliable   **render sth.**: (here) present sth.
35 **disposition**: (hier) Bereitschaft   43 **let sth. sink in**: wait until sth. has been fully understood or realized   46 **unanimous** [ju'nænıməs]: einstimmig

Chapter 30

At three o'clock in the afternoon the jurors in the trial of Kabuo Miyamoto filed out of the courtroom. Two of the reporters tipped their chairs back precariously and sat with their hands clasped behind their heads, speaking casually to one another. Abel Martinson handcuffed the accused man, then allowed his wife to speak to him once before urging his prisoner toward the basement. 'You're going to be free,' she said to Kabuo. 'They'll do the right thing – you'll see.'

'I don't know,' her husband replied. 'But either way, I love you, Hatsue. Tell the kids I love them, too.'

Nels Gudmundsson gathered his papers together and slid them into his briefcase. Ed Soames, in a generous mood, kept the courtroom open to the public. He understood that the citizens in the gallery had no warm place to go. Many of them sat languidly along the benches or milled in the aisles discussing the trial in hushed and speculative tones. Ed stood with his hands behind his back beside the door to Judge Fielding's chambers in the obsequious pose of a royal footman, watching everything impassively. Occasionally he checked his watch.

In the gallery Ishmael Chambers mulled over his notes, looking up every now and again to take in Hatsue Miyamoto. Listening to her testify that morning he'd been keenly aware of his private knowledge of this woman: he'd understood what each expression suggested, what each pause signified. What he wanted, he realized now, was to drink in the smell of her and to feel her hair in his hands. It was all the more acute for not having her and wanting, like the wish he had to be whole again and to live a different life.

Philip Milholland's notes were in Ishmael's front left pants pocket, and it was just a matter of standing up, crossing over to Ed Soames, and asking to see Judge Fielding. Then bringing the notes out and unfolding them, and watching the look on Soames's face, then taking them back from Soames again and pushing his way into the judge's chambers. Then Lew Fielding blinking down through his glasses, pulling the candelabra on his desk a little closer – the flickering taper dancing left and right – and at last the judge peering over his glasses at him as the weight of Philip Milholland's notes began to press against his mind. *The freighter began its dogleg at 1:42. Carl Heine's pocket watch stopped at 1:47.* It spoke for itself.

What was it Nels Gudmundsson had said in closing? 'The counsel for the state has proceeded on the assumption that you will be open, ladies and gentlemen, to an argument based on prejudice ... He is counting on you to act on passions best left to a war of ten years ago.' But ten years was not really such a long time at all, and how was he to leave his passion behind when it went on living its own independent life, as tangible as the phantom limb he'd refused for so long to have denervated? As with the limb, so with Hatsue. Hatsue had been taken from his life by history, because history was whimsical and immune to private yearnings. And then there was his mother with her faith in a God who stood at the wayside indifferently while Eric Bledsoe bled to death in the surf, and then there was that boy on the deck of the hospital ship with the blood soaking his groin.

He looked at Hatsue again where she stood in the midst of a small group of Japanese islanders who whispered softly to one another and peered at their watches and waited. He examined her knife-pleated skirt, the blouse she wore with long darts through the shoulders, her hair bound tightly to the back of her head, the plain hat held in her hand. The hand itself, loose and graceful, and the way her ankles fit into her shoes, and the straightness of her back and her refined, true posture that had been the thing to move him in the beginning, back when he was just a child. And the taste of salt on her lips that time when for a second he had touched them with his own boy's lips, clinging to his glass-bottomed box. And then all the times he had touched her body and the fragrance of all that cedar ...

---

13 **languid**: (here) without energy or effort   16 **obsequious** (fml) [əb'siːkwiəs]: trying too hard to please sb., esp. sb. who is important or has authority   **footman**: (hier) Lakai, Diener   18 **mull over sth.**: spend time thinking carefully about sth.
31 **candelabra** [ˌkændə'lɑːbrə]: Kerzenleuchter   32 **taper**: long thin candle
42 **tangible** ['tændʒəbl]: that can be clearly seen to exist   45 **whimsical** ['--]: launisch   56 **refined**: elegant

He got up to leave, and as he did so the courtroom lights flickered on. A mute kind of cheer went up from the gallery, an embarrassed, cautious island cheer; one of the reporters raised his fists into the air, Ed Soames nodded and smiled. The gray, sullen hue that had hung over everything was replaced by a light that seemed brilliant by comparison to what had gone before. 'Electricity,' Nels Gudmundsson said to Ishmael. 'Never knew I'd miss it so much.'

'Go home and get some sleep,' answered Ishmael. 'Turn your heater up.'

Nels snapped the clasps on his briefcase, turned it upright, and set it on the table. 'By the way,' he said suddenly. 'I ever tell you how much I liked your father? Arthur was one admirable man.'

'Yes,' said Ishmael. 'He was.'

Nels pulled at the skin of his throat, then took his briefcase in his hand. 'Well,' he said, with his good eye on Ishmael, the other wandering crazily. 'Regards to your mother, she's a wonderful woman. Let's pray for the right verdict in the meantime.'

'Yes,' said Ishmael. 'Okay.'

Ed Soames announced that the courtroom would remain open until such time as a verdict was reached or until six P.M., whichever came first. At six he would let the gathered court know about the current status of things.

In the cloakroom Ishmael found himself beside Hisao Imada as they both struggled into their overcoats. 'Many thanks for giving to us a help,' Hisao greeted him. 'It make our day much better than walking. We have our many thanks to you.'

They went out into the hallway, where Hatsue waited against the wall, her hands deep in her coat pockets. 'Do you need a ride?' asked Ishmael. 'I'm going out your way again. To my mother's house. I can take you.'

'No,' said Hisao. 'Thank you much. We have made for us a ride.'

Ishmael stood there buttoning his coat with the fingers of his one hand. He buttoned three buttons, starting at the top, and then he slipped his hand into his pants pocket and let it rest against Philip Milholland's notes.

'My husband's trial is unfair,' said Hatsue. 'You ought to put that in your father's newspaper, Ishmael, right across the front page. You should use his newspaper to tell the truth, you know. Let the whole island see it isn't right. It's just because we're Japanese.'

'It isn't my father's newspaper,' answered Ishmael. 'It's mine, Hatsue. I run it.' He brought his hand out and with some awkwardness slipped another button into place. 'I'll be at my mother's,' he told her. 'If you want to come speak to me about this there, that's where you can find me.'

Outside he found that the snow had stopped – only a few scattered flakes fell. A hard winter sunlight seeped through the clouds, and the north wind blew cold and fast. It seemed colder now than it had been that morning; the air burned in his nostrils. The wind and the snow had scoured everything clean; there was the sound of snow crunching under Ishmael's feet, the whine of the wind, and nothing else. The eye of the storm, he knew, had passed; the worst of it was behind them. And yet there was still a blind chaos to the world – cars turned front first to the curbs, abandoned where they had skidded unpredictably; on Harbor Street a white fir fallen against the snow, its branches snapped off at splintering angles, some of them piercing the ground. He walked on and found two cedars across the road, and beyond that the town docks were mostly swamped and under water. The outermost pilings had broken loose, the wind had shoved against the outside piers, and two dozen boats had piled up against one another and finally up onto the sunken piers, where they listed against their mooring ropes.

The white fir's root wad had pulled out of the ground and stood now like a wall more than twenty feet high with a tuft of snow-laden ferns and ivy sprouting over the top of it. Whitecaps roiled among the capsized boats and caused them and the docks to surge and roll, and the tops of the cabins and drum reels and gunnels were loaded down with snow. Occasionally sea foam broke across the boats and water washed through their cockpits. The tide and the wind were pushing in hard now, and the current funneled through the mouth of the harbor; the green boughs and branches of the fallen trees lay scattered across the clean snow.

---

4 **sullen**: (here) dark and unpleasant 52 **curb** [kɜːrb]: Bordsteinkante 53 **snap sth. off**: break sth. off 54 **splinter** (v): zersplittern 59 **list against sth.**: (of a ship) lean to one side against sth. 62 **roil**: (of water) strudeln **capsize** ['kæpsaɪz]: (of a boat) turn over in the water 63 **surge** (v) [sɜːrdʒ]: move with force in a particular direction 67 **funnel through sth.**: move through a narrow space

It occurred to Ishmael for the first time in his life that such destruction could be beautiful.

The reckless water, the frenzied wind, the snow, the downed trees, the boats dashed against their sunken docks – it was harsh and beautiful and disorderly. He was reminded for a moment of Tarawa atoll and its seawall and the palms that lay in rows on their side, knocked down by the compression from the naval guns. It was something he remembered too often. He felt inside not only an aversion to it but an attraction to it as well. He did not want to remember and he wanted to remember. It was not something he could explain.

He stood there looking at the destruction of the harbor and knew he had something inviolable that other men had no inkling of and at the same time he had nothing. For twelve years, he knew, he had waited. He had waited without knowing he was waiting at all, and the waiting had turned into something deeper. He'd been waiting for twelve long years.

The truth now lay in Ishmael's own pocket and he did not know what to do with it. He did not know how to conduct himself and the recklessness he felt about everything was as foreign to him as the sea foam breaking over the snowy boats and over the pilings of the Amity Harbor docks, now swamped and under water. There was no answer in any of it – not in the boats lying on their sides, not in the white fir defeated by the snow or in the downed branches of the cedars. What he felt was the chilly recklessness that had come to waylay his heart.

It was a boat builder who lived out on Woodhouse Cove Road – a gray-bearded man named Alexander Van Ness – who was primarily responsible for holding up a verdict in the trial of Kabuo Miyamoto. For three hours – until six o'clock – he persisted in the same inexorable vein: that Judge Fielding's admonitions should be heeded with the utmost seriousness and that reasonable doubt existed. The twelve jurors had argued over the meaning of the word *doubt*, then over the meaning of the term *reasonable*, then over both put together. 'Well,' Alexander Van Ness had concluded, 'I guess it comes down to a feeling, doesn't it? If I feel uncertain, if I feel that I doubt, that's all that matters, right?'

It had seemed to the others that he would not budge, and they had prepared themselves, by five forty-five, for another long night at the

Amity Harbor Hotel and for the necessity of taking the matter up with Alexander Van Ness at eight o'clock the next morning.

'Now look here,' Harold Jensen argued desperately. 'Nobody ain't ever sure about nothing. It's *un*reasonable to be so dog-headed stubborn. What's reasonable comes out of the rest of us, right here. You're what's unreasonable, Alex.'

'I can see what you're driving at,' Roger Porter added. 'I know what you're trying to say, Alex, and I've thought that way about it myself. But look here and think about the straight-off evidence. That mooring line come off his boat. That blood was on his fishing gaff. Mostly he lied about replacing his batt'ry, things like that, it was *fishy*. He just didn't show me nothin'.'

'Me neither,' put in Edith Twardzik. 'Didn't show me a thing, either. It was just suspicious how he sat there like that and said one thing about it to the sheriff one time and then later changed his melody. A person can't go changing his tune 'thout the rest of us thinking on it, Mr. Van Ness – don't you believe that man's a liar?'

Alex Van Ness agreed amiably; the defendant had indeed lied. But that made him a liar, not a murderer. He wasn't accused of lying.

'Now look again,' said Harold Jensen. 'What do you figure drives a man to lie? You think a man's got to go and lie when he ain't done nothin' worth lying about? A lie's a cover-up every time, it's something a man says when he don't want the truth out. The lies that man's been telling about this, they tell us he's got to be hiding something, don't you agree with that?'

'All right,' answered Alexander Van Ness. 'Then the question is, what's he hiding? Is he necessarily hiding the fact he's a murderer? Does that follow for sure and nothing else? I'm telling you I have my doubts, and that's all I'm trying to tell you. Not that you're wrong, just that I have my doubts.'

---

3 **frenzied** (adj): violent, out of control   8 **aversion** [əˈvɜːrɜn]: strong feeling of not liking sb./sth.   12 **inviolable** [ɪnˈvaɪələbl] (fml): unable to be hurt or damaged   23 **waylay sb.**: jdm. auflauern   28 **heed sb./sth.** (fml): pay careful attention to sb./sth.   **utmost** (adj): greatest   46 **fishy** (infml): suspicious   57 **cover-up**: action that is taken to hide a mistake or illegal activity from the public

'Now listen to this,' snapped Edith Twardzik. 'Supposing a man's got his gun to your son's head and 'nuther one at your wife. He tells you to take yourself exactly one minute and decide whether he ought to shoot your son or your wife, which should he shoot, and if you don't decide, he'll shoot them both. 'Course you're going to have some doubts no matter which way you decide. There's always something to fret about. But meanwhile, while you're fretting, the man's getting ready to pull both triggers, and that's all there is to it, all right? You aren't ever going to get past your doubt so you have to face it head-on.'

'It's a good example,' answered Alex Van Ness. 'But I'm not really in that situation.'

'Well, try looking at it another way, then,' said Burke Latham, a schooner deckhand. 'A big old comet or a chunk of the moon could come crashing down through the roof just now and fall on top of your head. So maybe you'd better move yourself case such a thing might happen. Maybe you'd better have your doubts 'bout whether your chair is safe. You can doubt everything, Mr. Van Ness. Your doubt ain't reasonable.'

'It'd be unreasonable for me to move to another chair,' Alex Van Ness pointed out. 'I'd run the same risk anywhere in the room – same risk you run from your seat, Burke. It's not worth worrying about.'

'We're not talking about the evidence anymore,' Harlan McQueen told them. 'All these hypothetical examples aren't getting us anywhere. How're we going to convince him what's reasonable without talking about the facts presented by the prosecutor, step by step, each one? Now, look here, Mr. Van Ness, don't you think that mooring line has to tell you something?'

'I think it does,' said Alex Van Ness. 'It tells me that Kabuo Miyamoto was probably on board Carl Heine's boat. I don't have much doubt about that.'

'That's one thing,' noted Edith Twardzik. 'That's something, anyway.'

'That fishing gaff,' said Harlan McQueen. 'It had a man's blood on it, Carl Heine's blood type. Can that slip past your doubt?'

'I don't much doubt it was Carl's blood,' Alex Van Ness agreed. 'But chances are it came from his hand. I think there's a chance of that.'

'There's a chance of everything. But you add a chance from here and a chance from there, too many things get to being a chance, they can't all be that way. The world ain't made a coincidences only. If it looks like a dog and walks like a dog,' Burke Latham asserted, 'then most prob'ly it is a dog, that's all there's going to be to it.'

'Are we talking about dogs now?' asked Alex Van Ness. 'How did we get on to dogs?'

'Well, what about this?' said Harlan McQueen. 'The defendant heard about Carl's body being found, but did he go to the sheriff and tell him how the night before he'd seen Carl out fishing? Even after they arrested him, he just kept saying he didn't even know a single thing about it. Then, later, he changed his story, came up with this battery explanation. Then he even altered that, said he put in a spare battery, but only on cross-examination. At this point it's his story against the prosecution's, and I'm finding him a little hard to believe.'

'I don't believe anything about him, either,' Ruth Parkinson said angrily. 'Let's get this done and over with, Mr. Van Ness. Stop being so unreasonable.'

Alex Van Ness rubbed his chin and sighed. 'It's not that I can't be convinced,' he said. 'I'm not so stubborn I can't be made to see the light. There's eleven of you and one of me. I'm all ears and I'll listen to anything. But I won't be in such a hurry as to go in there while I still have what I think are reasonable doubts and condemn the defendant to the hangman's rope or fifty years in prison. You ought to sit back and relax, Mrs. Parkinson. We can't hurry this.'

'Been here almost three hours,' said Burke Latham. 'You saying there's a way to move slower?'

'The mooring line and the fishing gaff,' Harlan McQueen repeated. 'Are you with us on those things, Mr. Van Ness? Can we push forward from there?'

'The mooring line, okay, I'll give you that. The fishing gaff's a maybe, but assume I'll go with you. Where do you take me from there?'

'The different stories he told. Prosecutor really cornered him on having two batteries on board. If he'd really loaned one to Carl Heine, there should have only been one.'

---

2 **'nuther** = another   13 **chunk**: thick solid piece that has been cut or broken off sth.   32 **slip past sth.**: (hier) etwas überwinden   37 **made a** = made of
54 **see the light** (fig): finally understand or accept sth., esp. sth. obvious
67 **corner sb.**: jdn. in die Enge treiben

'He said he replaced it. He explained that well enough. He – '

'He added it in at the last minute,' cut in McQueen. 'Made it up only when he was cornered, didn't he? He had his story pretty well lined up, but he left that detail out.'

'True,' said Alexander Van Ness. 'There should have only been one battery. But let's suppose he did board Carl's boat – maybe it was to talk about the land business, maybe Carl attacked him, maybe it was self-defense or manslaughter, an argument that got out of hand – how do we know this was murder in the first degree, planned out ahead of time? All right, it could be the defendant's guilty of something, but maybe not what he's charged with. How do we know he boarded Carl's boat with the intention of killing him?'

'You heard what all them fishermen said,' Roger Porter answered. 'No one ever boards a boat at sea except in an emergency. He wouldn't have come aboard just to talk, you see. Fishermen don't do things that way.'

'If they only board in an emergency,' said Alex, 'then the battery story makes good sense to me. A dead battery – that's an emergency. It kind of shores up his story.'

'Oh, come on,' said Edith Twardzik. 'Harlan's right about the battery story. Miyamoto didn't anytime loan one to Carl Heine, otherwise he'd only a had one himself. That battery story just won't wash.'

'It was a sucker's ruse,' Burke Latham explained. 'Just like the prosecutor said. Miyamoto pretended he was dead in the water, drifted right down on top of Carl and took advantage of him. That's exactly what happened.'

'Wouldn't put it past him,' said Roger Porter. 'The man looks damn sly to me.'

'That sucker's ruse story,' said Alex Van Ness. 'To me that's just a stretch too far. Drifting down out of the fog like that and exactly into the very man you've got it in your mind to kill. Here it is the middle of the night, fog as thick as pea soup, thicker, and you're expecting you'll just neatly drift in and find the boat you're looking for? That, to me, is a stretch.'

At six o'clock Ed Soames made the announcement: the jurors had adjourned for the night. No verdict had been reached thus far. The courthouse was going to be closed, he added. Everybody should go on home and get a good night's rest, turn up their electric heaters. They could return at nine o'clock in the morning if they wished to know where matters stood.

The jurors ate dinner at the Amity Harbor Hotel and talked of other matters. Alexander Van Ness ate meticulously, wiping his hands on his napkin often and smiling at the others, saying nothing.

---

3 **line sth. up**: (here) arrange sth., esp. a testimony, so that it matches with sth. else, e.g. evidence or sb. else's testimony   18 **shore sth. up** (fig): support sth., esp. sth. weak or likely to fail   21 **sth. won't wash** (AE): sb.'s explanation, excuse, etc., is not valid or not acceptable   26 (**I) wouldn't put it past sb.** (infml) = I think sb. is capable of doing sth. wrong or illegal   28–29 **a stretch too far**: (here) too implausible and therefore not to be trusted

Chapter 31

The power was not yet on along South Beach, and as Ishmael Chambers drove through the snow he glanced into the candlelit windows of the homes he'd known since childhood. The Englunds, Gunnar Torval, Verda Carmichael, Arnold Kruger, the Hansens, the Syvertsens, Bob Timmons, the Crows, Dale Papineau, Virginia Gatewood and the Etheringtons from Seattle who seven years ago had moved to the island for good; he supposed they regretted it now. Foot-long icicles hung from their eaves and the snow lay in drifts against the north side of their house: they should have gone on being summer people. The Crows had both passed away years before, and now their son Nicholas inhabited the place, steadfastly carrying on the border war with Bob Timmons, who had phlebitis in his legs these days and walked stiffly to clear the branches from where they fell among his cedar trees. Nothing had changed and everything had changed. Dale Papineau still drank too much and had no money to speak of. Verda Carmichael was gone.

Ishmael found his mother at her kitchen table once again, reading the last chapter of *Sense and Sensibility* by lantern light and drinking tea with sugar and lemon concentrate. She wore a coat and boots in the house, and her face looked bland and old with no mascara, for which she asked Ishmael's forgiveness. 'I'm getting to be so old,' she admitted. 'There just isn't any way around it.' Then just as before she gave him soup to eat, and he told her how the jurors had not reached a verdict and how the lights were on once more in town and how the docks had been destroyed by storm winds. His mother railed against the possibility that the jurors would be driven by hatred and prejudice; she hoped that in such an eventuality Ishmael would write an editorial. His newspaper, she said, had a responsibility at such times; his father before him had known that. Ishmael nodded and agreed with her; he would write a strong editorial. Then he suggested they pass the night at his apartment with its electric heat and hot water. His mother shook her head and claimed she was content to stick it out at South Beach; they could go to

Amity Harbor in the morning if they wanted. So Ishmael loaded the cookstove with firewood and hung his coat in the hall closet. Philip Milholland's notes stayed in his pants pocket.

At eight o'clock the power came on again, and he flipped the furnace switch. He roamed through the house turning off lights and turning up the baseboard heaters. The pipes, he knew, would begin to thaw now, and he decided to sit and listen to the house while it came back to itself. He made tea and took it into his father's old study, a room with a view of the water in daylight and of his father's much-loved rhododendrons. And he sat in silence at his father's desk, in his father's chair, with a single light on. He waited while the furnace gradually warmed the house, and then Ishmael heard water moving in the pipes and the drip from the taps he'd left open. He waited awhile longer before moving through the house again to see that the pressure was strong everywhere, and then he shut down the taps. Everything seemed to have held up.

At nine o'clock his mother kissed his cheek and said she was going to bed. Ishmael returned to his tea in the study, where he pondered his father's books. His father had been, like his mother, a reader, though his idea of good literature differed from hers; he was far less given to novels, in the main, though he read his fair share of them, too. His books stood neatly along the glassed-in shelves of four vaultlike oak bookcases: the collected Shakespeare, Jefferson's essays, Thoreau, Paine, Rousseau, Crèvecoeur, Locke, Emerson, Hawthorne, Melville, Twain, Dickens, Tolstoy. Henri Bergson, William James, Darwin, Buffon, Lyell, Charles Lamb, Sir Francis Bacon, Lord Chesterton. Swift, Pope, Defoe, Stevenson, Saint Augustine, Aristotle, Virgil, Plutarch. Plato, Sophocles, Homer, Dryden, Coleridge, Shelley, Shaw. *A History of Washington State, A History of the Olympic Peninsula, A History of Island County, Gardens and Gardening, Scientific Agriculture, The Care and Cultivation of Fruit Trees and Ornamental Shrubs.*

7 **icicle** ['aɪsɪkl]: Eiszapfen   8 **eaves** (pl): lower edges of a roof that stick out over the walls of a house   11 **steadfast**: not changing your attitudes or aims
12 **phlebitis** [flə'baɪtɪs]: Venenentzündung   15 **no ... to speak of**: such a small amount that it is not worth mentioning   26 **eventuality** (fml) [ɪˌventʃu'æləti]: sth. that may possibly happen, esp. sth. unpleasant   46 **hold up** [ˌ- '-]: keep working effectively   51 **in the main** (AE): used to say that a statement is true most of the time   59 **peninsula** [pə'nɪnsələ]: Halbinsel

His father had loved his fruit trees. He'd tended quietly to his apples and rhododendrons, his chinaberries and mulberry hedges, his rows of vegetables and flowers. He could be found on fall afternoons with a rake in hand, or a splitting maul perhaps. One year he'd painted the eaves and dormers, the clapboards and the deep-shaded summer porch, taking his time, finding pleasure. He never hurried. He did not appear to wish for something else. There were his evenings reading and dozing by the fire or working slowly at his desk. In his study lay two large Karastan rugs, woven in a mountain village in Turkey, the gift of a soldier he'd fought beside at Belleau Wood long ago. Each had knotted, carefully combed tassels, fleur-de-lis borders, ornate medallion designs, and minute scalloping amid a motif of connected eight-spoked wheels, all in rust and fire orange. The desk, too, was pleasing – his father had built it himself. It was a vast expanse of cherry wood the size of an English baron's dining table; smoked glass covered most of its surface. Ishmael recollected his father at work here, his neatly arranged manila folders spread out before him, his yellow legal pad laid off to his right, an array of heavily scrawled index cards, onionskin typing paper in both goldenrod and white, a thick dictionary on a stand, a thicker thesaurus, and a heavy black Underwood typewriter, the desk lamp pulled down low over the keys and his father blinking through his bifocals, slow and expressionless, absorbed in his words, afloat in that pool of soft light. He'd had a cordial, lonely, persevering face, and Ishmael turned now to stare into it, for there was a portrait of Arthur hung on the wall just to the left of a bookcase. There he sat in his high, stiff collar, no more than twenty or twenty-one, a young logger on his day off from the woods. Ishmael knew his father had come to logging with a romantic's sense of grandeur, viewing it at first as grandly heroic, in keeping with the spirit of manifest destiny. He'd come to outgrow this with the passing of time, and then he passed his evenings reading; sleep had seized him like a dark claw while other boys drank their hearts out. He'd educated himself in his spare time, had saved his money with the earnestness of a Horatio Alger, started his own newspaper, gone to war, come home, pressed on, moved forward. He'd built his own house, hauling river stone, milling lumber, a man prominently and wondrously strong far into his forties. He did not mind writing garden club features, school board reports, horse show notices, golden anniversary announcements – he pruned them as carefully as he pruned his hedges, rounding them toward perfection. He'd been, at best, an anguished editorialist; he was incapable of fully indulging himself when it came to condemnation. For he'd recognized limits and the grayness of the world, which is what endeared him to island life, limited as it was by surrounding waters, which imposed upon islanders certain duties and conditions foreign to mainlanders. An enemy on an island is an enemy forever, he'd been fond of reminding his son. There was no blending into an anonymous background, no neighboring society to shift toward. Islanders were required, by the very nature of their landscape, to watch their step moment by moment. No one trod easily upon the emotions of another where the sea licked everywhere against an endless shoreline. And this was excellent and poor at the same time – excellent because it meant most people took care, poor because it meant an inbreeding of the spirit, too much held in, regret and silent brooding, a world whose inhabitants walked in trepidation, in fear of opening up. Considered and considerate, formal at every turn, they were shut out and shut off from the deep interplay of their minds. They could not speak freely because they were cornered: everywhere they turned there was water and more water, a limitless

2 **chinaberry**: originally Asian tree that is widely cultivated in the USA
5 **clapboard**: Schindel   11 **tassel**: Quaste, Troddel   **fleur-de-lis** [,flɜ:r də 'li:]: Schwertlilie (königl. Wappen Frankreichs)   **ornate** [ɔ:r'neɪt]: covered with a lot of decoration   12 **minute** (adj) [maɪ'nu:t]: very detailed and carefully arranged   **scalloping**: bogenförmige Verzierung   **eight-spoked**: mit acht Speichen   13 **rust**: reddish-brown color   15 **smoked glass**: Rauchglass   17–18 **array of sth.** [-'-]: collection of sth., esp. one that is large and impressive   18 **scrawl sth.**: write on sth. quickly in an untidy way   **index card**: Karteikarte   **onionskin** (adj): very thin writing paper   21 **bifocals** (pl) [,baɪ'foʊklz]: Zweistärkenbrille   22 **afloat**: floating   28 **in keeping with sth.**: in agreement with sth.   29 **manifest destiny**: phrase much used in 19th-century America, meaning the right of the US to own and occupy land across the continent   **outgrow sth.** [-'-]: stop doing sth. or lose interest in sth. as you become older   32–33 **Horatio Alger** (1834–99): US author of more than 100 books for boys, most of which were about poor boys who became rich and successful through hard work and good behavior   41–42 **endear sb. to sth.**: (here) make sb. like sth. very much   45 **blend into sth.**: (here) adapt to sth. so well that you can no longer be seen as an individual   51 **inbreeding** ['- - -]: Inzucht, (hier: fig.) (unnatürlicher) Rückzug auf sich selbst   53 **trepidation**: great worry or fear that sth. unpleasant may happen   **considerate**: thoughtful   54 **interplay**: interaction

expanse of it in which to drown. They held their breath and walked with care, and this made them who they were inside, constricted and small, good neighbors.

Arthur confessed to not liking them and at the same time loving them deeply. Was such a thing even possible? He hoped for the best from his fellow islanders, he claimed, and trusted God to guide their hearts, though he knew them to be vulnerable to hate.

Ishmael understood, sitting in his father's place, how he'd arrived at the same view of things. He was, it occurred to him, his father's son, and now he brooded in the same spindle-back Windsor chair his father had brooded in.

Ishmael remembered following his father one afternoon as he roamed the grounds of the Strawberry Festival in search of photographs and winning quotes. By three o'clock the sun had swung down over the west goalposts of the high school football field. The tug-of-war, sack hop, and three-legged races were over, and a languidness had inevitably crept over things, so that here and there grown men slept in the grass with newspapers over their faces. Many of the picnickers had eaten to excess and now sat heavy and dulled in the sun, which poured over the scene a clear, clean radiance, a piercing island summer light. The odor of baked salmon hung stale in the air, slightly bitter and slightly acrid from the long smoldering smoke of burning alder leaves, and lay like an invisible pall over the exhausted revelers.

Ishmael walked beside his father past the concession booths where shortcake, bagged popcorn, and caramel apples were sold and down toward the displays of strawberries. And then his father stopped to bring his camera to his eye and photograph the fruit that was the point of it all, and at the same time, peering through his lens, he held up his end of a conversation: 'Mr. Fukida,' he'd called out. 'A banner year for strawberries. How are prices holding up?'

Mr. Fukida, a leathery old farmer in overalls and a billed cap, answered in English that was too precise, too perfect. 'Prices are very good,' he said. 'In fact, excellent, berries selling very well. Mrs. Chambers just now purchased sixteen crates.'

'I see,' said Arthur. 'Sixteen crates. No doubt I'll be asked to help with them, then. Can I trouble you, Mr. Fukida, to move a little to your left? This should make an excellent photograph, you and your beautifully displayed strawberries.'

Mr. Fukida, Ishmael recalled, seemed to have no eyes. His lids had sealed themselves nearly together; occasionally a thin tear trailed out. Working its way along the cracks in his face, it would eventually end as a shine against his cheekbones, which were prominent high points in an otherwise gaunt set of features. He smelled of ginger and onion root tonic and, when he smiled – teeth large as old beach stones – of powdered garlic, too.

'Mrs. Chambers will put up some excellent jam,' Arthur had said, without pride. He shook his head now, admiring with genuine avidity the spread of fruit before him; strawberries arranged in turned-up cedar flats, heavy and pungent, deeply crimson and firm, a regal abundance of them. 'Fit for a queen,' Arthur had said. 'My hat is off to you.'

'Good soil. Good rain. Sunshine. Six children.'

'There must be a secret you're not mentioning. I've tried growing strawberries myself, a few times, and with most of the same ingredients.'

'More children,' said Mr. Fukida, and grinned so that his gold crowns glinted in the sun. 'More children, yes, that is the secret. That is important, Mr. Chambers.'

'Well, we've tried,' said Arthur. 'We've tried hard, Lord knows. But Ishmael here, my boy Ishmael here – he's a match, easily, for two lads, for three! We have high hopes for him.'

'Oh, yes,' Mr. Fukida had said. 'We wish good fortune for him, too. We believe his heart is strong, like his father's. Your son is very good boy.'

---

2 **constricted** (adj): eingeengt, beschränkt   14 **winning quotes**: (hier) lohnende Zitate   19 **dull sb.**: (here) cause sb. to be sleepy or less lively   21 **acrid** ['ækrɪd]: having a strong, bitter smell or taste that is unpleasant   23 **pall**: thick dark cloud of sth.   24 **concession booth**: (hier) Ver-kaufsstand   29 **banner year**: year in which sth. is esp. successful   43 **gaunt** [gɔːnt]: hager   43–44 **onion root tonic**: onion juice that is rubbed into the skin to make your hair grow   46 **put sth. up**: (hier) etwas einkochen   47 **avidity**: enthusiasm   49 **regal** ['riːgl]: (hier) prächtig   **abundance** [-'--]: more than enough of sth.   50 **my hat is off to you**: used to say that you admire sb. very much for sth. they have done   59 **match for sb.**: person who is equal to sb. else in strength, skill, intelligence, etc.

Ishmael went up the worn-out stairs to the room he'd slept in for so many years and dug the book on boatmanship out of its box in the closet. There was the envelope with Kenny Yamashita's return address, the upside-down stamp, her smooth handwriting. There was the letter written on rice paper, fast fading after all these years, as brittle as old leaves in winter. With his one hand it would be possible in seconds to squeeze Hatsue's letter into motes of dust and obliterate its message forever. '*I don't love you, Ishmael. ... When we met that last time in the cedar tree and I felt your body move against mine, I knew with certainty that everything was wrong. I knew we could never be right together ...*'

He read the letter a second time, gravitating now toward its final words: '*I wish you the very best, Ishmael. Your heart is large and you are gentle and kind, and I know you will do great things in this world, but now I must say good-bye to you. I am going to move on with my life as best I can, and I hope you will too.*'

But the war, his arm, the course of things – it had all made his heart much smaller. He had not moved on at all. He had not done anything great in the world but had instead reported on road-paving projects, garden club meetings, school athletes. He had coasted along for years now, filling the pages of his newspaper with words, burying himself in whatever was safe, typesetting the ferry schedule and the tide table and the classified advertisements. So perhaps that was what her eyes meant now on those rare occasions when she looked at him – he'd shrunk so thoroughly in her estimation, not lived up to who he was. He read her letter another time and understood that she had once admired him, there was something in him she was grateful for even if she could not love him. That was a part of himself he'd lost over the years, that was the part that was gone.

He put the letter away in its box and went down the stairs again. His mother, he found, was asleep in her bed, snoring a little, a rough rattling in her throat; she looked very old in the light from the hallway with her cheek buried against her pillow, a sleeping cap pulled low on her forehead. Her face was a map of wrinkles, and looking at them he felt more deeply how he would miss her when she was gone. It did not matter whether he agreed with her about God. It was only, instead, that she was finally his mother and she had not given up on loving him. His trips to South Beach, he understood now, were as much for his own heart as they were for hers; he had fooled himself for years into thinking otherwise. He had acted as if her death someday – for someday he would have to face the fact that her death would leave him alone in the world – would not pose a problem for him.

Beneath the stars, with his overcoat on, he wandered out into the cold. His feet took their own direction through the cedar woods and underneath the canopy of branches he smelled the old fragrance of the place of his youth and the clean scent of the newly fallen snow. Here under the trees it was fresh and untouched. The branches of the cedars were hung with it and beyond them the sky lay immaculate and decembral, the stars chilled points of light. He followed his feet to where the path met the beach – where a wall of honeysuckle bloomed in summer, intertwined with salmonberries and wild roses – and cut through the dell of snow-covered ferns to the hollowed cedar tree of his youth.

Ishmael sat inside for a brief time with his coat wrapped tightly around him. He listened to the world turned silent by the snow; there was absolutely nothing to hear. The silence of the world roared steadily in his ears while he came to recognize that he did not belong here, he had no place in the tree any longer. Some much younger people should find this tree, hold to it tightly as their deepest secret, as he and Hatsue had. For them it might stave off what he could not help but see with clarity: that the world was silent and cold and bare and that in this lay its terrible beauty.

He got up and walked and came out of the woods and into the Imadas' fields. The way was clear between the rows of buried strawberries and he followed it with the starlight striking off the snow, bathing everything in an aqueous light. And finally he was on the Imadas' porch and then in the Imadas' living room, sitting with Hatsue and her mother and father where he had never been before. Hatsue sat beside him, just beside him, close, wearing a nightgown and her father's old bathrobe, her hair awash in light along her back, falling in cascades around her

11 **gravitate toward sth.**: be attracted to sth. and move towards it   19 **coast along**: put very little effort into sth. (disapproving)   22 **classified advertisements**: Kleinanzeigen   24 **live up to sb.**: do as well as or be as good as sb.   58 **stave sth. off**: prevent sth. bad from affecting you for a period of time   64 **aqueous** [ˈeɪkwiəs]: like water

hips, and he reached into his pocket and unfolded the notes Philip Milholland had written on September 16, and Ishmael explained what the shorthand meant and why he had come at ten-thirty in the night to speak to her after all these years.

Chapter 32

There was no way to call Lew Fielding with the news because the phones were all dead along South Beach. So the four of them, cups of green tea in hand, the barrel stove murmuring and clicking in its corner, spoke quietly about the trial of Kabuo Miyamoto, which was for them the only subject possible, as it had been for many days. It was late now, the room very warm, the world outside frozen and bathed in starlight, and Ishmael told Hatsue and Hisao and Fujiko that as a reporter who had covered the courthouse in Seattle he felt comfortable offering a present conjecture: that Philip Milholland's notes would force Judge Fielding to call for retrying the case. That the judge would declare a mistrial.

Hatsue recalled that in the course of his testimony the sheriff had described finding a coffee cup – tipped on its side, the sheriff had explained – on the floor of Carl Heine's cabin. It meant, she said, that Carl's gill-netting boat had been rocked by a freighter in the middle of the night – *something* had knocked that coffee cup down, and since Carl had never picked it up it had to be that the very same something had knocked him down as well. It *had* to be, she repeated. Her husband's case should be thrown out.

Spilled coffee didn't really prove very much, Fujiko urged her daughter to see. Hisao shook his head in agreement. There had to be more than spilled coffee, he said. Kabuo was facing something very large. He would need more than a coffee cup tipped onto its side to get him out of jail.

Fujiko refilled Ishmael's teacup carefully and asked how his mother was faring. She said she had always thought highly of his family. She complimented Ishmael on the quality of his newspaper. She brought a

---

3 **barrel stove**: Kanonenofen   10 **retry sth.**: examine a case again in court
10–11 **declare a mistrial** (fml): ein Verfahren aufheben   19 **throw sth. out**:
(at court) say that sth. is completely wrong or not worth considering

plate of butter cookies and pleaded with him to eat one. Finally Hatsue's baby began to whimper – they could hear him plainly from one of the back rooms – and Fujiko disappeared.

Just after midnight Ishmael took his leave, shaking hands with Hisao and thanking him for the tea and asking him to thank Fujiko, too. Then he went out. Hatsue followed him onto the porch, wearing rubber boots and her father's old bathrobe, her hands deep in her pockets now, the fog of her breath streaming out of her mouth and billowing over her nose and cheeks. 'Ishmael,' she said. 'I'm grateful.'

'Look,' he replied. 'When you're old and thinking back on things, I hope you'll remember me just a little. I – '

'Yes,' said Hatsue. 'I will.'

She moved closer then, and with her hands still buried deep in her pockets kissed him so softly it was like a whisper against his cheekbone. 'Find someone to marry,' she said to him. 'Have children, Ishmael. Live.'

In the morning his mother roused him at six-fifty, saying that the wife of the accused man was here, waiting for him in the kitchen. Ishmael got up and splashed cold water against his face and put on his clothes and brushed his teeth. When he came down his mother was standing by the cookstove and Hatsue was at the table sipping coffee, and when he saw her he remembered once again how softly she had kissed him the night before. 'Do you want me to leave?' his mother asked from her place in front of the woodstove. 'I'll leave, of course, so you can talk.'

'We'll go in the study,' answered Ishmael. 'Why don't we try the study, Mrs. Miyamoto? Why don't we go in there?'

'Take your coffee,' his mother suggested. 'I'll top it off for you first.'

They made their way to the study, Ishmael leading. The first light of morning – a wintry orange hue dappling the sky – appeared high and far in the distance above the salt water, faint beyond the leaded windows. The rhododendrons were all loaded down with snow; icicles hung from the eaves. Everything looked seized by a white stillness.

Hatsue had plaited her hair into a long braid, glistening, dark, and thick. She wore a thick-ribbed woolen sweater, a pair of navy dungarees, and a pair of calf-high fisherman's boots, and she stood now looking at the portrait of Arthur from long ago, in his logging days. 'You look just like him,' she said to Ishmael. 'I always thought you looked like your father – the eyes especially.'

'You didn't walk over here in the dark and snow just to tell me that,' answered Ishmael. 'What do you have on your mind?'

'I thought about it all night,' said Hatsue. 'Do you remember when my husband testified? He said that Carl had a lantern up. A kerosene lantern lashed to his mast. That he'd put it there because his lights weren't working. He'd lashed a hand-held kerosene lantern high up on his mast.'

Hatsue rubbed her hands together, then separated them again, lightly. 'My idea,' she said to Ishmael, 'is that if that lantern's still up there, right now, wouldn't it mean his batteries really *were* dead? Supposing you looked up Carl's mast and saw a kerosene lantern lashed up there, just like Kabuo said. Wouldn't that tell you something? That his lights were out and he'd lashed up a lantern as a sort of emergency measure? Don't you think that would prove something?'

Ishmael sat down on the edge of his father's desk, scratched his chin, and thought about it. Art Moran's report, the way he recalled it, hadn't said a word about a kerosene lantern lashed up high in Carl's mast, but on the other hand Art could have missed it. Such a thing was possible. At any rate, it was worth finding out.

'All right,' said Ishmael. 'Let's go into town. Let's go in and have a look.'

They took the DeSoto over snow-dazzled roads decorated with cracked and fallen branches and with the green twigs of cedars and hemlocks. The storm had passed and on the west side of Lundgren Road five children stood at the crest of the hill with sleds and inner tubes at their feet, looking down at the run-out below, a bowl surrounded by slender alder trees and a thicket of low bare vine maple. Ishmael turned west on

---

27 **top sth. off**: add fresh coffe to a cup   29 **dapple sth.**: (here) make sth. appear in patches or spots of color   60 **snow-dazzled**: (here) coated with snow that reflects the light so brightly that you cannot see   63 **inner tubes**: Gummischlauch aus einem Reifen   64 **run-out** (n) ['--]: (hier) Auslauf, Hang   **bowl** (n): (hier) Mulde   65 **thicket**: group of bushes or small trees growing closely together

Indian Knob Hill Road, and they passed the Masuis' strawberry fields and then the Thorsens' milk cow barn and Patsy Larsen's chicken houses. Hatsue sat with her mittens in her lap and her hands held close to the car heater. 'We ought to go to see my husband first,' she said. 'We ought to tell him what's going on. I want to show him the coast guard notes.'

'The jury reconvenes at eight,' answered Ishmael. 'If we can get a look at Carl's boat first, we can go to the courthouse with everything. We can put a stop to the whole business. We can end it all,' he said.

She was silent for a long time, watching him. She looked at him closely and pulled her braid down over her shoulder so that it lay against the front of her sweater. 'You knew about that freighter,' she said finally. 'It wasn't something new, was it.'

'A day,' answered Ishmael. 'I sat on it for a day. I didn't know what I should do.'

She said nothing in the face of this and he turned toward her silence to see what it might mean. 'I'm sorry,' he said. 'It's inexcusable.'

'I understand it,' answered Hatsue.

She nodded and rubbed her hands together, then looked out at the sun-dappled snow. 'Everything looks so pure,' she said. 'It's so beautiful today.'

'Yes, it is,' agreed Ishmael.

At the sheriff's office in Amity Harbor they found Art Moran hunched down at his desk beside an electric heater. When Art saw the two of them come through the door, he dropped his pen at the edge of his desk blotter and stood and covered his eyes with his hands. 'Wait a minute, let me guess,' he said. 'You people are on a mission.'

Hatsue brought out the coast guard notes and, smoothing them down with the palm of her hand, laid them in the center of his desk.

'Mr. Chambers discovered these,' she said. 'He brought these to me last night.'

'And?'

'A freighter out there,' said Ishmael. 'The night Carl Heine died, a freighter came through Ship Channel Bank, just like – '

'You playing detective?' Art said. 'You trying to be Sherlock Holmes? We got the mooring rope and that fishing gaff with Carl's blood on it – those things speak for themselves, don't they? What else does a body need?'

'Look, Art,' Ishmael answered. 'I suggest that if you're capable of reading shorthand you take a look at those notes there. I think they ought to make you consider at least going down to take another look at Carl's boat, okay? See if there's anything that's been missed, Art. In light of what's on your desk there.'

Art nodded. He nodded at Hatsue, too, for just a moment, and then he sat down beside the electric heater again and took the coast guard notes between his fingers. 'I kin read shorthand,' he said.

He was in the middle of reading the notes to himself, Ishmael and Hatsue watching him, when Abel Martinson came through the door in a pair of knee-high logger's caulk boots and a military issue polar parka, its fur-lined hood pulled tight around his head, his nose and chin a deep red. 'The phones are up,' he announced to the sheriff. 'They just got 'em up, about half the island. Town's got phones and south from there, all the way out to the lighthouse.'

'Listen,' replied the sheriff. 'Listen here, Abel. We're going down to Beason's Cannery dock, to Sommensen's warehouse, okay? You, me, Ishmael here, the lady'll wait at the cafe or something, get herself a breakfast. Can you get yourself a breakfast or something? 'Cause you're a little too close to all of this. You're a little too close to this already. I don't like the smell of it, okay?'

'It's me,' said Ishmael. 'It isn't her. This comes from me all the way.'

'Just the same,' said Art Moran. 'Go get yourself some eggs, Mrs. Miyamoto. Read the papers, maybe.'

Abel blew his warm breath against the lock before opening Sommensen's warehouse – a mildewed barn built of creosoted timbers, put up more than fifty years earlier. Even in the snowstorm it smelled of salt and tar and more faintly of diesel fuel and rotting lumber. Its sea doors opened onto the harbor so that boats could motor in and then out again once repairs were made. Its tin roof kept island rains out; with its two hoists, scaffolding, and wide-elbowed piers, it was a good place to overhaul a

---

6 **reconvene** (fml) [ˌriːkənˈviːn]: meet again after a break   16 **inexcusable**: too bad to accept or forgive   45 **kin** = can   48 **military issue**: military supplies
67 **hoist** (n): Hebezug, Winde   68 **scaffolding**: Gerüst   **wide-elbowed**: arranged at wide angles over a large area

boat in winter. For the past two and a half months the sheriff's department had rented it from Arve Sommensen for the purpose of sequestering the *Susan Marie* and the *Islander* in berths side by side. It had been padlocked and on occasion patrolled by Abel Martinson, who kept the key in his pocket. Nothing, he insisted, had been tampered with. The boats had sat in the warehouse untouched since the seventeenth of September.

Abel opened the sea doors wide and a gray light flooded in. Ishmael looked immediately at the *Susan Marie*'s mast and then all along her cross spar. No lantern hung anywhere.

They went into Carl Heine's cabin. Ishmael stood in the doorway looking out while the sheriff ran a flashlight across everything – the cased sausage beside the binnacle, the short bunk, the ship's wheel, the battery well. 'You know,' said Ishmael, 'when you were testifying, Art, you mentioned a coffee cup on the floor here, remember? Where was that exactly, the coffee cup? Do you remember exactly where it was?'

'I picked it up,' said Abel Martinson. 'It was right there, in the middle of the floor.'

'Everything else was neat and clean? Just the cup, that's all?'

'Like you see it,' said Abel. 'We didn't change anything – just the cup. I picked it up; a habit, I guess. Something's on the floor, a mess, I pick it up. Can't help myself.'

'Next time, help yourself,' said Art Moran. 'You're making a sheriff's investigation, don't change anything a-tall.'

'Okay,' answered Abel. 'I won't.'

'The cup,' said Ishmael. 'A cup on the floor. Doesn't it suggest this boat got waked? Don't you – '

'There's no *other* evidence,' cut in Art Moran. 'A guy gets waked hard enough to go overboard, you'd expect maybe more 'n a coffee cup on the floor. Everything's so neat and clean.'

They went out and stood just to port of the cabin door while Ishmael maneuvered a flashlight beam up and down the mast. 'You remember that business about the lantern?' said Ishmael. 'How Carl hung a lantern up there? Did you guys take that down?'

'Hold your flashlight still,' answered Abel. 'Just above the cross spar. There.'

He shone his own flashlight upward then, so that two beams shone against the mast now. There were cut lashings of net twine visible there, loose ends dangling, ten or twenty figure eights, cut through cleanly on an angle.

'That's where his lantern was hung,' said Ishmael. 'He'd hung a lantern up there, lashed it up, because all his lights were dead. That's where Carl hung his lantern.'

'We never took no lantern down,' said Art. 'What are you talking about?'

Abel Martinson hoisted himself on top of the cabin, propped one foot against the cowling, and shone his flashlight upward one more time. 'Mr. Chambers is right,' he said.

'Listen,' said the sheriff. 'Climb up there, Abel. Haul yourself up there and take a closer look. And don't touch *any*thing.'

'I'll need to push off your hands,' said the deputy, shoving his flashlight in his pocket. 'Give me a boost and I'll go up.'

The sheriff gave Abel Martinson a boost, and he lunged in his polar coat toward the cross spar. He wrapped one arm over it and hung there, the boat rocking, while his other hand fished for the flashlight. 'Looks like a rust streak 'crost these lashings,' he said. 'Like it could be off the handle of a lantern, maybe. Where the handle rubbed against them, maybe.'

'Anything else?' said the sheriff.

'You can see where the lashings been cut,' observed Abel. 'Somebody took a knife to 'em. And hey – something else – this stuff on the mast? It looks like it might be blood.'

'From his hand,' said Ishmael. 'He cut his hand. It was in the coroner's report.'

'There's blood on the mast and the spar pole,' said Abel. 'Not much, but I think it's blood.'

---

2 **sequester sth.**: (here) keep sth. deliberately separate from sth. else in order to make sure that nobody has access to it   5 **tamper with sth.**: make changes to sth. without permission, esp. in order to damage it   9 **cross spar**: Quermast   26 **get waked**: (here) be hit by the wake (= Bugwelle) of another ship   37 **lashing**: piece of rope or wire used to fasten sth. tightly to sth. else   38 **figure eight** = figure-of-eight knot: kind of knot for which a piece of rope is arranged in the form of the figure (= Zahl) eight before tying it   46 **cowling**: metal cover for an engine   51 **boost** (n): (here) act of pushing sb. up   52 **lunge** (v): make a sudden powerful forward movement   55 **rust streak**: Roststreifen   '**crost** = across

'He cut his hand,' repeated Ishmael. 'He cut his hand making room for Kabuo's battery. Then he got his power back up. Then he climbed up there to take his lantern down because he didn't need it anymore.'

The deputy slid down and landed hard. 'What's with all this?' he said.

'Something else,' said Ishmael. 'You remember Horace's testimony? He said Carl had a shuttle of twine in one pocket and an empty knife sheath knotted to his belt. You remember Horace saying so, sheriff? How the knife sheath was empty, unbuckled? A shuttle of twine and an empty knife sheath. I – '

'He climbed up to take his lantern down,' said Abel. 'That freighter came along and knocked him from the mast. The knife and the lantern went overboard with him – the knife and the lantern were never found, right? – and – '

'Pipe down a minute, Abel,' said Art Moran. 'I can hardly hear myself think.'

'He hit his head on something,' said Abel. 'The freighter wake hit, the boat rolled over, and then he fell and hit his head on something and slid on out of the boat.'

Ten minutes later, in the port side gunnel just below the mast, they found a small fracture in the wood. Three small hairs were embedded in the crack, and Art Moran carved them free with his pocketknife and tucked them into the sheath in his wallet that also held his driver's license. They looked at the hairs in a flashlight beam and then they all fell silent. 'We'll take these up to Horace,' decided Art. 'If they end up to be from Carl Heine's head, the judge will have to take things from there.'

At ten o'clock Judge Fielding sat down with Alvin Hooks and Nels Gudmundsson. At ten forty-five the jurors were told that they were released from any further duties; the charges against the accused man had been dismissed; new evidence had come to light. The accused man himself was set free immediately and walked out of his cell without leg irons or handcuffs; standing just outside its door, he kissed his wife for a long time. Ishmael Chambers took a photograph of this; he watched their kiss through his viewfinder. Then he went back to his office, turned up the heat, and loaded paper in his typewriter. And he sat staring at it for some time.

Ishmael Chambers tried to imagine the truth of what had happened. He shut his eyes and exerted himself to see everything clearly.

The *Susan Marie* had gone dead in the water – the bolt shook loose in her alternator pulley bracket – on the night of September 15. In a drowning fog, impatiently drifting – and too proud to just lay hard on the air horn he carried in anticipation of times such as these – Carl Heine must have cursed his misfortune. Then he lit his two railroad lanterns, slipped his twine shuttle into his back pocket, and hauled himself up to the cross spar on the mast, a lantern slung temporarily down his back, his rubber bib overalls slipping. The cotton twine he used for mending net bound the lantern to the mast easily, but Carl put in extra lashings anyway, figure eights laid one over the other, pulled taut and finished crisply. He hung for a moment, his armpit against the spar, and knew that his light was futile against the fog; nevertheless he adjusted the flame higher before clambering down. And he stood in the cockpit listening, perhaps, with the fog closed in around him.

And perhaps after a while he took his other kerosene lantern and picked out the five-eighths wrench from his toolbox to tighten the alternator pulley belts, cursing again just under his breath: how was it possible he'd neglected this, failed to check it as a matter of course, come to such a pass as his present one (which ordinary seamanship might have prevented), and he a man who prided himself silently on the depth and purity of his seamanship? He tightened the belts, pressed his thumb against them, then went out once again and stood leaning against the port gunnel. Carl Heine listened to the fog and to the sea, to the other boats moving off the bank with their whistles sounding incessantly and to the water softly lapping against his boat as he drifted with the tide, moving east. He stood with one foot up, the kerosene lantern handy, the air horn clutched in his hand. Something in him would not use the horn, and for a good long time, an hour or more, he debated whether he should use it anyway, and he wondered if there were fish in

4 **What's with all this?**: Was soll das alles?   15 **pipe down** (infml): be quiet
31–32 **leg iron**: Fußfessel   34 **viewfinder**: Sucher (einer Kamera)   40 **alternator pulley bracket**: board on which the electric generator is installed   50 **futile** ['fjuːtl]: without chance of success, pointless   51 **clamber down**: climb down with difficulty
57 **seamanship**: skill in sailing a boat or ship

his net. It was then that he heard a boat not far off, the sound of a foghorn blown deliberately, and he turned his ear in its direction. Six times it came, nearer at each blast, and with his watch he timed the precision of its intervals – one minute went by between each. When it drew inside of one hundred yards he gave a single blast on his air horn.

The *Islander*, her hold full of fish, and the *Susan Marie*, dark and dead on the water – a kerosene lantern lashed to her mast, her skipper poised in her bow with his chin set – came together in the fog. Then Kabuo's mooring lines were made fast to deck cleats in the efficiently wrought half hitches Carl Heine could lay out with no thought or hesitation. A battery changed hands, it was somewhat too large, a metal flange was beaten back. Carl's hand was sliced down the palm, there was blood on Kabuo's fishing gaff. An agreement was arrived at eventually. The things that needed to be said were said between them, and Kabuo pushed off into the night.

Maybe it had seemed to Kabuo Miyamoto, alone on the sea shortly afterward, a fortuitous thing to have come across Carl Heine in circumstances such as these. Perhaps it had seemed just the sort of luck he'd long thought he needed. His dream, after all, was close to him now, so close that while he fished he must have imagined it: his strawberry land, the fragrance of fruit, the fold of the fields, the early-summer ripening, his children, Hatsue, his happiness. Oldest son of the Miyamotos, greatgrandson of a samurai, and the first of his lineage to become an American in name, place, and heart, he had not given up on being who he was; he had never given up on his family's land or the claim they had to it by all that was right, the human claim that was bigger than hate or war or any smallness or enmity.

And all the while he was thinking this way, celebrating this sudden good fortune in his life and imagining the fragrance of ripening strawberries, he was drifting in the darkness, drifting in fog, with the low moan from the lighthouse barely audible and the steam whistle blasts from the S.S. *Corona* growing louder and coming closer with each moment. And a half mile to the south and west of the *Islander* Carl Heine stood in his cabin door and listened uncertainly to the same whistle blasts now penetrating through the fog. He had made black coffee and held his cup in one hand; the kettle had been stowed in its place. His net was out and running true behind as far as he could tell.

All of his lights were burning strong now. His volt meter showed thirteen and a half volts charging, and the *Susan Marie* ran hard and steady, her spotlight suffused in the fog. It was twenty minutes before two o'clock in the morning, enough time left to catch plenty of fish – the coffee would keep him awake long enough to fill his hold with salmon.

Surely Carl had listened to his radio, the lighthouse radioman dispensing advice, the freighter's navigator calling in positions, taking readings off Lanheedron Island, then suddenly deciding on a bisecting dogleg right through Ship Channel Bank. Carl had tried listening into the fog, but the thrum of his own engines masked all other sound, and he had to shut down and drift. He stood again listening and waiting. At last there came another steam whistle blast, closer this time, definitely drawing closer, and he slammed his coffee cup to the table. He went outside then and considered getting hard waked, the big swell from the freighter going right through him, and it seemed to him he was secure to take it, there was nothing to get bounced around very much, everything was in its place.

Except the lantern lashed to the mast. A big freighter wake would smash it to pieces; Carl would have seen it that way.

And so he paid for his fastidious nature, his compulsion to keep things perfect. He paid because he had inherited from his mother a certain tightness through the purse strings. Drifting on the water, the *Corona* bearing down on him in the fogbound night, he figured he needed less than thirty seconds to haul himself up his mast. Save a lantern that way. What were the risks? Does a man ever believe in his own imminent death or in the possibility of accident?

And so because he was who he was – his mother's son, tidy by nature, survivor of the sinking of the U.S.S. *Canton* and thus immune to a fishing boat accident – he climbed his mast with confidence. He climbed it and in so doing opened the palm wound he'd incurred banging against

---

10 **half hitch**: kind of knot used in sailing   23 **lineage** [ˈlɪniːɪdʒ]: ancestry, family members living before you   27 **enmity**: feelings of hatred towards sb.
35 **penetrate through sth.**: go through sth.   44 **dispense sth.**: provide sth. for people, esp. a service   48 **shut down**: (here) turn the engine off   57 **compulsion** [kəmˈpʌlʃn]: Zwang   59 **tightness through the purse strings** (AE): Geiz   67 **incur sth.** [ɪnˈkɜːr]: sich etwas zuziehen

the battery well's metal flange with Kabuo Miyamoto's fishing gaff. Now he hung by his armpit from the cross spar, bleeding and listening into the fog, working his knife from its sheath. Again there came the blast of the freighter's whistle, the low hum of its engines audible to port, so close he twitched in surprise at it, and then with his blade he exerted pressure through the figure-eight lashings he'd made a few hours earlier. Carl came away with the lantern's handle between his fingers and went to lock back his knife.

It must have been that in the ghost fog that night he never saw the wall of water the *Corona* threw at him. The sea rose up from behind the fog and welled underneath the *Susan Marie* so that the coffee cup on the cabin table fell to the floor, and the angle of deflection high up the mast was enough to jar loose the astonished man who hung there not grasping the nature of what was happening, and still he did not foresee his death. His bloody hand lost its grip on the mast, the rubber of his overalls ceased to grip, his arms flew out and his fingers opened, casting the lantern and the knife into the water, and Carl Heine fell swift and hard against the *Susan Marie's* port gunnel. His head cracked open above the left ear and then he slid heavily beneath the waves, water seeping into his wristwatch, stopping it at 1:47. The *Susan Marie* rocked a full five minutes and while gradually she settled once again the body of her skipper settled, too, into his salmon net. He hung there in the phosphorescence of the sea, gathering light and undulating, and his boat moved now on the tidal current, brightly lit and silent in the fog.

The wall of water moved on. It traveled a half mile speedily and then gathered beneath the *Islander* so that Kabuo felt it, too. It traveled with nothing more to interrupt it and broke against the shore of Lanheedron Island just before two o'clock in the morning. The whistle of the freighter and the lighthouse diaphone sounded again in the fog. Kabuo Miyamoto, his net set, his radio off, the fog as palpable as cotton around him, replaced the line he'd left on Carl's boat with a reserve he kept stowed in his galley. Perhaps he'd squatted for a moment, building a bowline into the manila, and heard the steam whistle of the passing freighter sounding low across the water. It would have been as sorrowful a sound in that heavy fog as anyone could readily conjure or imagine, and as it grew louder – as the freighter drew closer – it would have sounded all the more forlorn. The freighter passed to the north still blowing, and Kabuo listened to it. Perhaps in that moment he remembered how his father had buried everything Japanese beneath the soil of his farm. Or perhaps he thought of Hatsue and of his children and the strawberry farm he would one day pass to them.

The steam whistle from the freighter faded eastward. It sounded at intervals with the fog whistle from the lighthouse, a higher note, more desolate. The fog closed it in, muffling it, and the freighter's note went deep enough so that it seemed otherworldly, not a steam whistle but a cacophony of bass notes rising from the bottom of the sea. Finally it merged with the lighthouse signal so that the two of them sounded at the same moment, a clash of sound, discordant. There was a dissonance, faint, every two minutes across the water, and finally even that disappeared.

Kabuo Miyamoto came home to embrace his wife and to tell her how their lives had changed; the lighthouse dogwatch drew to a close, and Philip Milholland stuffed his notes into a folder and threw himself into sleep. He and the radioman, Robert Miller, slept steadily into the afternoon. Then they awoke and left San Piedro Island, transferred to another station. And Art Moran made his arrest.

Well, thought Ishmael, bending over his typewriter, his fingertips poised just above the keys: the palpitations of Kabuo Miyamoto's heart were unknowable finally. And Hatsue's heart wasn't knowable, either, nor was Carl Heine's. The heart of *any* other, because it had a will, would remain forever mysterious.

Ishmael gave himself to the writing of it, and as he did so he understood this, too: that accident ruled every corner of the universe except the chambers of the human heart.

---

8 **lock back a knife**: ein (Taschen)messer zusammenklappen   11 **well** (v): aufsteigen, anschwellen   12 **angle of deflection**: Neigungswinkel   13 **jar sb. loose** (v): (here) receive a sudden sharp knock that makes sb. lose their grip of sth. 46 **cacophony** [-'---]: mixture of loud unpleasant sounds   47 **merge with sth.**: mit etwas verschmelzen   48 **discordant**: (of sounds) not sounding pleasant together   **dissonance** ['dɪsənəns]: combination of discordant musical notes 51 **embrace sb.**: put your arms around sb.   62 **give yourself to doing sth.**: spend all your time and thought on doing sth.

The Author

David Guterson was born in Seattle in 1956. His father was a distinguished criminal defense lawyer and as a child David would often attend his father's court cases.

His choice of career was very much influenced by his father's advice to choose a job that he really wanted to do and that would enable him to make a positive contribution to the world. He took a creative writing course at the University of Washington and within a week decided to become a writer.

After graduation he moved to Bainbridge Island in Puget Sound near Seattle, where he still lives with his wife and his four children. He taught English at the local high school and began working as a journalist and author.

Snow Falling on Cedars (1994) is Guterson's most widely known novel. It has won many awards, including the 1995 PEN/Faulkner Award.